READING PETER READING

READING
PETER READING

Isabel Martin

BLOODAXE BOOKS

ISBN: 1 85224 466 6 hardback edition
1 85224 467 4 paperback edition

First published 2000 by
Bloodaxe Books Ltd,
P.O. Box 1SN,
Newcastle upon Tyne NE99 1SN.

Bloodaxe Books Ltd acknowledges
the financial assistance of Northern Arts.

Cover printing by J. Thomson Colour Printers Ltd, Glasgow.

Printed in Great Britain by
Cromwell Press Ltd, Trowbridge, Wiltshire.

To my family

ACKNOWLEDGEMENTS

This book is based on my doctoral dissertation written in German for the University of Kiel, *Das Werk Peter Readings (1970-1994): Interpretation und Dokumentation* (Heidelberg: Universitätsverlag Carl Winter, 1996). It has been updated, revised, rewritten and drastically shortened for a new readership.

I am particularly grateful to the *Frauenbeauftragte* (Women's Representative) of Kiel University, Dr Lesley Drewing, for the generous financial support given for this book. Thanks also to my German publisher Dr Carl Winter for granting permission for publication in this revised English version.

I am indebted to those critics who wrote perceptive reviews of individual volumes and helped my own appreciation of Reading's poetry when I first started (a few of the misinformed reviews had the same effect). I am also grateful to some critics for giving me access to unpublished material. For reasons of space, I have not been able to quote from them as much as I would have wished; however, their contributions are discussed in my German book and properly acknowledged here when they occur. Many other people were helpful in providing information; the list is too long to be reproduced here, but this help, too, is fully acknowledged in my German publication.

Without the following people this book would not have been finished. Profound thanks are due to my 'troublesome subject', for his openness and sincerity over 12 years. To all of his family, who have been most hospitable, helpful and friendly. To Deborah, for all she has done. To my husband, Edward Martin, for his untiring practical, critical, and stylistic help, and for blood-axing the final manuscript by 100 pages (too daunting a task for me) – his contribution to the book is significant. To my parents, Dieter and Marie-Hélène Metzler, for helping to look after Marielle and Benjamin over the long summer. To John Coggrave, for his helpful comments on the manuscript and a number of literary references that I had missed. Last, but not least, sincere apologies to my children, whose resilience was and is essential.

CONTENTS

EDITORIAL NOTE

This study gives readers a book-by-book analysis of Peter Reading's work, prefaced by a chapter sketching his biographical background and literary influences. A general introductory essay on his work as a whole is to be found in his *Collected Poems 1*. Page references given for Reading's poems are to *Collected Poems 1: Poems 1970-1984* for the collections up to *C* in the first eight chapters, and to *Collected Poems 2: Poems 1985-1996* for the collections up to *Eschatological* for the later chapters. In the last chapter, page references are to the individual collections published by Bloodaxe since the *Collected Poems*. When untitled poems were published in newspapers and magazines, Reading always gave them titles. This explains references to poem titles which are not to be found in the *Collected Poems* or the original editions.

The following abbreviations in square brackets refer to previously unpublished material:

[LI]: Interview with Peter Reading conducted in Liverpool over three days (4-6 June 1993), transcribed 6-hour tape-recording;

[C]: Conversations with Peter Reading (1988-2000), notes;

[M]: Material other than the above (transcribed audio and video material, letters, unpublished material by other authors).

The use of square brackets in quotations indicates minor changes in the quotations for reasons of clear syntactical cohesion.

Full bibliographical information on reviews is given in a Note to each chapter. All further quotations in the respective chapters are taken from these sources, but the critics' names are not explicitly quoted again where their identity is clear. Frequently quoted interviews and essays are given in abbreviated form after their first full listing.

The repeated reference 'Preminger' refers to the enlarged edition of the *Princeton Encyclopedia of Poetry and Poetics*, edited by Alex Preminger (Princeton, 1974). *The New Princeton Encyclopedia* was published in 1993. The use of technical poetic terms to describe Reading's highly complex versification is necessary for the sake of precision and concision. Readers may either ignore them or refer to the glossary at the back of the book.

PETER READING

'I knew when I started that if I wanted to get anywhere – not knowing anybody in the business – I had to bombard them with books' [C]. Between 1970 and 2000, Peter Reading published 24 poetry titles, and the 25th is forthcoming in 2001. The first 18 books have been reprinted in two volumes by Bloodaxe as *Collected Poems*.

Recognition came quickly. The distinctive start was made in 1976 with a Poetry Book Society Recommendation for Reading's second book, *The Prison Cell & Barrel Mystery*, followed by Poetry Book Society Choices for *Perduta Gente* (1989) and *Work in Regress* (1997), and Recommendations for *Tom o'Bedlam's Beauties* (1981), *Diplopic* (1983), *C* (1984) and *Collected Poems* (1995). Only once did he submit a poem to a poetry competition: this was '15th February' (*Diplopic*), winner of a small prize in the National Poetry Competition of 1981.

His first literary prize, the Cholmondeley Award, came relatively early, after the third full-length book in 1978. In 1983, he was the first poet to be given the newly inaugurated but short-lived Dylan Thomas Award for *Diplopic*, and in 1986 received the Whitbread Poetry Award for *Stet*. In 1988, Reading was elected Fellow of the Royal Society of Literature, and in 1997, he was shortlisted for a Paul Hamlyn Award and for the T.S. Eliot Prize. The most prestigious distinction of his career came in 1990: the international Lannan Literary Award, judged anonymously, is one of the biggest literary prizes, worth $35,000.

Peter Reading was born to Gray and Mary Reading on 27 July 1946 in Liverpool. His father, an electrical engineer, had been a prisoner of the Japanese during the war, and returned home after three years of isolation, forced labour and brutality with permanent injuries to his shoulders.

From 1948 the Readings lived at the rural periphery of Liverpool, but the fields next to their house have long since made way for redevelopment between Liverpool and Kirkby, just as the canal and the small river where Peter Reading went fishing as a child have been polluted. He witnessed the steady ecological collapse of the area as he grew up, and from his first collection made it one of his main subjects.

From the time I was a boy, and aware of the sorts of environmental issues which affected my principal interest – ornithology – I was alarmed and angered by the balls-up in areas like the tipping of pollutants into water sources. I and my colleagues could see in the late '50s that the Dee was shit-filled. We assumed it would come to the attention of the people who could do something about it. [Later] it was incredible to me that nothing whatever had been done to check the – what seemed to us then, in a despairing mood – inevitable chain of events.[1]

Gypsies sometimes camped along the canal between the Reading home and Kirkby, and they always had horses, fascinating for the boy. In the high grass there, he once found the green corpse of a gypsy, and paid regular return visits to this interesting find. Reading's obsessive poetic vision of a peaceful death covered in leaves goes back to the *Odyssey* (Book V), but has its seed in this discovery [C].

His interest in ornithology and natural history started at the age of 12, when he would walk out to Hilbre, a bird island accessible on foot from West Kirby at low tide,[2] joining an ornithological group that helped the warden at weekends, including an older boy, Michael Donahue, who was to become a close friend. For the next few years, Peter camped on Hilbre every weekend during the warm months, equipped with a toothbrush and a few soup packets, and the two young ornithologists went off to other bird islands twice a year to chart the migration; in autumn their destination was the bird station on Bardsey, off the coast of the Lleyn Peninsula.

R.S. Thomas was there; he had a parish on the mainland. There were quite a few *rarae aves* on the island, Thomas not least. There was an Icterine warbler. I was fortunate enough to catch the Icterine at the lighthouse. We thought Thomas a bit M, because he didn't seem interested in any of it. But we were young and intolerant.[3]

After 25 years of friendship, Donahue was killed in a car accident. Reading's first elegy to him is 'Ob.' (*Stet*, p.104). Reading did not attend the funeral; he remembers him in another way: 'I can't go birding and not think about Michael' [C].

The natural sciences figure in Reading's work as a continuing preoccupation with ornithology, biology, astronomy, mycology and œnology. Their literary function within the overall subject-matter is that 'that helps to maintain a sensible distance'.[4]

The other boys who went to Bardsey made a career out of their passion; for Peter (and Michael) one thing was more important: literature.

For me, it always seemed the best thing to be some kind of artist – it was a kind of hero-worship. Sportsmen heroes didn't really appeal to me as a boy. I was interested in a way by Len Hutton and Roger Bannister and Stirling Moss, but ultimately I found them fairly trivial people, and I thought that if I could be outstanding at something I'd prefer to be someone like Samuel Beckett. I first heard about him on an early *Monitor* programme – I used to stay up on Sunday nights –

and I was overawed. Clips from early productions of *Godot*, for example: not really understanding what was going on exactly but thinking here was something I was impressed and amused and utterly convinced by. I fell head over heels for it; I was eleven or twelve (Jenkins, 1985, p.5).

After Beckett it was Pinter, whose play *The Caretaker* also produced this feeling of witnessing, but not understanding something salient. The boys started discussing books, and Peter discovered W.H. Auden:

...from completely isolated passages I found that I liked Auden; from poems like 'The Unknown Citizen', Mr and Mrs A's dialogue from *The Ascent of F6*. I thought that poetry was rather good stuff, very powerful. When you're a teenager you like a certain sort of worldly cynicism, and those bits of Auden provided that. I read *Timon of Athens* and liked it... Frost's 'Out, out'; there's another (if you like) violent thing I read at about the same time (Jenkins, 1985, pp.5, 7).

At the age of 14, Peter was writing Keatsian poems:

I followed my heroes only in that I wrote poems, execrable attempts which appeared in the grammar school magazine. Poems about capital punishment or spiders' webs bedecked with dew (Jenkins, 1985, p.6).

The sentimental 'Death of a Grouse' was used satirically later in *Diplopic* (p.213), and 'Early Stuff' (pp.69-70) coldly discusses juvenile romanticism and confessionalism. Still: the 'foolish, romantic image' of the artist that Peter aspired to stayed with him, as he admitted, 'I mean romantic as in Romantics.'[5]

At 15, he read the *Odyssey*, and was deeply influenced by the image of shipwrecked Odysseus, who finds shelter under two olive bushes:

At school in those days you had to know a bit about this. We were fairly busy kids at that State grammar school...I probably read it because of reading Tennyson's 'Ulysses'...at school...I remember our being told a resumé about the Trojan War and Odysseus being ten years there, ten years drifting back to home. I think it was then that I picked the book up and thought I'd just clue myself up about this a bit, it was E.V. Rieu's translation...[LI]. Then I found, by accident, Cotterill's translation and I've been very fond of that (Jenkins, 1985, p.5).

In 1962, at 16, Reading started studying art at Liverpool College of Art, but kept his distance from the pop culture going on around him. His teachers apparently left him alone (he spent many mornings in the Anglican cathedral listening to the organist practising), as long as he had the required exhibition pieces ready by the end of the year; he produced many etchings and dark abstract landscape paintings. This liberal 60s art education gave him an understanding of modern art, a historical perspective and formal openness. In those years, Reading was also trying to get poems published [LI]:

I had sent stuff to... more or less every magazine that's on the main list...in the back of the *Writers' and Artists' Yearbook*...It just came back, of course...Sometimes I sent the same poem again to the same place. I don't think I that I'd had anything published until George MacBeth on the radio programme *Poetry Now* took some stuff... Amongst the places I tried to bombard with stuff when I had any was *Outposts Magazine*. Howard Sergeant...wrote to me saying, 'I don't want to use the enclosed, but...would you like to produce a small book?' ...That was how *Water and Waste* came about...Because I'd had contact with George MacBeth and he was very kind and generous to me. I sent him a copy of *Water and Waste*...And he...suggested that I send a copy to Anthony Thwaite...who had then just taken up the position of Poetry Editor with Secker's... Anthony wrote back...saying...had I considered doing a book and would I send him some stuff for him to think about for the Secker list that he was just establishing... Eventually...*For the Municipality's Elderly* was published. And then the others under his auspices up to...and including *C*... So that's the story. That's why I've had a very easy ride...I didn't ever have to tout stuff around too much.

Water and Waste (1970) was dedicated to the poet Jack Bevan, who taught Liberal Studies at his Liverpool college. There Reading came into contact with Old and Middle English poetry – *Piers Plowman*, *Gawain*, Chaucer – which had a lasting influence on him: 'I wasn't very well read, but I was attracted by the vigour of those works...to what isn't messing about' (Jenkins, 1985, p.5). He was especially grateful to Bevan because he encouraged him to write and let him collaborate on his own translations of Quasimodo.

Asked later about his favourites in art [C], Reading named the École de Paris; the beginnings of modern abstract art and cubism (Picasso, Kandinsky, Miró et al); the abstract expressionists (especially American); English painting from the 1930s; and Robert Rauschenberg, Jasper Johns and Jim Dine, aggressive and provocative modernists who shocked museum-goers with their collages, ready-mades and combines. Rauschenberg's and Dine's combines clearly inspired the structure of Reading's books – he, too, has incorporated found poems and disparate material. Johns rejected the expectation that art was, among other things, self-expression; this may have bolstered the idea in Reading that the personal ego was best eliminated from the artistic process.

At the same time Reading was reading widely, particularly the English novel of the 18th and 19th centuries:

> It would certainly be my choice of reading. I wouldn't sit down and read collections of modern poetry from choice. My choice would be to turn to Smollett, to Fielding, to Dickens, to Thackeray; also *Gil Blas* and the translation of *Don Quixote*...or perhaps Rabelais, something like this.[6]...I'm also a great admirer of Joyce and have since my student days dipped into the *Wake* regularly' [LI].

After Keats in poetry came Tennyson and Swinburne. He admired Tennyson's 'resounding grandiloquence' [C], while Swinburne impressed him because he was so well-read in poetry and '*au fait* with all the metres in accepted poetical literature in the 19th century' (Potts, 1990, p.94). In 1984, when the *TLS* asked various poets which works of literature had most influenced their own understanding of poetic form, this was Reading's response:

> *Paradise Lost*, in that it clearly defined iambic pentameter but demonstrated a sinuous freedom available within strict discipline. Frost's use of the same metre, for its casual ease but adherence to structure. All Hopkins flabbergasted me (still does) for explosive vigour strengthened by rigorous, odd, appropriate structural law. H.B. Cotterill's (1911) translation of the *Odyssey*, in that it made what I felt to be a classical hexameter equivalent (incorporating accentual and quantitative considerations) without sounding silly-quaint but vigorous, fast-moving, modulated, conversational – with the dignified distancing of order throughout. All Auden, for the above qualities and the idea that 'Blessed be all metrical rules that forbid automatic responses,/ force us to have second thoughts, free from the fetters of Self.'[7]

He has also cited Charles Dickens as a literary influence. Dickens's exaggerated characters and grotesques within a realistic framework, his cross-section of society and his creation of an entire fictional world are all features playing a large role in Reading's books. Interviewers who insisted on hearing about contemporary influences received these answers:

> The sort of poetry that I started off wanting to write, would have been full of admiration for, say, Robert Frost and Edward Thomas, people whom I admire tremendously as amongst my favourites for their attitude to nature, metrical formalism, and unassuming humanism.[8]
> ...I suppose it would be silly not to mention Auden, because clearly every schoolboy of my generation who wrote anything was influenced by him. And Eliot, obviously... But it doesn't somehow work out that you can do that. You find that all sorts of things occur which in some peculiar manner force you to take a different line – just the general sort of stimuli that prompt the writing of anything... In a way I don't seem to be able to control what I do. I don't seem to be writing what I would want to write. I'm almost like some sort of agent that is drawn into these things... I don't think I have...taken anything too literally from any of these people. One of the things I suppose I wanted to do was not be like anybody else (Hamilton, M; Edgar, p.20).

In 1967 Reading graduated with a First. A few exhibitions in Liverpool followed, but the end of his studies also brought with it the end of painting, first of all for practical reasons:

> I liked painting and am immodest enough to say I was quite good at it. But...I didn't continue as a painter because I thought it would take too

much hard work to be successful, and I didn't want to just paint on Sundays. Especially as the sort of painters I liked were large-scale painters – American abstract expressionists, de Kooning, Motherwell, Rothko; I was very impressed by Soulages; really big painters. You can't really fit painting in with having a job. Poets don't need as much sit-down time; the things that happen for a poem happen in small doses, and you don't need a twelve-hour stretch to sit down and type it. Also I couldn't drive, which meant that I wouldn't have been able to carry large canvasses about. When I left the College of Art I did a lot of small things, which you could pack into something the size of a wine-case, to convey from one place to another if you were having an exhibition. That dealt with the problem of scale (Edgar, p.59; Jenkins, 1985, p.5).

At the same time, oil and brush no longer satisfied Reading's artistic needs:

At some point I decided that the sort of things which I wanted to try and talk about were not best dealt with in painting... So I packed it up. By then I was writing a lot anyway; though I didn't know what I wanted to write. I liked the idea of writing, like all people who start doing any of the arts – they like the idea of it before they find that they have, or haven't, got anything of great moment to say (Bailey, M; Jenkins, 1985, p.5).

After three years in teaching posts, he moved to Ludlow, a deliberate move away from academia and city living. There he got work at an animal feedmill, doing a poorly paid but undemanding job which left him free to think. Writing required mental energy, and for him was not compatible with a teaching job. With a few interruptions, he stayed at the feedmill from 1970 until 1992:

Like the bloke in Philip Larkin's 'Livings', I deal with farmers, things like dips and feed...I've done various jobs in the mill, from hauling unwieldy sacks around the warehouse to pushing the buttons of the blending plant which brings together various ingredients in propor- tions formulated by a nutritionist for the production of the cattle, sheep, pig and poultry feed compounds that are the company's domi- nant concern. – Nowadays I operate the weighbridge, a cushy enough number, checking and recording the weights of incoming raw materials ...and weighing out the finished products.[9]

Asked whether he had also deliberately intended to distance himself from the London literary establishment, Reading replied:

Yes, that's correct. It's a bit unreal and of no particular attraction to me. Or at least its component parts do not attract me...The literary business can be done perfectly well by post...I neither despise nor court any literary scene. There is a kind of schizophrenia about it in a way...: I don't particularly feel that I fit in at the mill where I work. On the other hand, I don't feel that I fit in with the literati, either. But that's okay. It's a sort of prestidigital balance of the two (Edgar, p.54; Hamilton, M).

Four years later, in 1974, Reading's first book *For the Municipality's Elderly* was published by Secker & Warburg, after which the books kept coming in quick succession, with roughly 16 months between each. He only made about £300 to £500 per book, but accepted this: 'Poetry's an unmarketable commodity and why should it be otherwise? I'm not asking any favours.'[10] He did not regret taking the job at the mill:

I have always preferred to have a job which is still in touch with some kind of reality. I never wanted to be pretentious or set myself up in any self-conscious way as a "poet"...We take ourselves rather too seriously as writers. The writing isn't any kind of subject. It doesn't seem to me that you're a writer, first and foremost. That's one of the reasons I've got a job: an honest and ordinary job of work. I would feel guilty and silly if I was just a writer.[11]

Reading repeatedly named two factors which made his job attractive to him. First:

...some knowledge of a specialist working area like [the mill] is rather useful in that it can help to make credible a character or situation which one may choose to set in a similar context. – As for the sorts of characters to be encountered (and utilised for literary purposes) in this arena, there's more or less the same burlesque mixture as one would meet in any other declining parochial British industry of the late 80s: reps are, of course, a seedy bunch; sub-literates proliferate as much in the board-room as on the shop floor; company cars help to inflate what Auden identified as 'all weak inferior egos'; opinionated whippersnappers tinker with hi-tech; ill-read incompetent jackasses are catapulted to positions of grandeur for which they are grotesquely inadequate (no names – no pack-drill); integrity is inversely proportional to hierarchical position. – The farmers with whom one has dealings are a curious breed, varying from the genial Hodge to the spoilt churlish agrestic (*O fortunatos nimium, sua si bona norint,/ Agricolas!...*) There's a plentiful supply then, of ready-made *dramatis personae* – ghastly, funny or just plain bonkers – from which to draw (*Observer*, 'Muse').

He also felt that the different registers, dialects and styles of speech he encountered were helpful:

A more obviously useful and enjoyable literary resource to be found in a weighbridge, though, is the continually mutable demotic of lorry drivers' ordinary banter. It's this rich Rabelaisian linguistic inventiveness which compensates for the drudgery of the job and makes a day's work not unamusing to someone like me whose natural parlance is of the gutter (*Observer*, 'Muse').

Nevertheless, a writer's residency in 1981-83 at Sunderland Polytechnic (now University) gave him a welcome break from the job at the mill, and he wrote two and a half books in those two and a half years. One particular friend from Sunderland was John Coggrave, an erudite man who would recommend books. Some were of immediate practical relevance to Reading's writing and an important stimulus, such as Preminger's *Princeton Encyclopedia of Poetry and Poetics* and Saintsbury's *History of Prosody*. According to Cosgrave, the concept of the virtuoso appealed to Reading's ambition – he wanted to master as many instruments as possible [C].

Throughout the 80s, Reading produced poetry books which chronicled his country's moral, cultural and political disintegration. In an article for the Australian magazine *Island* called 'Going, Going: A View from contemporary England', he linked the literary tradition of English pessimism with the 'national sense of decline', listing Henry Francis Lyte, Gibbon, Hopkins, Dickens, Smollett, Thomas Hardy, H.G. Wells, Evelyn Waugh, Eeyore, Auden, Roy Fuller, Philip Larkin and Margaret Drabble. Reading, who firmly places himself in this literary line in *Stet*, sees four factors contributing to this attitude:

> ...a congenital English pessimism (maybe something to do with our economy?, our climate?); an English tendency to self-denigrate (attributable in part to an inherent reticence, in part to a native caution, and it causes us sometimes to portray ourselves as even worse than we actually are); the actual English experience of loss of Empire; and, arising from this last, all the connotations suggested by such a fall as had been delineated by Gibbon as early as 1776. Gibbon saw History as 'little more than the crimes, follies, and misfortunes of mankind', as 'vicissitudes of fortune, which spares neither man nor the proudest of his works, which buries empires and cities in a common grave'. His conclusion that 'all that is human must retrograde' completes the gloomy, if realistic outlook which many of his countrymen have subsequently inherited or adopted. We register our own degeneration when we observe external decay, and view our personal disintegration as a metaphor for universal entropy.[12]

This aside, Reading sometimes suffers what he calls 'a measure of misanthropy and a sort of depressive moroseness', an earlier example of which he sees in Smollett's 'Ferret' [C]:

> I see change and decay in all around – in microcosmic England, at least ...Perhaps many of us believe that nothing can be done, that these are the mere manifestations of an incontrovertible, irremediable change and decay. We may be perplexed and dismayed, but are also impotent...I think that things in England are worse now than they have ever been. Things are always worse than they have ever been; the newspapers, and their correspondence columns, corroborate this... Newspapers are the sumps of our society, draining off, and holding for our inspection, our own superfluous concentrated slurry...To hand, as I hack this, are the morning's journals, retailing with relish the ordinary mayhem and muck of a State farctate with feculence, violence and subliteracy. There are too many of us...Like Larkin, I just think it will happen, soon.[13]

By the end of the decade, when Reading was struggling to finish *Evagatory*, his mood was black. He told Robert Potts:

> If I can finish *Evagatory*, I've nothing else to say...In years gone by I've had sufficient resilience. This isn't a life that I like, or accept, but it is one I'm prepared to acknowledge. Nothing has meant more to me than writing. Without any satisfaction – indeed, with great dissatisfaction – I feel I'm facing the end (Potts, 1990, pp.96-97).

Not writing would mean 'not earning the justification to exist'. This made him restless and unstable, as he later recalled:

> In 1990...I was experiencing a period of low literary productivity. My fourteenth book, *Perduta Gente*, had been published in 1989 and seemed to have left me something of a 'lost person' myself – drained of ideas and artistic resources. The dozen or so (apparently desultory) pieces which I had subsequently written, had been gathered together, under the title *Shitheads*, in a volume published by a small press in a limited edition. This constituted a convenient intermezzo, but I was completely at a loss as to the direction my next concerted work should take. – Furthermore, the tedious job which I had held for about twenty years ...had become unconducive to literary activity and a source of only indifferent financial recompense. I had recourse to regular book reviewing for newspapers – a welcome supplement to my income, but a fatiguing adjunct to a full-time occupation and an additional obstacle to my own 'creative' writing [Lannan Report, M].

The Lannan award changed everything at once. International renown and $35,000 came in September 1990, a month after the gloomy interview with Potts. The artistic block and financial worries were wiped away:

> At a time of such personal disquietude, to receive, unsolicited and unexpected, an honour as prestigious and substantial as that...was at once a thrilling endorsement of past work and an invaluable stimulant for future production. It is no exaggeration to say that this sense of sincere encouragement engendered by the Foundation was the most important part of my award [Lannan Report, M].

In the meantime, Reading's workplace, which had been run by a local farmers' cooperative ('very small and rustic and rather inefficient and simple, but surprisingly successful'; Lannan Video, M), was taken over by a national agribusiness, which Reading called 'deeply unsatisfactory, the worst elements of commercialism, of trade':

> ...traditional values have gone to pot. The old hands have been bullied, badgered and baffled by new-fangled phenomena such as security fencing, an arty-farty logo and the inevitable bandying about of cant and shibboleth by a bunch of fresh execs at once callow and megalomaniacal. The Mill Manager's office, so crammed with computerised bleeping

gimcracks as to resemble the worst excesses of an amusement arcade, contains a diminutive bookshelf with two eye-catching titles: *Dealing with Difficult People* and *Don't Do, Delegate*.[14]

After 22 years at the mill, Reading was suspended from work in January 1992: 'the first time I have experienced such chastisement since 4th Form days, when I was copped for swaggering about the bike-shed with a Peterson full of acrid smouldering navy shag' (Reading, 'Freelance'). On the same day that Daisy Goodwin's film *Day Jobs* featuring 'one of our better poets, Peter Reading' [15] was shown on national television, he was summoned for a 'verbal warning' – 'a piece of theatrical irony', according to Reading. After a second warning, he was sacked 'with a month's notice' [C], the point of conflict being 'a very simple, perhaps silly, one'. Reading was told to wear the company's new green uniform (for 'Corporate Image' and 'Corporate Identity'), but 'declined the offer':

> There's nothing wrong with the things sartorially...but this is just fancy dress and toy soldiering...regimentation...Most people are glad to leave uniforms behind when they finish school...It's not as though I am refusing to wear a hard hat on a building site or protective clothing for health or hygiene reasons. – I suppose some bastard had been to a seminar somewhere and came back with this hare-brained notion... There's a rigmarole that these grown-up people have to go through. I've had a verbal warning; I've had what they affect to call a written warning, which constituted a syntactically appalling letter; the margins aren't quite wide enough to correct the syllogisms. – It was magnanimously decreed that if I were to return to work and don the offending garment, all would be forgiven and forgotten.[16]

While voicing his regret at having lost a job which had left him time to think, he was also relieved: 'it's refreshing to be away from there', and 'if it hadn't been this, we'd have fallen out over something else', because since the takeover his job had been 'a pain' [C]. Reading's satirical version of the story was published in the *TLS* (7 February 1992) and featured in a videotaped reading.[17] The anecdotal version covers up the private seriousness of the matter; this is Reading's interpretation of what happened:

> I've always hated commerce. My dealings with the previous company were the closest to compromise I could get. I suppose I was fleeing from what was clearly the end of England, and now that's caught up with me. It's a fair cop (Potts, 1992).

The Lannan Award enabled him to work on *Last Poems*. After that was complete, and he had finished illustrating his children's book *Rana*, he spent a year in Australia in 1993, returning to Britain to finish work on a joint exhibition with Peter Kennard,

Erosive, shown in London in 1994. This welcome move back to visual art was followed by the poster *Leasts* (poem and artwork, 21 October 1994, signed by the author, in an edition of 20); [*thence to this silence,*], an installation of six poems from *Evagatory* for the 100th anniversary of the Stedelijk Museum in Amsterdam in 1995, which was also printed as a pamphlet; and *Six Poems* (2000, in an edition of 5), six A3 pages of handwritten poems with photographs.

In 1994 he was able to combine readings for the Lannan Foundation in Washington and New York with ornithological excursions to Florida and the Everglades. Resettled in Shrewsbury, he worked with his new publisher Bloodaxe on the two-volume *Collected Poems*, which incorporated what would have been a new book, *Eschatological*, and had finished the next one, *Work in Regress*, when he took up a six-month fellowship in 1997 at the University of East Anglia.

In 1998, he was the first writer to hold the newly inaugurated Lannan Literary Residency, and lived for a year in the small town of Marfa, on the Texan-Mexican border, which he portrayed in somewhat unflattering terms in the next poetry book, *Marfan*. There he also began work on the next book, to be titled [*untitled*] and scheduled for publication in 2001.

In January 2000, Reading was given a two-year Continuation Grant from the Lannan Foundation to enable him to work on his next book or books.

For the Municipality's Elderly (1974): Looking for a Stance

For the Municipality's Elderly includes almost all the poems from Peter Reading's first pamphlet, *Water and Waste*, published by Howard Sergeant's Outposts Publications in 1970. George MacBeth had recommended the Outposts pamphlet to Anthony Thwaite, who solicited a first book-length collection from Reading for the new Secker & Warburg poetry list.

The book is influenced by Reading's literary mentors Frost, Hopkins, MacNeice, Auden, Eliot, Edward Thomas, Larkin, and by Anglo-Saxon and Middle English poetry. A few times Reading openly refers to Eliot, Auden, and Larkin, but his admiration of Robert Frost also makes itself felt, as Reading realised:

> Some early things were, I suppose, quite Robert Frost-like. What I admired about him was a directness and a lucidity in apparently very simple ways. Also the way that he managed to push the iambic pentameter to a casual recording of speech and things... It was a big development, in my opinion (Edgar, p.59).

At the same time, an individual voice and style are emerging in this first book, and Reading's distinctive thematic, stylistic, structural and metrical qualities can be identified in bud: the central theme of the *condition humaine*, the link with the specific situation in England; an elegiac tone counterbalanced by exact observation (and later, humour); the production of hypertexts of old literary texts;[1] the choice of a formal-structural basis for a number of poems (e.g. 'Juvenilia', 'Brabyns Park', 'Lapse'), combined with an instinctive tendency towards the dactylic-spondaic foot in a falling cadence, which was appropriately chosen for the 'already gathering maelstrom' ('Severn at Worcester'), Reading's main theme throughout his œuvre.

Nineteen out of the 22 poems in *Water and Waste* were reprinted in *For the Municipality's Elderly*. Reading decided not to include 'Horticulture', 'Dead Horse' and 'Dirty Linen', which had been placed at the end of *Water and Waste*. They were however reprinted in the *Collected Poems* (pp.64-66).

In 'Dead Horse' (p.65), the epanaphorical refrain 'Not to be born is best, said Sophocles' gives the source of this poem's motto. 'Dead Horse', though, is a 'Sophocles-by-way-of-Auden' poem, a hypertext.[2] The self-ironical disillusionment which surfaces in the (unsuccessful) attempt to disprove Sophocles corresponds to the unexpected debunking of the lyrical speaker by himself in the last stanza:

Not to be born is best, said Sophocles,
(the second-best is an abysmal bore)
a view which he would re-assert, I'm sure,
hearing the second-rate asthmatic wheeze
of this ephemeral trite Audenese,
the product of a brain long dulled and clogged,
the patter of a dead horse being flogged.

So, a salient feature regarding metrics surprisingly originates in one of the very first poems from *Water and Waste*: 'Dead Horse' brands metrical utterances a dead drumming art by exemplifying this art itself – but as such it is a successful example of a well-made poem which makes its point via its form, thereby rehabilitating poetry. Making negative statements about poetry in poems which are lively examples of poetic potential and potency is a logical and aesthetic paradox which Reading elaborated and stretched to its limit in later years.

For *For the Municipality's Elderly*, Reading wrote 17 new poems in four years, roughly the second half of the book. This relatively meagre yield coincided with a busy new phase in Reading's private life (marriage, job, moving). Aged 28, Reading comments on his 'Juvenilia' (p.43), with the characteristic inversion facilitating the dactylic beat:

But having found love I am left with nothing to say.
...
Thus, satisfactory poems have been,
through, first over-need, then through absence of need,
unwritten.

The old poems were tidied up in places: a few small points in punctuation, orthography, word-choice, and syntax and enjambement. Excluding three poems from *Water and Waste* was a result of thematic focussing and a lesson in self-criticism. Reading decided early on that the wastepaper basket was more useful than the desk drawer; so-called 'lesser poems' were not to be tolerated.[3] At the same time, mirroring his attitude to material things, Reading stuck to his dictum of economy: 'I don't like wasting things' [C]. This meant recycling the poems that did not go in the bin, which explains part of the œuvre's unity. Later, another measure of economy with respect to commissioned poems went as follows [LI]:

Say something had been commissioned – I'd do that particular job...and then I would find a way of incorporating it into what I already had or what I was going to do.

Even the 'naff juvenilia, chucked in the Parkray' (*Final Demands*, p.118) were distilled into new poems after the slag was drawn out of them (p.69, p.213). The impulse to preserve is granted – as with the Romantic image of a clear mountain spring on Bardsey Island in *Stet*, for example – but in *For the Municipality's Elderly* this is already interpreted as a futile gesture against transience, a stance that Reading takes to extremes in the eroding poems of the last books. The north wall of the nave in Ludlow Church bears a plaque with these words ('New Year Letter', p.48):

                              ...HIC JACET
A.E.H. is that which remains, while
his poems are not in the library here
today.

Even this is not a lasting memorial to the poet of Shropshire, A.E. Housman, because the plaque will erode and become illegible (like the 'five slabs' of the 'charabanc trippers' on Gorse Hill, p.29).

The blurbs of poetry books often make the point that the homogeneity of a volume is provided by a voice of integrity, which prismatically reflects on the multidimensional experiences of modern life and/or binds them together in a unified vision. One reason for the diversification of content in many books of poetry is exopoetic: the longer the time of gestation, the more disparate the subject-matter is likely to become. Interest in the sequence grew in the 70s with Hughes, Hill and Heaney searching for meaningful myths in unified works. Gavin Ewart pointed out in 1989 that this was not the normal course of events:

Most poets, when they're putting together a new book of verse – and 'putting together' is exactly the right phrase – sit down and sort out the poems they have written since the last book was published...The poems will be of different kinds: light, solemn, satirical, lyrical, narrative. They may cover a whole range of moods and techniques, and deal with very different subjects. Peter Reading is not a poet of this kind. [7]

For Reading, whose writing over 28 years averages out at one page per week, the situation was different. The condensed time span alone concentrated his choice of subject-matter. He was determined not to select poems retrospectively for publication, but to look ahead and draft his books *as books*: as mosaics, as elaborations on a complex theme with many variations. *For the Municipality's Elderly* was the exception to this trend as far as its composition went, but, as Reading said in an interview, 'even that I wanted to work as a gradual development of themes though they were what people call proper poems with titles and all that stuff' (Edgar, p.57). (In fact, this also goes for the next two books.) The formal discipline and structural tightening which Reading continually took further, evolved naturally from the thematic objective. Especially as from *C*, Reading planned his work more in accordance with the architectonic schemes and relatively fixed subject-matter of novelists.

His practical inclination towards economy may have been at the core of his later strategy, which combined many artistic devices to multiple effect and thereby led to a multi-dimensional network of self-referentiality unusual in poetry books. Economy was the principle that was given more and more functions, and so it became the general tool for cohesion. The arrangement of layers was not only achieved in the individual books: iconic, metaphoric, thematic, formal, narratological, and structural layers permeate the œuvre as a whole; it is devised as a unified corpus, as a *Gesamtwerk*.

In the first two volumes, unity is achieved mainly through the thematic exploration of the eternal lyrical sine qua non, transience and love. According to the Introduction in *Essential Reading*, *For the Municipality's Elderly* had not been conceived as a book. As it is, the choice of subject-matter, the tone and style, and even the table of contents all give evidence of unity: the first three poems are each individually bracketed together with the last three poems ('Fall' with 'Lapse', 'Embarkation' with 'Night-Piece', 'Earthworks' with 'Burning Stubble'), thus framing and holding the middle part like an envelope, but also giving the central subject of the book in shorthand: seasons, life-spans and nature metaphorically and linguistically overlap, and they are all bound under the big arch of death, exemplified by the structural bracket of the book. Also, the laconic titles (mainly nouns) anticipate the process through different stages of life. At the same time, in an allusion to Robert Frost's 'Fire and Ice' the first and last poems, with their respective images of death through cold and heat throughout the seasons, exemplify the beginning and the end of life. All this, no doubt, must have been conscious tectonics. Reading confirmed this [LI]:

> I've always found it very important. As soon as I've got the minimum to get by on ... then I have always had the luxury of putting them all out on the table and getting them into some sort of order which works sequentially or thematically or has some unifying factor. Certainly did that with *For the Municipality's Elderly* ... so that it wasn't just a rag-bag magpie collection of stuff.

Apart from this, the ever-more refined and surprising structures of the works also testify to the fact that there must have been unifying factors to start with, which were integrated into the writing itself as soon as a certain direction or principle emerged. This is how novels and plays are written, or indeed long poetic sequences, like Eliot's *Four Quartets* (five movements) or Bunting's *Briggflatts* (sonata form), which use musical structures already in existence. Rather than using the form of such models, Reading used the methods. Again, this was an eclectic measure resulting from the principle of economy – for Reading, poetry books were too slim not to make the most of all technical possibilities, so everything right up to pagination was scrutinised as potentially usable for structure, thereby extending the scope of poetry generally.

Perhaps it was due to Secker's reputation and to the interest in newcomers' books that *For the Municipality's Elderly* was reviewed in a few big newspapers straightaway. It was no bad start: there were some prominent poet-critics among the first reviewers (Peter Porter, Dannie Abse, Terence de Vere White and Martin Dodsworth), and their reviews were published in the big dailies.[5] It still took a while, though, for Reading to be given a lengthy review all to himself, and according to Alan Jenkins of the *TLS* it was the single review of *C* in the *TLS* which started 'the breakthrough' in his reputation [C].

The title *For the Municipality's Elderly* is a common inscription on community benches. It evokes a place to rest and reflect on the end of life, which happens in the title-poem. A related association is produced by the title *Water and Waste*, also a municipal term, but more literally about decomposition than death. 'Juvenilia' refers to this title:

> The Goyt, from the overhang of this bridge,
> changes in characteristic from,
> on one side asthmatic but indisputable
> life, to a moribund slack on the other
> where, deeper, the undercurrent remains
> towing a slack immobile body
> of water and waste away involuntarily.[6]

The perspective from the bridge corresponds to a change in life phases, but the metaphor also works on a higher level – the river carries away waste as time does lives, until they too turn to 'waste'. Taken together, the two titles bear the altogether unsentimental implication that while the poet may follow his poetic ruminations about death, the community's job is to dispose of the decaying bodies. (Dual vision is often present in Reading's books, most notably in *Diplopic*.)

The subject in *For the Municipality's Elderly* – the mirroring of the *condition humaine* in the natural cycles – was chosen with a certain aim in mind. The first axiom of Reading's aesthetics is that art has to deal with humanity in order to become important and to move readers. As a consequence, a perspective first had to be found from which to view human life. The question 'did you search for a stance?' was answered in the positive: 'Yes. Yes, very much so' [LI]. For this purpose, the eschatological stance is the best choice, because without an interpretation of death, pertinent comments about the value and meaning of life can hardly be made.

In *For the Municipality's Elderly*, decay and death are studied in a matter-of-fact way and are presented as purely biological fact without any transcendental dimension, i.e. as a datum that simply demands acceptance: 'each cell resumed decaying / to only chemically recur' (p.63).[7] An intensive investigation of religious questions is not to be expected of Reading, who already as a child put his faith in nature and the natural sciences and saw religious beliefs as anachronistic constructions: 'We are awaiting yet another Christmas, / giving a last chance to a disproved theory' ('Advent', p.33). Like everything else, ecclesiastic content falls victim to decay: 'Livid fur smothers an Old Testament' (p.63).

In 'St James's' (pp.57-58), Reading writes his response to an influential poem in the same tradition, Larkin's expedition poem 'Church Going',[8] where the speaker, an atheist, still feels an irrational longing and reverence in the church and tries to understand why; at the same time, Larkin's punning title points to the decline of the Church. One generation later Reading's speaker is already completely free from metaphysical unease – ecclesiastical concerns are *passé* to such a degree that the visitor, 'having to have a sense of history', instead inspects art-historically and architecturally relevant details and examines tombstones. The last signs of life in the holy building are skeletons and feathers left by jackdaws in the tower, and 'doodles in the roof' made by woodworm. The laconic omission of the eternal is most pronounced in the last verse (after which there is nothing): the visitor makes ready to go, 'turning from font to underground stone kist'.

In *For the Municipality's Elderly*, Reading lays the existential foundation for his works, turning to it again after the fourth book and then developing it into a more comprehensive world-view. This foundation deserves detailed attention because the other focal points of Reading's works – socio-political, but also aesthetic – have been over-emphasised by critics.

In a distanced stance, the lyrical title-poem provides the blank

parameters: 'Things here grow old and worn with untragic logic.'
The way to a stoic outlook on death has to be paid for with one's
whole life (p.50):

> Still there persists
> a smile of attained appeasement in worn
> grained skulls, streaked knobs of warm butter with no more
> of life left in them, misericords.

Observer and observed in the end are all equal: 'we...brown / and
burn out'. One of the most frequent words in *For the Municipality's
Elderly* is 'decay', with many synonyms (opposed by 'permanence').

So, the practical consequence of finding meaningfulness without
help from the hereafter becomes central, 'Lof the Saxons called
it'. ('Lof', fame in one's lifetime, is again recalled in *Evagatory*.)
In all of this, Reading avoids the tone of grave seriousness (*gravitas* is secured stylistically); nature alone is granted his unmodified
respect. The only mention of eternal life, for example, occurs in
the ironically titled 'Easter Letter' (pp.54-56): [9]

> I fade through years to a fair with a schoolfriend,
> quite beyond contact now, the Big Wheel
> sickeningly revolves, we first glimpse
> immortality – our insides
> keep going for ever after our bodies
> have stopped.

According to Reading the fauna-specialist, after the 'maelstrom'
only insects will find resurrection; on the opened Bible 'big black
dormant flies tremble in Genesis' (p.64) – this is the last verse of
the book. The division of lines per stanza in this poem also hints
at the lack of a spiritual alternative, and at decay. According to the
symmetrical structure, one more verse would have had to follow
(6-2-1-2-6), but Reading leaves the poem with an expressive 6-2-
1-2-5; the title is, appropriately, 'Lapse'. [10]

What comes down from Heaven is not exactly reassuring, either:
'Aeschylus' is a deceptive, amusing aside, pseudo-philosophising
about the grotesque end of the heathen Greek, and becomes a
metaphor for the unscrupulous religions and their attacks on dissenters (this is a recurrent target in Reading's later works, too).
An eagle mistook the writer's bald pate for a stone and let his prey
tortoise fall on it so as to split open its shell (p.42):

> I view all life now with grave disbelief,
> find all on earth reptilian and hideous,
> and Heaven sly, potentially perfidious.

The speaker strikes up solidarity with Aeschylus, the first author of tragedies, as one of the 'poets quietly in pursuit of grief'; this, however, is mockingly deflated by the light verse-rhymes, the skipping rhythm, and the limerick-like beginning ('There was a...').

As is now evident, in *For the Municipality's Elderly* the only basis for thought is nature, but Reading circumnavigates any conceivable pitfalls by acting as his own first critic. Aesthetic doubts are voiced in the poems themselves (see 'Raspberrying', 'Aeschylus' and 'Dead Horse') with all necessary clarity, and in this new context the hackneyed pastoral nature-metaphor of golden times becomes unpredictable again, interesting, and contemporary.

For the Municipality's Elderly uses different situations and images, especially observations of nature and related sensations, thoughts and associations, to record the all-pervasiveness of death. The poems, all darkened by the 'shadow of the quiet harvester' (p.61), can be grouped according to subject-matter: observations of nature with philosophical implications; time travelling, both to one's own ancestors and to people hundreds and thousands of years back who lived in the same place; the phases of life and marriage; paintings as starting-points for associative ruminations; old people. (The personal 'Mnemonic (For N.H.)' falls outside these.)

Reading sees the universal in the particular, thus complying with scientific induction; his eye for significant details and his sensibility introduce a new thematic nuance in each poem and generate a quiet continuity of the lyrical mood.[11] His composure may produce a certain counterweight to the dark views, but this is denounced as 'surface-calm' (p.44) and shows its shaky basis especially in the turbulent night agonies of 'Night-Piece' (pp.62-63), which as the penultimate poem relinquishes the controlled, cool stance in the face of the approaching Armageddon (Rev. 16.16), accompanied by Bach's 'Great G minor Fantasia', choreographed by the three goddesses of fate and engendered by 'the unrevealed player'. As Jenkins remarked, the 'infinitely unimpressed' tone, the 'complete social attitude, knowing, detached, almost Olympian' was a 'note that did not satisfy Reading for long'.[12] Unmistakably, in *For the Municipality's Elderly* we find the first examples of Reading's sarcastic tones and black humour, too.

The scope of the book is clearly defined, and the beginner's tendency to 'over-write' is also avoided. Dannie Abse was pleasantly surprised by this début: 'Mr Reading's poems... have an attractive modesty and in aiming for small effects frequently succeed.'

'Fall', for instance, the first poem (p.27), is an exact vignette. The sudden snowfall seems to announce winter, as the title suggests, but in fact it is spring, the birds' mating-season (ornithological, botanical, and other scientific details are, on principle, always 'straight'; 'Plashy Fen School' metaphors, as Reading labels them in *Diplopic* – what Ruskin called the 'pathetic fallacy', i.e. anthropomorphism – are out of the question). The 'fall' that destroys fertile life shocks people into 'that peculiar brand of politeness / that only climatic extremes, / or a war, produce'. The sluice manages to control the extra water, just as the politeness reins in feelings of panic, but it is a thin dividing line.[13] The poem's imagery seemed good enough to keep, but in a second version, 'Fetial' (*Stet*, p.84), improvements were made in direction, impetus, metaphorical and linguistic concentration, and polished metrics. Reading likes 'paring down' [C], as he says.

From an eschatological perspective, cyclic dying in nature lends itself easily to metaphor. The surprising thing is that not only fall and winter are taken as foils, but that spring and summer do not give any relief at all, as they too generate and symbolise decay. Reading also gives his poems cyclical titles – 'Letter in Winter', 'Spring Letter', 'New Year Letter', 'Easter Letter', implying recurrent sameness – and always only encounters transience: dying takes place all the time everywhere. A Botticelli spring seems anachronistic in the face of the continual destruction of nature and so Readings's spring appears as a brown reflection in the Severn. Summer heat stifles, suffocates, burns fields. Traditional counterweights like love, birth, and innocence only eke out a short existence, overshadowed by death, as in 'Calvary' (p.40):

Today
on the Nob hunched over this black northern splatter
of chimneys, lapwings whip down like Stukas
spun in a vortex, an inch from the ground
pulling-out, urged by an instinct to love
(though it seems courting death – and the two are fused
on this dead spring day; all coming alive
too late at the end of a season).
A lamb,
joints stiff, brittle, jabs at maternal clogged fleece,
spattered red (which is ruddle but looks already
like blood and soon must be).

The blurb for the first edition, written by Thwaite, highlights another aspect of the book:

Peter Reading, who lives in Shropshire, shows an individual talent exploring and accepting the 'routine passage' of a way of life geographically provincial but very close to the rhythms of life. The poems are rooted in particular places, with their own histories; but equally they draw on people and on human activities observed with quiet skill and exactness.

While *For the Municipality's Elderly* already bears unmistakable
hallmarks of Reading's style, it also reverberates with the poetic
tradition that impressed him: first of all, the exact topography and
setting in time recalls Middle English 'poetry of place'. The kind
of nature poetry that Reading encountered as a student in *Piers
Plowman* and *Sir Gawain and the Green Knight* appealed to him: 'I
loved the topography of the beginning – then I knew the area: "On
a May Morweninge on Malverne Hills" ' (Jenkins, 1985, p.5). As
Michael Alexander points out, 'For many people... such poetry
was part of an appreciation of the English countryside, a souvenir
of natural beauty to town dwellers, like the watercolour landscape
on the living room wall.' [14] While the topographical poem belongs to
'*local poetry*', of which the fundamental subject is some particular
landscape ...with the addition of ... historical retrospection or inci-
dental meditation', [15] in Anglo-Saxon poetry (and in the Bible) places
are used as *topoi*, without much detail or colour: 'The landscape of
the Old English Elegies is symbolic...the weather is expressive, not
meteorological. The central place on Middle Earth is the hall, the
home of feasting and recitation, the house of light and life.' (This
was taken up by Reading in his last books, especially in *Evagatory*
and *Last Poems*.)

The local-historical past is made visible in the present, while
the non-linear time references to the present suggest a cyclical
convergence. Reading maps out a many-layered chronography and
topography of two English countrysides, the Cheshire/Derbyshire
area and Shropshire. (Until 1970, Reading lived in the north near
Marple Bridge, the setting for *Water and Waste*. The new poems
for *For the Municipality's Elderly* explore his new surroundings
after the move to Ludlow.) In these atmospheric sketches time
and place in England are captured by a modern voice searching
the map for human remains. The famous kings of Mercia of the
6th and 7th centuries, Caradoc ('Earthworks', 'New Year Letter')
and Penda ('Severn at Worcester'), for example, left buildings ('Caer
Caradoc') or at least 'rubble' in Shropshire and Northumbria, but
'what they left is unimpressive / compared with their having been
here and left it' (p.50). Even the leathery bodies of 300-year-old
bog corpses are still visible; in 'Plague Graves', Reading layers
three time zones into three stanzas, the past of the five preserved
fingers in the moor, the present visit to them, and future reactions
to the visitors' own five tombstones (p.29): 'no one to know them,
extol them / or give them permanence in the now prevalent / sense
of fame; and their mark will be not / in palpable stone but that they
were once, / walked here, and did wonderful things'. The swinging

rhythm goes with the word 'wonderful', stressed even more for being surrounded by more factual monosyllables. Most people who lived here, however, remain unknown ('Easter Letter', p.54):

> The castle gleams like roasting duck,
> south-facing corners irradiate
> nine hundred years. Forty or so
> generations like us who have willingly
> browned, flaked-dry here, steam from the walls
> and nettled moat.

The present itself will leave hardly any significant traces. Some artistically attempt the *Exegi Monumentum* ('New Year Letter', p.48):

> My best friends are fifty and seventy,
> most of their lives being over. One keeps
> his manuscript autobiography locked
> in a safe against fire. The other will leave
> two softbacks a hardback and one translation.

But the reception of these 'inadequate drafts of them' beyond their grave is doubtful as well. Still, such self-assertion is brave (p.29): 'To see / the same future waiting and still to continue / seems our most noble attribute' – an early version of Viv's virtue in *Ukulele Music*. However, even this modest solution is not exempt from ambivalence. Anticipating allusions to Aeschylus and Eliot, a quotation of a popular song of *c*.1950 dismisses the speaker's own reflectiveness as superficial: 'Turn the switch, join in the chorus / "what to do about it? let's / put out the light and go to sleep" ' (p.55).[16]

In *For the Municipality's Elderly*, this question still calls for an answer. The questionable survival of mankind – which *in extremis* becomes the theme of the radical later phase – is already considered in 'Severn at Worcester': 'Appeasing to leave behind some record / of what our achievement was, provided / someone remains to read it.' Subliminally, the 28-year-old Reading still expresses the hope that things will turn out differently from what his intellect tells him.[17] Different philosophical variants are tested in different poems in order to find 'appeasement' despite the evidence, and the sceptical tension between wishful thinking and rationalism determines every line of thought (p.47; see also p.50):

> If I die
> tonight, I say to myself each bedtime,
> what will remain is either the abstract
> intangible fact of any anonymous
> ghost's former being – millions of wonderful
> things done, fun had, luscious and sour food
> and drink savoured, wife wallowed-in, despair,
> boredom, curious incidents – or

> the limp parenthesis of this
> in a palpable soft cover.

The secret unreasonableness of a troubled nobody is openly tolerated in *For the Municipality's Elderly*, even if it is unmasked as philosophical acrobatics, or 'devious thinking' (p.49). An uncomfortable conclusion is approaching in 'Brabyns Park' (p.30): 'The only permanence is, I suppose, / in having been and whether known or not / to others hardly enters into it.' In the end, the shocking insight in the volta of 'Plague Graves' makes plain that all agnostic consolation is futile: 'I suppose we secretly hope for some permanent / monument left of us, some recognition / by those coming after. No chance', abruptly ending the regular dactyls. Reading compares himself with his grandfather, whose photogravure he recalls when seeing his own reflection 'from unbiased uncompassionate / depths of a butt in a wilderness corner' ('Chiaroscuro'). There is a vital difference between the two men (p.44):

> But whereas the surface-
> calm of the goon in the barrel is rippled
> with frowns, the framed memorial (facing
> a mirror) exhibits the Old Boy's commendable
> talent for staring bald anonymity
> straight in the face unperturbed.

The central question of the book – 'what remains?' – is answered in 'Removals' in the end, even if the intellectually labile thinker leaves open another escape door (p.45):

> Will there be any tangible thing to remember us by?
> I think not; but living with being anonymous
> has almost equipped us to face leaving nothing behind.

Anonymity, as a taste of the things not to come, is woven as a *ploce* through the volume (see also pp.28, 44). From this array of thoughts, two tiny concepts are picked up, almost unnoticed, but they have great significance for the later books: 'human acknowledgement' and 'those coming after' are the only irreducible valid concepts and provide the basis of Reading's ethics. In view of the denial of transcendence in Reading's books, meaningfulness boils down to the need for human acknowledgement. And the 'almost' leaves room for an emotionally helpful function of art.

The personal character of *For the Municipality's Elderly* touches on a problematic point at this early stage. Reading, who in 1993 had not looked at the book for a long time, thought he had steered clear of the confessional mode as far as possible [LI]. But *For the Municipality's Elderly* has an undeniably autobiographical narrative frame and springs directly from personal experiences, told by an often unmasked lyrical 'I', with references to places of residence and of work, to commuting and walking, and to wife, mother and father, grandfather and great-grandfather, friends and to a bygone love. The phases of life are linked to the natural cycles: the 'Embarkation' into adult life involves several moves, and finally the author has to go past an 'Almshouse and graveyard' on his daily walk to the mill where he worked at the weighbridge (p.57), watched by an inmate as he is 'crossing towards the other side'. An echo of this is heard in the young marriage, whose stages are also metaphorically linked to natural cycles, even if presented unchronologically: a beautiful start, followed by careful scepticism and retreating passion, but with a rewarding togetherness up to the final drab loneliness of the widower.

The impulse to avoid the lyrical 'I' and an autobiographical stance is already there, but the avoidance of proper names, i.e. the de-authenticating of personae, and the abundant use of personal pronouns have only a slight generalising effect, so that the addressing of his wife or former love as 'you' or 'Love' may facilitate identification for the reader, but does not solve the aesthetic problem. The same applies to the abbreviations of authentic names ('N.H.' and 'K.J.'). On the other hand, the rivers, castles, parks, and graveyards with *their* proper names feature all the more clearly, being the more prominent "protagonists" – just so there is no mistake: to reach *their* durability, human generations must be added up in numbers of two to three figures.

Another consequence of the uncertain 'I' is that the narrative angle in *For the Municipality's Elderly* oscillates. Mostly we hear a specific (autobiographical) 'I', but sometimes there is another, older voice, which cannot be distinctly isolated. Considering the careful thematic balancing of the poems, this change seems arbitrary, if not disturbing. It does not provide a new perspective, either, as the tone remains the same. (One exopoetic reason could be the long genesis of the volume; an endopoetic explanation would suspect the speaker's function of being unresolved.) Reading, after looking at the book again, conceded this was the case [LI]:

> Some of the 'I's are just general, philosophical things. There's quite a lot of 'I's, quite a lot of personal stuff, really. It was something that I was unhappy with, though I certainly didn't manage to iron it out here... probably didn't know quite how to. The first thing I started to try and do was simply not use an 'I' at all. I haven't really used any personae in the way that I did later. No, most of these 'I's are personal, almost all of them, I'm afraid.

Only three poems avoid the 'I' or 'we' entirely ('Baigneur', 'Raspberrying', 'Nomenclator'), as in the title-poem, which as the first 'fairly dead-pan statement rather than any kind of declaration' [LI] assumes de-personalised authority. How to put individual aspects behind universal ones without losing authenticity remained a task to be solved; and the relation between autobiographical detail and non-private, but nonetheless personal writing had to be worked out.

An acute awareness of a problem of an entirely different nature shows in Reading's cursory remarks about the dark future of England and our planet (pp.36, 38, 42-43, 45, 62-63). As Dennis O'Driscoll, one of the most percipient critics on Reading, points out: 'The darkness which pervades *Water and Waste* (lightened by brio and wit rather than compromise) is that of a poet concerned about environmental issues long before it became fashionable.' [18] The gloom is punctured in places, be it through a black futuristic joke (p.29) or the convenient sarcasm of a young person for whom factual knowledge and joy of life are still two separate things ('in thirty years time she'll be gulping for real./ Top up your larynx', p.62) and who also sees that the establishment of a domestic existence and having a job can induce political apathy, as admitted in '(Advent)' (p.32).

A harmless weather forecast turns into an débâcle-oracle ('Early Closing', p.39), but in view of the devastating prognoses the pseudo-sermonising 'may we then, in the event of our general / annihilation' gives way to an angry outburst: 'You can stuff Conservation Year – let's get it over with quickly' (p.45). The effectiveness of such sudden changes of tone first became evident here and was later used as one of Reading's most important stylistic devices. That mankind has a realistic chance of survival is still an option in this book, where hope is vying with doubt (p.48) – a "soft" outlook that Reading does not allow himself again.

Another subject in *For the Municipality's Elderly* is art; there are several thematic allusions to paintings, painters and poets. Reading had just changed jobs, and just as he occasionally used the mill environment later on, one point of reference in this volume is the department of art history in Liverpool, where, for instance, he is seen cataloguing slides.[19] Following the Horatian *'Ut pictura poesis'* (*Ars Poetica*, 361), which claims poetry is of the same essence as art, poems about paintings had become very popular.

In the end, the obvious drawbacks to name-dropping – borrowing readymade connotations while addressing only those readers with art-historical knowledge – made Reading keep his distance. In *The Prison Cell & Barrel Mystery*, the endless list of artists in 'Ballad' occurs for reasons of poem-genre only, and after the biting asides in *Nothing For Anyone* about art-historical half-wittage (pp.119, 127, 145), no more was said about the subject. In his writing, Reading clearly wanted to be as close as possible to the "real" world. This impressed Martin Booth, who thought that this 'was a new book in a number of senses. The poems most definitely shaped up a lot of the time to the type of material that would appeal to the writers of real verse.' [20] That Reading was going to disappoint Booth's hope for a 'new popular poet in the mould of Logue or Mitchell or Patten', however, should have been clear. Not only does Reading cite other mentors in the book, but he also denigrates the 1960s leftovers as 'derrière-garde play-ettes' (p.35), complete with linguistic "mistake" ('arrière-garde'). Tom Paulin, also an admirer, is another critic who measures Reading with external yardsticks; he cannot salute the unpolitical début:

> His first volume … is a shaky recuperation of deeply exhausted, traditional images – graves, castles, cottage hospitals, pleached hedges, alabaster knights. However, Reading litters Deepwood Lane with some of those ephemeral consumer items which also fascinated Larkin – Kleenex and Lucozade, for example – though these contemporary markers are too obviously strategic and fail to redress the pre-first World War ruralism of the poems. The language is sometimes innocently archaic… and this increases the reactionary and nostalgic effect. These poems appear to be insulated from a society which was deepening in economic crisis (in 1973 a miners' strike brought down Edward Heath's Conservative government, which was replaced by a shaky series of Labour governments until what now looks like the final defeat of British socialism in 1979). [21]

Another poetic camp had been occupied by the so-called 'Movement' poets, who defended the traditional 'English line' against Modernism and Neo-Romanticism. While Reading shared their pragmatic no-nonsense outlook, his poetic range was greater. The direct literary lineage of *For the Municipality's Elderly* goes back to the two big names in 20th century poetry [LI]:

> I wouldn't have actually recognised the fact, but Eliot was at the back of my mind, as was Auden, as they would be for anybody of our generation who had the audacity to try and write things. There was a review of *For the Municipality's Elderly* by Terence de Vere White in the *Irish Times*… It spoke quite highly of my book and invoked Eliot, but went on, quite rightly, to say that this wasn't anywhere near as profound as *The Waste Land*, but that that was at the back of my mind.

The image from *The Waste Land* of the 'commuters over London bridge' – invoking the Charon myth and transposing it into modernity via Dante – is used for Reading's own commuting across the Cheshire Plains and over the Mersey (with the bitter taste of Charon's Toll in his mouth), always on the way 'between departure and the terminus', especially in 'Embarkation' (p.28) and 'November 5' (p.32).[22] In contrast to the fertile connotations of the river in *The Waste Land*, Reading uses it as a metaphor for time; also, rivers in the 1970s are near dead themselves. The Goyt, for example, 'brownish and throaty, / choked with smoke from the valley homes' (p.42), seems like an infected lung, 'slack', rotten, stagnating, not really much of a river any more.

While avoiding Eliot's concept of 'difficult poetry', Reading used other modernist elements in shorthand, such as the linking of the old and the new world, the fragmented view of the world, the impressionistic opening of a poem with an epigraph or motto, the intertextual references (Dante), cohesion by way of hidden allusions, learnedness, or the anacoluthic interruption of a poem and continuation in a completely different register or tone.

Auden was more easily digested than Eliot when Reading first read him: serious subjects presented in accessible ways, and a good deal of disillusioned sarcasm were features which impressed the schoolboy, who only later discovered the poet's technical talent. Auden's interest in Old and Middle English poetry as well as his penchant for alliteration were picked up, but it was mainly the stance of 'let's make the best of a bad world', the informal voltas, the social issues, and the view that industrial malaises were symptoms of a deeper sickness which were assimilated into Reading's own writing. In *For the Municipality's Elderly*, Auden's influence first becomes apparent in a few direct allusions,[23] but then can be heard in the diction and tone. Not all critics had approved of the diction in this book. Jenkins had just interviewed Reading about this and knew the background:

> The sombre diction, dignified movement, and 'rough edges' of the poems ...the mix of Latinate constructions...with heavy alliterative stress (deriving from Middle English poems such as *Piers Plowman*, but most likely via Auden), all combine to give them an air of considerable *gravitas*, a whiff of something ancient and serious (Jenkins, *DLB*, p.470).

Two other critics also had something to say about Reading's originality and technique. First Peter Porter:

> Peter Reading has an easily recognised tone and a strange fondness for inverting the clauses in his sentences. He is entirely his own man, but at the moment many of his poems are wrecked by poor technique.

Dannie Abse:

> Mr Reading has already a distinctive style, if only by virtue of his syntactical idiosyncracies. His is a rather sardonic voice, continually saddened by impermanence... He seems relatively sophisticated in terms of technique.

Stylistically, the archaic, circuitous, faltering syntax, the inversions
and Romanic word order (Hopkins' influence) are indeed prominent
and seem thematically appropriate. The semantic-syntactical focus
is often on the end of the sentence, which produces an exhausted
movement reaching towards the end, finally sinking and letting go.
Appropriately, this is most pronounced in the last poem, 'Lapse'
(p.63), where the syntax hardly has the energy to go beyond verse
ends, or in 'Combine', in which rural autumn and the departure
of migrating birds ('the dark swift coming and going', 'the vast
departure') blends into an image of death (p.61; it is repeated in
the final poem of *Last Poems*; see also p.51):

> I seem to have been with you only an instant here;
> idyllic becomes fearful grave silence as I awake
> to you already arisen, the steady thresh
> and much nearer shadow of the quiet harvester.

Words often oscillate between different parts of speech ('oak rattles
leaves'), which adds to the overall retarding effect, as do the numer-
ous grammatical conversions ('whorily', 'insufficient dies'), the
omission of articles and relative pronouns, and some neologisms.
Words like 'photogravured', 'uncurtained', 'nettled', 'molassed',
'parsleyed', 'rearguarding', 'unfunny', and 'unbreathing' are rem-
iniscent of Hopkins, too. In 'Lapse' (p.63), Reading also makes
very effective use of pauses, as indeed he often did later.

> It's an intuitive thing. It is just something that I have always, rather
> stiltedly, done and enjoyed, and I do it in conversation a bit as well.
> The circuitous syntax is simply a way that I find I've operated, and it
> has come about largely because of trying to concentrate ideas. It can
> be a nuisance, I suppose, to the reader – but it's... a difficulty that I
> don't mind because I think that it is part of the general deal concern-
> ing poetry as something rather different from ordinary linguistics [LI].

While the deviant syntax aims at more concision and complexity,
the metrics and rhythm, in contrast, are rather loose and ensalada-
like: sentences extend over an irregular number of lines, and run-on
lines often cut iambic or dactylic feet in half, which also are padded
abundantly with anacrusis and hypercatalexis. Also, 'Curfew' (p.52),
for instance, is supposed be a dactylic five-footer, but iambic inter-
ference creeps in (or vice-versa, as in some other poems, see pp.51,
58, 59). Reading's comment [C]:

> My early stuff is sort of *vers libre*, but fairly tight-structured by way of
> pauses, line ends, sense ends. Anything you read at the time of writing
> will strike you in certain ways and then you nick it. [The sense/line
> ends were 'nicked' from Louis MacNeice.] To be honest it was all
> mainly ear-operated then, but also partly trained up by Hopkins, whose
> contrived magniloquent-sounding stuff impressed me.

However, the indentations of stanzas make it evident that Reading at times was counting feet, without necessarily minding the exact number of unstressed syllables – the first step towards his later use of stress metre. In the new poems, the feet were more regular, and sentence and stanza length were more clearly organised, as in 'Brabyns Park', where the number of verses corresponds to the movement from the general to the specific and back (see also 'Juvenilia', 'Embarkation', 'Removals', 'Lapse').

The question of the right metrics was looming large already [LI]:

> It's been something that's caused me a great deal of questioning, actually, that I didn't really know why – what I was supposed to be playing at, or, by that I mean what anybody was supposed to be playing at. I found very few things which seemed to have a *raison d'être* for their metrics. Very few things. Some of the ones which I did find would be Hopkins, say.

Reading's metrics can be discerned in bud in this first book. Not only did the dactyls seem 'right', but their extension starts here: there are aeolic verses, choriambs sounding strangely dactylic ('arms round his wife'; see also p.41), even three hemiepes (dactylic half hexameters), as in 'flickering into the dark' (p.38).

> In *For the Municipality's Elderly?* But I didn't know that I was doing that. I find that very, very interesting. And this corroborates what I was saying; that in this rather airy-fairy manner … the music is somehow right for me. And I think, though I'm not entirely sure why, it is appropriate to the things I'm talking about [LI].

Interestingly, the iambs which dominated the pamphlet *Water and Waste* (1970) are on the retreat in *For the Municipality's Elderly* and give way to dactylic-trochaic/spondaic feet, the first indication of the metrical development to come. In *Water and Waste*, two-thirds of the poems are iambic, the last third is either dactylic or free verse; the new poems for *For the Municipality's Elderly* are two-thirds dactylic. When this drift was pointed out to Reading, it came as a pleasant surprise [LI]:

> Really? That's interesting… I didn't consciously set out to do that. They just seemed to sound right for the kind of things I was doing and I didn't know why. Completely intuitive or thoughtless or how you'd wish to phrase it.

In this book dactyls get ripped apart between lines and are used in run-on lines with or without enjambement, possibly for semantic reasons, if, indeed, for any conscious reason at all (see for instance the first two verses of 'Severn at Worcester' or 'Raspberrying'). Also, the metrics in 'Fall', for example, underline the thematic concern, but, as the different treatment of the same thing in the very next poem shows, they could have been a stray hit.

Reading's intuitive choice of falling cadences maybe owes something to his 'Beethovian ear' [C], as he speculated in an allusion to the famous opening cadences of the Fifth Symphony (metrically speaking, they would be fourth paeons or choriambs). However, the logaoedic verse with dactyls joined by trochees (a shortened fall) or spondees (as alternative or stopping point) was not worked on until Reading had finished his early explorations in both structure and in stress and syllabic metre: it became his metrical basis as from the "middle period", starting with *Ukulele Music* (1985).

Other unassuming structural features include occasional rhyming, highlighting words by accentuation (i.e. an odd metrical or phonetic choice), as well as the devices of envelope and alpha-omega metaphor. As in the syntax, there is the same penchant for sounding archaic lexically, to stress the thematic juxtaposition of the past and the present. The sporadic use of Latin, French, or Italian expressions, however, sometimes appear rather heavy-handed;[24] the Latinate diction, though not unnatural for Reading even in spoken English, goes better with the elegiac metrics of the later books.

In this context, a few 'Readingisms' are worth mentioning that already feature in this book: monosyllables, abbreviations, and the slang-register. There is only one instance of sham-coyness in using explicit language in this volume ('effing', p.28); the next volume already presents the first four-letter word, and nobody's linguistic propriety is spared after the third book, where the use of such language is indirectly explained (p.110). Puns, on the other hand, are comparatively rare as yet (the unreligious 'Morning Star' later becomes the effective 'Mirror' in *Ukulele Music*).

As from the next book, Reading wrote more idiosyncratically. In *For the Municipality's Elderly*, 'Stills' and 'Fossil' already stand out in this respect as they make use of an unconventional idea, suggestively presenting the world with the volume turned off. However, humorous poems like 'Earthworks', which revolves around a jokey parallel ('precursor'), or 'Prologue', which plays word games with an idiom and is the first kind of semi-sonnet, are not up to the same standard. Dodsworth thought:

> There is something to Peter Reading, most obviously his ability to perceive a range of different kinds of event, but he has yet to put this to good use. Too many of these poems fail to stand quite clear of the circumstances in which they were written, and a general effect of muzz-iness obtains, derived from an altogether wasteful expenditure of words.

While the 'muzziness' could also come from the uncertain identity of the speaker, words like 'deliciously' and 'appeasingly' (p.28), or poeticisms like 'pressed-transparent mummy forms of brown' (p.35) are not repeated in later books. Reading's economy was not yet being used with respect to the lexicon and syntax. Many details, many qualifying adverbs, long appositions and brackets leave as much room for a thought, scene or image as they require; a stanza is as long as the syntax demands, making poems alloestrophical. Some reviewers disliked the Latinisms, but there was no doubt about Reading's potential:

> None of these criticisms seems to me to matter very much as I said at the beginning, I find him a very good read and I am sure time will make him a better one...
>   I feel that there is only one wholly successful poem in the book – 'Nomenclator' – yet I was impressed at the end. The language is alive, though dense; the feeling real inside the strangled sententiousness. And he can handle the long poem (Graham; Porter).

With this last tagged-on remark, Porter meant the 'Letters', which over several pages remain interesting through a simple and effective focussing of seemingly disparate observations. While Reading perfected this technique in later books, Porter's comment was also the first critical comment to be parodied in a poem later (p.166).

In the next three volumes, Reading got rid of the technical flaws described above, and the foundation laid in *For the Municipality's Elderly* turned out to be elaborate enough – and stable.

The Prison Cell & Barrel Mystery (1976): Life's Little Ironies

For the Municipality's Elderly had taken Reading three to four years to write, a normal span for a book of poems. His second volume and first Poetry Book Society Recommendation was published in March 1976 – 16 months later – and Secker had taken up half of that time. Colin Falck was only one of the many critics who wondered 'how long he can go on turning the stuff out at this rate'.[1] But this speed was kept up for 20 years, and Reading was to publish a new book every one or two years – 'shows no signs of slowing down', the reviews reiterated – and became as prolific as Peter Redgrove, George MacBeth, or Seamus Heaney.

'Juncture' from the preceding volume was the seed of *The Prison Cell & Barrel Mystery*:

> So strange to see you, whom I loved
> ten years ago...
> ...whereas you never loved me
> while I loved you, you might love me
> after I had ceased to love you.

All Reading's books are variations on one theme; so this central occurrence with its tragicomical implications is refracted into narratives with very different voices, perspectives, situations, moods and forms. Brief excursions into other experiences of loss enlarge the radius a little. The locality of the poems is comparatively peripheral here: Liverpool is only referred to indirectly by the symbolic detail of the dividedness (the Mersey);[2] and the places in Shropshire are interchangeable. The rootedness of the poems is provided this time by the aura of these places: Reading's past years at the College of Art in the Liverpool of the 1960s as well as the rural working world ('South Shropshire Farmers') in Shropshire ten years later. The post-1960s urban milieu is impregnated with oversated sexual liberation, *eros furens* gives way to broken dreams and confused lives, past mistakes take revenge upon the present. By contrast, the people in the country discuss and sublimate their frustrations in more conventional ways – seemingly casually, or with drastic directness. Reading's personal experiences, but also those of his ex-fellow students, friend, wife and relatives, along with farmers' conversations overheard in pubs, provide the raw material of these poems, blended into a typical *loss-of-love story*.

In 1976 Reading was still prepared to communicate his ideas on poetry and aesthetics to the members of the Poetry Book Society. His strong reservations against confessional (and sentimental) poetry, because of which he only rarely allowed himself to write celebratory, private poems, were aired for the first time here:

> *'Autobiographer, please don't tell me the tale of your love-life:*
> *much as it mattered to you, nothing could marvel me less.'*
>
> In spite of the fact that the poems in *The Prison Cell & Barrel Mystery* are about love, I trust that I have been sensible, throughout the volume, of Auden's cautionary words, inasmuch as I have earnestly endeavoured to avoid the difficulties which attend this somewhat thorny topic. These difficulties are fairly obvious and probably the foremost of them is embarrassment, which is to be sedulously avoided, not only as far as the reader is concerned (because embarrassing sentiment is generally sentimentality), but also I suppose that any writer is anxious to distance himself, through his writing, from matter which is rather too close for comfort and therefore a potential embarrassment to himself. At the same time, of course, as attempting to distance deeply personal matter (with the intention of transforming the purely personal into something of more general significance), one wishes to try and retain any originality of experience and convey any moving quality, poignancy and so on, which may have characterised the initial motivation. The crux is to get the balance right...
>
> One very simple way of achieving distance from an experience is to distort it – even to be a downright liar about it. So what is said in a poem is not necessarily journalistically accurate, though it aims, of course, at being the truth. Lying about people and events, then, can be a most useful poetic device (though it enrages and estranges acquaintances by the dozen).[3]

Therapeutic emotional disburdening in poetry is 'not the function of art' [C].

Reading's artistically fabricated 'I' is not wholly congruous with the real person. Dramatic monologues have always been used in poetry; but to devise, set up, and maintain a coherent, posited authorial instance and to employ it as an artistic device – a development originating in *The Prison Cell & Barrel Mystery* – is unusual.

At the same time, Reading makes sure that his œuvre remains a genuinely and deeply personal one; the decoding of the artistic functions of the posited authorial stance reveals his personal positions. The discussion about the worth of such personal communications is, in turn, incorporated into his œuvre with persistent, elaborate self-referentiality.

By contrast, authentic facts (such as the breakfast table or the colour of his wife's hair) function as representative narrative, iconic or metaphoric details, just as the authentic persons who figure in the early works serve as characters which 'were meant to be stereotypes

which anyone could empathise with, sympathise with, get cross
with the attitudes struck'. Reading would never write about 'per-
sonal likes or dislikes, unless they are monitored by the artistic
process' (Potts, 1990, p.97).

In *The Prison Cell & Barrel Mystery*, 'Life's Little Ironies' – as
the Hardy quotation in 'Thanksgiving' puts it – mainly revolve
around the modern relationship. With the pivot of a triangular sit-
uation, lost love is the theme and the *mal marié* the motif. Peter
Porter's objection – 'what obsesses Reading may not interest us' [4]
– is justified, but without consequence, as this can of course be
said about any writer at any time. The real irritation concerns the
question of "poetic" or "unpoetic" subject, to which we will return
later.

Stylistic and linguistic levels are adjusted to the socio-regional
provenance of the protagonists and the particular speech situation:
thus the contemporary clichés of student psychologising clash with
the dialectal "nuggets" of rural received wisdom (' "we may be mad,
Michael, but, GOD, IT'S REAL" ', p.102; ' "Once you marries the
wrong un youm never the same somehow" ', p.100). In view of the
subject-matter in question, they ironise and relativise each other.
The same antithetical effect is achieved by juxtaposing them with
the lyrical language from the authorial voice, which again relativises
them, as well as making them a source of amusement.

With the narrow, almost age-specific choice of subject-matter
and the "unpoetic", loose, sometimes satirical language in the *con-
versation pieces*, which here goes with ironic distance, Reading marks
his borders clearly. It is no coincidence that young, inexperienced
readers can be won over to poetry with the help of this volume:
not just thanks to the portrayal of familiar relationship problems
and the easy diction, but also because of the skilful tackling of the
form-content dichotomy in poems like 'Trio', which unfailingly
produces key technical insights. *The Prison Cell & Barrel Mystery* is
not, as Martin Booth remarks, just a 'book for poets' (Booth, p.159).

The reviewers reacted differently. Some were amused and enjoyed
the good entertainment, others felt negative about this "unlyrical"
book of poems.[5] One of the most important controversies as
regards Reading originates here: how far may a poet venture away
from what is accepted as poetry without being reprimanded or even
falling into disrepute? Who is to say what "poetry" *is* (and thus
should be) in the first place, and how it is that poetic conventions
never stop changing? The prescriptive answer of 1976 in the reac-
tions to Reading's book was: can't go far. It is traditionally the
disappointer who gets the blame for disappointed expectations,

not the expectations (in this case, post-Romantic expectations with regard to the function and diction of poetry). Literary expectations of this kind, however, are based on an essentialist notion of literature and insist on the medieval, pre-Kantian concept of meaning and value residing *in* things, although the 'Copernican Revolution' (started by Copernicus, and continued by Marx, Freud and Lacan) has indicated that no centre of meaning can be located anywhere, thus generating a modern, relativist (or functional) theory of literature, which differentiates between the properties of a text on the one hand and the ascription of meaning and value by the reader on the other, and which takes into consideration that *any* method of interpretation projects a poem that corresponds to it and thus "works". *The Prison Cell & Barrel Mystery* never once claims to be "high art"; at most it asks some pertinent questions: why fetter poetry to its traditional frame? Why should poetry not be "allowed" to use the colloquial register, too?

One reviewer implied that Reading's dramatic talent had chosen the wrong medium, as if poetry could not contain dramatic elements and genre and style demarcations did not need to be continually re-drawn. Indeed, looking back on Reading's richly diversified œuvre, one sees his poetry repeatedly operating in between standard categories.

Apart from literary taste, another reason for the critics' diverging opinions about the artistic value of the book is their different perspectives on Reading. Martin Dodsworth (*Guardian*) and Peter Porter (*Observer*) had already reviewed *For the Municipality's Elderly* and remarked on the young writer's progress: 'here is a poet who is actually getting *better*' (Dodsworth), 'a considerable advance on his first book' (Porter). Colin Falck (*The New Review*) and Martin Bax (*Ambit*) also knew Reading's first book. Despite the 'fewer very good poems', Bax deemed the new volume more lively and recommendable, and Falck liked Reading's 'indifference to the received pieties [imagistic tentativeness or contemplative polishing]'. On the other hand, D.M. Thomas thought Reading's art was not sufficiently literary; he was not familiar with *For the Municipality's Elderly*.

Reading does not make a representative impression if read in single doses; he is better read in instalments. Of course individual books have to prove their worth without the context of the others, but in the early books one will not yet find the answer to the question of what overall purpose and concept Reading is pursuing. In the 1970s he was still looking for his artistic identity, and the three books after *For the Municipality's Elderly* – *The Prison Cell*

& *Barrel Mystery*, *Nothing For Anyone*, and *Fiction* – reveal a logical and "intentional" development – seen retrospectively.

The impressive thing about *The Prison Cell & Barrel Mystery* is that although the author's voice can be recognised and there is again one main theme, one mostly encounters new possibilities and precise improvements. Just as before, the title is traditionally denotative, but the volume contains only about half as many poems, while the book length is almost the same (55 pages in the original edition) – the first indication of a material change. The most extraordinary poem in the book, 'Trio', claimed 9 pages in the original edition (10 with the title), and other poems also venture beyond the one-page limit.

The words, however, are placed more economically than before, the syntax is completely different for all its linear straightness, and the stylistic level is lowered, using demotic speech and pastiche. Reading starts consciously planning the structure of poems and co-ordinates them in a new metrical arrangement: one will look in vain for dactyls in this volume; instead one encounters metres not commonly used in English. In 'Nocturne' und 'Trio' Reading realises his first original formal ideas.

The lyrical 'I' is already keeping a greater aesthetic distance from the authorial 'I'. Ways of achieving this include extending personal utterance with dramatic monologue, atmospheric vignette, narrative reportage and miniature drama, but also simply by 'lying', as Reading calls his fictionalisations. This is the beginning of the employment of fictional stances in Reading's œuvre, a device which has been deemed too complicated by some, and taken at face value by others. The phrase 'ninety per cent misanthropy' (p.43) from *For the Municipality's Elderly*, for instance, seems to have automatically disqualified its author in some minds; the poem 'Cub' (*Ukulele Music*) was also taken literally and scandalised a number of dons. Poetry was expected to provide other things: if not confessionalism, then at least depersonalised abstraction. Reading helped to change this notion.[6]

The first function of distance is the avoidance of directly confessional poetry. Reading will not tax readers with confessionalism unless it is veiled in fictions [LI]:

> I know that my attitude would definitely have been to try and destroy the narrative 'I', the first person, the Poet-'I'... simply in the interests of avoiding the personal and the mawkish and so on... then you can work a double bluff and introduce an 'I' which *is* personal and, well, confessional...

Most poems in *The Prison Cell & Barrel Mystery* are still told from a first-person perspective. In the early works, Reading does not avoid the 'I' through depersonalisation, but by using a simple postmodernist strategy. The introduction of the real author as a fictional character, 'Pete' (p.87), 'Peter' (p.101) or even 'Peter Reading' (p.102) destabilises the basis for an identification of the lyrical 'I' with the author. The result: every speaker, every protagonist becomes a fiction. (This is taken to its logical extreme in the fourth volume, *Fiction,* and as from *Tom o'Bedlam's Beauties* the problem of the first person is resolved.) In the lyrical or pugnacious passages an authentic voice is to be heard, but one cannot ascribe it with full certainty to the authorial 'I'. Falck is on the right track when he suspects 'poignantly personal-sounding experiences behind these tales', but at the same time understands that Reading first had to get 'his more urgent subjectivities out of his system'. Reading was still a little in Reading's way.

Examples of the 'double bluff' are 'Trio' (pp.76-82) and 'Memsahib' (p.83). In 'Trio' Reading has three voices speak in the first person, making them the dramatis personae of a typical triangular relationship. The authentic details about himself and his wife (his deep blue eyes and taste for good wine, her beautiful hair and first name), also about his past love, cannot be recognised by readers, and anyway their authenticity is utterly irrelevant – the poetic function is to engender the impression of authenticity, not to vouch for it.

A confessional background can perhaps be suspected because of the parallels of the plot to the title-poem, whose lyrical 'I' seems to have the least distance from the authorial 'I', but in order to deflect the reader's attention from the inessential personal element, the tracks are covered. For instance, the agitated dramatic monologue of a 'Memsahib' (p.83) remembering her escape from her Indian husband, whose drinking and social habits regularly embarrassed her in public, does not invite personal speculation, but this is the typification and fictionalisation of a domestic conflict; making it "foreign" clearly accentuates the perceptive problem involved.

Similarly, in 'Thanksgiving' (p.97) the vocabulary of manners is contrasted with the undomesticated 'low type' who cannot stand inconsequential 'claptrap' and flees the festivities, 'rude and outrageous'. Typically, the 'low type' includes himself in this assembly of unsufferables – his own theme, 'sotted / No-God and Species Decline stuff', is perhaps equally difficult to sit through. Indeed, the corrected Leo-horoscope in 'Early Stuff' (p.70) – Reading's sign of the zodiac – warns right at the beginning: 'avoid Leos, they're losers, /... they're bloody fairies, / they end up in the Arts or in the boozers.'

Another change from the first book is that the elegiac ground-note starts to give way to Reading's notorious humour, befitting the theme. *The Prison Cell & Barrel Mystery* guarantees entertainment: wit, mockery, irony, satire, black humour, teasing remarks, and cheap insults, sometimes tongue-in-cheek, sometimes 'straight', and always at the expense of his protagonists, including 'Peter Reading'.[7] Reading's admiration of Jonathan Swift – whom he often mentions – may throw some light on his turn of mind; poetically, however, these elements need a certain basis. Peter Porter explains: 'He is concerned with conduct, feeling, dialogue, human tension: not for him the notion of no poetry but in things.' This is another reason why hardline novel-readers find they can make an exception for Reading. His slant is a combination of a strong emphasis on narrative and dramatic elements with the subtler preoccupations of perception, identity and consciousness, not giving up one for the other. This disregard for expectations linked to literary conventions became one of Reading's hallmarks and was consistently developed by devising new forms, thus opening new territory for new generations of poets.

The dramatic poems 'Trio' and 'Luncheon' received so many accolades from the reviewers because they produce the strongest effect in a seemingly effortless, but purely technical way. Reading developed this new strength, which enabled him to discard the less sophisticated summaries and punchlines which drew attention to themselves in *For the Municipality's Elderly*. Instead, there is an enriching mix of different 'poem genres' and tones, another discovery of dormant potential that was continually developed and soon made a structural principle.

The title *The Prison Cell & Barrel Mystery* alludes to escapologist Harry Houdini, whose shows were popular around 1900 and whose talents led to international fame. Reading explained [LI]:

> Yes, that sort of thing, an escapologist. Though, of course, the phrase is just invented to sound good... I don't think I saw anything saying *'The Prison Cell & Barrel Mystery'*, but it's meant to be an equivalent to some of these strange and incongruous things that you do see like announcements of circus acts ... 'The Greatest Show in the World'.

The image speaks for itself: a Houdini may be able to escape from multiple chains and impossible situations – the rest of mankind, though, gets hopelessly entangled in the intricate net of *l'amour*, and nobody wins the 'GREAT HANDCUFFS CONTEST' because everybody's hands are bound one way or the other. Missed opportunities, misunderstandings, mis-chosen spouses, still-flickering adolescent loves, Godot-like pregnancies all bring about a huge emotional, psychological and sexual mess. Happiness in love sooner or later becomes susceptible to breakdown; loneliness, jealousy, and frustrations are longer-lived. However, one will not find pervasive sadness in this volume – despite the sorrow, sympathy and bitterness which resonate in the poems, the fundamental mood of the book is – just like most of the language – matter-of-fact, and the presentation is meiotic: [8] such incidents are far too commonplace to warrant over-dramatisation. Apart from that, Reading even gives himself over to romantic emotion in the title-poem sequence, alluding to Dante and Beatrice without undermining himself anacoluthically – a rare occasion in his œuvre.

The speaker of the title-poem has arranged to meet his early love in the 'Post House' (p.96), the last station of the renewed relationship, and reads the old posters on the wall ('The Change Up' and 'The Change Down' refer to the change of horses in this previous post coach-station), which he relates to his own complicated situation. [9] Instead of presenting melancholy introspection of the lyrical 'I', the speaker prefers a self-deprecating, distanced attitude. 'THE GREATEST SHOW IN THE WORLD' is his ironic label for the universally muddled matters of the heart – his lover never turns up.

Additionally, the circus-programme metaphor has a structural function. The different poems of the volume can thus be presented as a colourful programme, as a variety of acts in the one arena (the same principle holds *Nothing For Anyone* together). This, too, becomes a typical Reading feature: idioms or images work two ways, both symbolically and structurally.

The opening number 'Early Stuff' (pp.69-70) also operates on several levels. A woman reads, quotes from and comments on old poems by her ex-boyfriend, which chronicle the stages of the relationship. Thus a story with a frame story can be presented in an unusual way. At the same time, the boyfriend's poem titles – 'Poster Girl', 'Au Pair', 'Umbrae', 'Cemetery', 'Misprint in Last Year's Horoscope', 'Caricature Angel' – are authentic juvenilia by Reading, which are to be both preserved and ironised here as purple patches [LI]:

> Yes, I was just using them before they were thrown away, really. 'Early Stuff' was the one that D.M. Thomas thought was a bit of a sell-out because he'd thought it started off all right, but what he liked was the thing which was then eventually debunked.

D.M. Thomas would have preferred the book to continue in this lyrical vein:

> 'Early Stuff' has a spring and zest, lyrical yet realistic, that promises excellence...However, it turns out that this is deliberate parody, and the book settles into drab, rhythm-less demotic, without distinction of style.

This is, though, what the poem announces at the very beginning of the book in the prosaic comments of the protagonist reading lyrical poems: the description of amorous encounters and dreamy reminiscences may warrant the lyrical intensity and extensive imagery of the juvenilia paraded here; naked facts, however, had better be rendered as unjudgmental, uninfluenceable, and hard (p.70): 'He seems not to have known I loved him then / (he married someone else) but found out later.'

The lyrical passages are perhaps placed at the beginning of the book also as evidence that this emerging young writer deliberately avoids accepted poetic diction (not because he cannot master it) (p.69):

> Relinked
> in the park palmhouse hot glass cranium,
> temperature rises with each opening door,
> tormented steamy ferns drip, your tights stick,
> air clings to lungs like candyfloss. Outside
> lovers are strewn like white stones on the banks
> of the brown lake. I wither for your love.

This complication and the following lyrical poems, which lack irony, ensure that the poetic functions of the other stylistic levels can be recognised as such. One reviewer saw through the plain surface. Falck singled out this 'sardonic look-back at some "Early Stuff"' as 'one of the most effective pieces'. Thomas, however, although granting 'there are moments where talent shows through, as in "Widow" and a few lively Shropshire dialect pieces', measures the book by yardsticks outside and alien to it. His criticism – 'the book as a whole produces an embarrassed voyeurism rather than any sharing of pain or any transcending of pain through art' – represents such a fundamental error with respect to Reading's poetic proceedings that Reading used it in the meta-critical poem 'Opinions of the Press' (*Fiction*). Reading's ideas about what art is able to do and should do, are diametrically opposed to Thomas's. However, Thomas's verdict is so representative of a certain reaction among some critics to Reading's œuvre that Reading found it necessary to discuss the underlying problem in his poems again and again. For the time being, the following should suffice as refutation: voyeurism can only occur to a reader who overlooks the fictionalising, i.e. distancing, device. 'Sharing of pain' is an affective, therefore personal expectation that cannot be generalised. Thomas's last point, though, is the most inappropriate one: 'transcending of pain through poetry' is a dangerous axiom. Several years later Reading said [C] he thought it was an arrogant assumption – one he would never uphold to art, his readers, and least of all those afflicted by pain (see the chapter on *Ukulele Music*). Reading accompanies pain with poetry.

In order to allow the unassuming, litotic language its natural flow as far as possible and to proceed in the narration unhindered, Reading chose a generous metrical framework.

What Thomas derided as 'rhythmless', is almost exclusively (excepting 'Early Stuff', 'Nocturne', 'Trio' and 'Ballad', which follow different patterns) written in neat stressed metre throughout, which was first used in Old English poetry. (The original Germanic metre is perhaps not wholly inappropriate for the time-honoured Little Ironies between the sexes.) This metre was later taken up again by technically adventurous poets such as Yeats and Auden, and Reading went on using it mainly for narrative poems and dramatic monologues. The rhythm may not be heard by inexperienced readers because it is unusual, but whenever Reading introduces new metres there are visual hints, usually indentations, for discreet scanning instruction, as here in the very first poem.[10]

Even metrical details carry significance now: the opening poem 'Early Stuff', which indulges in 'verbal pickling' and with an ironical touch preserves Reading's juvenile love poems, is adequately rendered in iambic pentameter; not only did he use it as a youngster, but it is also the most frequently used metre in English and therefore potentially the most monotonous one – befitting the lyrical cliché of thwarted love re-enacted here. Following this, an irregular, more permissive, rather freer rhythm dictates the course of modern loss-of-love stories, varying in stress between poems (two to six). The fewer stresses, the more condensed the image and the more tersely serious the tone; comical-grotesque pieces generously ramble on in long lines of four, five, or six stresses (with an unspecified number of unstressed syllables in between), giving the fuller picture. Even the exact number of stresses usually has endopoetic reasons, a spill-over from the contents.[11] Only the two stresses in 'Us in The Ship' (p.74) verging on the choriamb remind one of the 'Beethovian' beat started in *For the Municipality's Elderly* $(-\smile\smile-)$, which later grew into hemiepes and Reading's favoured logaoedic verse.

'Nocturne' is a first taste of Reading's technical development and warms the reader up for the unusual 'Trio', which for Alan Jenkins was 'the first of many Reading tours de force' (Jenkins,

DLB, p.471). Reading has said that in 'Nocturne' he was 'trying to find a way of dealing with concurrency on a single page' [LI]. This eye poem visualises two lovers dreaming each other's death. In the context of the book the voices can be identified as those of the husband and wife. The two columns printed alongside each other suggest both the concurrence and the two bodies lying in bed. The narrative and bed frames merge into one, adding a spatial dimension to the chronology of both the time narrated and the reading process. The metrical framework is similarly simple, logical and lucid: the ground beat is not stress here, but in the dream columns a trochaic dimeter, i.e. a falling cadence in double step for two; and in the frame, which typographically joins together their newly awoken consciousnesses in one line, both sets of trochees add up to four.

'Trio' (pp.76-82), a composition in syllabic triple metre for the three voices of a love triangle, works on the same principle, revolving around the number three and its multiplications. 'Trio' shows in a convincing way how an "unlyrical" poem can still be a little masterpiece and how the reader's interest can be aroused by the creation of suspense and an imaginative arrangement. The force and expressiveness of details, especially in the choice of words and their typographical arrangement, is considerable.

Three voices (or perspectives) are distributed into three columns. Each verse of this triple metre is strictly syllabic; [12] all contain three syllables. [13] The effect is complete neutrality: no voice carries more weight than the other two.

The dramatic action of a married man visiting his early love, who after a divorce has ended up in an unsatisfactory relationship with a married man, develops in nine stages over nine pages in the original edition, with the respective thoughts and feelings of the husband, wife, and ex-lover set in columns alongside each other, either as direct monologues or else with concurrent activities presented by an omniscient narrator. Dialogues are accordingly typeset in succession, but this visual device is also used to encode more subtle points. (The typesetting of dialogue on the same page-level, by contrast, marks the nervousness produced by speaking at the same time, as in 'sorry I' and 'That's all right'.) The level typesetting of 'He'll be now / at her door' is especially meaningful in this respect (p.78), [14] as are the typographical "condescension" of the wife towards the ex-lover (p.79), [15] and the biggest possible distance between the married couple in 'How was she?' and 'Seemed OK' (pp.81-82), which allows the ex-lover's lonely drama to unfold once more across an entire page.

The number of verses is distributed in unequal amounts – here the wife (116) is between her husband (112) and the ex-lover (145); typographically, too, she is in the way, between the other two. In a comparison of the individual stages, though, the ex-lover squeezes in between the married couple, whose verses grow continually further apart in number, until they are re-united in the end on the lowest possible level of communication (only one verse each), with the biggest possible distance between them, and with the ex-lover further away (in quantity) than ever before. The numerical principle is all-pervasive: the telephone and house numbers of the ex-lover are based on 3, the hours of contact are also aligned accordingly,[16] the number of flowers brought to her equals the number of passengers on the bus taking him away again (divisible by 3).

The personae are first characterised and contrasted by their outward appearances and habits – reasons for past disagreements are hinted at. The only person given a first name is 'Diana', the wife, as the only one who can be trusted to maintain a stable, reliable identity – while she knows all too well that the 'reticence' in the ex-lover's letter to her husband is not to be expected in the uninhibited, winey atmosphere during his visit to her house; she is aware of her husband's potential instability (p.79). Her resulting fear expresses itself in the fact that she lets herself go a little in his absence, but even more so in her aggressive, condescending choice of words, which is in stark contrast to the verbal – and emotional – harmony of the other two. The indecisiveness of the husband, who loves them both (p.80), shows itself in senseless repetitions (p.77) and lastly in a drunken, slurred declaration of love; in neither case does he say the truth ('That's all right', p.77; 'simly a / soshul call', p.81). He also distinguishes himself at the first meeting by remarkable clumsiness (p.78). He ends as he started, only worse, late at night, hopelessly drunk.

For Reading, 'Trio' and 'Nocturne' were a test of his first publisher's tolerance [LI]:

> They're metrically... fairly straightforward things. But there are, by comparison with what you normally see done, a couple of difficulties. There's the three-column thing and I didn't know whether I'd ... get away with that, either because it might seem too outré or it might be too difficult to print, but I did manage to do that and subsequently didn't have any problems with any of the other things.

The italics, big letters and the use of the historic printing-'V' for 'U' (p.97) were also first examples of the imaginative typography to come. Reviewers sometimes point out that this kind of experimentalism is hardly revolutionary these days. However, there is no other poet who consistently makes such forceful, effective use of the visual element outside of concrete poetry. Reading decided after a few years to send in completed bromides to his publisher, both to avoid printing errors and to save his publisher trouble with type-setting. Several years later Margaret Drabble observed in a review of *Final Demands* that Reading was to be envied for his good relations with his publisher, but the truth of the matter was that Secker was never put in the position of having to reject a manuscript because it would demand complicated (and costly) typesetting.

Two poems do not sit easily in this volume: 'Equinox' (p.73) is a complete outsider and one wonders why it was not saved for the next volume: there is no solemn frame to contain these heavy-handed lyrical, metaphorical observations. The ithyphallic 'Mycologia' (p.75) draws on Reading's special knowledge of fungi and stands out for both its mood and the absence of personae. In a clean-cut, well-made form it presents us with the slimiest image of this volume. The shape of three old, unappetising fungi at the edge of the brake is described in such unerotic sexual terms that queasiness is practically guaranteed.[17] Nowhere else in the book are the sexual instincts connoted in this revolting manner – sexual impersonality is drastically exposed (no verbs, no pronouns) and the undeserved pain of the third party bitterly accentuated.

The other poems relate to one another more closely than it may seem – another thematically relevant structural detail. As in *For the Muncipality's Elderly*, groups of poems can be identified, here with regard to the personae involved. The former lover, met again by chance after 10 or 12 years, speaks in 'Early Stuff' and 'Discarded Note'. The latter starts with '*Dear Pete*, (to whom she did not ever post this / discarded note)' in an entertaining tone, but soon changes into a muffled cry for help. To have stayed childless many years for rational reasons, and to display a callous attitude to abortion ('*squirt it down the bogs*'), is one thing ('*All very well*'). Not being able to bear children any longer because of the removal of the untrained uterus is another. The shock to the instincts goes so deep that now everything is interpreted biologically (p.88):

'unable to have babies' leaves me a stunned
primeval craving pregnancy –
the outmoded evolutionary urge,
to which you are immune being a male
and biologically unsympathetic
to mere irrational femininity.

In 'Kwickie Service', 'Us in The Ship', 'Prolonged Look', 'THE PRISON CELL & BARREL MYSTERY'[18] and 'A•MON•SEVL•DESIR' the ex-girl-friend is directly addressed by her former lover ('Pete'), who by now is married (and loves his wife, too). The different stages of their former and present love affair and the different reasons for their limited duration are shown in single vignettes which express the loss, sadness and the absurdity of non-concurrent love (p.75):

> The dead channel.
> The foetid swamp.
> Eurydice.
> NEXT BOAT LEAVES AT…,
> rotted away,
> the hour is gone.

'Near-Miss' (p.98) and 'Luncheon' (p.86) is humorous light verse from the by now distanced man's perspective. Five verses and a laconic slapstick-rhyme suffice to describe the scene of a proposal rejected by the Miss a long time ago ('fell in love / each with the other quite genuinely / – but not, regrettably, concurrently'). The comical effect of 'Luncheon' is based on the fact that the poet, who is waiting to read on George MacBeth's Radio 3 poetry programme his poem about a 'desperate phone / conversation with a young woman whom / I had been much in love with years before', kills time hedonistically in a fancy restaurant, apparently without registering the irony that the Italian waiter, in between serving his elaborate courses, has to endure a telephone drama with his girlfriend. The poet's senses are occupied by a 'fat sleek black olive'; and his enthusiasm for 'blood welling at the raw centre' only refers to the roast beef, while the Italian, who is in the middle of emotional rawness, only has a limited vocabulary for the things the poet is about to read across the ether – for each of them, the other's preoccupations are now just a job. As Porter wrote, 'Luncheon' 'deserves a place in the next anthology of comic verse anyone may be assembling'.[19] The other poems rendering the man's perspective deal with the fear (or the fact) of his wife now leaving him (indirectly in 'Absentees' and 'Nocturne', directly in 'Mem-sahib').

'Trio', 'Correspondence' and 'Ballad' soon open up the whole circus arena: 'Correspondence' (p.84), a satire about the free choice of partners, consists of six letters (stanzas) of eight verses with four stresses each: one for each of the four personae forming the love-clover leaf – but somehow luck or happiness are slow to materialise. The speed and ease with which these four change their bed-and-table partners becomes a frightful merry-go-round for the reader, and the separate strands of relationships can only be disentangled with some difficulty (we eventually discover that Karen and Martin, who in the old days left their partners and then each other, end up alone). The mendacity of the proceedings is exposed by means of the most economic measures; the pseudo-psychoanalytical slang takes care of the rest.[20]

'Ballad' (p.89) is a modern tongue-in-cheek version of the old doomed love stories written in easy-going, affable conversational diction. John and Joan loved each other once, but everything went wrong. In 26 ballad metre stanzas their story is told ('I'll tell you all a story / concerning John and Joan; / in student days each clung to each / as flesh will cling to bone') with all the features of this poetic genre: description of an episode with a bad ending, dramatic presentation, dialogue, simple formulaic language, an abundance of similes, repetitions and enumerations,[21] deictic references for heightening the atmosphere as well as "comments" by the first-person narrator representing the public: 'It's cliché but it's sound / – what they say about no good coming / of love on the rebound.'

The pace of the book picks up after 'Duologues' (p.99). There we have two seemingly detached conversations between farmers in Salopian dialect about love affairs with fatal results, whose heartless, but not heartlessly meant, comments are unwittingly rather comical ('a bit loony like'). This is followed by a third conversation, held by women who themselves were enmeshed in such stories; this comes across as somewhat milder, but confessions such as 'as I loves im an all' or 'once you marries the wrong un youm never the same somehow' basically have the same effect. These bucolic poems are funny enough on their own but their effect is heightened considerably by the finale, two pages on, which seems to have brought its dramatis personae in from another planet: 'Ménage à Trois' (p.101) resumes the main theme like a last circus act and, as light verse or *vers de société*, draws on plentiful resources. So this is what love can also be like: a romping sketch spins out of Michael's 'visit' to 'the psychologist's mistress and the / psychologist's wife and the psychologist'. It begins relatively harmlessly ('"Make yourself coffee, and *feel* the place"' is the first invitation), but within minutes escalates into a catastrophic drama of plain old-fashioned jealousy – '"we may be mad, Michael, but, GOD, IT'S REAL."'

The Prison Cell & Barrel Mystery ends with these verses, focusing on and linking together the terrible and the funny, qualities which infuse this entertaining, melancholy book:

> Outside the gate he thought 'I must remember
> this for my novel. Meanwhile I must tell
> my friend Peter Reading about it – he'll
> probably find it terribly funny.'

Nothing For Anyone (1977): Postmodernist Games

Nothing For Anyone is a loose bundle of 21 very different poems and short sequences in which Reading marks out the territory he is planning to occupy. Social satire in light verse and personal themes are again present, but he also takes on broader subject-matter, integrates bizarre drôleries, and explores new poetic possibilities. As for its status within the œuvre, *Nothing For Anyone* seems more like a warming-up exercise than the performance proper – not a very substantial book, but interesting and entertaining, especially in its use of postmodernist techniques.

Nothing For Anyone – and even more so the very clever book *Fiction*, which followed – are sillographical mixed bags and exercises in formal artistic acrobatics; although they offer considerable aesthetic entertainment value, they have detached perspectives without any balance elsewhere in the volumes. Even if this lack of balance is interpreted as thematically relevant (i.e. quotidian trivialities suffocate the big issues), the impression of sketchiness remains. Also, *Nothing For Anyone* is the only one of Reading's books which dispenses with effective structural cohesion, and there is no functional reason for this. While the bracketed epigraph, a device which in subsequent books functions as a motto, is used for the first time here, it does not appear to be the concise expression of an organic, inherent principle, but more of a legitimising afterthought: to prevent the volume from falling apart into separate poems, a common denominator is formulated:

> *(Mercifully, we're only*
> *molested by the Big Issue*
> *in the watches of the night:*
> *in daylight hours we busy*
> *ourselves with the Trivial.)*

The day-to-day trifles are presented in entertaining satire, which makes the seriousness of the 'Big Issue' seem rather more oppressive. In this context, the title, *Nothing For Anyone*, is a sarcastic pun on different levels. 'Something for everyone' is a cliché, inflated and indiscriminate in its enthusiasm and optimism: it is used here in a poem as a circus advertisement and implicitly serves as a poetic and self-ironising legitimation of the book's colourful mixture. Its validity is debunked by the ominous title-poem, but – unlike with later works

– the laughter comes easily in this book; even the protection of
species and of nature turns out to be a joke in the hands of the
'Con Men' (p.132):

> It isn't that we care about the *Hippo*,
> but that we want our children's children's children
> to see it for their entertainment.
>
> It's
>
> our children's children's children precisely who
> make the extinction of the Hippo (and
> themselves) inevitable.
>
> …and 'Conservation'
>
> meant *what a shame the kiddies got slick-oil*
> *between their toes on seaside holidays*
> or *Save the Hippo!* (for Safari coach-trips)

Metrically, *Nothing For Anyone* is comparatively unambitious;
clearly, the raising of the artistic platform by other means was on
the agenda. The chosen metres are the same as before, but the
accentual poems seem rhythmically less vigorous than their prede-
cessors and are placed alongside iambic pentameters and free verse
without any discernible differentiating function. The only metrical
novelty is provided by two sonnets, 'Sonnet' and 'Zygmunt'; new
also is the use of (unmetrical) long-winded, banal, disorganised
prose to characterise intellectual vapidity.

The critics were nevertheless mostly positive.[1] Along with Gavin
Ewart, Dennis O'Driscoll thought it 'the best of Reading's early
books' (O'Driscoll, p.210). It was especially Reading's out-of-the-
ordinariness and his poetic oddities that were repeatedly hailed as
'refreshing'. Gavin Ewart even suggested in the *TLS* that the merits
of *Nothing For Anyone* were singular in contemporary poetry:

> We are surrounded by poetry that is well-intentioned but dull; Reading's
> book is an oasis of intellect and wit. Experimenting with styles and word-
> games, he achieves some very entertaining and interesting effects…He
> is also master of a narrative and descriptive strain ('Travelogue', 'Dr
> Cooper's Story', '10 x 10 x 10' – the last being the invention of a new
> art form). A bitter wit marks almost all these poems. Of their kind – and
> there are not many poems of their kind now that George MacBeth has
> temporarily gone out of business as a poetic experimenter – they are
> quite remarkably good.[2]

Only Jenkins had expected more of Reading and in a later appraisal
in the *DLB* concentrated on the book's shortcomings:

> *Nothing For Anyone* (1977) seems the most uncertain and 'undirected' of
> Reading's books…The book shows Reading at his most formally ingenious
> and adventurous, but its inventiveness and technical sophistication seem
> unfocused. Its oddness – both in the writing and in the 'oddities' which

it picks up – is appealing but also a little pleased with itself (Jenkins, *DLB*, p.471).

The air of self-contentment in the book comes from the pervasive tone of bitter wit and wise-sounding phrases such as 'the most we can do, Little Mortal' (p.105). There is entertainment value in the critical intelligence which instantly spots potential for ridicule in every phenomenon observed, but in the long run it generates the wish for some kind of relief provided by, for instance, a more naive or vulnerable or otherwise undistanced perspective.

As *Nothing For Anyone* has no firm thematic or poetic centre, one might expect to find lyricism, or a poetic exploration of linguistic possibilities. Instead, Reading addresses a rationally accessible and morally urgent set of problems according to the principle of veri-similitude, as if – in view of the impending global disaster – it was no longer adequate to practise linguistic-aesthetic contemplation and akyrologic condensation in poetry, let alone indulge in 'pure poetry', hermeticism, mythopoeia or even poems-in-things. The necessary consequence is the iconic adjustment of diction and style, as well as the frequent use of the dramatic monologue as the safest way of keeping bookish tones at bay. This led to the accusation that Reading was writing journalism and social criticism rather than poetry.

Indeed, for Reading poetic licence was the most important device – and he did not use it only in devising his own tone, style, diction, and structure, but also in choosing his subject-matter. Over the years, he had played an important role in making it more acceptable for poetry to confront the modern menaces. In the mid 70s the oil crisis and continuing destruction of the environment were bringing about a slowly growing awareness of a possible global catastrophe, of the possibility that *all* human life was at risk.

As a consequence, some poets avoided the lyrical mode. The tendency towards *désinvolture* and to the dramatic and narrative mode has since grown even stronger, as can be seen in recent anthologies. In *Nothing For Anyone*, Reading is not interested in the potential of lyrical language, but in specific poetic techniques and the sub-ject of humanity. It was therefore understandable that some critics reiterated the suspicion that he had chosen the wrong artistic medium. Joan Forman saw in Reading the qualities of a novelist:

> Occasionally one wonders why a writer chooses prose rather than poetry as a medium for his observations. Or vice versa. Prose is very near to Peter Reading's verse: he is an observer par excellence. There is a cer-tain verve and thrust, not to say impudence in much of this writing, but all are refreshing qualities and *Nothing For Anyone* has a bit of everything for someone, if not for this reviewer.

Shirley Toulson, on the other hand, declared the unlyrical orientation of the volume to have been consciously chosen, as a counterbalance to pretentiousness, escapism, or transcendentalism:

> Impatient with any departure from the immediate and rational, suspicious of any trace of romantic superstition and false posings, Peter Reading uses his sharp wit and technical agility to shape urban jokes in entertaining verse forms... Yet this delight in the trivial and more bizarre aspects of everyday life is combined with a real compassion for human ills.

What makes Reading's early poetry interesting is just this attempt to find new unlyrical ways for poetry to go: to find a fitting form of expression to match the "unlyrical" subject-matter, a form which would nevertheless work in a poetic way. This could possibly be catalysed by the combination of new form and new content, similar to the principle that minus multiplied by minus equals plus. Hence the independent and – at that time – rather bold experiments with different "materials" and "processing techniques" in *Nothing For Anyone*. Even in the *poésie engagée* pieces, the clear aim in this volume is to achieve 'Good Art' first of all. The means Reading chose for this were entirely his own.

In *Nothing For Anyone* Reading first used found poems, reworking other texts which seemed to him worth preserving, and which would fit in his own book and generate a certain effect. As is the case with readymades and combines in art, literary objects and their new contexts can throw new light on one another and provide additional stylistic, structural and semantic layers. Reading remarked on this [LI]:

> Well, it's something that's always interested me. And in a way, almost all poems are found in that you sort of snap bits of this and that... I suppose it's a development of a Dadaist and Surrealist set of possibilities, but at their best these things can, out of their own original context, have some more general significance, metaphorical or otherwise. I don't use them a lot, or at least I would say that they are *always* tempered with a bit of invention as well.

' "Iuppiter ex alto periuria ridet amantum", 15s 6d' quotes from 'A lady's album of 1826 in my possession' (p.106), a commonplace book which relates her small-scale amorous tragedy in restrained clichés (the album is quoted from again in *Stet*). Ironically, Helen's verses and those of both her suitors', as quoted in Reading's poem, only come alive through the Ovid quotation the bookseller had written on the flyleaf (along with the price), which Reading chose as the title of this found poem. Reading had bought the book in a second-hand bookshop (' "NEWINGTON BOOKSHOP LIVERPOOL 1962" on the endpaper', p.108) [LI]:

Yes, that *did* exist. That's three parts a found poem. I've used the phenomenon later in some other things, talking about such volumes in my possession, and they don't actually occur, but that particular one did, as did 'Iuppiter ex alto periuria ridet amantum'.[3]

Reading's interest in unusual documents about lives in previous centuries had resulted in a small collection of such items, which he repeatedly drew on for his poems. The last poem in *Nothing For Anyone*, 'Receipt (1793)', which describes how to boil up Turkish figs with hot milk for fomentations against 'Cancer', is also taken from a historically authentic source [LI]:

That's another partly found one from one of the manuscript books that I had of that date, an 18th century manuscript book. I used to collect such things, or *own* such things, in my days of considerable wealth. And this was a book of receipts, or recipes... Though I've altered it slightly.

The next specimen, a prose-poem, appeared in the following book, *Fiction*, and was highlighted and "authenticised" further by old orthography and period typography ('Mens Talents in Difcours Shadowed out by Muficall Inftruments', p.156). The force of these texts is released best by their being presented on the page without comment, thus charging up the literary context, often by means of stark contrast. Welcome side-effects include the ludic character these stylistic outsiders take on in their new surroundings, as well as the usually imposing diction of former times. As O'Driscoll sees it,

[One manifestation] of Reading's resourcefulness [occurs] in his 'found' poems, his invented poets... and his pseudo-poets... If he has not yet made poetry from the telephone directory, he has at any rate proved his ability to draw on crossword puzzle clues and wedding gift lists for inspiration (O'Driscoll, p.210).

Later Reading granted himself the pleasure of writing such texts himself but still presenting them as found poems, another device for interpolating stances so as to ensure a convincing perspectivism. Later still, he reproduced dictions of former centuries as if he had learned a few new languages. Eventually this led to the need to preserve old texts, old language, old insights, old human concerns – in short, the past – Reading's main theme in the four books which followed *Last Poems*. Over time, his works have become linguistically more varied and alive, and at the same time more concentrated and suggestive.

Gavin Ewart was the first to fall into the found poem trap: he reckoned ' "Iuppiter ex alto periuria ridet amantum' 15s 6d" ' was a fake, which no doubt reinforced Reading's decision to incorporate more found poems in his books. Obviously, the authentic text already in itself bore poetic elements that were usable. The reviewers eventually became somewhat cautious in their assessments of these matters, as Reading's (reworked) originals and fakes could not always be told apart. The prose-poem from *Fiction*, for instance, was thought by some critics to be authentic but by others a fake. Both the postmodern conclusions following from indistinguishable pre-texts and hypertexts and the subsequent epistemological dissolution of the concept of "reality" open up a fascinating field of study with regard to Reading's art. But at this early stage of his writing, and on a much simpler level, Reading deemed the difference between original and fake to be unimportant:

> Linguistic accidents play a large part, always. I want to incorporate 'found' material, and, deriving from that – a more difficult job – to invent found material. I've been rather happy to find people mistaking found things for bogus and vice-versa. The point, although it's an enchanting exercise, is that there's not much difference, the found and the invented are all extraordinary, just as people are all exaggerated (Jenkins, 1985, p.12).

Reading's instinct for 'poetry in strange places' (Mackay Brown) did not just cover material already in existence, but also tackled the question of "unpoetic" language and subject-matter. The poems called 'oddities' by critics can also be seen as asking whether there *is* really anything such as a "poetic subject" that can only be approached in a set number of ways; or, conversely, whether everything can be turned into poetic subject-matter as long as the means of transmutation is not an artistic dead-end.

This hypothesis is here enacted in the numerical '10 x 10 x 10' (pp.129-31) – the decastrophical poem uses ten decasyllabic lines per stanza. It sets out to recount the absurd adventures of a certain 'Donald' (main protagonist of the following volume) in such a painstakingly detailed and deadpan way that the reader cannot help but be interested in the remarkably silly storyline. The poem is always under artistic control: when, after a ridiculous accident, Donald falls unconscious, the period of his unconsciousness is filled in with asterisks over two-and-a-half verses: 26 asterisks replacing 26 syllables. In 'Trio' (pp.76-82), the subject-matter had the syllabic form; here the form is the subject: Donald happened upon a stage, on which a stage had been erected, 'a stage on the stage – 10 x 10 x 10'. The poem itself has – and is – the third level; it is like an autotelic, metaleptic, three-dimensional version of Pope's 'And ten low Words oft creep in one dull Line' (*An Essay on Criticism*). Before the reader quite grasps what has happened, the experiment has worked: the moment the reader starts counting asterisks, the discovery that there are other poetically functional ways of writing poems – and quite amusing ones too – is underway. The end of this deceptively simple poem states:

> *   *   *   *   *   *   When he regained
> consciousness, he was considering the
> arbitrary nature of the Sonnet –
> 'One might as well invent any kind of
> structure (ten stanzas of ten lines each
> of ten syllables might be a good one),
> the subject-matter could be anything.'

By successfully acting out its own hypothesis ('the subject-matter could be anything'), the poem verifies it. Reading's (relativist) answer to the (essentialist) question of "poetic" *v.* "unpoetic" subject-matter is clear-cut. In this poem, he proves his point along theoretical lines; in the books to follow, the evidence is more on the practical side. In a rather unorthodox way, '10 x 10 x 10' is also a personal poem on the subject of aesthetics, as Reading reveals [C]: 'Good execution matters' – it can even be made the subject. For Reading, this strategy originated in his training as a painter. His last painting had employed the same modernist techniques [LI]: 'Execution becomes part of the subject-matter; in the case of the paintings a very important part, almost *the* part'. Like a large proportion of modern art and music, this poem has no "message", it does not *mean*, it *is*. For Reading, if the reader was stimulated to think [C], 'it's well done, never mind about the contents', the poem had achieved its purpose.

A verse from Eliot's 'Ash Wednesday' illustrates what Reading does in his poetry: 'I rejoice, having to construct something/ Upon which to rejoice'. The "substance" comes out as "form", the act of writing is made transparent, the structure is circular, and the "message" falls back into itself. At the same time, the first echoes of Beckett are heard: there is nothing to say, so I say it. Reading agreed there was a connection [LI]: 'Yes, I think that that probably *does* apply in a fairly complicated way, yes. Also to the other structured ones, I suppose, and the other mathematical, or sham-mathematical ones'.

'Response' is structured in a similarly circuitous and paradoxical way and also uses the stage metaphor, which warns the reader that a game is being played, mind the trap doors and the false floors. (The poem commissioned by Alan Brownjohn *about, or in some way deriving from, Shakespeare*[4] gives Reading 'nine nights of recurrent nightmare', after which 'I balls up Act 1 Scene 2 thus'.

The pun on 'I balls up' (eyeballs up) promises quite a few contortions to come. 'Response' is the commissioned poem, presented within the frame of a written reply to Brownjohn. This letter then quotes the full commissioned poem, which, in turn, quotes from *Julius Caesar* (I.2.102-10 and the first half of 111). This Shakespeare quotation ('Caesar cried, "Dar'st thou, Cassius, now"') starts the Reading poem afresh three times, giving evidence of Reading's centrifugal nightmare about his inability to write such a poem.

The Chinese-box principle, perhaps best known to readers from Robert Graves' poem 'Warning to Children', first applies to the hide-and-seek that Reading, allegedly out of his depth, starts playing. The boxes are empty: Reading cannot come up with any verses of his own. But Chinese boxes have no contents; their point is in their very walls: the poem resides in the spaces *between* the boxes. As soon as the first space outside the innermost box is scrutinised, i.e. when one looks up the Shakespearean verses which do *not* get quoted (starting where Reading keeps breaking off just before the second half of verse I.2.111), then a logic materialises from which everything can be unravelled. As Reading recoils twice from quoting these verses fully and starts afresh from the beginning of the quote, they must bear some significant clue; the key to the poem is thus only quasi-lost – and the missing half makes it whole. Reading quotes: 'Caesar cried, "Help me, Cassius, or I sink!".' This is how verse 111 continues (*Julius Caesar*, I.2.111*n*.):

> I, as Aeneas, our great ancestor,
> Did from the flames of Troy upon his shoulder
> The old Anchises bear, so from the waves of Tiber
> Did I the tired Caesar. And this man
> Is now become a God, and Cassius is
> A wretched creature, and must bend his body.
>   ...Ye gods, it doth amaze me,
> A man of such a feeble temper should
> So get the start of the majestic world,
> And bear the palm alone.

The parallel between Caesar / Shakespeare and Cassius / Reading thus established can be seen to work in the space between the next two boxes as well: Reading is booed off the stage and goes to Hell, i.e. he falls through a trap-door into the lower part of the Globe stage. This is where, on the one hand, he rightfully belongs ('I am with dust and other discarded props'), but, on the other hand, also where he at last hears the muffled cry for help from Caesar ('Help me, Cassius, or I sink!') – at a safe distance from the stage itself. This is an intriguing image of the paradoxical situation of the modern poet, who cannot possibly live up to Shakespeare's grandeur or do him justice in a poem, but who is "needed" by Shakespeare as a matter of life or death: the Capitol 'is brittle polystyrene', money for the Globe must be raised, poetry must continue.

'Response' is directed at two addressees, Brownjohn and Shakespeare. But the ultimate joke is on the reader. Reading first finishes the commissioned core-poem with 'this is not how I had envisaged it', and then ends the commissioned frame-poem by adding: '– nor, I imagine, what you had in mind. / I think perhaps you'd better count me out'. Apparently addressed to Brownjohn, these verses are a decoding directive addressed to the reader, asking him to step back from traditional reading strategies, 'counting' here meaning the reconstruction of the various poetic steps at three removes. Note, too, the author's damning verdict on inattentive readers: 'those in the cheap seats who're not bored are angry'. The poem claims it is impossible to write an adequate poem while doing exactly the opposite.

From the beginning Reading made sure that he could be understood (or, in some cases, decoded). He therefore did not consider it his problem when the reading clues he inserted were overlooked by reviewers [C]: 'that's literary 1x1, Part One, for tiny-tots', was his standard comment in such cases. From *Nothing For Anyone* onwards, he no longer wrote for popular tastes. He admitted that a certain literary education – or an education like his, coming from modern art – was necessary to fully appreciate his work. However, there are also readers whose understanding of artistic processes grows with each reading of Peter Reading's books, volume by volume; they may not understand much on first hearing the poems, but are very taken by them and go in search of meaning. He certainly gives a helping hand to 'anybody who bothers to look' [C].[5]

In 'Diptych' (p.109), for instance, a poem dealing with Reading's ideas about art, Reading the painter speaks on the left wing, and Reading the writer speaks on the right wing (two stresses per verse for each wing). Both expressly exclude 'the wish to communicate' as a reason for producing art, but of course already the spatial arrangement on the page starts communication with the viewer.

'Dr Cooper's Story' (p.122) masquerades as a mere narrative poem, but it turns the tables on the reader: the contents of Cooper's parcel are harmless, although a bomb was suspected in it, whereas the harmless-looking "packaging" that is the poem actually turns out to be a joke bomb, waiting to be detonated. The poem can be read as a postmodernist allegory of the communication process between writer and reader, a process termed here 'intercourse'. (There is no town called 'Intercourse' in Pennsylvania, as the poem claims – but there is one called 'Reading'.) To start with, the poem's title is suspicious, because 'Dr Cooper's Story' is not his story at all: someone else is telling it. The story is this: 'Dr Cooper' receives a parcel from 'Intercourse', but he does not know anybody there. Suspecting danger, he gets the bomb experts to examine it for him, which they do, declaring it safe, and he then finds some very tasty jam inside, without ever getting to know who sent it. The poem's allegory, or joke, is that the author (in Pennsylvania – pencil-vain-yeah) has his poem first misunderstood and mistrusted by the reader, then understood by an agent on the reader's behalf, and finally enjoyed by the reader while the author remains mysterious. (In other words, Dr Cooper had better get some help in unravelling poems like this – a doctorate alone may not be enough.)

By definition, reviews cannot delve deeply either. Shirley Toulson, for example, showed herself to be impressed by the precision with which Reading captured places and their ambience, especially in the poem 'Placed by the Gideons': 'I particularly like his reconstruction of a seedy hotel bedroom'. (This unfortunate sentence was rendered in the passive in 'Opinions of the Press' [*Fiction*], and thus made to sound patronising and incompetent.) Her one-dimensional reading is probably just a consequence of hasty reviewing and does not do the poem much justice (p.116):

> The top stair creaks. At the end of the landing
> the carpet changes to faded flesh.
> An exponent of the compliant smirk
> welcomed me, carried my case for pence.
> Plywood firedoors snap shut.
>
> A warped latch forced (yellow *Times* lines the wardrobe)
> rattles bone shoulders to hang your coat on.
> YOU MAY DRIP-DRY IN THE WASTEPAPER BIN.
> A varnished oblong, ruled-round with dust, is
> left by the Book.
>
> Where to find help, when assailed by... Doubt... Debt...
> Death – John 11. 25, 26.
> ... the resurrection and ... though he were dead...
> and believeth in me, shall never die.
> Believeth thou this?

Toulson: 'He is a painter as well as a poet, and many of these verses are strengthened by being set in a location that is exactly visually realised.' As with most poems in *Nothing For Anyone*, the

expressiveness of the poem is even greater if its structural hinge is
taken into consideration, hinted at in a double-edged question at the
end of the poem. The Holy Book here lies untouched in a desolate
room where *everything* is cheap, dusty, and antiquated. The religious
context is developed by quotations from John (11. 25-26), and
concluded with a question which could also be addressed to the
reader. The full text reads: 'Jesus said unto her, I am the resur-
rection, and the life: he that believeth in me, though he were dead,
yet shall he live: and whosoever liveth and believeth in me shall
never die. Believest thou this?' In other words, the poem addresses
the notion of resurrection, and thus carries the comical insinuation
that Heaven looks like this seedy hotel room and that the behaviour
of the landlord corresponds to St Peter's at the Gates of Heaven.
The traveller, once ferried over to the other side ('carried my case
for pence') with the fire doors snapped shut, 'MAY DRIP-DRY IN
THE WASTEPAPER BIN'.

Reading's atmospheric accuracy was the most easily recognised
feature, though, and also singled out by George Mackay Brown:

> Even this genial poet can put barbs in his tongue. I have tried to write
> 'Calendar poems' myself; so I appreciated, and was rather envious of
> 'Almanac'; because this is a witty abrasive comment on a twelvemonth
> of England in the seventies.

He accordingly deemed 'Travelogue' (pp.118-21) to be 'a series of
brief brilliant sketches of French holiday places'. Similarly, Alan
Jenkins excepted these travel notes from his criticism of the book
and saw retrospectively how a 'new expansiveness' was budding in
them (Jenkins, *DLB*, p.111). While 'Response' is the most impres-
sive poem in the volume, the six travel pieces make an interesting
sequence in their variedness. The exact evocation of surfaces and of
what lies beneath them is rendered in economic images. A deserted
winter holiday resort that has been ruined by tourist architecture;
a bathing resort on the Mediterranean that looks a sham as soon as
summer is over; the paintings ('doodles') hanging in the Château
d'Antibes masquerading as art in their opulent gilt frames, complete
with knowledgeable explications larded with art-historical nomen-
clature and reverent coach-hordes; the rules of a 'Camping Provençal',
which feature the usual translation howlers ('These rules must be
respected under / penalty of your time expiring here'); Les Grottes
de Niaux with 20,000-year-old cave paintings inside and obscene
graffiti outside ('partly both convey, / and partly were inspired by,
mortal fright'); finally Lourdes with its 'distempered congregate',
which heals everything except 'Catholic superstition'. The sequence

ends with a quotation from Auden, showing the same irreverence that marks the whole sequence:

> Precocious of me, I know, but: 'Irreverence
> is a greater oaf than Superstition'?,
> W.H.A., *really!*

A similar mini-sequence is 'The John o'Groat's Theory' (pp.110-13), which takes up the plot from *The Prison Cell & Barrel Mystery*. We hear four contributions from semi-educated middle-class people, who give us the benefit of their opinions about life and love. Reading's talent for satire draws its impact from the simple observation that the most effective exposé of shallowness is achieved by having the protagonists philosophise "themselves", unhindered by authorial intervention. The author then only has to fix *in print* what they say, in a painstaking no-comment way: this gives the platitudes a status they cannot live up to, and they promptly break down, to the reader's amusement.

The first poem (p.110) can be seen as the outside perspective on 'Correspondence' (*The Prison Cell & Barrel Mystery*), i.e. stereotypical gossip pretending to be a psychological report: ' "When Alison left Gregory for Miles / Gregory went to pieces. Angela / – that's Miles's wife – was not resentful, but / she went to pieces also." ' Two men's joint outrage about the gutter language which Reading introduced in *The Prison Cell & Barrel Mystery* (' "he said to Howard 'You can "eff off", too' – / in front of *women*" ') is visually presented in Amoebean verses as ripped-up, tautological-dialogical give-and-take (pp.110-11): thus, and in its syntactical incompleteness, it is itself nothing but a mutilation of language. The third text (pp.111-12), a humdrum Christmas letter from sister and mother, which 'Sue' reads out to 'Donald', echoes parts of *The Prison Cell & Barrel Mystery* (tedious in-laws, and the – just ended – relationship with another woman). None of the speakers develops a single thought; this is also brought home by the lack of structure in the sequence (no stanzas, just complete sentences or paragraphs) and by the fact that everybody ends with the same words they began with. Tellingly, in the fourth part an exception is apparently made from ' "normal social and matrimonial / codes" ' (p.113): but real thoughts – ones which are unfortunately not 'comfy to realise' – are here tapped from the television set, and (as an uncomfortable truth) are not integrated into the circular structure of mental immobility.

In these sequences themes are developed as they were in the first two books, but with tighter, smaller circles of cohesion. The

technique of perspectivation starts here. It is then elaborated in
Tom o'Bedlam's Beauties, while in *Diplopic* it is combined with
cross-referencing in the narrative: the first time Reading produced
an absolutely unified book of poems.

Reading's hopeless love of England is not mentioned much in
reviews or articles, although it is one of the most important rea-
sons and starting-points for the documentation, criticism, satire
and elegy with which Reading accompanies the signs of decline in
the country. Already as a young boy Reading was infatuated with
everything that dealt with the exploration of fauna and flora. His
love of nature made itself felt as a strong driving-force in his very
first book, expressed in the descriptions of English countryside.

In *Nothing For Anyone*, Reading's 'Hymn' (p.105), placed at
the beginning of the book, clarifies the premises of his ecological
worries. In very regular stanza structure, three-stress metre, and
simple diction, what is hymned is not eternal peace in the here-
after, as the title would suggest, but an early-morning walk in a
'puny dignified gesture / ... / that today we are here'. Reading's
addressee in hymns is always nature, and his hymns are really
reverdie-updates. Here, he is content with recording the transitory
moment of happiness 'at 8 / on a summer morning /... / ...17th /
of June 1975'. The poem is noteworthy for the ease with which
Reading makes it possible for the reader to remain unaware that
he is actually hymning dew on English roses in an enchanted
country churchyard on a honeyed morning – an accumulation of
lyrical clichés *par excellence*, but freshened by their self-denigrat-
ing context and the matter-of-fact conclusion.

'On Hearing the First Cuckoo in Spring' (p.109) is written in
the same way.

> Unbearable: (1) listening
> to music any more (unless
> in the safe company of others),
> (2) vegetal spring stirrings –
>
> each an insufferable glimpse,
> a split-second's primal clarity,
> of Not-Quite-Graspable Potential/
> Dimly-Recollected Guilt.

The self-important, capitalised title calls up the literary tradition of
Romantic Odes, but the first word immediately undermines it and the
first stanza consists merely of a list of facts. Nonetheless, the first song
of the herald of spring is finally made all the more moving (and,
indeed, Romantic) by its unexpected, and untraditional, effect –
'unbearable', 'insufferable' – especially for the ornithologist Reading.

In later works Reading continued along this path, which had
started in 'Raspberrying' (*For the Municipality's Elderly*), and
always avoided the traditional nature poetry stencils; different
impulses and emotions are always allowed to contradict each other
openly. The interfering agent in these troubled idylls invariably is
man – in *Nothing For Anyone*, this is still only indirectly implied.
But man is disruptive on more than one front. In 'Address
Protector' (pp.122-23), Reading uses a misunderstood word as a
starting-point for rambling on amusingly about his anchoritic
longings to escape from unnerving 'fellow-men', who even in cold
England like their garb slight and orange:

> *everyone* now lives in some clapped-out farmhouse
> with weaving on a *real* Indian loom
> and dung-grown carrots that you have to talk to
> with love to make them extra full of *goodness*
> and hand-thrown coffee-mugs with shit-brown glazes
> and stone-ground flour and Whatsisname just back
> from being a Transcendentalist (goose-fleshed
> under a shaved pate in un-English drag)
> – no, loonies were ever far too *numerous*.

Unfortunately, it is not only the loonies who are too numerous.
What here is skittish, turns earnest a few pages on, close to the
end of the volume. 'SOMETHING FOR EVERYONE!!!' (p.126) is a
shrill prelude in big letters to a circus act about to take place on
the 'SHEEP SALES FIELD, LUDLOW'. The invitation to the
sawn-lady show reads like an insane attempt at distraction from
the 'Big Issues' ('ILLUSION SUPREME'), and as such is uncom-
fortably connoted in the last verse, which draws attention to itself
by use of an extra stress: 'LAUGH?, YOU'LL SIMPLY DIE!'
    The title-poem 'Nothing For Anyone' follows (pp.127-29),
explaining it all; the capitalisation of even the preposition does
justice to the 'Big Issue' announced in the epigraph. 'Lord Ashby
spells it out for us': 'Population, Energy, Food'.[6] Grim thoughts on
leafing through the 'Dailies and Monthlies' disseminate a matter-
of-fact *Endzeitstimmung* which can hardly be countered today, over
20 years on. The simple enumeration of the main global disasters
which will dominate the existence of *Homo sapiens* until the end
corresponds to their actual status in people's consciousness: they
are catchphrases from the headlines, denotation-less with regard to
the imminent dangerous changes. The zenith of wealth has been
passed and the freedom from dependence on raw material-producing
countries is over. The Western world, according to Reading (quoting
Lord Ashby) is not in a crisis, but in a climacteric. New strategies

and global cooperation are required, but this will not be popular with the vast majority of people, because rational argument does not carry much clout:

> Of course
> it will still take us by surprise –
> nine out of ten oafs in the street,
> a census informs me with cheer,
> fondly imagine we'll find
> deposits of copper and oil
> ad nauseam, or find substitutes.
> Possibly; possibly not.

This theme goes back to the first volume, *For the Municipality's Elderly*, where the foreseeable catastrophe was glimpsed as a 'deeper already gathering maelstrom' (p.37); it got a fleeting mention in the second book, *The Prison Cell & Barrel Mystery*, as 'No-God and Species Decline Stuff' (p.98); but now, in *Nothing For Anyone*, the theme is not treated with lyrical reticence, but with existentially incensed sarcasm. Tom Paulin wrote:

> Reading's imagination responded to that lacklustre, blank decade, the 1970s... a new demotic voice – driven and anguished – ripped the poems apart. The new style was a kind of satiric prophecy which ten years on from its first appearance seems tensely able to ride the currents of an analytic desperation... And as Britain regressed more and more into a nasty and brutal form of populism, Reading observed the national sickness and chucked torn gobbets of verse at his readers (Paulin, p.288).

Even the most innocent newspaper article is imbued with a nasty double meaning in the light of the imminent catastrophe ('EARLY RETIREMENT IS COMING'), or else appears insignificant, abstruse, ridiculous. The reviewing page is no exception from this, and neither is poetry itself (p.128):

> Some snivelling Celt reviews verse.
> Compared with De Witts' Black Holes,
> a handful of weighed syllables
> has no future (nor has future).

Nowhere else has Reading commented so directly on world politics, but his 'loonies', 'oafs at Blackpool' or *'Homo erectus autophagous'* are only ever contrasted with exceptional individuals like Byron, Catullus and T.S. Eliot; the effect can therefore only be polemical. The remaining iota of hope contained in the word 'Possibly' was allowed here for the first time, but also for the last.

In view of the crazy actions of the human race depicted here even Reading becomes indirectly confessional in a laconic reference to a strained liver (p.127):

> This sot's liver – a metaphor
> for sterling's swollen decease
> and Technological Man
> and before him Roman, Mayan,
> Minoan, all *Homo erectus*
> and what he conceives as Cosmos
> in his own petty perspective
> blown oversize by an ego
> too big to survive itself. [7]

The background to Reading's 'No-God and Species Decline stuff', summarised in 'The Con Men' (p.132), is also personal. The 'dormant flies', the last surviving creatures in *For the Municipality's Elderly,* are joined here by the ant and *Penicillium.* Reading's stance of the unmoved onlooker is derived from a strictly scientific perspective. Natural science is the basis of this author's worldview and consequently also that of his works:

> To have devised
> a Theory of Evolution, yet
> to imagine *we* remain somehow outside
> its sensible advance, has been our costly
> luxury up till now; ...
> ...
> replaced now by the *sapiens* conceit
> that somehow we must organise our course
> of Evolution to preserve *ourselves*!
> (unable to accept that nasty 'Nothing',
> we long ago evolved the comfy Spook).
>
> The Ant inside the Test Zone (that 'survived,
> despite exposure to large overdoses')
> and *Penicillium* and Stone and Vacuum
> are queuing up impatiently behind.
>
> The only thing it matters to is us.

After the predictions of Sir Harold Hartley in 1954, Reading's observations of 1977 simply followed Lord Ashby's prognoses and referred to processes already starting to take place. They have all escalated: football hooliganism[8] ('terraces / dripping with apes' gore'),[9] skinhead attacks, higher crime rates, traffic chaos on the streets, energy crisis, recession, the Gulf War, pollution, Chernobyl.

Two cross-rhymes, which contradict Lord Ashby's faith in the adjustment faculties of the human species and his hope for 'value changes in society', end the title-poem in an authoritative manner:

> F.T. Index down 1 p.c.
> Frankly, we couldn't care less.
>
> Never let it be said that *we*
> ever stood in the way of regress.

Seventeen years later, an uncanny confirmation, both aggressive and resigned, is given in *Last Poems* (1994). Of course nothing has changed. The impotent, futile warning poem '*Nothing For Anyone*' is reiterated four times ('Reiterative', 'Erosive' and pp.279, 280) – first as an annotated rewrite, then as 'eroded, faded text', and, on the last two pages of the volume, so strongly eroded (through photographic manipulation) that it can hardly, and then not at all, be decyphered – a disdainful, poignant presentation of a useless text.

Fiction (1979):
Death of the Author

Fiction was Peter Reading's fourth volume, and contains 23 longish poems. It picks up the thread from *Nothing For Anyone* and ends his early phase. With its inventive sophistication, *Fiction* displays both the strength and weakness of the previous book to a heightened degree; this time, there are no new contours. The book seems unbalanced, yet technically it is an essential and defining contribution to the œuvre and, like its predecessor, a brilliant and entertaining little firework with much sparkle in the details, but the material has less substance.

The reviewers dealt with the book rather briefly and gave it only a superficial reading.[1] However, once the poeticistic manoeuvre and the word games, jokes and postmodernist structures are understood, the book's poetic agenda and technical complexity become clearer. In *Fiction*, as in the previous volume, the syllabic, accentual and numeric metres appear alongside rather loose iambic pentameters, prose, and another visual parallel text (p.155, see before p.72 and 109), but there are formal and metrical novelties, too: concrete poetry, prose poems, a dramolett – altogether a similarly diverse quodlibet as in *Nothing For Anyone*.

Fiction is a small emblematic excursion into the vast land of metafiction, 'slightly tongue-in-cheek' [LI], and inspired by the self-reflexive novels of Beckett and Robbe-Grillet and the riddling heterocosms of Borges, which Reading was familiar with. (Behind it all probably lie *Alice in Wonderland* and *Alice Through the Looking Glass*.) Before the reader even sees the first poem, Reading stages a collision between the title and epigraph: '(*Verse is not Fiction –/ ask any librarian*.)' The tension created by this non-definition charges all the poems. (Both true occurrences and fictions are presented as fictions, and these fictions are rendered either in prose or verse.)

Again, a poem from the previous volume provides the core of the current book. 'Donald', the protagonist of the meta-poem '10 x 10 x 10' in *Nothing For Anyone*, is given the function of being an authorial mask (p.130): 'He...said "Damn and blast it all to bloody Hell!", / ran his fastest (unhampered by Measles / and now using conventional techniques) / and thought "This could be good to write about / – but in the third person, naturally." ' Similarly, he is identified with the husband who returns to his wife in

Nothing For Anyone. In *Fiction*, he is a prominent figure, but the reader is deliberately disorientated about his identity in the very first poem, '*Fiction*' (pp.137-38). 'Donald is a fictitious character' and, as he is no good at rhyming, a 'writer of fiction'. 'Donald' is writing a novel ('*Fiction*'), in which the protagonist 'Donald' or 'Don' – his *alter ego* – writes poems, which he sends to magazines under the pseudonym 'Peter Reading'. (The poem titles attributed to 'Don' are identical with those in the table of contents of Peter Reading's *Fiction*.) In Donald's novel, the poet 'Don' with the pseudonym 'Peter Reading' sues

> a man whose *real*
> name is 'Peter Reading' for having once
> written a fiction about a poet
> who wrote verse concerning a novelist
> called 'Donald' whose book *Fiction* deals with 'Don'
> (a poet who writes satirical verse...)

But that is not all. The fictional poet is up against the real author of fictions:

> In 'Reading's' fiction, the poet who writes
> verse concerning the novelist 'Donald'
> is sued by the latter who takes offence...

Likewise, the fictional novel author is dissatisfied with the implied poet, who is the only one not to be identified by name (a significant hint). To further confuse the reader, more court cases and stolen quotations are listed.

The point of this verse-fiction, which destabilises the differences between "reality" and "fiction" and is also a mini-introduction into different authorial stances in narration (another poem warns 'You Can't Be Too Careful'), is this: real author, implied author, protagonist and his under-protagonist are easily mixed up, but absolutely must be kept apart, even if they can be partially identical. This is the first lesson in reading, and presented in an entertaining, postmodern, Chinese-boxes manner.[2] The poem concludes: ' "Even one's self is wholly fictitious." ' Besides being amusing, this also alludes to the 'Copernican Revolution' about the absence of centres of meaning (in the universe, in history, in language, in the self), which makes the epistemological notion of any stable "reality" seem highly dubious. Even more importantly, though, as far as his own person is concerned, it announces what Reading regards as his most important aim in this book.

The narratological potential for suspense, structure and perspective that resides in the interplay of different authorial stances becomes a favourite with Reading in this volume and is kept up until *Last Poems* (to which 'John Bilston' writes the foreword). The aesthetic possibilities for the real author increase with every new stance: the literariness and attractiveness of a text increase, and the confessional mode is switched off. Jenkins describes one of the consequences:

> The reader might consider the opening piece another evasive stratagem, a way of ducking responsibility for some of the more grotesque imaginings that follow; rather, it frees the poet and his words from the burden of literalness and casts a harsh ironic light on his freedom, which is a freedom thus to "play" with others' lives or deaths – even invented lives, invented deaths (Jenkins, *DLB*, p.472).

Even more important is that the implied author Reading is shown ridding himself of the real author Reading. Other poems corroborate this: the author has a fictionalised part in the ensemble of the syllabic-numerical, autotelic 'Choreograph' (pp.148-49), for example, and is outside of the literary proceedings at the same time. The poem includes a chart of nine letters and nine numbers representing nine people in nine rooms in part of a high-rise block viewed through 'this window opposite', and the verses describe what the people are doing in the different rooms: alongside perfectly banal activities such as E painting a wall, there is a theft by A and a scene of presumably illicit sex between B and C, but everything is presented in the same detached way. Finally, the poem drops a tactful Venetian blind on B and C, then puns on its use of the ninth letter 'I' to refer to the first person singular: 'I, slouched over office 9's desk, may / be generously assumed asleep.' The poem's reflexivity hinges on the same pun: the authorial 'I', here seen in his traditional (pre-Modernist) function as a moral commentator on human behaviour, has been put to sleep. The poem 'Remaindered' (p.168) is even more explicitly reflexive, and after this Reading employs deixis when referring to himself.

Reflexivity in writing opens itself up to postmodernist interpretations, which can neglect the overall aesthetic balance of a given book.[3] Reading is not first and foremost a postmodernist, nor does he think the term itself is precise enough [C]. In *Fiction*, his main object is to free his poetry from the only "fallible" element which has so far disrupted its literariness, which, in the end, is the aesthetic level supposed to make his œuvre convincing. The dramatisation of this process could equally well have been conducted behind the scenes, but it is openly and comprehensively shown for two reasons. First, the 'I' as the centre of lyrical articulation has been historically fettered to the personal author's 'I' for so long that the loosening of those ties cannot remain uncommented. Second, Reading wants his readers to know where they are with him: the personal element, even if used in an identifiable way, henceforward only carries a fictional, i.e. generalising function.

Apart from that, these steps were also preparatory measures for achieving what is in the end a humanistic goal. Reading agreed [LI]:

> I'm loth to try and sound grand about this, but I *do* think that I'd want some sort of accessibility and that anything that I wrote was, really, *not* to do with me – though that might be the triggering-off point – but to do with any possible human being who was able to read the thing.

Apart from working towards a possibility of identification and an authoritative generality, a stance which would also allow the combination of sympathy with irony, Reading also welcomed the 'double bluff' [LI], which facilitates the author's use of his personae as alter ego, as voices for his own thoughts and emotions, which do not run the risk of sounding pompous or sentimental, as long as they are not pronounced ex cathedra but evinced from the relativised stance of a character (in later works: of an older literary text). And even if utterances can be identified as authorial, they cannot, after the definitions in *Fiction*, reach the egocentric status of confessional poetry. Reading does not want to communicate himself, but something, and this is supposed to happen as inobtrusively as possible in the sense that the stance of the autocratic "poet" has to be avoided at all costs. According to Reading, such a figure is close to ridicule, considering the complexity of the world today [C].

Donald, who in *Nothing For Anyone* devised a new structure (10x10x10), for which 'the subject-matter could be anything' (p.131), does it again in *Fiction*, but on a larger scale: the self-referentiality is extended and intensified. A new 10x10x10-poem ('Inter-City') calls up the poetic principle in question and is just as self-referential under the surface; footnotes, which were introduced in *Nothing For Anyone*, abound; "explanations" in the appendix, which alternate between being correct notes and splenetic fantasies of 'Donald', question the fiction of alleged authenticity (and satirise the note-writing in poetry books). The competition within the hierarchy of authorial stances is ironically exemplified by death and violence. Donald, the would-be literatus who secretly reads adventure novels, meets the eerie 'Dr Liebgarten' – a protagonist of the *Biggles* book Donald is presently reading on the Inter-City. A 'funny-sinister, mad anecdote' follows – as in Dürrenmatt's *The Tunnel*, the journey leads into the underworld of death.[4] Direct and implicit links between 'Y – X', 'Festival', 'And Now, a Quick Look at the Morning Papers',[5] 'Inter-City', 'Parallel Texts', 'Clues' and the absurd 'Notes' also make clear that 'Dr Liebgarten' is the same train passenger who is trying to solve the crossword puzzle as the train mows down a farmer and some cows at an unmanned level crossing. The human significance of that accident is hidden by design in 'Parallel Texts', where the equally unfeeling descriptions reduce the accident to the status of anecdote and reportage.[6] The same happens in another Salopian dialect poem, which then equally unemotionally reports the suicide of the train driver whose identity (as a transvestite) had been unstable. In 'Festival', 'Don' (who shares a compartment with 'Dr Liebgarten') confounds a American lady from 'Noo Joysey', who understands neither art nor French, with French art explications, and himself becomes the victim of a car accident on the A49 (which in fact runs parallel to the train tracks in question). His creator, 'Donald', seems to be the victim of the heart attack described in '5'.

The obscure crossword puzzle 'Clues' (p.159) hides the key to *Fiction*: both are creative language games, which – like Donald's literary talent – are not to be taken quite seriously. The last word of the book is 'dupe', addressed to the reader. In the poem 'Clues', it is also the solution to '25 down' ('Toll or fee split softly to hoax'), making fun of the linguistic distortions of crossword puzzles.[7] Next, the 'dupe' (both persona and solution) in line 11 of 'Clues' is surrounded (both literally and linguistically) by a human tragedy without noticing it – an oblique acknowledgement of the fact that this is only a literary game involving fictitious personae, and that *Fiction* does not deal with human concerns, while also showing human tragedies in the midst of mundane goings-on. 'Dupe' also goes with the plot and personae in 'Inter-City', who – like the reader – do not solve the puzzle they are themselves a part of. In short, the 'Notes' and the poem 'Clues' are instrumental in pointing the way out of this maze; and the word 'dupe' provides the 'clue' to the literary riddle of *Fiction*. Revealingly, 'PX' (p.170) is the only 'answer' without a question to go with it – this is the point of the book in a nutshell: the reader is not supposed to harbour any more curiosity about the author, Peter X. *Fiction* despatches pseudo-art, pseudo-art-lovers and pseudo-identities, performing the 'death of the author' in an unusual, funny, and almost literal way.

The other poems, with subject-matter outside the metafiction, are still thematically connected with it insofar as they stage further casualties,[8] expose further examples of pseudo-art ('*King Lear* done in dirty macs') and pseudo-identities,[9] and transpose these

issues onto the material, linguistic level.[10] 'Festival' (pp.145-46)
and 'Interview' (p.160) are heartlessly funny satires about precious
and semi-educated artists, about art-lovers 'who like art a lot once
a year / [and] who really do say "*Darling,* / I haven't seen you for
ages!" ', and about art sponsors whose development in taste peaks
with 'Blue Nun Liebfraumilch'. 'The First Three Minutes &c.'
(p.161), a history of the universe in 18 verses, is not only a sur-
prising synopsis of these various strands in a new context, oscillat-
ing between fact and fantasy, but also an imaginative "summary"
of Steven Weinberg's astrophysical Harvard lectures about the
problem of Genesis. Weinberg's detailed philosophical conclusion
about the universal absence of meaning[11] is summarised by a terse
two-liner: 'Which knowledge is no excuse / to cease behaving like
Gentlemen.'

Pseudo-identities and displacement also concern the "authors"
Kokur Niznegorsky and Pedro Ximénez. Niznegorsky's 'heroic
anthem *The / Soya Bean Canning-Plant Operative*' (p.152) is quite
obviously mock-communist nonsense, but Niznegorsky can still be
viewed as influential on Reading insofar as it is a Ukrainian wine.[12]
The Spanish author's name is reminiscent of a type of sherry.[13]
Reading explained his reasons for the heteronyms in his works –
'bogus translations of bogus names of people' [LI]:

> I like translationese anyway and it enables you to actually say things in
> a way that you couldn't otherwise. But it is also to question the idea
> that... anything slightly obscure (especially if it's, say, South American
> literature) would be regarded as immediately marvellous and to become
> a kind of cult straightaway. So you had the dredging up of all sorts of
> obscure names and because they were South American and had some
> sort of political inclination they would be immediately highly thought
> of in any intellectual circles... Also it's just a pleasant sort of joke.

Reading uses the distancing Niznegorsky stance again for some
erotic poems in *Tom o'Bedlam's Beauties* (p.186) and in the epi-
graph of *Diplopic*. Also General Señor Conde de Torregamberro,
who is accused by 'Pedro Ximénez' in an pseudo-imagistic, pseudo-
suggestive polit-miniature in 'In State' (p.159), is hailed by a
fanatic in *Going On* (p.59). In *Tom o'Bedlam's Beauties* (p.198) and
Diplopic (p.224), the distinguished circle is extended by the tankas
'after' Sanraku Koshu; but in *Tom o'Bedlam's Beauties* the inspira-
tion derived from 'Noval *Nacional* '63' (p.201) gives away the true
(vinic) identity Quinta do Noval (port wine), thus inviting suspi-
cion of the previous "authors'" authenticity. In spite of this dis-
closure, Reading teases readers once again in a Poetry Book Society
comment:

references to such justly celebrated names as Kokur Niznegorsky and Sanraku Koshu have only been cited where it was felt that the reader might benefit from direct contact with these congenial sources of inspiration ... Noval's 'Nacional', 1963, to which I allude in 'Legacies' is of such profundity that I urge readers...and non-readers alike to make haste in acquainting themselves with it.[14]

These "authors" are also the first "personae" in Reading's ensemble, who by their repeated appearance contribute to the emergence of a distinct little world in the œuvre.

Two poems deserve special mention: '5' (pp.141-43) and 'Opinions of the Press' (p.166). '5' merges the visual and numeric devices which were used separately in *The Prison Cell & Barrel Mystery*. In the first edition, five pages present five stanzas each, which are all arranged like the five dots on a dice, every stanza consisting of five lines which consist of five syllables each, which makes 5x5. The five stanzas on each page represent the five senses (their arrangement roughly corresponds to the location of the sensory organs), which chronicle their respective sensations of the successive stages of an old man's (Don's?) heart attack: the heart attack itself, followed by first aid in the ambulance; the heavy sensation on the chest triggering a flashback to the first accident in childhood; the time on a clock triggering thoughts of a memorable night of lovemaking; then death. The senses are separated, as is to be expected in a situation of physical excruciation, where consciousness collapses and only one sensation can be processed at a time. Reading's arrangement is therefore not merely fanciful invention, but an apt reversal of the normal synaesthetic experience of life.

'Opinions of the Press' is an example of masterliness camouflaging as a piece of apprenticeship. Ironically, reviewers saw it in the very same unliterary way that the poem debunks in the snippets of reviews (of previous poems) presented.[15] Of course the poem is a sarcastic counter-attack against critics on one level, but if that was all then Reading's opinion would simply stand against his critics' opinions in deadlock. The reviewers' comments are not always wrong as such, but they all miss the point. Reading's slight adaptation of their opinions about his poetry by including the first person ('I contain some clever rhymes') highlights their basic mistake: if Reading's poems were "life" and not "art", more prosaic explanations would be appropriate; paradoxically, "life" categories are what the reviews seem to expect of him.

This significant negligence is most obvious in the literal readings of the last verse, the culmination of the poem. Like a photonegative, the ridiculous question '*but am I Art?*' enacts and ironises the fact that the right question was not once asked (let alone answered) in the reviews. Even Longley stated: 'This question is partly rhetorical (in placing such questions as rhetorical), partly the real question that stays for an answer.' Jenkins concluded that 'Reading in this book seems finally and unequivocally to have "found his voice" – economical, witty, *very* mordant' (and, accordingly, the poems he chose for *Essential Reading* were more often funny than artistically demanding); he was thus led to describe this poem as a 'splendid piece of self-examination' (Jenkins, *DLB*, p.472).

The poem follows the rules of *Fiction*: life is not art and the real author is not necessarily identical with the implied author, who does not have to be the 'I', either. As already explained, this opens up highly productive artistic functions which can explain why the features applauded or found missing by the reviews are present or absent. Furthermore, by repeatedly using the jarring 'I' (ludicrous in the context), then capitalising 'Art' and using italics for even more emphasis, the problematic aesthetics suspected behind the language of reviewing are exposed as being an essentialistic idea of "Art". The "essence" of "Art" has been a Holy Grail for centuries, so any (explicit or implicit) checklist of "poetic ingredients" is determined by historical context ('I do not transcend pain with Poetry') and personal taste ('I am not as mellifluous as Sir John Betjeman'), as the word 'Opinions' in the title also indicates. In debunking the essentialist question by asking a question that leaves the literary arena altogether ('*but am I Art?*'), 'Opinions of the Press' shows that criticism by the yardstick of axiomatic "Art" does not lead very far. Asking '*what is his art?*' instead would lead further – for example, to the discovery of an artistic relation between Reading's authorial stance ('I') and its aesthetic functions.

In the end, the categories of fiction and verse, if understood as genre demarcations, have undermined each other, and the author 'Peter Reading' has met his certain death by fictional overkill. In 'Clues' the strategy was named: 'Un pom led me to writer's disguise', the anagram 'Nom de Plume' leading to 'Don'. Therefore, the alliterative Anglo-Saxon riddle 'Remaindered' (p.168) about the cremation of the "unsaleable" author is logically placed at the end of the book, where the top wines mentioned ('Bordeaux Crus Classés') also identify 'Reading' as 'Don' by referring back to the first poem, where they were first mentioned. About the "author", Reading said, 'Yes, I wanted to get rid of him. I wanted the stance of Addison in "Thus I live in the world rather as a spectator of mankind than as one of the species"' (Edgar, p.57).

The road was now clear for the following works, which are neither traditional poetry books nor novels, but a hybrid of the two, and for a voice which could freely move between the personal, distanced and superpersonal stances.

The epigraph had announced problems of definition. One possible solution in the end is: (*Art is not Life and the Poet is not Reading –* *ask Donald*).

Tom o'Bedlam's Beauties (1981): Risky Reality *v.* Illusion

Tom o'Bedlam's Beauties was the first book of Peter Reading's "middle period", and received a Poetry Book Society Recommendation. The *TLS* featured the first long review of a book by Reading – by Grevel Lindop – and the other papers also carried extended reviews.[1] From almost all sides, there were positive comments: 'The book is a brilliant, scathing achievement' – 'a *tour de force* of great originality' – 'a very disturbing book' (Jenkins, *DLB*, p.473; Ewart; Curry). According to Lindop, Reading had 'steadily made his way into a territory explored by no one else in contemporary British poetry'.

However, the 'Martians', Ulster poets and several new women writers were attracting more attention at that time, and Reading narrowly missed being included with them in the influential *Penguin Book of Contemporary British Poetry* (1982), whose editors Andrew Motion and Blake Morrison decided to restrict their selection to only 20 poets. Since Secker & Warburg were only producing print runs of 500 copies of his books in hardback only and were doing little to publicise them – and Reading himself was not giving many readings – he was not widely read. But there was another factor, if Philip Larkin's words about 'the Reading Public' are true: 'to be a popular writer you must not bang on about age, misfortune, sickness, grief'.[2] Indeed, A.A. Cleary started her long review of *Tom o'Bedlam's Beauties* by saying, 'It's not customary to dwell on the world of the mad'.

Tom o'Bedlam's Beauties is the first 'typical Reading': variations on one large, unusual theme are bound into a mosaic structure by novelistic devices. It marks a new phase, leaving meta-poetological concerns largely behind and tackling weightier subject-matter in technically and structurally more elaborate poems, although the grave authority of Reading's voice in later works is still some way off. Lindop characterises Reading's early poems thus: 'A typical Reading poem greets us with a beguiling grin and welcomes us into situations so terrible that they pass into black comedy and out on the other side, while in the margins paradoxes and uncertainties multiply to infinity.' What he omits to say, though, is that there is no book by Reading without a meta-level; Reading will himself mention contentious features, both to pre-empt criticism and to guide readers. In *Tom o'Bedlam's Beauties*, he dismisses

himself as 'whippersnapper' (p.197) and says: 'This writer has
never tackled / a single *major* issue. / (Was unaware there *were* any.)'
(p.187). Starting with *Diplopic*, Reading was to pursue his uncom-
fortable, serious, contemporary themes with a rare degree of
intensity in tenacity and passion. Dodsworth saw this coming in
Tom o'Bedlam's Beauties: 'these poems are very sharp instruments
indeed, forged from an unyielding and troublesome pessimism'.

Reading wrote in his Poetry Book Society author comment:

> *Tom o'Bedlam's Beauties* features lunacy. There is material about bona
> fide Bin-endorsed idiots as well as the more day to day mad (presi-
> dents, meths-drinkers, the Welsh). Those items not directly about
> insanity do imply some backdrop of irrationality ('65th', reprinted in
> this *Bulletin*, is the grateful acknowledgement of a promoter of sanity)
> and those touching on the Major Issue or the Amorous fall by
> definition of their subject within the compass of the central theme.[3]

Tom o'Bedlam's Beauties is Reading's first step towards integrating
"unpoetic" themes into poetry. (Since Aristotle "truth" and
"verisimilitude" have been discussed as poetic categories, and
Romanticism added "beauty".) Wordsworth's comments on his
'Idiot Boy' are an early example of aesthetic self-defence: 'You
begin what you say upon the Idiot Boy with this observation, that
nothing is a fit subject for poetry which does not please. But here
follows the question, Does not please whom?'[4] Madness remained
a thorny subject, despite the fact that Wordsworth, Anglo-Saxon
and Elizabethan writers, Shakespeare, Pope, Swift and Crabbe had
all written about the subject, and in alluding to almost all of these
(e.g. pp.186, 195), *Tom o'Bedlam's Beauties* places itself in the same
largely comic, satirical line.[5]

The first 'therapy poem' quotes 'Modern Maladies', such as
'Dyslexia, Anorexia' or 'Road Signs in Welsh' (p.191). Despite the
humour, Reading shares a Wordsworthian drive to enlarge readers'
sensibilities.[6] Indeed, the epigraph reveals a moral interest – even
though it is immediately belittled: '*I once considered nursing them /
– even went for an interview / – magnanimous of me, eh?*' The typical
twist undercuts any potentially egocentric motif: the objects of
compassion deserve attention, not the compassionate subject. At
the same time, the sharp self-irony demonstrates the paradoxical
ambiguity of his empathy: the wish to help is mentioned, but writ-
ing a book about lunatics also means taking literary advantage of them.
After Reading's job interview and visit to a clinic for the mentally
ill (described in 'Visit', p.189), he concluded [LI], 'I couldn't put
up with it. I was inadequate.' The epigraph continues: '*Backed out
– like them, eschewing / the risky Real for Illusion.*' This paradox

makes looking away seem morally dubious, too. All this was material for a single carefully interrelated book.

The epigraph toys with the question of whether a neutral coexistence of ethical urge and artistic volition is possible, or whether the moral foundation is corrupted by the artistic act, or, conversely, whether the literary presentation could be morally charged. (In the next book, the role of the 'poet vulture' is investigated in more detail, and the tension resolved in the book after that, *C.*)

A footnote claims the title derives from an 'Old Herefordshire name for variety of eating-apple'. A closer look at its contrived literary context makes one sceptical, and Reading conceded [LI]: 'completely bogus. An invention... But it's the sort of name that apples get called, "Lady in the Snow" and all this sort of stuff.' The fictive name is an allusion to the literary ancestor of this book, an anonymous Elizabethan poem, 'Tom's Song', 'Tom o'Bedlam's Song' or 'Loving Mad Tom',[7] in which an inmate of Bedlam describes the maltreatment he suffers ('Poor Tom' is a recurrent figure in Elizabethan drama, best known in *King Lear*). The abuse of Bedlamites is notorious; visiting 'St Mary of Bethlehem' (founded 1247) was a popular pastime, where visitors could pay tuppence to see the torture of inmates. 'Tom o'Bedlam' was also a name for the homeless, who sang in the hope of earning money. Several centuries on, for some the situation has not changed. In the 1980s hospital capacity was reduced by 3,000 beds, releasing the mentally ill into the streets of London.

'*Tom o'Bedlam's Beauties*' are green apples thrown at helpless inmates by green boys. The real "Beauties" however are the dramatic monologues of the personae: painful variations of 'Tom o'Bedlam's Song' in which they tacitly ask for nothing more than attention. Following the dictates of the epigraph, there is no appeal for empathy. Instead, Reading exposes the perpetrators: seducers, frauds, tormentors, mockers, but here again, 'the poet's design cannot, of course, be entirely free from suspicion in this regard, and he knows it' (Jenkins, *DLB*, p.473). Sometimes 'doubting Reading's motives' (Curry) means overlooking the paradoxical ethical danger set up in the epigraph. Reading never fails to address his paradoxes; besides, in *Tom o'Bedlam's Beauties* Reading starts using the Robbe-Grillet perspective, a stance of mere recording, and of projecting mirror images (see 'Four Poems', p.187).

The historical parallel indicates that the "Beauties" also are the specimens paraded in *this* Bedlam, first spotted by the ignorant boys in the title-poem. The reader is being taken round the asylum

with a good deal of good-natured humour – some of the oddballs
are simply 'mildly amusing' (p.203). The soothing effect of humor-
ous attitudes is celebrated in '65th' (p.197), a laudatio on Gavin
Ewart's light verse, 'learnt by heart in bits / to keep us sane whilst
dealing with the shits / daily we've the misfortune to confront'.
But fun has no place alongside primitive cruelty to the sick, and
'every snigger becomes a wince as the exactness of the suffering
and the pity makes itself felt between the lines of Reading's terse,
alliterative utterance' (Jenkins, p.60).

The table of contents and the 'Notes' show that the 27 poems
"inside" are held together by the firm bracket of two poems entitled
'?', emblematic Riddles in Anglo-Saxon style (p.173):

Say, supple-minded   master of wit,
wealthy in words,   what my name is.

Behind this stands an old pre-text – 'I always enjoyed [Anglo-
Saxon poetry], and since student days had copies of the transla-
tions from the Exeter Book, *Beowulf* and so on' [LI] – but the
answer can be guessed without knowing the source: 'men will
attest me a tight-fitting raiment' gives a clue at the outset, and the
last page specifies the case: 'Without my weave, un-wise would
wave their arms weirdly' (p.207).[8] If the caesura is an appropriate
form for ripped-apart minds, the securing knot of the jacket is
tied in the arrangement of '?' and '?'.[9] The affliction of insanity is
timeless and a matter of ill-luck ('don't think it couldn't be you'
in *Perduta Gente*). 'About How Many?' asks (p.196):

What kind of people?
People like us.
Who hasn't wanted
to scream the house down?
Felt there was no point
carrying on?
Sat day-dreaming
at place of employment?
Wouldn't be human
if you hadn't.

Like radioactive pollution or Aids in other works, mental instability
can hit 'All walks of life' (p.196), be it through chromosomes,
accidents, or nervous breakdown: '…Classless; / vassal, my stiff
canvas fits tight, or viscount' (p.207). The lucky ones are not
lucky forever, either (p.204): 'appalling / age, like a fuddling nar-
cotic, / has the same effect on the rest of us.' The 29 formally
very varied poems parade a weird conglomeration of patients, all
with different stories and different symptoms. The only rational

element of order in this state of emotional and perceptional imbalance is the rigorous shaping power behind the poetry – a measure of mental self-discipline helping the sane to stay so.

Tom o'Bedlam's Beauties combines sharp images with a sometimes moving directness or simplicity, while the cross-references mentioned by Reading in the *PBS Bulletin* ('one piece may inform another or a sub-plot unfold in a footnote', p.3) contribute to a sophisticated structure that fully reveals itself only on re-reading. Lindop felt reminded of other literary genres: 'a tangle of riddles, a maze with [a] dual enigma…a labyrinth that has no exit…the book as a whole reads rather like a detective story with half the clues left out'. The clues are well hidden, as a jokey example may serve to illustrate. The main character's name is 'Tom', mentioned casually towards the end. His opponent all the while has been 'Gerald', fondly abbreviated to 'Gerry' by Tom's adulterous wife.

The first half of the book reports on different lives and calamities leading to hospitalisation. As Jenkins notes, 'The point about them is not so much that they are mad, but that they have such good reasons to be so' (Jenkins, *DLB*, p.472). The partly absurd and partly correct information in the 'Notes' and the steady accumulation of clues help towards the dénouement.[10] Some of the characters clearly live together in the euphemistically named 'Les Lauriers Nursing Home', which is identical with 'Bay Trees Mental Hospital', the very asylum with the 'red brick buttressed wall' the green boys discovered. Torturing Tom with electro-shock therapy, the modern counterparts of the Elizabethan poem's 'hag and goblin' are the Nurse and a Dr Snieder (*alias* Snyderson, Schynieder and Snyde – his identity also seems to be disintegrating). None of their patients ever gets better, nor do they grow very old, either. The ex-sales manager Tom, whose farcical fate can be traced through 'Concord', 'Some of Their Efforts', 'Between the Lines' and 'Commitment', is committed to hospital by his wife and her lover, 'Gerry', the slippers rep ('it's a step / up in the world to ride round in a Merc.'). 'Concord' (pp.174-76) is Reading's third 10x10x10 poem and already established as a special form for amusingly crazy narratives. Here Tom hallucinates about the things that have driven him insane – terrible headaches after a motorcycle accident, illnesses, gambling debts ('Turfster', *'the three-o-clock Haydock'*), his wife's infidelity, stress, and practical jokes at his expense.[11] After a failed suicide attempt in adolescence (p.199), Tom's second attempt on a railway line is obviously successful.[12] Another inmate, Brigadier Peregrine ('Perry') Fashpoint-Shellingem, recounts fabulous yarns (p.184), similar in style to the sea-story of 1765 (pp.178-79):[13]

Fell through the floes with a dog-team in Labrador,
slashed free the harnesses, swam for the nearest ice,
stripped off my garments and beat the freeze out of 'em,
still couldn't last the night, had to kill all the dogs,
skinned 'em and made a rough coat with the hair inside,
piled up the dead bodies, cuddled up close to 'em,
lasted till morning, relief-ship arrived, by Gad.

As in Tom's case, the Brigadier's 'Wandering' monologue ends
with a brief comment by Nurse to Doctor 'Snyderson' – the
'plaque ready-labelled HIC+IACET / PEREGRINVS+NON+COM-
POS+MENTIS' (p.191) is soon required. Glimpses of the Brigadier
can be caught in 'Some of Their Efforts' and *Tom o'Bedlam's
Beauties*', where he is chewing a rose. The unconventionally
rhymed sonnet 'A Departure' describes how he dies dressed in
expedition gear facing the river, and in the following poem
('Legacies') he, at least, is mourned by his widow. (His old mili-
tary persona is revived for *Ukulele Music* and *Final Demands*.)

The other two inmates who appear several times are the 'soli-
tary boy' (p.177), whose incoherence and imbecility were probably
caused by the Birmingham 'Spaghetti Junction petrol fumes' [14]
(p.191) and who also does not live long, like the dotard Johnny
Weissmuller, who is still playing Tarzan ('beating his wizened
dugs like bongo-drums', [p.192]).

There are even indications of the presence of 'Artemus Ward'
in the clinic, who claims in 1973 to have been born in Maine in
1834. 'Artemus' Wardrobe' (p.188), a parody of the successful
malapropian style of Charles Farrar Browne (*alias* Artemus Ward,
1834-1867), is a funny slapstick poem about the protagonist's
unsuccessful visit to a 'Booteek':

But, hitchin up the trowzerz, as I stood
balansin on wun legg, I nearly cumm
a cropper – hopt ter save meself, an lent
on the accursid daw. It throo me owt.
I hopt a pays ore too, wylst givin vent
too me emowshunz, & herd someone showt
'A Bedlamite, got luce without is droors!' –
the most embarrassust I ever bean.
The ground flew up and hit me on all fores.
I girdid up my Lions & fled the Seen.

The ill, unstable, or eccentric who manage to avoid hospitalisa-
tion are still so damaged that they perish miserably or at least do
not dare to venture back into the "real" world. These characters
are neatly matched with the inmates: the American sailor David
Flat, whose last voyage ended much more harmfully than the

Brigadier's (pp.178-79); the deceived girl, who goes the same desperate way as Tom after her lover's last visit ('Amulet', p.190), singing (like 'Tom') her 'Song of the Bedsit Girl' (p.204) and holding an empty Valium phial;[15] the great satirist, authentic like Artemus Ward and much valued by his contemporaries (and by Reading), who after a long, excruciating illness lost his mental faculties;[16] and finally, another special case like the young boy, 'he' in 'Limns' (p.183) is grouchy to an acute degree, as is amusingly evident from this typified miniature portrait in five tankas (5-7-5-7-7).

The limns represent some of the poet's own traits in Dickensian exaggeration, and 'he' (the poet) appears again in 'Eclogue', being offensive to the local Councillor about a hypothetical nuclear attack ('if you are spared I'm happier lost / I'm old-fashioned', p.180). Also, in a reaction to the tittle-tattle heard in a hairdresser's ('Interior', pp.187-88), 'he' goes into a double-edged offensive:

perhaps I should retrain to program
dumb Artificial Intelligence
in unmeasured no bull-shit language –
ALGOL and COBOL and FORTRAN.

Too late: the poet despairs of his dactyls and is hospitalised, too (p.191). In the same poem, the Shakespeare trio of 'The lunatic, the lover and the poet' (*Midsummer Night's Dream*, V.1.7), who all share heightened imaginative powers, is made complete by amorous insanity: one lover experiences rapturous moments of love-trance; another is transported by 'L'amor che muove il sole' into Bay Trees Hospital (p.191).[17] Meanwhile, Ronald Reagan, the wrinkled 'cadaverous Thespian' who occupies the Pentagon, also contributes to quotidian madness (p.180); another old man, expert at ancient farming techniques, cannot even begin to understand the modern world ('Bereft', p.182): 'when his wife died he sat in the dark, hungry. / Dialled the Surgery with my assistance, / held the phone in two paws like a sad dog / gnawing a bone, not knowing which end spoke.'

This display of doomed destinies is followed in the middle of the book by five poems entitled 'Some of Their Efforts' (pp.191-93). A note refers to the (fictitious) publication of hospital psychologists 'Glibber & Crass': '"Therapeutic value of Poetry practised amongst the mentally disturbed"', which is not followed by evidence, but by five poems written by the Sales Manager (or the hospitalised poet?), Peregrine Fashpoint-Shellingem, Johnny Weissmuller and the boy. These all reveal disintegrating minds (one case is even caused by 'Writer's Block, Spondee / Trochee / Dactyl'), while the

tidy outward forms clearly have no beneficial effect whatsoever
(three poems are in accentual verse, one is a villanelle, the other a
Shakespearean sonnet), as the grotesque misquotations from Dylan
Thomas and Eliot also indicate. If compassion is not the first aim
of poetry, as hinted in the epigraph, then poetry perhaps cannot,
in turn, claim any therapeutic power, either. Gardening, fine art,
music and drama seem better suited (p.189), but best of all, patience,
tolerance, acceptance, as research shows (pp.196, 204).

After anamnesis and therapy, the appropriately fragmented third
part of the book charts the course of the malady: chaos, disinte-
gration, in the end the straitjacket. This structure is not presented
linearly, but a-chronologically, the technique of literary collage
also having the advantage of creating more density, suspense, and
surprise. The remaining 'Songs' include statistical background
information; a quasi-ithyphallic tanka about a puzzling situation,
allegedly 'after' Sanraku Koshu;[18] a Petrarchan sonnet mimicking
birds' voices, whose cries are homophonically and phonolectically
connected with a 'madness' and 'sex' wordfield (p.194); two harrow-
ing dramatic monologues; a Catalogue verse listing 79 synonyms
for 'mad' in septenaries ('The Euphemisms'), which includes
political separatism; newspaper headlines; an advertisement poem;
two prose-poems; and a commissioned birthday poem for Gavin
Ewart's '65th' (p.197):

> and [you] remind us that, as well as bruising,
> poems, and life, can also be amusing
> and dignified and common-sensed and sexy
> and much more fun and certainly more flexi-
> ble than they seemed before.

Of course, these are qualities the 'whippersnapper' Reading him-
self felt a close affinity with and wanted to achieve in his own
books, too; one of his comments on *Tom o'Bedlam's Beauties* in the
PBS Bulletin confirms this: 'All these pieces are what I believe is
called "accessible" and some may be found funny by some people'
(p.2). Variation had also been one of the main aims, as Reading
went on to explain (pp.2-3):

> To minimise tedium I have varied the forms and tried to retail the
> sad, the amusing, the horrifying, the absurd and the rattling good
> yarn...I have varied the starting points too. There is no authentically
> 'found' material, though a number of things are composed of more or
> less butchered originals...The complete simulation of what is meant to
> seem like convincingly 'found' matter also occurs.

Tom o'Bedlam's Beauties indeed features an unusual number of
different metres, stanza forms, and poem-genres: Anglo-Saxon

alliterative poems, a 10x10x10-poem, narrative poems with two to four stresses, triplets, tankas, poems with abundant alliteration, rhymed poems, iambic pentameter, dactylic tetrameter, a villanelle, one Petrarchan and two Shakespearean sonnets, another sonnet that links octet and sestet by cross-rhymes (abcdcefg / aefdbg), septenaries, rhymed quatrains, prose-poems, dactyls / spondees / trochees. About the use of prose-poems Reading said [LI]:

> 'Between the Lines' seemed the kind of narrative that didn't require versifying. And I just wanted to write about the image of the gypsies... And so it was partly to ring changes, partly because it seemed to me to be most appropriately served in prose. Or, at least, not to merit being put into verse. Generally, to sustain interest and to sustain my interest.

The poems are not all of the same standard – compare, for instance, the accomplished sonnet 'Ornithological Petrarchan' (p.194) with the malapropian 'Testimoliums' (p.202), a pastiche of newspaper verse – but all clearly are fragments of the 'cracked pot' that even 'Fixo' (p.202) cannot make whole again. Jenkins' assessment is to the point:

> One or two pieces, tending to a clichéd neatness or oversimplification, or to facile grotesquerie, are unsatisfactory; but for the most part the poems are persuasive, unsettling, and memorable. Among them are two of the strongest single poems Reading has written, the historical dramatic monologues 'Hardfhip Aboard American Sloop The Peggy, 1765'... and 'Phrenfy'...These... seem not quite found, but not invented either... the air of documentation is very powerful, the atmosphere totally convincing; the stories... are extraordinary (Jenkins, *DLB*, p.473; Jenkins, 1985, p.12).

In these poems, Reading continues the old tradition of maritime disaster stories. He based his regular 12-stanza poem in stress-metre on an authentic 18th century case, rendered as the dramatic monologue of a surviving sailor. The laconic style combined with the objectivity and acceptance in the terse narrative make his controlled voice moving (p.179):

> By January 26th
> the corpfe of the flave was ate.
> Drew lots to fee who was next,
> myfelf, David Flat, foremaft man,
> felected the fhorteft ftraw,
> afked to be defpatched quickly.
>
> Reft of the hands decided
> to wait till 11 o'clock
> next day before flaying me
> left deliverance fhould arrive.
> That night my fenfes quit me –
> 'tis faid they have not returned.

Booth had noted the auditory potential in Reading's poems: 'Reading's style is highly suited to the public reading; but he is not a performance poet, it seems.' Reading's grave, hoarse reading of this monologue is indeed memorable; and although he writes primarily for the page, the expressiveness and impersonation of different voices and dialects at readings charge his poems with intensity.[20]

Still, the entertainment value of poems on a painful subject can produce aesthetic and ethic doubts in some readers. Lindop underestimated the volume's self-awareness in this respect; but Curry was also uneasy:

> Where there *is* compassion, there are some very moving moments here, as in *Bereft*... But the dust jacket suggests that we will find Reading's work 'as witty and entertaining as ever'. And that disturbs me. Can madness be entertaining, and ought it to be a subject for wit?

Obviously, the fun is not an end in itself (there is also a lot to laugh about in *One Flew over the Cuckoo's Nest*). Reading does not want to bore readers, but to arouse their interest, and the fact that a certain amount of frisson is required in a painful story is a commonplace familiar to all readers since they first heard *Little Red Riding-Hood*. But variation for Reading also means the possibility of incorporating difficult facts, linguistic material, or imagery with strong emotive potential, as he does here in the dramatic monologues. In this light, it may not be far-fetched to interpret the lighter poems as comic relief. According to O'Driscoll, *Tom o'Bedlam's Beauties*, which he compares unfavourably to *C*, does not show enough empathy. While it could be argued that empathy is the foundation of the very structure of the book, direct empathy indeed can only occasionally be felt through the formal manoeuvres, ironic debunking, and comedy, as in the small-voiced title 'There seem to be so many of them,' (p.203).

The question in need of an answer then is, to come back to the original problem discussed by Wordsworth, 'not enough empathy for whom, and which kind?' Ethical and literary categories cannot be kept apart, as the epigraph conceded, and what interested Reading in this book was this very question: whether compassion could be kindled in readers by other than the tried-and-tested means, and whether the writer could also dispense with the basis of 'genuine experience' in trying to achieve this end:

> Similarly I have been attracted by the idea of trying to draw forth responses to entirely synthetic stimuli – to see whether the quite artificial fabrication of an event, a situation, an emotional state, could be as effective in producing a desired reaction from a reader as the faithfully rendered Genuinely Felt Poetic Experience is said often to

be. Conversely I have sometimes tried to fictionalise an actual experi-
ence until it is beyond the recognition of its original participants (thus
parrying embarrassment, legal action, actual bodily harm) and yet
retain something of it which is able to move the reader.[21]

Reading admitted it was 'difficult' to find the right balance [C]:
'the subject-matter is either deeply personally felt, so it is com-
pelling, immediate, then it works, or it is forced, wanted, made,
manufactured, so it might not come off the ground. On the other
hand only personal experience is boring to readers too.' For
Cleary, the desired synthesising effect was achieved; noting that
the inmates are not dangerous maniacs (these are only mentioned
twice, pp.189, 203), but defective people, she spins this thought to
a half-conciliatory end:

> It says something of Peter Reading that his book, a variety of formal
> poems on derangement, is always entertaining in Wordsworth's sense
> of usefulness ('The Ruined Cottage'), and never treats the subject
> [summarily]. In delineating with imaginative sympathy cases of mad-
> ness that were not inevitable, he raises consciousness of our own possi-
> ble culpability of such things; he also causes us to have pity on con-
> genital and incipient conditions, and finally to give thanks by valuing
> sanity and the human person.

In this early volume, Reading's success in reaching 'sensitive
nerve-ends' was obviously still largely dependent on the presence
or absence of readers' affinities to his style and spirit – in other
words, a matter of literary taste and personal character. This did
not remain the case for long.

Diplopic (1983):
Embracing Malodorous Humanity

In 1981 Peter Reading was given a writer-in-residence post at Sunderland Polytechnic, a welcome break from his job at the feedmill. In the two and a half years he was in Sunderland, he wrote two and a half books: *Diplopic*, *5x5x5x5x5* and *C*.

Secker printed 400 copies of *Diplopic* in hardback only, but Chatto's later reprint of *Diplopic* in *3 in 1* (1992) led to immediate critical attention at least in the USA, where the Lannan Foundation videotaped a reading by Reading of *Diplopic* and *Evagatory* for its Contemporary Writers series.

Diplopic was Reading's third Poetry Book Society Recommendation. Shortly afterwards, he received the Dylan Thomas Award. The judges Leslie Norris and D.J. Enright explained their decision:

> That the Award should have attracted so large a number of entries of high standard is extremely gratifying. This did of course make the work of the judges more difficult than is usually the case...
>
> The judges' decision is that the Award should go to Peter Reading for poems in his collection *Diplopic*. In these we especially admired the combination of comedy, intellectual inventiveness, fantasy (reaching outwards into a shared reality) and energy of expression.[1]

Peter Porter was impressed, too: 'Who would have thought that verse could deal with such a gallimaufry?...With this, his sixth book, he has become one of the most original poets in Britain.' The other reviewers shared this opinion almost unanimously, applauding Reading's audacity.[2] The title of Szirtes' long review became a frequently used label – 'COMEDY OF TERRORS' – and Cleary saw that 'he should provide an answer to those who say that "literature" as studied is too discrete'. Reading himself wrote another comment for the Poetry Book Society:

> Diplopic means pertaining to double vision. Every subject is treated from two sides. The funny and the ghastly are symbiotic. The artist is thought of as a scavenger adapting carnage for his own amusement into artificial form. Accordingly, every second view of a subject is ordered into a sonnet or sonnet-variant (because a sonnet is about as formal and artificial as you can get)... The book is meant to work as a whole, not just a gathering of poems, so that sub-plots recur throughout – a bit like a novel. The book is meant to be funny and horrible.[3]

The unity of *Diplopic* grows out of multiple heterogeneity: far corners of experience, outrageous characters, and strange material provide extreme contrasts, but are given a clear structure by firm tectonics and strong cross-referencing. Everyday and less everyday scenes from the England of the early 1980s are counterpointed by a prehistoric perspective. Like the poet, the palaeontologist dissects, prepares, orders. An instruction manual, a description of a First World War tank, a wedding gift list and newspaper headlines help to shape the poet's work, while his "unliterary" registers and jargon (scientific and restricted code, journalese) appear alongside neutral diction. The Dickensian dramatis personae from all parts of society do evoke laughter and horror – skinheads, an OAP, a romantic student complete with black boyfriend and hysterical mother, a scientist, newly-weds, First World War soldiers, circus folk, a drunk journalist, a hung-over poet, a murderer, etc. All are victims, perpetrators, or both, and their lives often intersect in unfortunate places (newspaper headlines, hospital, cemetery). In *Diplopic*, Reading obliterates any demarcation between entertaining fiction, poignant authenticity and poetic technique.

The book's intricate intertextual web delineates its macabre plot. Judging by the errors and oversights in the reviews, a short paraphrase would seem helpful. The book starts and ends with 'Gibbo', a 16-year-old Mackem (Sunderland) skinhead yob who, exchanging 'simian ululations' ('gerroforral getcher yafugga') with his pals, likes going on sprees of violence and destruction: first they attack a colony of gulls ('At Marsden Bay'); then they torture an 87-year-old woman and her mynah bird in a vicious robbery ('At Home'), all for £1.60. ('They don't pay poor Gib much, stacking them heavy sacks / off the conveyor', p.245.) She is the grandmother of the pharmacy student, who later remembers her in a lecture about Huntington's Chorea, a disease she had been suffering from.

As a young girl, the grandmother Sally Hibbert's family background was in imperial India. Her love was the soldier John Carew, who in April 1917 notes in his diary ornithological observations and memories of his polymath grandfather (born 1800), who translated Virgil, did art and natural sciences and participated in the nascent dinosaur research.[4] The 22-year-old Carew has just seen the first tank, which was developed as a new land weapon and first used by the British in 1916. This he jots down, as well as a farewell note to Sally, and after lights-out puts his head on a grenade and then detonates it (1917). The official war artist Eric Henri Kennington paints a watercolour of his remains.[5] Carew's friend Thomas Gibb, who mentions this incident in a letter, turns out to be the great-grandfather of the same skinhead Gibbo, who 66 years later attacks Carew's widow. 'Tommy' Gibb is then so

badly injured by another novel First World War weapon – nerve
gas – that he is sent home. He is buried in the cemetery where
his great-grandson Gibbo and his girlfriend later go for their
'trysts'. A little later Gibbo's arm is ripped off in an accident with
the new pacepacker at the feedmill – poetic justice for his treat-
ment of the gull – and he dies in hospital.

Except for the two chroniclers (journalist and poet), all inter-
mediary dramatis personae die or come to harm: circus-artist Miss
Jill is thrown to the big cats by the deceived Miss Herculess, or
drawn into a threesome, or both.[6] Her lover – Señor Garcia, Miss
Herculess' husband – is killed by a load of Portaloos falling off a
lorry: he dies next to Gibbo in hospital ('Admissions', another
pun). The Scottish student Flora Mackenzie gives the writer-in-
residence her sentimental poems to comment on, and then elopes
with a black '3rd Year Mining Engineering student' to Zimbabwe,
where she is first married, then cooked and eaten by him.[7] The poet's
mother-in-law dies suddenly, and her death has to be explained to
her five-year-old granddaughter: "'Yes, Grandma's bones *might*
fossilise, of course, / like those in your *First Book of Dinosaurs*.'"
The palaeontologist's ten-year-old daughter, who is blind, gets mown
down by a train and is buried in the aforementioned cemetery.[8] The
palaeontologist himself, who works on dinosaur fossils, happens to
be standing next to Señor Garcia at the bus stop and also dies the
Portaloo-induced death in Gibbo's hospital room (which does not stop
him from voicing his ideas about the Holocene again in *5x5x5x5x5*
and *C*). A young woman tears up her ex-boyfriend's Valentine and
is raped, stabbed and strangled by him the next day. Two other
young women – Crystal the bride and Gibbo's girlfriend, who also
both work at the feedmill – have their sexual ordeals to endure too,
but at least they are not killed in the act (pp.240, 245).

A cynical, alcoholic journalist, who goes boozing in Reading's
Sunderland pub *The Vaults* (and re-appears in *Stet*), reports on
these (doubly barbaristic) *Supa Scoops*, published as sanguinary
headlines between the usual national and international disasters.[9]
One of his readers is the palaeontologist in his laboratory, who in
his coffee break reads the newspaper.

The poet works in similar ways to the journalist and palaeon-
tologist. He cannot stomach triteness, especially in contemporary
poetry (p.228):

> *Look at the high tor!*
> *The rocks are older than men*
> *and will last longer.*

Thank you very much
for pointing this out to us,
PBS Spring Choice.

His haiku and tankas build up to sarcastic epigrams, among other
things about bardolatry and incestuous reviewing practices (where
he disrupts anadiplosis antistrophically – a simple, effective device;
p.229):

In last week's press, X
reviewed Y: *One of the best
poets now writing.*

In this week's press, Y
reviews X: *One of the best
poets writing now.*

This poet is also irritated with the biological poetic licence in his
colleagues' poems: 'unscientific fauna / is a bore in verse' (p.230).

Phoney-rustic bards,
spare us your thoughts about birds,
butterflies, fish, snakes,
and mammals (including us) –
biologists write more sense.
Down the lab they think
these crows, peasants, pikes, eels, swifts
are twee, ill-observed.

In these attacks against the pathetic fallacy the poet's voice merges
with Reading's, for whom anthropomorphism is anathema.[10] In
Diplopic, Reading writes diametrically opposed poems about natural
phenomena, using expert knowledge to make them palatable to
informed readers or scientists. In this context, the use of Latin
nomenclature is essential to exclude the traditional connotations of
nature poetry.

The poet welcomes a night sobering up in a police cell as 'Raw
Material'. Artistically, he models himself on the stoicism and empirical
exactness of the official war artists on the front, and on the Victorian
polymath Carew: he 'Englishes' two passages from Virgil's *Georgics*
as an antithesis to the lyrical features criticised before (pastoral;
anthropomorphism; *savoir vivre*-stance).[11] Subverting Virgil's pane-
gyric on country life (itself an adaptation of Hesiod), and alluding
to Dryden's translations of Virgil, Reading's sharp bucolic satires
ridicule the yokels from the fertile Midlands and the barbarians
from up North; thus, Virgil's '*O fortunatos nimium, sua si bona
norint...*' is rendered as 'farmers are fortunate fuckers, / wanting
the wit to know it' ('no wit').[12] The festivities surrounding 'Crystal's'
wedding were also grist to his mill; the relish with which Reading

reads 'Epithalamium' (pp.238-39), especially the wine-related words 'MEGOD CHAMPAIN' and 'dégustation' with wrong word stress, is funny. The poem's title, originally denoting a fertility song, puts the newly-weds under a pressure they cannot take, as their names 'Crystal' and 'Mal' indicate. After all this, Reading gives an ironic comment on his satirist stance, always undercutting any sense of self-importance that might be automatically generated in some readers' minds by his role as "poet" and "satirist" (p.229): 'I am / a good man and know what's what.'

The synopsis of the various narrative threads is tucked away in a footnote featuring the 'jabbering night-hag' Sally Hibbert's delirium in the form of a Petrarchan sonnet (p.227). Sally's last exclamation is clever. 'I hates a trochee!' is hypercatalectic: her speech muscles obviously cannot control the 'trochee', which is another word for 'choree' – and 'chorea' is the name of her illness, etymologically connected with 'choree' (pertaining to dance), i.e. she despairs of her illness. Snippets of other poems are unified choreophrasically, thus creating a new poem-genre, the 'auto-cento'.[13] The same effect is achieved in the inventive 'Between the Headlines' (p.240); its rhopalical structure builds up climactically, and the epanaphora 'not' links the 'Supa Scoop's' sensational headlines with the poet's equally inappropriate dry-mock comments about both the individual disasters depicted in *Diplopic* and world politics (Ireland, Lebanon) – in short, about "reality".

The subject of this book is identical with its structural, diplopic organisation, as announced in the three-part epigraph, which begins:

> *Optician, I am having Double Visions*
> *to see one thing from two sides. Only*
> *give me a Spectacle and I am delighted.*

This is not only 'one of the funniest [epigraphs] ever invented' (Jenkins, *DLB*, p.473), but a precise condensation of the double duplicity in *Diplopic*: to begin with, the tragicomic tension between Thalia and Melpomene is diplopically presented in the pun on 'Spectacle' and 'delighted', and then clarity of vision and fun merge into one way of perceiving the world. This dual principle was also evident from the original layout. In the Secker edition, the table of contents listed 17 poems on the left *and* right side of the page, indicating that the poems were to be read as pairs, a development of the idea behind 'Parallel Texts' (p.155), 'Nocturne' (p.72), and 'Diptych' (p.109). Updating the tradition of companion poems, Reading looks at what is usually a horrible 'Spectacle' from two perspectives. The implied author restricts himself to the scientifically objective and unemotional transmission of facts. Of course, this considerably heightens the horror at the violence described, because nothing is provided to fall back on, but without 'diplopic' counterweight the technique would be too facile. In juxtaposition with the emotional perspective of the personae involved, however, this is very effective.

The symbiotic principle also governs the total structure of the book. Not all poems describe 'palimpsests of horror' (Porter); some of the tandems employ black humour that provides comic relief, extra-dry (e.g. 'The Terrestrial Globe' or 'Epithalamium'). All the more shocking, then, are the 'headlines' poems; for example the ironically titled 'At Home', Reading's first depiction of cruelty, which left a strong impression on reviewers. Splitting up the diplopia in this way makes visible the creative, Apollonian/Dionysian tension within the entire œuvre: the humane perception of pain and the pity on the one hand, the artistic sine qua non of aesthetic order and precise technique on the other. Aesthetic distance, says Jenkins, 'can be very funny, or suggest a kind of insanity creeping in, or that the only alternative would be going mad'. Reading, however, was content with a more modest reason: 'There's a more literal justification for that' (Jenkins, 1985, pp.7-8). What he meant was mere 'recording' [C]. Reading later explicitly referred to the function of the camera-eye in Robbe-Grillet's novels, a technique he borrowed (especially in *5x5x5x5x5* and *Going On*) for the artistic aim of looking unblinkingly at the more unsavoury aspects of contemporary life, without any overt purpose or judgement. Ewart noted indeed that 'Ordinariness and the received idea are altogether absent'. He wrote:

> Poems that confront the bogeymen bring, at least, the consolation that they can be confronted. Articulate protest is a positive way of hitting back, and this is the great virtue of [this] very talented [poet] (Ewart, *TLS*).

Contrast is also a prominent factor within the tandems. One companion poem always is a sonnet; these, too, are diverse and include the Shakespearean sonnet, Petrarchan sonnet, blank pentameter 14-liners, a Meredithian sonnet of 16 lines ('Sortie'), and, as Reading informs readers in his *PBS Bulletin* comment (p.3), 'dispersed couplet sonnets…, a 12-syllable but 5-stress 14-liner' ('Englished'), and an invention of his own, 'a sham-Japanese job' (untitled, p.230), which is explained in *C* (Unit 62): 'I have invented / a brand new kind of sonnet / where the octave is / a tanka plus a haiku / and the sestet two haikus' (at least syllabically). Had Reading's immersion in *The Princeton Encyclopedia of Poetry and Poetics* been

greater at that time, *Diplopic* might well have featured Hopkins's
10-line Curtal Sonnet and the special forms of Caudate Sonnet
and Reverse Sonnet.

'The notsonnets go purposefully wild' [C]. A minimalistic free-
verse fragment ('Minima', p.217) was printed in diminutive type-
face in the original edition and stylistically adapted to the telegram's
content. A four-part pastiche (one part in Skin-speak) uses ham-
mering trochaic tetrameters ('At Home', p.220) in the so-called
'*Hiawatha* metre' from Longfellow's poem (1855). (Longfellow
had taken the metre from the Finnish folk-epic *The Kalevala*.)
Reading commented [LI]:

> I don't really know quite why I used that. It just seemed to fall out
> that way and seemed to be appropriate. The thing was going to be a
> longish poem – for me, for then; I had to make sure that it was going
> to go along with a swing to sustain narrative interest. And it has a sort
> of jaunty air about it as well which was in purposeful contrast to the
> rather sanguinary subject-matter.

To complete the metrical list: there is a recurrence of syllabic and
accentual metres with two, three, or four stresses ('At Marsden
Bay', 'Dark Continent', 'The Terrestrial Globe', 'Stedman's', 'War
Artistes', 'Finds'), blank verse ('P.S.', and of course some of the
sonnets), tankas ('After Sanraku Koshu' and some stanzas of 'Nips'),
and haiku (some stanzas of 'Nips'). New additions include the
approximative aeolic Sappho-stanza in 'Tryst' (p.245);[14] two Georgics
for the rendering of two passages of Virgil's *Georgics*; and two of
his own inventions: 'Between the Headlines' adapts the principle
of rhopalic verse by increasing the number of stresses per line
(amplifying headlines), and, rather more extravagant, the hyper-
trophied 'Baroque, or Super Tanka' ('Ex Lab', p.231).[15] Again
Reading did 'as much as possible for variation' [C].

The same structure (first polarisation, then diversification) is
achieved on the level of *Weltanschauung*: the palaeontological per-
spective collides with "received opinions", ensuring that the deaths
of *Diplopic* are seen within a framework grander than personal
microcosms. The reference-point of all deliberations is the chrono-
stratigraphical diagram of all known life on earth, reaching back
3,600 million years. As to the existence of *H. sap.* (p.233):

> On this diagram,
> the Holocene or Recent
> (last ten thousand years)
> is far, far, far, far too small
> to register on this scale.

While his work on fossil preparations is interrupted by having
to wait for certain tools, the professor of palaeontology in 'Ex

Lab' (p.231) glances at 'Supa Scoop' headlines in the newspaper, picks up Nietzsche, and all the while mutters to himself about existential questions. His thoughts on life, God, and the Universe are communicated in an understated, surly way, ensuring that the vast scope of his perspective does not seem self-important. What is more, his misanthropic asides make it clear that he means what he says. These days only pacepackers effect retributive justice; in earlier times it was the order of the day: '*Megalosaurus* et al / flenched, flensed these bastards to mince.' And in an attack on humans higher up the social ladder, he dismisses small-scale humanitarianism as complacent and ineffective (p.234). Mankind's cardinal error is not to see the human race first of all as just one of many species, and Nietzsche would have saved himself a lot of trouble had he acknowledged that simple fact. Here Reading's own outlook is voiced: Coggrave had argued that if Nietzsche was right, then the death of God was a cataclysmic event in the history of civilisation, but Reading was unimpressed [C]. In the persona of the palaeontologist (p.232):

'God is dead' – quite straightforward.
But why, then, go on
to think some mitigation
is needed for us to face

Godless cosmic dust?
Matter just gets on with it.

Religion is mere assuagement; 'sky pilots' are fools (p.233):

You live, then you die.
This is extremely simple.
You live, then you die –
no need to wear funny hats,
no need for mumbo-jumbo.

The 20th century is the era of the bomb, not the Bible: hydrogen and helium are the 'Original Sinners', not Adam and Eve; and scientific scrutiny is more fitting than metaphysical musing. With regard to evolution, this means the following: dinosaurs were dominant in the Jurassic Age, when the mammals were still primitive. Along with half of all other species, they became extinct in the Cretaceous, when the 'Great Dying' occurred. 'Ex Lab' finishes the story with a simple analogy (p.235):

That extinction seems
to have been protracted for
a few million years;
this one, now underway, will
have reached a similar scale

in a few decades.
The hiatus resulting
in some processes
of evolution will be
extremely fascinating.
...
Vacuum, cosmic dust,
algae, rhipidistians,
internecine us
(it is a fucking good job
that it all does not matter).

Still, the palaeontologist's occupational blind spot – 'the Holocene did
not concern me greatly' – leads to 'ham philosophy', as Reading sees
it [C]: the outlook does not exactly allow for much fellow-feeling.

This palaeontological leitmotif is reiterated in Reading's work
up until *Evagatory*, by which time the tone has become elegiac,
world-weary: 'one of those routine faunal extinctions'.

Diplopic opens with a poem giving geological instruction. Apart
from the language of ornithology, which runs through most books,
Reading uses a whole set of scientific terms for the first time here,
illustrating a particular area of knowledge as novels do, or the ancient
dit or *lai* did: 'I have occasionally used this sort of specialist jargon
in poems, but the very fact that so much of it is comprehensible
only to the initiated somewhat limits what one can do with it'
(*Observer*, 'Muse'). O'Driscoll explains:

> The scientific process... is all the more convincing for being expressed
> in scientific language... Reading is...evoking a milieu. The palaeonto-
> logical, medical and astronomical experts who inhabit his poems are
> fully-realised creations speaking a professional patois and not some
> simplified poetical version of it. Similarly, natural phenomena...are very
> precisely delineated. Reading's world is large not only because of the
> largeness of his linguistic resources... but because he knows – or is pre-
> pared to learn – more about the world than most poets (O'Driscoll, p.202).

At the other end of the intellectual scale an uneducated, misguided
skinhead has other linguistic resources – 'lookadembastabirdsmon'
– as he hurls chunks of limestone at kittiwakes' nests. 'At Marsden
Bay' (p.211) uses the clash of registers (skinhead and geologist) not
to show us a clash of cultures, but a clash of civilisations:

> Nests are dislodged, brown-blotched shells crepitate
> exuding thick rich orange embryo goo
> under a hail of hurled fossilised desert
> two hundred and eighty million years old.

The vicious assault on Sally Hibbert comes next and, rendering
it even more sickening, the perpetrators' assessment: 'that was

dead great like'. But worst of all is the mad voice of the rapist in '15th February' (p.225).

> The heart was scarlet satin, sort of stuffed.
> I sort of felt it was me own heart, like.
> SHE TORE THE STUFFING OUT OF THE SCARLET HEART.
> I sort of stuffed and tore her sort of scarlet.
> I sort of stuffed her, like, and felt her sort of satin.
> I sort of felt she'd tore out all me stuffing.
> I felt her stuff like satin sort of scarlet
> her stuff felt sore, torn satin whorlet scar
> I liked her score felt stiffed her scar lick hurt
> I tore her satin felt her stuffed her scarlet
> tore out her heart stuff scarred her Satan har
> I licked her stiff tore scarf her harlot hair
> tied scarf tore stabbed scar whore sin sat tit star
> stuffed finger scar ha ha ha ha ha ha
> felt stiff scarf tight tore scarlet heart her scare
> her scare stare stabbed heart scarlet feel torn mur

In a brilliant, torturous articulation of inarticulate resentment and violent, maniacal rage, Reading shows his protagonist – in a sickening spiral of linguistic permutations – pumping his fury up to its sexual and linguistic climax ('ha ha ha ha ha ha'), and then subsiding to abrupt silence with the realisation that he has murdered his victim. The monosyllabic cadence gives it a last sinister polish: it is masculine – in an embracing rhyme.

Reading's instinct for emotive force is particularly acute in both this impressive *abstract poem* and its companion 'Found', which intensifies one's nausea by the distanced description of the blood-lapping mongrel in the alley where the corpse was dumped.[16] Dismemberment is conducted on the sonnet itself, too: the vicious frenzy is noted alloeostrophically in regular iambic pentameters, but the octave and sestet happen to be in the companion poem (and are consistently ametrical there).

Mole spoke of his 'sheer amazement and despair' at the book, and touched on a sensitive issue: '[Reading] is obviously attracted to the desperate and awful but there's nothing gratuitous about the way he dramatises the...horrors.' Paul Bailey also wondered in an interview, 'you seem obsessed with grottiness'. Reading's answer – 'I suppose that anybody who lives in this country at this time would be hard pressed to avoid grottiness' – clearly re-routes the question, 'as if writing meant you mustn't touch on certain things' (Bailey, M). In literature, there are no 'Do Not Enter' signs, as Martin Amis says – one of the few writers with whom Reading shares a lot of common ground – they are notional and to be ignored.[17] It is unimaginative, absurd, and goes against all the evidence to think of

Reading as a macabrophile, or as posing in 'designer outrage', or as an 'on-stage dandy of destruction' creating an 'aesthetic of cruelty', or as indulging in an 'unhealthy interest in the callous and sub-human'.[18] He has to defend his choice of subject-matter, as did Wilfred Owen before him:

> There is a dismayingly large amount of unpleasant subject-matter about. In a way I don't really pick this and I haven't elected to do it. It's just that that's what's around; that's what moves me in a negative sort of way. – Someone… in what was meant to be a fair review, went on about *the beauty of pain*, which is appalling, because I find nothing beautiful about pain, I'm horrified by it (Edgar, pp.55-56; Jenkins, 1985, p.7).

Some critics presuppose that his writing is purely volitional, although Reading indicates his dependence on the Muse in this very book (p.218):

> We are always out there
>   with pencils raised,
> treacherous bastards,
>   Double Agents
> not working for *you*
>   but for some Secret Power.

The clearly Romantic implications surprised some of his inter-viewers, and perhaps, even Reading himself:

> I wanted to write like Frost. I still do. I don't actually write the things I wanted to – … in a way the writer is a kind of agent who has nothing to do with *you* – as in Beckett's *From an Abandoned Work*, 'my body going on, doing its best without me…'; a strange detached quality. I don't really *like* the things I do any more than anybody else does (Jenkins, 1985, p.7).

Owen, who was mentioned in 'Thanksgiving' (p.97), writes in his famous Introduction: 'All a poet can do today is warn. / That is why the true Poets must be truthful.' For Reading, this means 'I sing the Grot' (*Going On, Stet*) – at the time doubtlessly new poetic territory, for which new ways of speaking had to be found. In 'Mnemonics', the companion poem of 'War Artistes', the painter/author declares (p.219):

> Some matter is too delicate to define
> with muted chalks or the restricted palette
> implicit in small portable tubes of gouache
> (e.g. the whitish-tallows and wax-yellows
> and algal-greens of military flesh).

In other words, using an implied author's voice, or a stance or persona is an important device for handling difficult material, because then every utterance – in this case, one that is not 'restricted', i.e. any-thing up to plain insult – first and foremost has an artistic function:

> You couldn't possibly do it if it was just *you*, but by using personae
> you can cover the wilder side of things. Painting, again: there was
> always a tension between the wild, physical aspect of doing the thing,
> and the overall control which [one] must obtain if it wasn't to be a
> complete mess. It's an attractive thing to get that into poetry. As long
> as you make it clear in some way that it isn't *you*, or isn't even the
> text – it can be a footnote, or an afterword, or an appendix or some-
> thing – by distinctly separating it from what is 'normally' OK you can
> allow the wildness in, and the tensions to exist (Jenkins, 1985, p.6).

Where there *are* hard, shrill, and dark colours instead of 'muted
chalks', some reviewers immediately start talking about shock tac-
tics. To some degree, Reading said this was a factor: 'Yes. But
that would just be for the reason of simple crossness. I mean,
obviously we all get cross about certain things which don't seem
to be right' (Edgar, p.56).

As a strict empiricist, Reading has no time for mythical worlds
of the imagination in poetry (this is also evident from the hundred
or so reviews of poetry books that he wrote over the years). Instead,
as from an early 20th century philosophical materialistic outlook (but
without the Wellsian optimism about the future), his readers are
offered grotesque reality. Jenkins quoted Seamus Heaney's phrase
'England of the mind' for the works of Geoffrey Hill, Ted Hughes
and Philip Larkin, contrasting it with Reading's œuvre, which is
also 'full of historical reference and feeling', but 'seems far more of
its time than anything we get in Hill or Hughes, it's wittier, more
absurd and amusing…; it's far more democratic, and celebrates'.
With regard to the commonly levelled charge of 'morbidity' and
'pessimism', Reading's response (of 1985) is surprising again:

> You've cited poets who are all very different, yet I would agree with you
> that their kind of England is very much the same – even Larkin's who
> has more of the 'contemporary scene' in his poems – it's nostalgic, and
> longs for what isn't there. I may feel nostalgia, as everybody does, about
> certain things, but I'd hope that my stuff isn't nostalgic. Also, the poets
> you've cited I find rather gloomy, and I hope my things are more cheerful,
> I hope I'm not essentially gloomy – that is to say regretful. But I feel
> total impotence (Jenkins, 1985, p.11).

This aside, the terms 'pessimism' and 'morbidity' are inappropriate
in the modern context. As Heidegger said:

> The spiritual decline of the earth is so far advanced that the nations
> are in danger of losing the last bit of spiritual energy that makes it
> possible to see the decline…The darkening of the world, the flight of
> the gods, the destruction of the earth, the transformation of men into
> a mass, the hatred and suspicion of everything free and creative, have
> assumed such proportions throughout the earth that such childish cat-
> egories as pessimism and optimism have long since become absurd.[19]

To investigate facts and their consequences is first of all an empirical activity: 'There seems to be nothing but health-giving sanity in dealing with any issue that comes your way' (Jenkins, 1985, p.8).

'Stedman's' quotes Graham Greene: 'There is a splinter of ice in the heart of the writer.' [20] Impartial observation by artists, though, takes getting used to, as Thomas Gibb says about the official war artist: *'He seems not quite human. He drawers even when the heavy firing is on... I think he SEES things different to us'* (p.218). In 1983, some still attacked Reading for his aesthetic perspective – but he persisted, helping to establish "important subjects" in poetry. The difficulties were not glossed over, but put up front (epigraph; see also 'Widow', p.71, in which Reading first found an image for the distanced eye and cold pencil of the poet):

Vulture, manipulating still-bloody bones
on the white sand;
Poet, ordering the words of a beautiful sonnet
on the bare page.

The doubts are raised even before the reader can develop them. This image (another wine-vision 'after' Niznegorsky) is amplified in the hyperbolised parallel text of the palaeontologist with his bones (p.235):

What one enjoys most
is the manipulation
of these hapless things
at such impartial distance
to fit an imposed order.

Of course one does not
really care for the *objects*,
just the *subject*. It
is a Vulture Industry,
cashing in on the corpses.

The two possible reactions to the charges reliably appear in two poems, once defensively, once aggressively. First, the poet's role as double agent is explained (p.218):

We have a horrible
    kind of diplopia –
(1) straight, clinical,
    accurate, X-ray,
(2) refracted
    to serve our bent calling.

Soon after, Reading confronts the subject head on; instead of attempting justification, he draws a derogatory picture of himself (p.227):

                                    I savour
the respective merits of one
kind of mayhem over another,
contentedly ponder the species
of fourteen-liner most apposite –
Petrarchan? Elizabethan?

'A nasty versifier is researching, / sniffing historic carnage, adding salt...' (p.243). Later, when critics quoting these lines omitted the ironic dots, 'nasty' was taken literally, and Reading was accused of voyeurism and 'obsessional nastiness'. For several years, he did not comment, or at the most let such charges boomerang. Ian Hamilton asked: 'The nastier the subject, the more self-conscious the technique. I suppose an unkind listener might find that you are managing to get the best – or worst – of both worlds.' After a meaningful clearing of his throat, Reading answered in his most friendly voice: 'Yes, I suppose an unkind listener might think that' (Hamilton, M). In 1988, Paul Bailey – who said that 'no sensible person supposes that Shakespeare shed tears as he worked on *Lear,* or after he finished it' – at last extracted an answer to the question as to whether Reading did not himself invite such charges:

> Yes, yes, but it seems to me that you either don't bother *at all* examining the baser things that we have to confront as human beings...you ignore them, or, you in some way try to look at them, think about them, talk about them, and then, yes, of course, the cry goes up in certain quarters: 'VOYEUR!' I think that's unavoidable and, to a strange degree, I can sympathise with it. A lot of people spend a lot of time trying to forget about nasty things, myself included, but it isn't any kind of solution, and I can therefore understand why people might feel, 'oh, we've had enough of this sort of thing in the newspapers; we don't want to turn to a poetry book and find it there as well' (Bailey, M).

Later reviewers corrected the picture, but Reading still emphasised the difficulty of his position:

> Of course, there's an element of voyeurism, of dwelling on nastiness; of providing a frisson for the reader. There's a close border between expressing dismay at certain aspects of life and actually being as offensive as the original perpetrators (Potts, 1992).

Apart from this, both empathy and 'lack of sympathy' are required for sanity:

> We all have a lack of sympathy, or we wouldn't be able to tick over. We're spared real grief by the impersonality of most affairs. When they do affect us they affect us in ways other than artistic ones (Jenkins, 1985, p.8).

Therefore *Diplopic* explicitly describes the literal lapping up of human blood, first by a 'scabbed mongrel', and finally by the 'impartial houseflies'.

The adjectives used in the reviews – remarkable, shaking, sear-
ing, scathing, entertaining, chilling, sinewy, forceful, compelling,
shocking, hilarious, angry, painful, worrying, idiosyncratic, talented,
intelligent, outrageous, brilliant, disconcerting – are evidence of
the strong effect of *Diplopic*. The pain threshold is definitely vio-
lated: ten years before the murder of James Bulger, children are
called 'sinister dwarfs' capable of homicide (p.212), chickens are
sodomised (p.213), breasts marinaded and cooked as steak (p.214),
and the so-called 'transcending of pain' is turned on its head: this
is reality and should be seen as such. As Adorno said, the socially
most 'critical zones' of an artwork are those where it hurts.

> Stimulating compassion, then disrupting it, [Reading] makes the reader
> question that habituated response – sympathy more than horror is his
> subject... Provoking and denying the consolations of fellow feeling, he
> forces the reader back to ask the questions that the ideal society of
> consensus socialism had answered, and whose solutions were being
> undone through the decade.[21]

The question of taste and the didactic function of art aside, the
fact remains that aesthetic categories are subject to historical change
so that any normative concept of "the aesthetic" must be anachro-
nistic. The real issue is the adequate, convincing artistic transfor-
mation of an "unpoetic subject". In 1993, Sir Stephen Spender
wrote in his introduction to the *Forward* anthology, in which
Reading is also included:

> One can only rejoice that poets feel that poetry can be made out of
> many things and does not have to be about poetic subjects. There is,
> though, a danger attached to this view: it is that if poetry can be about
> anything, anything can be poetry...a poem must be a verbal artefact
> which in form, vocabulary, texture, rhythm, must be distinct from
> some possibly alternative version which would be in prose.[22]

Reading's solution to the problem could not be simpler: if "poetic"
subjects require the lyrical mode, then "unpoetical" subjects should
be poeticised in unlyrical ways. Imagine a lyrical version of the
murder in '15th February' – that indeed would invite the charge of
'nastiness' and 'voyeurism'. For Reading, developing alternatives
was what it was all about:

> The subject-matter is straightforward enough, that takes care of itself.
> ...And of course, the linguistics then are what the whole business is about.
> If you have missed doing that then you've missed the whole exercise
> (Edgar, pp.55-56).

The 'theoretical' proof of this position – see '10 x 10 x 10' in
Nothing For Anyone – is put into practice. Ewart saw that 'Reading
is [keen] to use unorthodox ways of writing poems' (Ewart, *TLS*),
and O'Driscoll concluded: 'So distinctive is his use of language, so

extraordinary his outlook and so abundant his technical skills that no topic can defeat his ingenuity…' (O'Driscoll, p.209).

The discussion does not quite end here. Even if Reading writes convincingly about "unpoetic subjects", the question sometimes arises why he does not write about what he does not write about. In a poem in *Final Demands* (p.125), Reading takes this up: 'doesn't he ever write about *happiness*?' (Even his wife once asked him, 'why don't you ever write about us?' The answer was: 'but I do' [C]). Are major writers only major because they do not omit things? Ask any admirer of Jane Austen.

Diplopic was only his sixth book, and Reading was at the beginning of his promising career when D.J. Enright named *Diplopic* in a *Observer* 1983 'Book of the Year' feature, sensing great potential: 'Perhaps he should strive to contain himself just a little: he has a lot to contain'.

A reading of *Diplopic* in Los Angeles was followed by a panel discussion. The following excerpt serves to close the chapter of "unpoetic subjects" (Lannan Video, M):

MICHAEL SILVERBLATT: I know that sometimes there is an audience response to your work as if you're making fun of calamity. What is your attitude towards that?

PETER READING: It would be one of shock – and I'd feel that I was being unfairly treated if that was the case. I'd probably even go so far as to say that whoever thought that that was ill-informed.

MICHAEL SILVERBLATT: Well, even Jenkins … in articles about you, will remind the reader that you are frequently perhaps going too far with the neutrality bit.

PETER READING: …I would say that this is part of what it's necessary to *do* in *any* work of art, not necessarily just literature, in order to treat the subject. Art isn't the raw material itself, it's some kind of resolution of that made by the person who aspires to be an artist. Whether it's artistically valid is a slightly different point.

CHRISTOPHER HITCHENS: But all [artists] deal with this kind of thing. Always faced with some question about their relationship to the vicarious and to the cathartic. In other words, are you really pacifying the feelings that you're stirring up?

PETER READING: I think it's very straightforward, simple and evident. You could say of Rabelais, and again of Swift, and more or less anybody you think of, that there is a certain ambiguity there, which is felt clearly. There's outrage, anger, dismay, but [you're almost saying] there's also… a sort of relish for the ordure – and what that metaphorically suggests as well – the ordurous behaviour of *H.sap*. And if you want that vindicated, I suppose you can say 'well all right, they embrace all this as well' – there *is* an ambiguity there, there is a kind of manic energy there amongst those writers I've just mentioned which is, I suppose, justifiable by saying that it is an embracing of humanity – with all its malodorous defects.

$5x5x5x5x5$ (1983):
Ludic Exercises

The interim booklet, $5x5x5x5x5$, was published by Ceolfrith Press in a poet and artist series in the same year as *Diplopic*.[1] Reading had met his co-author David Butler at Sunderland Arts Centre, where Butler worked as community artist; and, as Reading was working on *C* at the time and his residency was nearly finished, he was pleased that Butler was prepared to work fast [LI]: 'He'd been at the College of Art in Sunderland and he did a bit of free-lancing. I stayed with him when my family moved back home. He was a bloke I quite liked and I liked his work... So I just asked him and he fancied the idea and I think did a very good job on it.'

Ceolfrith had requested that the book should not exceed 50 pages; Reading and Butler then worked out its homoeomeral struc-ture together [LI]:

> It was simply a mathematical non-sequitur. 25 pages each, so that was
> 5 fives; so I thought I'd have...five stanzas, each of five lines, each of
> five syllables, up to 5 to the fifth. And they were only syllabics, so that
> it could be very informal.

'Once Reading has made a mould, anything will set' is O'Driscoll's verdict on the 'entertaining' $5x5x5x5x5$, in which Reading is 'at his most ludic'. The 'ingenious and often extremely funny or touching [and worrisome] work...which teeters on caricature (a lot of ordinary life does the same thing)', as Jenkins writes (*DLB*, p.473), is prefaced by an announcement of a plot: '5 personae are observed in 5 (licensed) locations.' (Three of those Sunderland pubs are named: the Museum Vaults, where the English staff regularly met, the Railway Hotel, and the Theatre Vaults.) The fates of five reg-ulars are sketched: the 38-year-old palaeontologist (downgraded from professor to technician in this book); Schultz, the professor of Logic; Ferdie 'Fats' Oliver, the '20-pint-a-night' binman; the 61-year-old unemployed ventriloquist ('The Great Maestro De La Voice'); and Jock, the Scottish Combined Arts student of the Sunderland Polytechnic rugby team.

In five sections, the book imitates the pattern of an antique tragedy in five acts. The appendix lists five 'Notes' quoting (ficti-tious) newspaper excerpts – 'W.C.P. Elliott, *Cheltenham Chronicle*' and 'His 'n' Hers Boutique' were already established as bogus sources

in *Tom o'Bedlam's Beauties* – as well as five (authentic) sources
referred to in the book, i.e. publications on logic, palaeontology
and ventriloquism, used to give convincing lines to the protagonists
[LI]: the ventriloquist 'wasn't a complete invention. I found a book
about ventriloquism and thought it was deeply amusing – to my
childish mind.'

The first part – the exposition – presents the personae separately
in their drunken states, all from different perspectives: their own
(1 I), their drinking pals' (1 III), and the author's (1 II, 1 IV, 1 V). As
the palaeontologist also conducts behaviourist research in the pubs
('I review the gross / sub-species', 1 I, see also 3 I), some of the sub-
units could also be his perspective, of course.

The stanzas of the second part – the complication – are ordered
on the page like the synaesthetic components of '5' in *Fiction*, with
one stanza by each of the five personae. Pub talk: everybody is
talking at the same time, probably as much to themselves as to
anybody else.[2] The ventriloquist, to whom usually nobody listens,
enumerates one ex-ventriloquist after the other, mourning the dying
of his art (*'distance* it was. Nah, / telly spoiled all that', 2 I).[3] The
logician explores the hypothetical possibilities of the Aristotelian
syllogism (2 III):

    …if it's 6 o'clock
    you can hear the News;
    if you hear the News
    you have ears. Therefore
    if it's 6 you've ears…

He talks to Fats as if he were a colleague: 'Can I win a prize / on
this fruit-machine / when it is not here?' Fats seriously strains to
keep up with Schultz: '… ang on, wait a jiff: / if it isn't ere / ow
the bleedin ell / *canyer* winna prize?' The palaeontologist is inter-
ested in the Pre-Cambrian and Oligocene Ages ('[which] sires
irreverence / for the Holocene', 1 I), but, after 15 years of marriage,
no longer interested in his wife. Her frustration vents itself in an
outburst (1 IV) depicted in expressive typography foreshadowing
the liberties Reading took in later books. In contrast, the totitest-
icular Jock can only think about one thing ('getcher knikersdoun',
2 IV) and considers himself an enormously witty, irresistibly potent
powerhouse. In the course of the evening articulatory abilities dis-
solve (1 III revolves around 'a fag' and 'a lager'); a slurred drunken
dirge is phonologically transcribed, just like Fats' sociolect and
Jock's dialect.

That 'the advance / of the sub-species' is imminent, forming the
climax (third act) of the book, is first perceived by the palaeontologist

(3 I). The logician, however, having failed to notice the skinheads'
grotesque obtuseness – threatening enough in the ungrammatical
correlative verses with hammering epanaphora ('& we') – and having
instead lectured them about his apparatus of non-standard possible
worlds, is taken by surprise: 'Young men, my friends! Why? /
Please, no, please, no, *please!*' (3 IV).

```
get him     in the bogs
shove his     head in it
rub his     face in shit
piss all     over him
get them     matches out

butt him     in the face
knee him     in the crotch
kick him     in the face
smash his     fuckin legs
stick one     in his nuts
```

The brutal imperatives are typographically severed into hemistichs,
like the victim's body. Destruction is all the skinheads know. The
'posh puff clever shite' should know that 'Bad Skins Rule OK' (3 V)
– and for this he is almost killed and set on fire. The result (5 II):
'Cabbage. A cabbage. / They can't do no more. / Ave to spend all
is / life in a wheelchair / jabberin nonsense.' Binman Fats weeps
for him, 'I *loved* that man' (4 II), while in the fourth part the other
three look deep into their beer glasses. (One possible reason for
alcoholism is elucidated in 5 III by the palaeontologist with a quo-
tation from Eliot: 'Human kind / Cannot bear very much reality').

Meanwhile, the observing author is getting fed up with the stu-
dents' 'Formative Minds' (4 III): 'Too much confidence, / no
respectful fright / or awareness, yet, / of mortality, / too much
decibel…'. In a postmodern aside, he steps on to the meta-level –
as before in 'Raspberrying' (*For the Municipality's Elderly*) and
'Stedman's' (*Diplopic*), and in later works marked by square brack-
ets and/or italics – and makes short work of Jock (4 III):

[Here the author snatched
up his Bic and scrawled
on his beer mat:
In next Saturday's
match, regrettably,

Jock was savagely
tackled, losing 8
teeth, and choking on
his gum-shield. He died
in the ambulance.]

Danger looms for the other personae, too. Fats is apoplectic, the palaeontologist has a weak heart ('still, what's 40 years / here or there on the / chronostratigraph?', 5 III), and the ventriloquist cannot endure his insignificance.

The fifth act brings the catastrophe to its logical completion. The heartless palaeontologist is punished: smashed by a Portaloo in a book called *Diplopic* by Peter Reading, as one of the burlesque 'Notes' informs readers (at the same time parodying the tradition of postscripts in Victorian novels). The ventriloquist breaks down crying on the toilet and soon after commits suicide in an almost amusing way. The severely handicapped logician becomes the victim of a second attack. The other two are spared: loyal Fats receives the bonus of a public weight-reduction campaign ('Slim for Health' – the only authentic detail from the 'Notes' [LI]), and the author saves Jock in 'An Act of Mercy' (the title of 5 IV in a magazine publication) and punningly reaches the 'magnanimous decision to revoke sentence' ('Notes'). As the local newspaper reports, only one handicap remains (5 IV):

[In a quite unique
collaboration,
Author and Surgeon
today succeeded
in reviving a

hopeless cadaver
killed last Saturday
in the *Wasps'* home match.
Tipp-Ex and scalpel
joined forces to clear

a throat obstruction.
AUTHOR ADMITTED
'I ACTED IN HASTE'.
EX-SCOTTISH PATIENT
EXHUMED AS *ENGLISH.*

Mick Imlah wrote in the *TLS*:

We look on these kinds of death and pain as the legitimate fictions of the light-verse black comedian; grotesque retribution on those who are only invented to deserve it, redeemable in joke resurrections. In *5x5x5x5*, poet and surgeon alike have the power of life and death; in *C*, by a bold intensification of its author's morbidity, poet and surgeon have no power at all.

Indeed, *5x5x5x5* is a kind of loosening-up exercise and an indirect announcement of the other book Reading was writing at the same time: *C*.

C, however, is not jokily morbid: it is pervaded by a humanity earned in the most relentless and troubling way.

C (1984):
Art, not Ovaltine

C was Reading's seventh book, and the fourth to receive a Poetry Book Society Recommendation. It was published 15 months after *Diplopic* in 1984, and later reprinted by Chatto in 1992 in *3 in 1*. Once again, Reading wrote a comment for the PBS:

> *C* is about having terminal illness and ways in which people confront dying and death. It tries to look hard at these despite La Rochefoucauld's famous maxim. The vindicability of verse under duress is also considered (few of us in circumstances of, say, an amputated breast or a tube stuck up the penis against a cancer, will busy ourselves with dactylic tetrameter catalectic, I think)... Prose and, although their unvindicability is implied, divers verse forms are used (iambic pentameter, haiku, tanka, sonnet, Spenserian stanza, Adonic, dactylic hexameter, tétramètre, elegiac distich, trochaic tetrameter, acrostic, choriamb). A few parts of *C* are quite funny; many are horrible, of course. The blurb says that it *challenges, shocks, entertains.* I hope not to be portentously gloomy like Thomson (*Dreadful Night*, not *Seasons...*) – nevertheless, *C* is perhaps (outwardly) a cheerless little number, just getting on with it.[1]

The reviewer for *Poetry Review*, Dennis O'Driscoll, saw *C* as a seminal book. In a later critical essay on Reading, he described the 'supreme achievement' of *C* as combining 'the intensity of the early poems with the inventiveness of Reading's subsequent work to produce not only his best book but what is surely one of the major post-war volumes of poetry' (O'Driscoll, p.213). Leaving aside such high praise and the fact that *C* is not really a poetry book, it is still surprising that *C* did not attract more attention. Most reviews were positive,[2] while the negative criticisms again accused Reading of 'morbidity' and generally were unhelpful to the point of ignoring evidence.[3]

There had been depictions of terminal illness in poetry, but, as O'Driscoll says, 'The "big C" has never loomed so large in literature as it does in this relentless book' (O'Driscoll, p.214). About his motivation to write *C*, Reading said: 'I contemplated it for a number of years before deciding to go ahead because it's a subject which more or less everybody has experience of and can relate to' (Susan Press).

Unblinking and meticulously researched, *C* is a *tour de force* that confronts terminal illness and slow, painful death from the perspectives of those involved. To the charge that life is difficult enough, Reading gave this response, much quoted since:

If you want art to be like Ovaltine then clearly some artists are not for you; but art has always struck me most when it was to do with coping with things, often hard things, things that are difficult to take (Jenkins, 1985, p.7).

At the same time, Reading wanted to play down the importance of *C* in this respect [LI]: 'I don't think that it's achieving anything.' Questioned further, he admitted having received grateful letters from bereaved readers [LI]:

I don't think that generally happens with my stuff – I'd *like* it to be the case... – but I've had letters about that which meant a great deal to me. From quite different people who've had relatives that have been in the process of dying or had just died, and said that they didn't quite know why, but they felt very grateful for the book because it seemed to them to talk about the issues that were uppermost in their minds. And that is the best kind of praise that's ever happened to me. I was really very, very pleased...

Paradoxically, this bleak confrontation ultimately shows the most respect to the victims, and Reading had learnt this from two sources:

the important thing is being alive or dying easily, and it doesn't, unfortunately, come to many of us to have that privilege... I *had* read Elisabeth Kübler-Ross, and I had also read, many years ago when I was a student – and maybe the idea first occurred to me in the 1960s – John Hinton's book, simply called *Dying*, which was one of the first realistic looks at dying which I have ever encountered... It was perhaps trying to be helpful... in a way which actually took the problem, looked at it very closely, and then set out to say 'well, what, if anything, can we do about it? If we can't do anything about it then at least let us accept *that* and learn to go along with the fact.' Now that's the sort of thing which I might be looking for in the kind of art that moves me most – in some short Beckett tracts, say, or in late Shostakovich string quartets. You're not looking for immediate peace of mind or soothing, but in the end you are stimulated beyond the harrowing things which those works deal with to something sympathetic, compassionate and to do with human beings (Bailey, M).

Asked by Alan Jenkins how he could combine the 'ingenuity of the writing' with such a subject, Reading replied:

That's become a kind of nervous tic, by this stage in the proceedings... and it is a sort of self-preservation. Everybody who lives has different ways of dealing with what he has to deal with, and it simply happens that mine is a kind of metrical way. I felt the book was OK. I worked very hard at it (no, that's nonsense, working hard is carrying bags around, but I put a lot of time and effort into it) and got very tired... I honestly didn't think of it shocking anybody, and I don't think it has. Shocking isn't really the right word. People don't *like* that sort of thing, and of course not. I thought it might receive some minor accolades. It's jolly good of my publishers to bother with me, because I do a lot of things that aren't attractive to people, I'm never going to be a popular chap on the campus (Jenkins, 1985, p.8).

'C' explicitly stands for incurable illnesses of the 20th century, cancer and cardiac illnesses (and for the fear of death). But, as a Roman numeral, it specifies the number of days left to the poet-narrator, 'probably between three and four months, perhaps one hundred days' (unit 1):[4] '(*Incongruously I plan / 100 100-word units*)', as he announces in his epigraph. 'C' also stands for the hundred words which he writes daily about aspects of his dying, altogether a 'neat' idea, as the narrator himself puts it (98, p.316). This arbitrary structure is functional insofar as it highlights the arbitrariness of the illness itself – which may attack some parts of the body and indeed some people, but not others. On the book's larger scale, the 10,000 words also allocate one word to every year of the existence of *Homo sapiens* in the Holocene. The book had obviously been carefully planned [LI]:

> I thought of it as the complete thing to start with, with all its connotations of C being 100 and so on... except that I'd been thinking about it for many years...C was exactly as I had planned... though I wanted it really to be more comprehensive than it is, or, rather, I wanted it, in a way, not only to be about cancer, but simply about dying – and about all the things that in the retrospect you consider when you *are* dying. So it was *meant* to have all those sort of things as well.

The 100 epherimide Units are a heterogeneous mix of "misplaced" poetry and eloquent prose. Individual poem titles are abandoned (as they are in the next six books of the next decade). Instead, Reading orchestrates his continually changing perspectives, tones, registers and voices, as well as different text-genres (excerpts from letters, medical dictionaries, lists, anecdotes, etc.) into a cacomorphous polyphony, generating in the reader a degree of disorientation, tension, and shock that intensifies the portrayal of what the victims are undergoing.

The narrator calls himself 'C' in the third person (wife and daughter are 'A' and 'B'), or else 'Master of the 100 100-Word Units', and the cancer is, of course, spreading in his colon. *C* is also C's (fictitious) literary legacy, as C himself explains meta-textually (87, p.310); this text is critically and sometimes palinodically annotated by the implied author (who always appears in square brackets, as in *5x5x5x5x5*).

Finally, 'C' also stands for 'Char' (40, p.293), aka 'Mort', whose last name is 'Tucker',[5] and who frequents two pubs by the river, 'used by ferrymen and travellers calling for a quick drink before crossing' (2, p.277). 'Our hero' (26, p.287), the true main protagonist, is allegorised death, 'infernal' (40) Charon, whose palm is 'constantly grey from receiving pennies' (2). He is silently omnipresent in the

proceedings, coldly tracking down his doomed passengers and ferry-
ing them over the Styx and Acheron to Hades, sometimes with
diabolical hatred (26, 63).[6]

'Char' introduces himself to C 'with importunate familiarity' (2)
after having inspected him once before at a family picnic (21, p.285):
'He knew who I was all right.'[7] Appearing either in the guise of an
outcast (gypsy, vagrant), or as a lone man carrying out a series of
sinisterly appropriate jobs (stoker, stretcher-bearer, ferryman), he is
often accompanied by a horse which C – in a strange premonition
– studies in great anatomical detail (a Beckettian device to focus
readers' attention). He muses: ' "That's a pale one ye have there,
Mr Tucker" ' (21). 'Pallida Mors', pale death, a literary motif since
Horace, is one of the four horses of the Apocalypse: 'And I looked
and behold a pale horse and his name that sat on him was Death,
and Hell followed with him' (Revelation, 6.8).

Apart from the main protagonist, an unspecified number of
dramatis personae, whose thoughts are recorded, are gathered in
some hospital by the sea. The central figure here is C, the 'Master
of the 100 100-Word Units', a writer-in-residence who does not
always manage to combine his fatal illness with the first person
singular (67, p.303):

> He keeps
> a sort of journal, so they say, in which
> *he chronicles his death in the 3rd Person,*
> partly in prose, part verse, peculiar, hey?
> He's only youngish too.

The reason for using the third person is evident enough, as is also
clear from his emotional breakdown: he has ceased to be the Master
of his own life, so the imagination and courage needed for con-
fronting pain and death are not always available (81):

> And I can't believe it – that I am really going to   It is as if I were
> just writing about someone else d – just as if it were yet another of the
> things about those poor *other* people that I write (*used* to write) about.
> Why am I writing about it?

In the bed next to him the palaeontologist is also dying from cancer
(89, p.311). Their wives, a little daughter, an Indian doctor who
operates on C, nurses, a psychologist, and other specialists move
in and out of the picture, as do the other patients whose cancers
and complications amount to a representative cross-section of the
affliction. It can hit anybody, and, as Reading shows in other books,
'their reaction to / terminal pain democratises them' (86, p.310).
Daily dying in hospitals is the subject of the book, and so is poetry –

which, like the hospitals, is not properly equipped to cope. Reading insisted the medical 'found material' (as with the palaeontology in *Diplopic*) was there for a good reason [LI]:

> Natural History, ornithology and biology wouldn't be any problem and I probably know a bit about the stuff that I was talking about in those contexts. With other things I've very self-consciously researched things to slip in the same way as any writer of fiction would. If you were a novelist...you would have to research various subjects to make your characters or the narrator be sufficiently credible so as to carry weight. And so I've done the same sorts of things on bits about astronomy and about medicine and various other things... If I'm talking about a certain trade or science or small specialist part of life then I want it to be absolutely convincing. Otherwise the whole thing is null and void.

Apart from this, specialist subjects provide an 'extra bonus' [LI]: 'the rich language itself'.

The book's concerns are also now more openly literary. Its first line ('The brass plate polished wordless. Stone steps hollowed...') focuses briefly on the erosion of metal, stone – and words. C emerges from the diagnosis like Betjeman's death candidate in 'Devonshire Street W.1', and having just received his death sentence, he snarls at the reader (1), 'What do you expect me to do – break into bloody haiku?', providing one instantly:

> Verse is for healthy
> arty-farties. The dying
> and surgeons use prose.

Henceforward, in a style and tone unsparingly curt and hard, the book subjects poetry to a Final Judgement: 'Why write it? Why ever wrote any of it? Poetry all weak lies, games' (6, p.279). Just as the surgeon examines with a scalpel parts of C's abdomen, testing their remaining working order so as to determine further treatment, C sceletises his verse forms, repeatedly pronouncing them unworkable. Given the subject, poetic transformations are no longer justifiable, the realisation of which always throws C back to matter-of-fact prose. C's obsessive, repetitive attempts to connect up to poetry again goes with his irrational instinct to hold on to life. With the help of a metrically stable framework, he tries to oppose his disintegration: the clash between bound and unbound speech, which runs through the whole volume, finds its paradoxical solution only on his deathbed.

Meanwhile, as from unit 3 (p.278), the 'specialist' material begins its attack on the reader's composure. A catalogue verse after the *'McGill-Melzack Pain Questionnaire'* clinically lists 78 capitalised adjectives denoting pain. There is one notable omission – 'painful',

probably the most commonly used word of all, but for the techni-
cians it is obviously too vague. For C, who is actually experienc-
ing pain, it will do, though he stoically hides it in brackets: '(par-
ticularly painful)' (4, p.278). Similarly, the self-satisfied language
of the 'trained' or 'Terminal Caregiver' (4, 92, p.312) ('there is
much comfort') with its 'patronising tone' (86, p.310) does not
reach patients. Also out of touch are the meek doctors who with-
hold the truth from patients, thus depriving them of the chance to
prepare for death – 'about 80% of us rarely, if ever, tell them' –
while a study conducted by the American Cancer Society reveals,
'about 80% of patients say they would like to be told' (15, p.283).[8]
Relatives can be equally inadequate, some not even being able to
hide their revulsion or give simple help (19, 20, p.285). One rep-
resentative humane voice is heard through the dissonance of dis-
tance and distaste – probably the Indian doctor from the Intensive
Care Unit – and in despair speaks in parabasis to the reader (33,
p.290):

> It is bad for us as well, you know, looking after them. Can you take
> any more? I can't. I'm ready to give up. What's the use? All our
> patients die eventually. They should do six things for their 'Death
> Work': (1) become aware of their impending death, (2) balance hope
> and fear throughout the crisis, (3) *reverse* physical survival instincts,
> (4) relinquish independence, (5) detach themselves from former expe-
> riences and (6) prepare 'spiritually' for death.

In the face of physical and psychological disintegration, hardly any-
one is able to do this grief and death work (93, 95, pp.313-14).
Indeed, the opposite happens (33):

> They go through six emotional states (outlined by Kübler-Ross);[9] (1)
> Denial, (2) Isolation, (3) Anger, (4) Bargaining, (5) Depression, (6)
> Acceptance. All, eventually. All.

The doctor gives heart-breaking examples of each state (34-38).
After the colotomy, C senses his doctor is overstrained and tense:
'He is afraid of what I am going to ask' (70). In the course of the
book, C himself experiences all those states himself.

The lack of chronology in the units eventually puts the reader a
few steps ahead of the protagonist, so that the reader involuntarily
shares the doctor's half-secret knowledge about his patients. However,
the overriding mood, tone, and imagery of the units are so varied
that the reader continually has to adapt. The only peaceful passage
(5), in which C finds solace in the image of shipwrecked Odysseus
on the Phaeacian coast, finding protection, peace, and sleep under
two olive trees,[10] is followed by C's emotional breakdown, the

pleonastic, panicky intensity of which is punctured by the harsh palinode: 'Stupid childish helpless poor little frightened [Pusill-animous drivel.] frail poor me. Us *all*' (6). The very next unit begins with a comic rhyme about Tucker the Tramp, then moves on to 'Tucker's Tale' (authentic [C]; see 74), which seems to be a coarse joke but ends in nauseating violence and a terse comment on art and life. Relief is then granted only in the vision of a tablet-suicide after a bottle of Bual of 1894: 'Fat buttery fumosity of amber decanted Madeira. Sour chalkiness of the twentieth pillule' (8). The scarcity of verbs, though, indicates both the nascent narcosis and the unlikelihood of this event. The setting for the stoical acceptance of an early death is provided by the beautiful hills of the Salopian Long Mynd (authentically) called 'Hanging Brink', 'Ashes Hollow' and 'Callow Hollow', near Oakleymill Waterfall, the scene of earlier family idylls (21, 23, pp.285-86). But the recollections are rudely curtailed: 'where once my sweet wife, my dear daughter …(enough of that shite).' This Eliot-device of using aposiopesis in the parabasis is amplified by change of register and frustrates the reader's incipient empathy.

Never once is the reader allowed to feel straightforward pity: the death candidates themselves do not dare indulge in nostalgia for fear of intensifying the pain. And trips down Memory Lane only end in dark cul-de-sacs, as for example the family breakfast in spring ('bluebells on sun-dappled gingham'), when the narrator is served 'a dusty handful' of *Bran-Brek* and reads on the packet: '*Doctors say fibreless diets cause bowel cancer*…What was then fear has become shitless terror' (18). His moving love-letter to his wife and child is similarly counterpointed (23):

> *I recall our Callow Hollow alfresco. Our tiny child bathing in Oakleymill Waterfall pool. A gorse sprig suspended in an eddy. We were at the best of our lives. Such happiness never recurs. Never. Golden bright little flower, sharp thorns. Spätlese cooling in the gelid spring. Later, the gipsy with that pale gelding. I will remember these things until the day I die.* [Which is the day after tomorrow…]

Conversely, black humour, *drôleries*, and Fescennine verse temporarily counteract depression:

> It is a most terrible *bore*
> to haemorrhage, spewing-up gore,
> and, bubbling for breath,
> be blood-drowned to death.
> Je *ne* voudrais *pas* être mort.

You find the Limerick inapposite? Care for a cutely-adapted Adonic?

and promptly one is delivered ($-\smile\smile--$) (11, p.281). In the same gruesome joke a Marvell quotation ('Lilies without, roses within') is grotesquely de-sanitised in 'pretty Choriamb': 'Bed-sores without, swarm-cells within' (91). C still has the nerve to joke, as in his allusion to Charon, the Romany, in his choice of typeface (*Tedious Acrimonious roman*, 87). The peak of macabre self-irony is reached in his letter to his editor (87):

> *I am irritated to learn that I shall soon be dead. You will be irritated to learn that by then I shall have completed a final book. This epistle constitutes one of its 100 sections. I shall be dead by the time you receive this typescript.*
> ...
> *PS. Seriously, though, my wife will deal with proof correction.*

The first victim to break down is verse, the patient in the next bed. Dekubiti full of pus; 'tubes stuck up the nose, into the veins, up the arse' (9, p.280); 'Snot, gore, filth, suppuration of the arse-gut' – 'for these *no* metric is vindicable' (25, p.287). The first operation punningly calls for verse to be reduced to 'justified prose' (17, 7, 18, 75), depriving it of its elegant shape. Then, in a bad-tempered satire on the poetic practice of glossing poems with the varnish of European culture, the Master angrily rejects all cosmetic surgery on the object: 'I used to pepper my poetics with sophisticated allusions to *dear* Opera and *divine* Art... A tube is stuck up my prick, and a bladder carcinoma diagnosed. One does *not* recall Piccinni' (9). Even hard puns are brought in to mortify art: a soldier is shot in the back while sodomising – 'Vita brevis, ars ditto' – (7, p.279), and the poet himself is subjected to a colostomy, which inspires an antanaclasical triple pun (24, p.286):

> Terminal verse. Rain-pits 700000000 years old in Precambrian rock: a species evolved 696000000 years after that: a handful of stresses and punctuation: ars only as long as vita: pentameters, like colons, inadequate.

But there is a 'Nevertheless' with a capital 'N'. In the local library, the letter 'C' is the most thumbed in *Stedman's Medical Dictionary*. The Master says: 'We are beyond verse here. No one wants to write "On Last Looking Into Stedman's Carcinoma". Nevertheless, I have invented the 13-line sonnet for unlucky people (100 words, inc. title)...' (27, p.288):[11] the amputated sonnet follows, with the surgeons talking shop over lunch ('advanced C. uterine cervix / [just my damned luck to find that]') (28). A few pages later, bouncing 'catalectic tetrameters' rhyming in pairs provide the ultimate ironic form for a mastectomy (41, 43, pp.293-94). Reading's imagination in this book pulls out all the stops.

The more frenetically the Master argues against the use of
verse, the more extravagant and refined the appropriately inappro-
priate verse forms become: catalogue verses list adjectives for pain
and words starting with CARCINO; an ametrical, synoptic acrostic
(39) is arranged in a visual kaligramm as a pattern poem depicting
the hospital; the 'Great unvindicable idea: a 17-liner, 100-word,
pentameter acrostic, first letters forming CARCINOMATOPHOBIA'
(44, p.294) is promptly carried out (46), reporting such a case.
Further laments are poured into unfashionable *Ubi sunt* poems (47;
49; 72, p.304; 88, p.311) and into the measured tétramètre-form,
with caesura and divisions made visible (69, p.303). The 'Japanese
sonnet' of *Diplopic* recurs (62, p.301); a harmless quatorzain remi-
nisces about an ornithological adventure which 'incongruously
gladdens my last thoughts' (31, p.289), echoed in *Ob.* ('At Chesa-
peake Bay').

The doctor cannot believe it (37, p.29): 'One of them wrote verse.
Verse! Write about this: a Left Inguinal Colostomy. Shit, blood,
puke and a body no longer dependable, metastases, dyspnoea...'.
But the compulsion to versify proves as tenacious as the will to live.
Pentameters are rejected as 'blank' one moment, but get written
the next. Likewise, the elegiac distich, which Reading uses for the
first time in this book, apparently cannot do justice to excruciating
pain, let alone death, in its cadence (13): 'Even formed properly,
no elegiac distich can fall with / quite this sospirity: breath – out of
a black mask exhaled.' However, another one follows (13), 'None
of it matters except at a purely personal level: / pain, not oblivion,
hurts; as with me, so with all quarks'. After acknowledging that
'twee verse' (93, p.313) at least can provide 'comfort of make-
believe games / such as this one that I play now in distich, almost
pretending / verse has validity' (73, p.305), there is the by now
familiar retraction: 'No. Verse is fuck-all use here, now.' Any lyrical
transformation must violate the real situation, but the tension between
need and rejection, like the tension between life and death, is still
allowed to persist in the lyrical poems. Rumens explains the back-
ground:

> He cannot shift from physical disgust to moral disgust as could, for
> example, Wilfred Owen; cancer, unlike war, is more a matter of bad
> luck than of badness. As a result, such poems may exhibit a certain
> manic bravery, but they are not cathartic for the reader; pity and ter-
> ror have become redundant emotional responses just as metaphor has
> become redundant 'arty-farty' diction.
>
> Nevertheless, the volume does make room for poems of a traditional,
> redemptive aesthetic, and both kinds of writing gain added pathos from
> their juxtaposition.

Revealingly, there are two significant exceptions, where verse and life are both granted momentary dignity. A hexametrical epyllion about C's suicide vision (97, p.315) is exempt from the rage and confusion, and the elegiac distich *is* qualified to speak – once – for the lament of the widow who, faced with the task of tidying away her late husband's 'vacated clothes', cannot stop weeping at the 'Empty, amorphous and cold, blue tubes of Levi's' (83, p.309).

The question, 'But is there, today, / one ghastly experience / that vindicates verse?' (62, p.301), seems to retract Reading's position in earlier books that there are no "unpoetic subjects". At the same time, the ambiguity of the Master's convictions about unpoetic dying remains unchallenged (the question above is a haiku). The resolution of the apparent paradox is by now clear: on the narrative level of *C*, it is evident that the Master may not be able to grasp or contain the *subject* in verse, but against all reason looks for diversion, comfort and protection against the unbearable prognosis – in versifying. In his weakest moment – the bargaining state – he (almost) says it himself (76, p.306, see also 81):

> [He breaks down and sobs embarrassingly.] Oh! I shall miss you so. Why has it happened? Why has stuff inside me suddenly gone terribly wrong? I don't think I'm afraid of not *being* anymore but so terribly terribly frightened of not being *with you...* Oh my darling, help me! Look after me! Can't be brave or consoled by philosophy or by po – would willingly never have written anything *if only*

Even in imagining his last minutes, he appeals (in hexameters) to the protection and deliverance of the Goddess of Art (97): 'Thus do I bury me closely with leaf-mould and / wait for Athene's / Soft anaesthetic, benign soporific, ar- / cane analgesic...'. His last letter to wife and daughter – '*won't last (too weak) till Visiting Hour. Hope you find this*' – is written with 'Biro on Kleenex, fitting medium terminal words' (78, p.307). Awaiting death, C controls his confused thoughts by quoting poetry to himself: Shelley's and Spenser's lines on death at least steady him mentally[12] – in the absence of someone to hold him. Accordingly, the wish to write one last poem emerges, which impulse is duly kept in check by the Beckettian interjection in square brackets – '[Pah!]' – thus banishing any hint of quasi-religious undertones. But still C tries, one last time, to encompass his inconsolability and fear of death in two Spenserian stanzas (79) as if poetry was the Last Sacrament; to structure his thoughts metrically is his *personal* way of ensuring they do not run amok. As 'incongruous' and 'inadequate' this tendency may seem, in view of the atheist convictions permeating *C* it is nonetheless an instance of stability (albeit a highly idiosyncratic one). Perhaps it is even a sign of a moving bravery if C does not let himself be engulfed by the reality of his own death, but still tries to shape it partially, in a creative way. In poetics, experiencing something first-hand and then giving this experience artistic shape ironically bears the name 'autopsy'.

More importantly, while verse as an artistic and therapeutic medium for coping with terminal reality is subject on the narrative level to what must be the harshest attacks seen in literature, it is innocent of these charges on the structural level, with countless relativisations and contradictions going on in between. The structural framework of the book is elaborate enough to encompass this basic issue of the validity of verse, and it is convincing because the reader experiences how all imaginable doubts are confronted and therefore become manageable.

Reading's poetry does not declare its validity openly. The tension between the two opposing poles is unresolvable, because both are true in their own right, and on their own levels.[13] Rumens' depiction of how C works is lucid and to the point:

> C's philosophy seems to be akin to that familiar theory which states that there are certain areas of human experience which poetry cannot and should not attempt to reach, since by its innate powers of transformation it will make the unbearable bearable. However, he simultaneously demolishes such an objection by creating a 'poetry' that does not transform its subject-matter, that is, in effect, anti-poetry... It is not of course clear how much of the anti-aesthetic in C is Reading's own. His other books, however, contain evidence that he believes that poetry should seize on the ugliness of modern life (moral as well as visual) without recourse to the redemptive synthesis with which art 'cures' reality. There are poems so flatly shocking they might just as well be pieces of tabloid journalism. C shows a finer sense of balance. It allows poetry to argue with itself without committing suicide.

Paul Bailey asked Reading whether the Master's opinion expressed in the opening haiku – 'Verse is for healthy arty-farties' – was his own:

> To some degree. There is that paradox between the idea of fiddling away at verse and trying to... approach some subjects with it which are very serious, but which one is completely impotent to deal with... But of course the whole paradox hinges on the fact that one still persists writing it... In view of this impotence, I suppose the only possible usefulness... perhaps... is giving some people some sort of, if you like, sympathetic support, albeit ... – in my particular case – perhaps a hard-won kind of support and a rather grizzly one to come to terms with. But nevertheless I suppose that's the rather precocious intention...The whole point which was being put under question was that *verse* was inadequate (Bailey, M).

The reduction of poetry to a slice of validity accompanies and mirrors the actual deterioration of the suffering protagonist. The medical and personal details of his hospital stay become increasingly awful. After the first symptoms – blood in the urine – a successful operation, 'but [it] recurred, *massively*' (80, p.308). The sight of the other 'hopeless pyjamad cases in ghastly contraptions' as well as the daily 'meat waggons swing[ing] through the gates braying, pulsing blue light, their burdens already history scraped off the Tarmac' (53, p.297); lengthy preparations for anaesthesia and operations which the patient does not fully understand; the colotomy; self-delusion; dyspnoe, dysgneusia, dysphagia, metastases, chemotherapy; the consequences of the growth in the colon, causing pain and embarrassment (also for the 'bewildered' relatives): the colostomy and countless complications, vomiting blood, decubitus ulcers, haemorrhage, draining fistulae; the bitterness of some of the dying about 'the life that seemed unfulfilled'; then the attempt to at least die at home or in a hospice, which results in soiled bed-clothes, bed pans, diapers, lubricant, Special Laundry Services; in the end excruciating pain against which even opium is powerless, making a leucotomy of the brain unavoidable. 'The Unfortunates' are dehumanised and tortured to death, which means that in the end 'Of course Mr Tucker comes to help, a real help' (96).

But not everybody in the ward is tormented by extreme states of mental turmoil. Some patients are capable of admirable self-composure and dignity; it is a weakness of *C*, though, that their voices get drowned in the frantic loudness of the despair around them. Some turn to religion, encouraged by the hospital 'missionaries... clutching "Good News" bibles' (10). C despises the dogma that man is somehow exempt from natural law – '*The only way to cross the Acheron is on inflated egos*' (78, p.307) – but in his penultimate poem, a Spenserian stanza, at least concedes they have a beneficial effect on troubled souls (79, p.307):

Interdenominational claptrap,
from the Infirmary Chaplains, helps a few
cowardly of us bear our deaths. The chap
whom they leucotomised conceives this true:
that his soul is eternal. Such a view,
wholly unsatisfactory for me,
is genuinely good – he won't pull through,
but hopes to die without finality
accepting their dud-specious immortality.

For the micro-palaeontological scientist in the next bed, though, religion (as in the last two books) is *the* anathema, as his wife explains after his death (10, p.280):

He regarded it as an arrogant ('arrogant humility' is a phrase he used
of Buddhism, Christianity &c.), Quaternary, Hominid invention for
crudely pacifying the purely physiological characteristic of Hominid
cephalic capacity. He viewed the concept of theism as cowardly, con-
ceited, unimaginative and, necessarily, at the *earliest* merely Pliocene.
(His period was Precambrian, before god.)

His wife had broken the news of his imminent death to him in a
movingly meiotic scene, and he took it with uncanny calmness (55,
p.298). In dying, he displays formidable self-control (75, p.306)
and strives for composure by distancing himself, regarding himself
as the part of an evolutionary chain. Thus, he finds some solace in
the analogy of regular mass extinction of millions of species in
earlier geological eras (22, 75) and manages to fend off attacks of
panic, reminding himself that he will be 'Sedimented, sedimented',
like the first organisms on earth, the 'blue-green algae', and the
'good old rain-pits and ripple-marks so transiently formed about
six hundred million years ago' (47-49, 65).

C, too, finds some consolation in the parallel of earlier existence
become anonymous. In an *Ubi sunt* poem, he alphabetically gives
names of authentic VIPs listed in the *Who Was Who 1897-1915* –
whom nobody knows any more (72, p.304). This atheist's emotional
reaction is more problematic than the palaeontologist's: 'How we
hate you, busy, ordinary, undying' (1). First there are manifestations
of burning envy, then: *'His irascibility increased towards the end'*
(repeated four times, with diminishing print-size). It is directed
against hospital staff, priests, even other patients (no need any
more for sham politeness). Since everybody is in the same boat
there is room for mockery and even fun, as in the cruel treatment
of the folk-singer 'devoid of talent, mawkish and platitudinous',
member 'of the You'll-Always-Be-On-My-Mind-Girl/Nuclear-
Holocaust-Is-An-Awful-Shame School' (16, p.284), or as in the
belligerent attack, in accentual metre, against nature poets (com-
pare 'Nips' in *Diplopic*) and 'nature lovers' (29, p.289):

The sham the twee and the precious / phoney-rustic ignorant / wield
their sugary Biros / down in the safe Sticks / ensconced in the done-up
Old Wheelwright's. / Poetical mawkish duff gen / where a buzzard is
'noble' and lands / in a tree (surprise, surprise!) / to corroborate some
trite tenet / cum badly-observed Nature Note. / Their fauna is furry or
feathery / people like you and me, / cute or nasty – a raptor / becomes a
Belfast terrorist. / Bullshit bullshit bullshit / of the Plashy Fen School. /
Peterson, Mountfort & Hollom / write more sense than you / bloody
carpetbaggers.[14]

Nature deserves better treatment. Complicated human dying is
contrasted, if not shown up, by silent dying in nature. The doctor's

hand on the pulse reminds the patient of how the gipsy Tucker once gently killed a rabbit (14); artificial saliva and colons, oxygen flasks, sleeping pills and narcotics are counterpointed by the unostentatious disappearance of cancer-infested birds. Reading reports about the days of his youth spent on Hilbre (12, p.282):

> In ornithological days, at the observatory, we used, not infrequently, to discover moribund specimens. They seemed always to have grovelled into some niche to quietly get on with it – the stance would so often be trembling on a single weak leg, the lids half closed, the grey nictitating membrane half-drawn across the, by then, dull bead.

Only the old Cockney is capable of a similarly simple acceptance (86, p.310):

> 'The wife was upset, as she's never seen
> me like this. So I said "We've all of us
> got to go, Girl, I've ad a decent life;
> it's im in the next bed as I feels sad for,
> e's only young – they ad to stop is pain
> by a-leucotomising-of is brain." '

Also simple is the *Ubi sunt* manner in which *C*'s dead are simply listed by the implied author himself, who at this point relinquishes his contrastively regulative and distanced-critical stance, to express at least once his pity and empathy. He uses exactly the same words as C used in his breakdown – which he had then labelled 'pusillanimous drivel'. In this complete U-turn, there is even a faint echo of the 'poor naked wretches' (*King Lear*, III, 4) (88, p.311):

> [*Ubi sunt...*? All planted, at the time of going to press. Some feared oblivion; most feared pain. Poor frail dear frightened little vulnerable creatures.]

A broadening of perspective is also triggered by the Acrostic 'IN THE SAME VERTICAL COLUMN' (39, p.292). A pattern poem, or kalligram, it schematically visualises the five hospital floors – a pictorial summary of the narrative. In G (Ground Floor), and floors 1, 2 and 3 the death candidates lie, with the Master at the very top, with images of Hell, or the crematorium, in the basement (Charon feeding the stove and getting his Pale Horse ready for summoning the next candidate). The metaphorical implications ('all of us in the same vertical column...acres of soft white lint to one or another and finally all', 53, p.297) soon grow into a lament for a whole nation. This central motif in Reading's œuvre is specified here for the first time (57, p.299):

> (Not just me, but out there in the Pedestrianised Precincts. The filth gathers beyond clearance or control... New desolate sounds of Coke cans discarded tinkling rolling in windy streets... and cables slapped

clacking against tin masts of yachts in deserted lidos. In Department Stores staff outnumber customers now... something irrevocably dying is happening.)

In a last widening of focus, the whole world is suppurating to death (57, 61, 71). C's wife notices other women's pain at their husbands' dying – Northern Ireland and Lebanon already were a synecdoche for all countries in *Diplopic* – and incantatorily repeats her empathic lament several times: 'Newsflash, their women writhe unconsolable in the dirt of Ulster and the Holy Land. They are not actresses; that is how they really feel. How I feel also, my cancerous husband' (59, p.299).

Those husbands, ironically, could let each other live if they chose. C, who cannot choose, plans to ingest soporifics on the 100th day after the diagnosis, and, close to the end of his life, composes metrically complicated verse, the 'subtle grafting of a cdedee Spenserian sestet onto an abbaabba Petrarchan octave' (99), as started in the poem concerning his 'cadaver' (25, p.287; see 63). C's conflicting thoughts about 'lyric metre' are jotted down on a piece of paper found on his (imagined) cadaver (98) by one of Charon's shifting personae, who takes his obolus from the corpse's pocket. The imagined Odyssean suicide idyll in 'Ashes Valley' may be rendered in a quiet, simple epyllion in hexameters (97), recalling the quiet dignity of a cancerous bird's death earlier; these visions, however, cannot extend beyond his imagination to become part of the narrative (94):

> It is not as one can imagine beforehand. Dysgneusia (an altered sense of taste occasionally occurring in cases of advanced malignancy) prevents my savouring the cigar-box-spiciness, deep, round fruitiness of the brick-red luscious '61 *Cheval Blanc*, the fat, buttery, cooked, caramel-sweet-nuttiness of the 1894 Bual.

Besides, he is unable to leave his bed. Also, his wife and daughter would 'interpret my self-destruction as failure on their part to nurse me properly. Conversely, the grief my daily decline causes them is difficult for me to bear' (100).

C's final attempt at a literary synthesis of palaeontology and a conclusive nihilistic, stoical statement gets linguistically stuck in aposiopesis (99):

> Precambrian sub-division *Longmyndian*, ca. 600 million yrs. old. An individual Holocene *H. sapiens* with terminal pathogen. The coincidence of these two, thus: approaching oblivion (by ingestion of soporifics), *H. sap.* picks up, from scree in Ashes Hollow, a sample of rock imprinted with 600-million-year-old rain-pits...Vita b.; ars b. Nor does the Precambrian sub-division *Longmyndian*...[matter], nor Holocene *H. sap* with terminal &c., nor the *conception* of its not mattering, nor

Only the last but one word of the book – '*prosaic*' – gets any further, and is the necessary step towards achieving the hard-earned rest granted in death and in the final word, 'love'. It is the only thing that 'matters' in the story of life, as verse is the only thing that can matter in the 'Master's' poetic, imaginative world of the mind. In the end, C simply accepts the prosaic facts: 'My wife patiently washes my faece-besmirched pyjamas, for *prosaic* love' (100). From the haiku of unit 1, the wheel has come full circle. Poetry has been replaced. As O'Driscoll concludes (p.215): 'Never has the word "love" had such a difficult passage and never has it earned its place in literature so convincingly.'

Ukulele Music (1985):
Joining the Cimmerians

Published together for reasons of economy, *Ukulele Music* and *Going On* appeared in 1985, only seven months after *C*. A later American edition (1994) from American Northwestern University Press had *Ukulele Music* paired with *Perduta Gente* – a good combination, but strong meat for a first US publication.

Publication in Britain was preceded by a controversy in the literary columns. Alan Jenkins, then poetry editor of the *TLS*, summarised the episode as follows:

> the poem 'Cub', a dramatic monologue voiced by a cub reporter who witnesses a violent incident in Lebanon, was printed in the *Times Literary Supplement* for 23 March 1984. The poem was badly misunderstood; the most common misreading took it to be an anti-Semitic statement. It was virulently attacked as such, and fiercely defended as the ironic, antiwar poem it in fact is in the letters columns of both the *Times Literary Supplement* and the *Times* (Jenkins, *DLB*, p.475).

Asked about his reaction to the charge of anti-Semitism, Reading replied (and wrote about in an Alcmanic stanza, p.77):

> I was very, very surprised. Then I was rather alarmed, because the sort of response that rumbled on in the literary press for a while was the sort of response that I'd actually been moaning about in the original piece – a sort of atavistic violence which seemed to me to be completely hopeless...The response that was triggered off was concerning some remarks about characters from the *Old Testament* not having changed since the times of the *OT*. And this was seized upon by some people as referring exclusively to Jewishness [whereas] it was meant to refer to the pages of blood-curdling military history that occur throughout the *OT* from all and sundry... The *Times Literary Supplement*...received a bag of faeces through the post, and you start to wonder under these circumstances whether some incendiary device might be the next thing to plop on to the lino (Bailey, M).

The reception of the book itself was less fierce.[1] A.A. Cleary printed 18 pages from *Ukulele Music* in *Thames Poetry*; Neil Corcoran devoted a sub-chapter to *Ukulele Music* in his book on contemporary poetry, Tom Paulin praised the book as Reading's 'most brilliant and assured volume', P.J. Kavanagh listed *Ukulele Music* in the *Spectator* as the 'best book of the year' because it was 'unlike anything else' and 'because of [Reading's] tone and skill it enlarges the world that poetry can incorporate', and Robert Potts concluded: 'But he also stands out among post-war poets as a genuine social commentator, a journalistic or analytical dissector of the modern world, and of England in particular in 29 years of not uncontroversial writing.'[2]

The forceful social realism of the book's surface understandably attracted most attention, but this meant neglect of the finer and more far-reaching thematic functions of structure, metrics, and other devices. The desolate social situation is firmly embedded in the larger *condition humaine*. One notable exception to the general critical consensus was Fraser Steel's illuminating review:

> The standard objection to Reading sees him as the fat boy who likes to make your flesh creep, a garrulous retailer of vicarious horrors. The standard riposte casts him as the bard of immiseration of Thatcher's Britain, doing for poetry what Derek Jarman did for cinema in *The Last of England*. Both miss the point. These are the accidents of a poetry whose substance is the catastrophic nature of the human condition. If he'd lived in the 14th century, Reading would have written a great deal about bubonic plague. In the late 20th there have been some additions to the repertoire of natural and unnatural shocks, and these are in the centre of his gaze – not, though, to the exclusion of the sufficient reasons for misery and despair which have always lain around the human path.[3]

For Reading, any political angles on the book were simply 'off the point' [LI]. He commented on this subject in detail after a reading in Los Angeles. Christopher Hitchens asked, 'you obviously don't want to be thought of as political, and I think in a really deep sense you're not', to which Reading replied:

> The sort of things that I write about... can't really exist without being, in some broader sense, political in that anything that concerns humanity and is treated in literature and any of the other arts, is ipso facto political in that it is about the way that humanity conducts itself. So that's the only kind of political sway that holds there, I think... I wouldn't want to be thought of as a sort of radical or a left or a right...but to maintain an Addisonian position, if you wish...'Thus I live in the world rather as a spectator of mankind than as one of the species' (Lannan Video, M).

An Australian interviewer took issue with the alleged 'distance' and spoke of 'strong moral passion' and 'engagement' in his work: 'Yes, there is, but that isn't a political one... The sort of things I am talking about are really beyond politics. They're to do with simple kindness. Humanity, really'.[4]

After the close-ups of private deaths in *C*, the poems in *Ukulele Music* show a widening of focus: they look at the socio-political decay of England, while also pondering the foreseeable end of the entire world, Reading's theme in the late books. But as with *C*, readers still have to brace themselves, all the more so as it is not ill-luck which causes suffering: it is man-made evils.

In *Ukulele Music*, Reading again dispenses with poem titles, once more unifying the poems and prose into one large sequence. The book breaks down into three parts and consists of four distinct voices: a poet, his charlady, a sea Captain, and the text of a ukulele manual. They constitute four seemingly separate and metrically different narrative strands which later counterpoint and complement one another, until they are drawn together into one narrative and merged in one image in the finale. As in other books, it only becomes gradually clear how these strands and their dramatis personae are connected and where the plot is going. Reading's intention 'to build up an overall not necessarily story, but thematic development', is achieved again by means of *ploce* and other verbal echoes [C].

The book's "heroine" is the poet's charlady Viv, who comes alive in the many little notes she leaves on her employer's desk, creating a new version of the epistolary novel in endearingly malapropistic, illiterate working-class patois.[5] She is modelled on Dickens's Mrs Sarah Gamp, who also took great liberties with the English language, and on Mrs Frances Harris, the fictitious semi-literate menial of Swift's poem 'Mrs Harris's Petition'. Viv often asks for money in advance and rarely manages to keep to her schedule – for good reasons, as it turns out. She has a tough life: a delinquent son (Trev[or]), an unemployed (sick) husband, a traumatised sister to look after, cancer to cope with, a violent neighbourhood and endless financial worries, all typical of working-class lives in England in the 1980s.[6] No character in Reading's œuvre is as lovable as Viv (p.45):

> *not as I'm one for the books and that what with doing the housewort*
> *(no Womans Libbance for ME, what with that much things to do.*
> ...
> *Only I've never been happy but what I'm pottering, I ain't –*
> *always the pottering sort, that's why I hates coming DOWN*

On Tuesdays Viv cleans for 'the Capting', an old sea-captain, whose nautical register is highly specialised [LI]: 'Well again, that has to be to be convincing, yes. It's a mariner speaking and I didn't want some old sea-dog to pick the thing up and cringe with embarrassment because there was a lot of duff gen in it. So of course that's accurate.' Reading had learnt it from a source he was using as a literary pre-text [LI]: 'That register was very strong in the original accounts' (*Shipwrecks and Disasters at Sea*). The Captain sings his lyrical shanties about past adventures, raids, and catastrophes at sea. Just like Viv and her notes, the Captain and his narratives are of course a product of the poet's imagination, their function being to provide a comical or lyrical counterpoint to the journalese-reports that come from the third voice.

The poet-persona's voice is first heard in poems about the dis-integration of contemporary civilised life, poems that turn tabloid material and police reports into disengaged verse reportage. Later, encouraged by Viv's support, he openly confronts his critics by referring them back to his raw material – 'he don't invent it, you know' – and lashes out in angry Dunciads against the 'Poetry Wallahs' in Grub Street and their 'lame valedictory bunk' (p.20).

The fourth and shortest narrative strand is simply 'found mate-rial', slightly reworked from an American ukulele manual. Some passages from the handbook are so heavily ironic when read against the other strands that some critics thought the 'found material' must have been largely rewritten by Reading, but it was not [LI]:

> Well I bought one. You can get these little Teach Yourself pamphlets. I searched for quite a long time in music shops, but the ukulele is a bit out of vogue. And I eventually found – in Ludlow, of all places – in a music shop some sort of discarded thing that had been published about 20 years earlier and was very shop-soiled and was cheap anyway. It was an American thing. I've pepped it up slightly to make it slightly more bizarre in parts, but for the most part it's used verbatim.

The volume starts with Viv's address to the poet, '*Dear sir*': her confused explanation for her coming early is a comical description of an unfortunate incident involving her budgie – the first victim she has to look after in her household. Orthography, grammar, punctuation, idioms, tenses, syntax, cohesion and causality are riddled with malapropisms (e.g. '*REPRIMANDED IN CUSTARDY* ', p.20), solecisms, catachresis, cliché and general idiosyncrasy. In short: this is comic relief of the first order.

The poem following her note represents the starkest formal contrast: the elegiac distich is a new form in Reading's œuvre. Despite all the attacks on verse in *C*, metrics cannot be dispensed with if the aim is both to entertain and move the reader and to achieve supra-personal poetry.[7] Reading followed Auden in this [LI]:

> Auden, interestingly enough in elegiac distich, remarks: 'Blessed be all metrical rules that forbid automatic responses, / force you to have second thoughts, free from the fetters of self', which I take to mean that by the very act of writing verse and thinking about metrics you tend to analyse and perhaps revamp your original thoughts to fit in with what you're trying to do. You're in a bigger framework, and you're in a very artificial one, which is fine.

Previously, in *C*, Reading used distichs on only three single occa-sions, whereas here – contrary to *C*'s tendency to vary metres as much as possible – all the poet-poems are monostrophical. (The other two strands also move along on a beat of three.) The pacing and suspense are achieved by variations in voice, not metre.

Though barely familiar to English readers, this classical stanza based on dactyls and spondees is one of the oldest in existence (8th century BC) and was used for wholesale elegy because of its heroically falling cadence, to which Reading felt drawn for its 'grandiloquence and gravitas' [C].[8] Over the centuries, the elegiac mode became historically associated with this metre and thus part of its associative potential, which Reading, in approximative English, was able to make entirely his own, while nudging readers to tune into the tradition of 'heroic hexameter' (p.43) – 'heroic' pointing towards the resilience required to withstand elegiac subject-matter [LI]:

> The use of elegiac distich was very conscious in that I first of all felt…what I'm writing here is a sustained elegy and it's not inappropriate to use the earliest kind of elegiacs that we have…They have the kind of gravitas that I'm talking about and cadence. I think ordinary hexameters do as well, but they aren't used much by English writers, for some reason which I…don't at all understand. Again, I know that this sounds very silly and childish, but they have the kind of music that I simply respond to and feel at home with and feel is correct for me and for the sort of things that I'm saying and for that kind of weight. It's… trying to achieve a kind of gravity without looking as if I'm trying too hard, or at least operating several bluffs at once to try and gloss over the fact that in this day and age it's very difficult to write serious stuff with a kind of musical gravitas about it without looking simply ridiculous. And so it's a constant battle to try and bluff your way through – doing that.

However, the dactylic foundations had already been intuitively laid in *For the Municipality's Elderly*. From this followed Reading's distich, his Alcmanic and Alcaic strophe (as from *Going On*) and his asynartetic compositions (as from *Final Demands*) [LI]: 'It's simply a combination of dactyls and spondees that I feel good with in *English*… – more than I do with iambics although I might choose to use them occasionally.'[9]

The first elegiac distich is press reportage. A neutral voice hypomnemnically records a violent attack by two youths and quotes the mother of the eight-month-old victim at a police-station (p.11):

> 'He told me "This is how we earn our living, this and the dole like."
> Then he just wiggled the sharp, smashed slivers into her eye.'

> Promptly the mother gave over her golden wedding-ring, also
> three pounds in cash and a watch (silver, engraved 'My True Love'),

> but the attackers slashed Sharen twice more – in the mouth, and a deep cut
> neatly round one chubby knee. Then they strolled leisurely off.

The only comment comes form a C.I.D. officer, the hopeless inadequacy of which is emphasised by bold newspaper print: ' **"This is a callous assault…"'**. All the violent deeds in the book are preceded by a litotic haiku epigraph: '*Few atrocities / of which H. sap can conceive / remain unfulfilled*' – a shocking thought, amplified by the double negation of 'few' and 'un', and by being placed on the "wrong" side of the page, appropriately at the end of the line. The *ploce* 'H. sap.', which had so far been connoted with a scientific outlook, henceforward bears the mark of Cain.

The assault was observed by several passers-by, but 'nobody wanted to know' (a reaction doubtlessly shared by some readers). In fact, Viv is the only one who ever actually does anything at the cost of getting hurt herself, once rescuing a small boy from a dog attack (p.12); she also tells some impudent children off for spitting, only to be spat at herself (p.13). Ironically, though, one of the muggers can later be identified by his tattoo ('Mam') as Viv's unemployed son. His arrest thus produces more hurt, namely to his mother; as she tells the lady whose dog attacked the child, ' "still, you *must* still love your own; if he's bad, he's *still* my boy"' (p.21).

In *Ukulele Music*, the victims of a crime are usually children and old people, and the perpetrators unemployed youths or immigrants. (To avoid sociopolitical misunderstanding, Viv explains (p.41): '*So even if they are out of work it is NOT RIGHT they should hurt their own townpeoples. Any road it is too late now.*') Bottles are hurled from a bridge at people waiting for a bus (p.12),[10] an 88-year-old woman is robbed and raped (p.19), pedestrians are knifed for the hell of it (p.37). And, meanwhile, the criminals on the international, political level kill hundreds of victims at a time (pp.19-20). Nobody need wonder about the adolescents' morals as long as their governments 'function by mores / not altogether removed from their own bestial codes' (p.39).

The desolation evident in the city architecture, summed up in the image of the 'cast concrete span (aerosolled WANKERS and TREV)' (p.12), is mirrored in the sordid diction of the children who call adults 'Fucking bastards' (p.12). Ironically, what people mean by 'Them animals is disgusting' (p.17), is not themselves, but the neurotic animals in the London Zoo, a mirror of their own species, neatly illustrated by the image of the cardboard lion and its human faces.[11]

The crude language used by the young, and sometimes by the poet-persona, met with disapproval in some quarters, because it is repulsive rather than poetic language (the same had already happened with "unpoetic" subject-matter). Of course the restricted code is repellent, in print especially – but the shock has a function. However, it cannot be assumed that all readers are prepared to investigate this: 'Reading doesn't feel he'll ever be popular, widely

well thought of, because of bad language, gory detail, etc, even
though the language he hears around him every day is worse and the
gore isn't invented. People don't want to think about it' (Hart, M).[12]

The abuse Reading himself directs at his favourite targets
throughout his œuvre – i.e. on the 'Plashy Fen School', literary
critics, religious and political fanatics, 'reps and execs in *Plastics and
Packaging*', narrow-minded people, and of course himself – is less
of a problem. Reading: 'In contemporary British society insult is a
formality, as in the ranks of the Army, and a healthy deflation.' Much
more important is its literary function within the bigger context:
'The silly cheap insult, I repeat, has its place' (Jenkins, 1985, p.11).

> Making words new and inventing words is one of the ingredients...
> also using words from all ends of the spectrum – whether they're
> words that are not commonly used or words that are not generally for-
> mally used in literature because they are demotic or considered offen-
> sive in some circles, or obscene. All of these things have got a place
> and this is part of a general ludic exercise that anybody in the business
> takes up and takes part in (Lannan Video, M).

O'Driscoll quotes Updike to explain Reading's transgressions beyond
good taste: 'Our reading life is too short for a writer to be in any
way polite. Since his words enter into another's brain in silence
and intimacy, he should be as honest and explicit as we are with
ourselves"' (O'Driscoll, pp.207-08). What matters is that none of
the tastelessness is without a function, but nonetheless, even the
most experienced reader will not always be able to suppress a sense
of nausea and revulsion. However, as Martin Amis said, it is the
prerogative of the writer to be unshockable.

Urban violence is described in the dramatic present in *Ukulele
Music*, and different episodes are woven into a narrative web. The
leitmotif distich with its biblical echo (Isaiah 1, 1-2) and reference
to an early poem ('At Home', *Diplopic*) is repeated several times in
Ukulele Music and appears again like a *burden* in *Going On* and *Stet*
– it describes, among other things, the post-war increase in violence
in England:[13] 'Grans are bewildered by Post-Coronation disinteg-
ration; / offspring of offspring of *their* offspring infest and despoil.'

Tabloid press news becomes the raw material of this book because it
is part of the problem, as the poet angrily points out (p.38, see p.41):

> It has not been without usefulness that the Press has administered
> wholesale mad slovenly filth, glibly in apposite prose,

> for it has wholly anaesthetised us to what we would either
> break under horror of, or, join in, encouraged by trends.

> Horrible headlines don't penetrate. Pongoid crania carry
> on as though nothing were wrong.

The 'Mirror' records authentic cruelty, and hardly anybody thinks twice about it; if poetry does the same, the shock juxtaposition of content and genre can trigger a fresh understanding. Concerning Reading's 'generally successful' shock therapy, O'Driscoll quotes Stephen Vizinczey's assertion that 'great writers are not those who tell us we shouldn't play with fire, but those who make our fingers burn'. [14]

This aside, just as the deliberate provoking of revulsion in readers is not new in literature (see Swift, for example), the poetic treatment of public issues has been a matter-of-course before too – in the 18th century, that is. Why there is no further poetic transformation of the newspaper material in *Ukulele Music* is explained by the Captain towards the end, where the voices start merging (p.42): 'So, d'ye see, after putting our gear and tackle in order, / all we can do is observe, course set by helmsman and wind.' [15] Orientation by possible life-giving principles no longer works (p.45): 'During this voyage ye heavens has been so dree overcast that / no observation by stars, nor yet by sun can be got.' Asked if observation was really the only thing which was possible, Reading briefly answered [LI]: 'In Art, yes.' At readings, he gets dismayed by the question 'but is there no hope?' His answer [LI]:

> Of course not – and there's no need to elaborate on all this. And I'm not achieving anything in writing – I'm well aware of that. The whole thing is simply an expression of impotence in a way. I can't help *that*.

Nonetheless, the poet-persona eventually feels forced to defend his subject and forms (p.19-20):

> 'Life is too black as he paints it' and 'Reading's nastiness sometimes seems a bit over the top' thinks a review – so does *he*.
>
> Too black and over the top, though, is what the Actual often happens to be, I'm afraid. He don't *invent* it, you know.
>
> …
>
> **Sexual outrage on woman of 88 robbed of her savings.**
> **Finger found stuck on barbed wire.** Too black and over the top.
>
> Clearly we no longer hold *H. sapiens* in great reverence
> (which situation, alas, no elegiacs can fix).
>
> What do they think they're playing at, then, these Poetry Wallahs?
> Grub St. reviewing its own lame valedictory bunk.

This invective was emphatically repeated twice towards the end of the book, epanaphorically stressing the uniform nature of the criticism (p.40). How to compose Grub Street poetry is then exemplified in the extended metaphor of the ukulele course, the book's final narrative strand (p.41): 'those oldies we know and love!... Play each chord as indicated until a new chord is shown. Do not change…! Everyone's just got to join in and sing right along

there!') Of course, Grub Street poetry utterly disregards the condition the ship of state is in (p.13):

> Stubbornly, Taffs at their damn-fool anachronistic eisteddfods,
> still, with this breach in the hull, twang (ineffectual lyres).

> Mercury falls, it's no go, and the pink geraniums shrivel:
> ceilidh and Old Viennese drone as the packet goes down.

With this, the theme of the book is established, and the poem sarcastically closes with the first music lesson, a list of notes from the octave scale – with the last note missing.

The ukulele, the 1920s version of the oldest string instrument, the poet's lyre, has lost much of its ancestor's impact – it has a tinny sound and in this book it is appropriately accompanied by the drumming on other hollow bodies (grand piano, banjo, castanets, bones, gambas, bottles, and in another context, the fiddle).

The ukulele manual's comically imbecilic 'plinka plonk' advertises the underlying dactylic beat, but the 'Triple Roll' apparently calls for 'happytime songs' about 'Soft summer nights' (p.40), which the poet with his 'out-of-tune Uke' (p.44) is unable and unwilling to sing along with. At the same time, his ukulele produces rhythmic twangs rather than resonant music, the implication being (again) that metrical poetry is also unable to render the cruelty and desperation that this poet sees around him. As in *C*, these aesthetic worries are continually disproven by Reading's prodigious poetic imagination, yet they are tirelessly repeated throughout his œuvre.

Like the book's title, that distich ('Mercury falls...') is one of several allusions to Louis MacNeice's 'Bagpipe Music', whose answer to the world's imminent demise is dancing on the volcano, itself a reference to a poem by Auden.[16] Faced with the sinking of the 'packet', Reading's poet reacts differently (p.13):

> When all the cities were felled by the pongoid subspecies in them
> (Belfast, Jerusalem, Brum, Liverpool, Beirut) and when

> blood-swilling (Allah is wonderful) Middle-East Yahoos had purchased
> nuclear hardware, he found distich the only form apt.

The *topos* of the sinking ship of state is taken up by the politicising Viv and punningly transposed onto the narrative level (p.14):

> *well, Sir*
> *...where I thought it was just Underground Car Park ect. under ~~Civie~~ Civet*
> *Centre is not just Car Park but bunk for FALL if there is trouble, that*
> *sometimes seems likely with uSA and russiens with there bomb warfair. But*
> *what can you do? nothing and he say there are SARDINES stored in there*
> *for after siren. with DRINK. so we are all prepared thank God... So you*
> *can only keep CHEERFUL and keep trying your best. sir. for Exsample I*
> *have done the floors... I would not want sardines ALL THE TIME who*

*would? noone… But now they are on the streets the ARMY against thugs
and Mugers as that is where the REAL war is on NOW, cities in 2 halfs
with police and army and nice folks against dirty animals, so may HAVE
to go DOWN soon for THAT war.*

Viv is now actively starting to influence the poet's scheme for his
book *Ukulele Music*, just as she is influenced by him. She spends
more and more time hovering around the poet's desk: '*what can
you do as it gets worse like one of yr poetry Works that I saw when
cleaning desk with wax which I need more of soon as possible please*'
(p.15). She gets through an alarming amount of wax polish in the
book – the shining desk becomes her alibi for reading new poems,
adding new meaning to the phrase 'wax lyrical'. Thus, via notes
and poems, an amusing dialogue starts between Viv and her
employer about England, world politics, and poetry. The poet
incorporates Viv's accounts into his writing, and Viv starts voicing
her opinion about his poems, then makes 'literary' connections
(between youths in England and the sadistic crimes of Roman
Emperors), until in the third part of the book she suddenly starts
writing metrically herself.

The poet reacts differently from Viv, but is eventually affected
by her view of things. At first he concentrates on the social reality
in England and the political reality of the atomic threat of the 80s,
contradicting 'the child-soothing platitudes' – '*Life still goes on* and
It isn't the end of the world' (p.15). Then Viv introduces him to a
new thought (p.15): '*well what can you do only get on with it as you
can't sort it all out can you? we are like the man in music Hall song
that goes he play his ~~Uku uker~~ Youkalaylee while the ship went down.*'
Viv's husband (another 'Tom') plays the bones to a George Formby
song which was very popular in Blackpool during the Second World
War (p.20), which also provides the poet with a title for his book.
A variation on this theme, or rather the original image – Nero is
supposed to have recited his poetry and played the lyre to the
spectacle of Rome burning in 64 AD – is vividly illustrated in the
third part, where Viv has watched *The Twelve Caesars* on TV by
accident (p.36): '*stories about the roam Kings, dirty disgusting old lot /
… / this is called "Narrow" which plays on a fiddle, all the time Roam
burnd.*' This of course makes the poet look rather silly, especially
after his scathing comments about the 'Taffs'. He persists with the
elegiac distich for a little longer, but doubt has crept in, 'Lieder's
no art against these sorry times' (p.15).[17] Finally, in the last third
of the book, the ukulele handbook fully exposes the futility of the
poet's lyrical endeavours (p.38): 'plinkplinka plinkplinka plonk plink-
plinka plinkplinka plonk.'

In the middle section, however, Viv's other employer, the Captain, sings six sea shanties (pp.22-33) that were underread by a number of reviewers. Like many of Reading's pastiche-poems, they are written in fast-moving 3-stress metre, which Reading had used in earlier books. The Captain may sound deranged, but he is in fact re-narrating authentic disasters from the 18th century up to the H-bomb tests at Bikini. The nautical details are as authentic as the palaeontological or medical ones in previous volumes:

> The sea scenes are more or less stolen – this again is desultory reading
> …There are a number of accounts from the eighteenth and nineteenth
> centuries, which I like very much. In their context these are great feats
> of resilience, compressed into short, violently difficult stretches of
> time.[18]

Apart from their function as a counterpoint to the mundane horrors back home – '*worse things happen at SEA!*' (p.18) – the maritime poems also indirectly corroborate both the positive principle of the book, Viv's 'resilience' (see also the structural and metaphorical parallels between those two parts), and the poet's compulsion to versify. Another function is the allegory of the Ship of State going down (a conceit invented by Alcman), which on this level links up with the past glory of England's naval power. The stories also prepare the ground for the Captain's clairvoyance in the last part, and they are parables, too – as well as being a good, unusual read in their own right.

The catastrophes are litotically rendered in archaic, lyrical language and a distanced tone, bringing out their dramatic and historic potential. A fire on board detonates the barrels of gunpowder, killing 65 sailors, so that the only survivor 'hymned being simply extant' (p.24); after another shipwreck, a crew is stranded for six years in Patagonia under the most wretched conditions, sending the captain raving mad (p.26),

> and upon bleached seal bones he played
> hour after hour in uncanny
> tattoo as to harmonise
> with a wordless mindless dirge
> as he moithered, moithered, moithered,
> weird, xysterical airs,
> yea, even unto the end.[19]

After a fierce battle and shortly before going down, the survivors of two enemy crews sing through the night to the rhythm produced with an empty bottle (p.31). The impulse for rhythmic song 'e'en in pitching Gulphward' (p.33) – a kind of whistling in the dark – is deeply human and inextinguishable, as many more examples in the book suggest; in this image we also find this poet's poetic self-confession. The natives of Oroolong deliriously and literally 'dance till they drop' to fiddle-music (p.28); they have only just discovered the white man's fire-weapons, 'puzzling their foes, / who could not comprehend / how that their people dropped / without receiving any / apparent blow' (p.27). The same fate overtakes the white man himself in March 1954 'hundred miles off Bikini' (p.29):

Hands mustered on deck,
saw, to larboard, a fireball,
like a rainbow brand,
rise up from ye horizon,
silent, that was the queer thing.

Minutes passed; the blast
suddenly shook the ocean,
shuddered our whole hulk,
hands was belayed with affright,
none, howsomdever, hurt (*then*).

This anachronistic pastiche, which also draws attention to itself metrically (it consists of 5 tankas),[20] serves as the link between the 'bunks' mentioned to Viv by the Captain in the first part, and the atomic bunker in the third. (The bunker is, just like the atomic explosion, not mentioned by name: unspeakable.)

What the Captain says about the fifth disaster, shipwreck by fire, is a parable of endless warfare and the political and ecological cul-de-sac that the modern world has got itself into (p.30): 'the unfortunate / victims has only two / alternatives – to seek death/ in one element in order / to avoid it in another. /... / We, the spectators, ourselves / were the poor players also / in the bloody scene...' In the sixth and last narrative, the skipper finally explains why he sings shanties – a parable of the poet who charts the catastrophic development of civilisation ('no source of pleasure') because, like the Ancient Mariner, he must (p.32): 'I am impelled to convey / salt observations, a tar's / chantey habit, d'ye see?' (in hemiepes). In its uncertainty regarding the future of mankind ('we'), the third stanza is one of the most positive passages in Reading's œuvre: 'I know not whether... / we shall set forth again'. Later, however, there is no doubt that the deadly alternative – 'or rest in quiet' – is the only remaining 'choice', necessitating the decision to 'return to the deep' (p.42) – with devastating results. 'Our strange propensity / to undertake voyages, / ... / whatever adversity / befalls us' merges with the poet's need to record all of this and 'therefore continue to play'.

> And shall it, now, be counted
> as ye dignified defiance
> in us towards our fateful
> merciless element,
> or gull naiveté,
> cousin to recklessness,
> that, e'en in pitching Gulphward,
> our salt kind brings forth chanteys?

This lyrical stanza (p.33) contains one of Reading's rare, open statements of his poetic creed and is one of the core existential passages in his œuvre, reminiscent of Beckett. At the centre of Reading's poetry is this 'dignified defiance', this heroically stoical endurance, a worthy gesture at the edge of the abyss.

The subsequent third part of the book begins with the strong contrast of Viv's first own elegiac distich, which is simply touching and a moment of great tenderness in this book (p.34): '*Who would have thought it Sir, actually putting ME in a WRITING! / me and the Capting and ALL. What a turn up for the books.*' Of course she is polishing again and has just discovered what the poet does with her notes. That she then enters the poet's lyrical space is only consistent, and a measure of her solidarity with her employer's poetic problems. Besides, speaking in distich is not so difficult in the first place: '*Still, when you're USED to it like, then you can speak natural*'.[21] What is more – as she is now on the same level as her poet, she has the right to back him up against his uninformed critics (e.g. Roger Scruton, who had levelled the charge of anti-Semitism; p.40): '*Don't you go brooding and brooding and getting all of a state sir / just cos the LITARY GENT don't seem to like your nice books. / / Like the old man used to always say "When we wants YOU to chirp-up, / matey, we'll rattle the cage" – don't heed their old tommy-rot.*'

The unusual enjambement of two other distichs in this passage announces the structural 'enjambement' of the third part. Up to the end, there are no more pauses or spaces; pages 34 to 46 form one text. As a structural consequence and an existential necessity, the voices typographically run into each other in the last polyphonic part of the book, culminating in wild cacophony. Nothing holds together any more in this linguistic expression of the final detonation.

The Captain's 'yarns' are now mixed up with authentic reports from the newspaper, as Viv explains (p.45), and the deaths described are always accompanied by music (pp.35-36). The poet, in turn, takes up Viv's comparison ('*Roam is BAD TIME*', p.37) – and illustrates it with further reports of evil acts committed in British cities (pp.37-38). Meanwhile Viv's account of the broken barometer connects the storm brewing at sea with the atmospheric pressure at home, both literally and metaphorically, thus referring back to the beginning of the book (MacNeice's barometer poem) and also merging with the book's main thematic line (p.37): '*so it has broke and the needle now ALWAYS points to the STORMY – / he is a fool to have PLAYED (Formby)*'.

The direction is clear: 'Gulphward'. There is another, more literal reason for the typographical proximity of the voices. As from the beginning of the third part Viv, the poet, and the Captain all sit together in the said bunk under the civic centre (p.45; see p.39): '*What with the waiting and not knowing what on earth is the matter / up in the cities and that. Still, it was awful up there... not safe to walk in the streets – not that we could NOW, of course / / only it's funny for us being down here under the Civic / Centre – I thought it was all Underground Car Parks and that.*' 'Here' is the underground shelter, from where there is no return. As if at sea, where the alternative is destruction by water or by fire, today's personae have to face civic violence '*up there*' and then the final atomic strike in their underground fallout shelter under the Civic Centre. The Captain can still not name this last incident ('synne rises firey and red – sure indycation o' gales', p.39), but he is the first to perceive it and then talks about nothing else. He is not mad: these are not hallucinations. As Viv says, '*sometimes I thinks the Capting's the only / sane one among the whole lot*' (p.39).

The fable of the sheep in the ship's hull is the counterpart to the story of Noah's ark (p.42): one sail after the other has to be reefed because of the 'falling barometer'. By the end of the book, the slight breeze has turned into a roaring storm – as predicted by the Captain, prophesied by the Old Testament prophets, and announced by God.[22] The captain and his 'messmates' steer towards the dark Cimmerian land, the bottom of the ocean, death (p.42):

> Here is perpetual smoke of a city unpierced by sunlight
> where ye Cimmerians dwell, unvisible from above.[23]
>
> Here we make fast and drive up from the bilges, bleating, the
>   stunned sheep
> into these bunkers of lead, granite and greyness and stench.

This allegory of radioactively polluted humans (see 'highest grade sheep's gut', p.46) being driven to the bunker has a lyrical and metaphorical density that gives the unity of the book a universal dimension. Allegorical and archetypal supra-texts also make the supra-personal voice of the last pages more forcible. Invoking James Thomson (*City of Dreadful Night*), Pound's 'Canto I',[24] and

Homer's description of the very last journey in the *Odyssey* (XI.14),[25]
Reading has everybody in the same boat steering 'Gulphward'
towards the ultimate explosion. That there will be no escape is
clear from two nautical terms: the only light in the dark sky is the
'Fire of St Elmo' (p.45) – this ball of fire hovers around the top
of the mast of ships in distress; and the 'messmates' get ready for
'Davy Jones' (p.46), the sea spirit, whose 'locker' is a sailor's very
last destination.

In perishing, the individuality of the personae becomes irrelevant;
the voices run into one another in ever shorter intervals until they
become interchangeable; Viv (p.46): '*mind you the Powertree Bloke
and the Capting doesn't arf GABBLE – / what with the Capting his
YARNS: tother keeps chaingin is VOICE / / anyone'd think they was
Everyone All Times Everywhere…*'. What remains? One year before
Chernobyl took place, the '*Powertree Bloke*' asks journalistic ques-
tions (p.41): 'What was the level of contamination? Where had it
come from? / What is a "low level" leak? Why was the public not
told?' No answers are given.

In this sense, the chirpy ukulele instructions are not only grot-
esquely ironic in their cacophonic displacement, but take on a sec-
ond meaning. Here of all places the author encodes further poetic
statements about his recording of the Actual in orderly metres. It
had been made clear that he cannot achieve anything by metre,
but this of course is only one end of the Reading paradox (p.40):

> Let that wrist hang loose! Start slow and then increase speed until you
> produce a smooth, even tone. Well done! the speed you move the pick
> across the strings will depend on what we call *tempo* (that means *time*)
> of the number you're accompanying.

The exact 'tempo' used in *Ukulele Music* is also explained – this
time in the nautical register (p.43): 'make yr pentameters taut…keep
spondees and dactyls close-clewed, / trim yr heroic hexameter' ('The
Triple Roll is one of the prettiest of all Uke strokes!'). The term
'heroic' instead of 'dactylic' hexameter must not be underestimated
in its significance for Reading's art. The intention to muster a
'heroic' gesture of resistance in view of the 'gathering maelstrom' is
in the final analysis superior to the other, more specifically literary
aim ('all we can do is observe'). Morose and utterly nihilistic as
Reading portrays his persona in the very late books, he still com-
bines a depressed world view with formal elegance, as Larkin did:

> [I have] purposefully resurrected things like classical hexameters and
> classical elegiac distich… Now that's not only appropriate in logical
> terms but – this measure did not get invented by accident – it has a
> certain kind of cadence that is appropriate, a falling cadence…When I

said, rather foolishly, that Larkin is a bit cheerless for my tastes, what I meant was that he [puts forward] a genuine middle-class voice of someone who is genuinely afraid of dying, principally. Now we're all afraid of dying – there's no dispute there – [but] Larkin doesn't seem to me to want to engage in any kind of heroic approach. Now, that would be what I would want to do...not exactly [giving] comfort, but going one step beyond... And that again is where something of that selection of metre comes in... By that I mean actually being prepared to embrace the whole shitworks of it, and accept that and not whine about it (Edgar, p.56).

The penultimate verse is by Viv, whom by now the poet greatly admires (p.46): '*Whatsisname says to me "Viv you're the life and soul of the party' – / Viv, he says, MEANS life, you know (in Greek or Lating or French)'*. The Captain's narrated resilience is demonstrated in "real life" by Viv, not that she has a choice (p.45): '*get on with THIS Viv and THAT Viv and, well you has to LIVE don't you?*' As Reading told an interviewer, 'In *Ukulele Music* you also have a woman whose great quality is to *carry on*' (Jenkins, 1985, p.11).

The following, final tones of the sinking poet are hollow. The book ends, logically, with the diacritical notation of a perfect elegiac distich and an echo of last sound: 'plinkplinka plonk'.

Going On (1985):
Tension / Impotence

In *Going On,* Reading starts unifying. Subject-matter, structure, metrics, the leitmotif distich and other verbal echoes all carry on from *Ukulele Music,* with which the book was originally published in one volume, and many other Reading staples recur in modified form: the prominence of voices, the *topos* of 'inexpressibility', pre-emptive lampoon attacks on his critics, the sea storm apocalypse anticipated by the augur's observations of fateful birds, the messengers of death. However, new metrical patterns are introduced and explained, to instruct reader and Muse alike.

If one is familiar with the poetic devices favoured by Reading, *Going On* is probably his most direct and uncomplicated book. However, the reviewers did not have a lot to say about it,[1] and *Going On* seems to have left a somewhat diffuse impression. Indeed, more careful structuring and fewer tabloid pieces might have brought the book's agenda into focus better. It takes too long for the reader to understand how the book is structured; the impatience or irritation which has built up in the meantime cannot wholly subside until the end. Reading [LI]: 'It's probably a bit rough and crudely put together. I've noticed that a lot of people aren't anxious to reprint it... I don't really care too terribly, but it was material that I wouldn't particularly want to discard.'

The theme of the breach between omnipresent violence and impotent poeticising is again prevalent and accepted as such; so Viv's credo, 'just Going On, Getting On With It' (p.66), is the only thing left to do. As in Auden's 'The Epigoni' – an influential poem for Reading's 'poetic credo and practice', as his friend Coggrave wrote [M] and Reading confirmed [C] – it means, in Reading's case too, writing verse, as the Alcmanic epigraph explains:

> [Bit of a habit, this feigned indignation,
> various forms, Elegiacs, Alcmanics...
> gets like a game, the old global débâcles.
> Just Going On remains possible through the
> slick prestidigital art of Not Caring/Hopelessly Caring.]

Reading's use of the slash aptly expresses the by now familiar paradox. 'Not Caring' is a prerequisite for mental stability, achieved by versifying, which at the same time is also an expression of Reading's humanistic hopelessness – as are the allegedly neutral journalistic poems or the angry aggressive ones, which are all presented from behind literary masks refracting sensitivity and the pseudo-Protean stance.[2] Under the term 'persona', Preminger explains the functions of masks, which had also been discussed by Yeats, Pound, Eliot et al:

> The mask permits the poet to say things that for various reasons he could not say in his own person or could say only with a loss of artistic detachment; the mask permits the poet to explore various life-styles without making an ultimate commitment; it is a means for creating, discovering, or defining the self; it prevents the artist from being duped by the limitations of his own vision; it is a means for the expression of ideals that the poet may not be able to realise in his personal life; it is an indispensable condition for effective personal communication.

Masks, or stances, as Reading calls them, are used as from the very first book. Later, in *Final Demands* (p.135), he expressly names stances as a device he always uses; it is an integral component of his œuvre. Reading explained the mechanics [LI]:

> I've quite often tried to be, in a sort of Robbe-Grillet way, like a camera rather than actually participating. Of course, there are huge contradictions to that because I am very personally involved with all the things that I write about, but I'm pretending not to be always, and trying to find new ways of appearing not to be, and that's one of them. I think there is more or less a complete ironing out – the exception would prove the rule – of the first person... I have always liked that idea of complete impartiality, or at least apparent impartiality. Now I know that a lot of people think that in many things I have been wearing my heart very much on my sleeve, and it's to the detriment of the poems. Now they're probably right and I'm sorry about that. But... I don't really like saying this... I feel very passionately about the stuff that I write. That's why I write it. You know, everything, even when it may look very banal, like '10x10x10', is only done because of some strong personal reason. It's very, very personal poetry, but I hope that's not too apparent... So it's a constant pretending game that I'm impartial and this doesn't matter to me... Of course it *does*, but you can't go round saying that it does because...emotional unburdening is not the function of art. Of course it does it, but it should be an invisible element, and the personal element is to be experienced by the listener, spectator, reader. I wouldn't want to commit anything to print unless I felt that it was *not* to do with me but to do with human beings.

The many stances, personae, masks and Chinese boxes are indispensable for the artistic arrangement of all the alleged contrasts, paradoxes, and open secrets. As Reading told an interviewer, 'I had the energy to be bothered by these things. I was aware of the paradox and had the energy to grapple with it' (Potts, 1990, p.95).

This poet does not 'play games', nor is his stance 'Thatcherite',

as one misguided critic insists.[3] Reading himself thinks his artistic
strategies should not cause any educated person any problem –
'that's literary one times one, Part One, for tiny-tots' [C]; as he
says [LI]: 'It's what somebody called "the Protean stance"... And
it's this constant dancing about between "the slick prestidigital art
of not caring/hopelessly caring".' This way, it seems that there is
an equality of value in the opinions and attitudes depicted, as if
they were all equally valid or equally flawed. Reading [LI]:

> I'm only saying that they exist and then go on to slug them because
> there isn't really a Protean stance at all; there *pretends* to be. The
> poems are very tendentious if that's the word I want.

Not all stances are marked as such or are decodable in an un-
ambiguous way: '[*What's 40 years here or there on the chrono-strati-
graph?*, you wrote. / Striking a stance you were then; really believe
it, though, now]' (p.135) can of course be a new stance again – or
possibly not. Another ambiguity occurs in *Going On* where 'coded
behavioural special characteristics' are deterministically seen as lead-
ing to violence (p.78, 'Specific'). This opinion possibly complements
an explanation given in *Ukulele Music* – 'mindless and jobless and
young' – and is reiterated in *Stet* ('"Unemployed / Hopeless"
doesn't sufficiently / serve to explain Cro-Magnon atrocities, / vin-
dicate *Homo troglodytes*. / Dominant morphisms wield big cudgels',
p.113). How many stances are involved here? Reading [LI]:

> I was trying to draw sufficient distance between me and the subject-
> matter and to actually become aloof from it. There *is* a constant tension
> which is between despair, almost, and hatred and affection. Now, how
> you express this tension I don't really know and probably haven't done
> it at all successfully. But that tension exists is all I'm saying: that I
> have great misanthropic tendencies, but also at times feel great warmth
> toward humankind; that the two operate as uncertain yoke-fellows.

The contradictions of 'Caring/Not Caring' and their artistic pre-
sentation as well as the holding on to normality by way of versify-
ing are exemplified in the very first poem by an invocation (p.49,
'Subways'): 'Muse! Sing the Rasta, who stabbed out a baby's eye
with a Biro /... / down in the crazed uriniferous subway under-
neath Blake St. / (leading to Wordworth Estate)'. In this light,
even teaching 'Creative Writing' appears beneficial: 'Half-batty
Writer-in-Residence meets the / totally lunatic amateur hopefuls';
but even if poetry does not make anything happen, this is the
nearest that Reading comes to saying that poetry is *not* completely
impotent (p.76; 'All Together Now'): '[**Poets' & Novelists' Surgery**
– ballocks. / Still, I suppose, if it keeps them from other, more
harmful mischief...]'.

After this, the elegiac distichs (typeset differently this time) go
through another lengthy tableau of horrific atrocity, presented in
the usual journalese, so perhaps it is hardly surprising that *Going
On* did not meet with much enthusiasm. The first poem, a steno-
graphical protocol of a trial about the savage treatment of a prisoner
by police (p.50, 'Stenog'), implies with the pun on 'Constable
Renton is charged' that more villainy will follow, and so it does: a
representative cross-section, from domestic crimes to international
kakistocracies, almost always perpetrated by men and authentic all
the way through [C]. Satanic murders by members of the sect
'Rats Chapter' (p.52); the castration of a little boy on a public toi-
let by youths (p.55); injustice in a South African court of law
(p.56, 'Currencies'); the incomprehensible guerilla war politics of a
Central (or South) American terrorist (p. 59; 'Dilucidación'); Robert
Mugabe's lies about the massacre of his opponent Joshua Nkomo's
supporters, the kaffirs in Ndebele (p.65); the abuse or murder of
children because of bed-wetting (pp.61, 62) by British parents who
are not tried because there was no 'gross negligence'; and then the
lapidary sentence '[Clearly, then, some of us entertain scant regard
for the kiddies; / ditto the kiddies for us – malice reciprocal, dread.]'
(p.62) and the sadistic torture of an old lady by two teens (pp.57-58).
Mundus inversus, homo barbarus. Tom Paulin enthused:

> In his most brilliant and assured volume... Reading blasts the national
> consciousness into tacky fragments and exposes the insane ugliness of
> British life... His manic self-consciousness designs a poetry of extreme
> risk, and this is appropriate to the crazed astringency and philistinism
> of the present social moment (Paulin, pp.291, 290).

Hopelessness is universal, omnipresent: 'These are the days of the
horrible headlines', and relentlessly Reading summarises them
again (p.67); they traumatise this writer into obsessive re-writes
because tabloid evidence no longer hurts. Corrective measures
cannot be expected from the public, and even court sentences go
against the law and humanity. At this point, though, nothing can
counter his nagging awareness of his own pointless and tedious
impotence (p.58):

> [... page after page of trite news reports
> rehashed, vomiting squalor,
>> Over-exposure to vile
>> madness (from verse or the box)
>
> makes for immunity. None of the
> ghastly nasties he re-spews
>> eases or mends with the mere
>> telling *again* of its filth.]

A public reaction against the status quo is called for, but seems naive, which is why Viv loyally takes on the task. As in 'Mrs Harris' Petition', she writes a letter to the editor (a very long Alcmanic strophe, pp.70-71), expressing incomprehension of why the 'GOOD BRAINS / out of the BIG unerversity College' in politics and 'PRY MINISTERS' do not see that taxes should not be spent on Cruise Missiles, but on schools, hospitals, and pensions. (Viv's husband backs her up in *Stet*, p.88). Her unfailing logic: if all the money is spent on missiles the feared Russian invaders will not find anything worth having when they arrive (p.70).

> How to stop vilence and crime and the warfair
> that is the questions what faces the whole WORLD
> goverments nowdays and what is the answer
> I dont know nor does the HUSBAND we only
> have to get on with it just GOING ON...

In the middle of the book, the atrocities in elegiac distich are abruptly and anacoluthically cut short (p.66): '[Who wants to dwell on it all? / *Nil Carborundum*, OK?'. The poet considers which form could still be adequate after elegy; the Alcmanics, debunked as 'fun' even before they get properly started, are then paraded as the new product (used once before in the Epigraph; p.66):

> Shake off those gloomy and old-fangled
> boring, sad Elegiacs!
>> Try our own new-look re-vamped
>> Alcmanic Strophe, wherein
>
>> form, ham-philosophy, alcoholism
>> may not *transcend,* but do celebrate simply
>> just Going On, Getting On With It. Try our
> fun Catalectic Tetrameter, with Hexameter added!]

The first complete Alcmanic poem therefore depicts some current anaesthetic measures such as alcohol, sex, or blinkered vision, but not without a good proportion of sympathy: 'lovers seek refuge in succulent plump flesh, / booze themselves innocent of the whole shit-works' (p.67). Another way of enduring the present is to live in the past (as does the old dear who ends up in the mental hospital, pp.53-55), or, like 'Outraged of Telford', to vent one's anger in a letter to the editor, both a commendable and hopeless gesture (p.62).

However, as the astrophysicist's endless elaborations about the furthest detectable star in the universe and the inevitable end of the universe make plain, religion offers no escape for those who are more scientifically inclined. Apart from that, religion accounts for much of the mayhem in the first place. More than elsewhere Reading attacks militant religious fanaticism in abusive, blackly farcical *silloi* which could earn him a death sentence any time; this is especially true of the much-quoted hyperbolic tirade with its hammering alliterations and participles, which further intensify the abusive content (pp.72-73; 'Exegetic'): [4]

> This is unclean: to eat turbots on Tuesdays,
> tying the turban unclockwise at cockcrow,
> cutting the beard in a south-facing mirror,
> wearing the mitre whilst sipping the Bovril,
> chawing the pig and the hen and the ox-tail,
> ...
> loving the platypus more than the True Duck,
> death without Afterlife, smirking in Mecca,
> laughing at funny hats, holding the tenet
> how that the Word be but fucking baloney,
> ...
>> Started by *Australopithecus,* these are
>> time-honoured Creeds (and all unHoly doubters
>> shall be enlightened by Pious Devices:
>> mayhems of tinytots, low-flying hardwares,
>> kneecappings, letterbombs, deaths of the firstborns,
> total extinction of infidel unclean wrong-godded others).

Reading explained the juxtaposition of evolutionism and theology in his œuvre:

> I'm concerned with not being so *conceited* as to think that there's something special and privileged going on which we are somehow heirs to. That involves all sorts of terrible complications with people's theological beliefs, it cuts across and annihilates them. What upsets me is that people can't cope with seeing their own end, whether personal or wholesale, the end of a species. Of course we're unhappy about dying, and it would be nice to go on sipping Campari until the day is done. But I'm astonished and horrified by the beliefs opposed to the attitudes I'm assumed to have, by the things that people actually *believe*...When people are insulted by their gods being insulted, this is baffling and shocking to me, a simple man who is insulted hugely, in the normal course of events. The majority of people who have ordinary sorts of jobs are insulted every day – their appearance, beliefs, whatever...What horrifies me... and comes as a surprise... is that people continue to be bothered by such things, and that dangerous, violent, horrible, malevolent theisms thrive... So, one makes the silly, cheap insult. The silly cheap insult, I repeat, has its place (Jenkins, 1985, p.11).

The antithesis to both religious destructiveness and Cimmerian darkness is celebrated in rare, happy (and therefore all the more effective), pastoral hymns. Reading starts inventing his own metra episyntheta here, reshuffling classical metrical verses. The elegiac sequence is simply reversed for the hymn, 'it was a logical thing to do' [LI]: first the pentameter, then the hexameter, celebrating a secular Supper at Easter, outdoors, sharing the bread and wine, locus amoenus. The singularity of the experience and the special elation stand out all the more clearly as this is the only celebratory poem in the entire book, a sharp contrast to the horror elsewhere. O'Driscoll describes the ambiguity of Reading's lyrical songs of praise:

> Reading's wariness concerning readymade or inflated emotions towards nature has led him to respond with a blend of helpless celebration and sceptical asides. The effect, though, is to convey the fragile sense of beauty or celebration all the more convincingly for having over-whelmed his doubts... A punctuated idyll is offered as a sop to those who ask 'Doesn't he ever write about *happiness?*' His suspicion that he may be surrendering to 'mawkish platitudes' gives way to some ravishing lines (O'Driscoll, p.204).

If love, nature, food and wine satisfy emotional and bodily needs, the intellect turns to the natural sciences – the second antithesis, in the form of an astrophysicist's explanations about the end of the universe. The successor to the palaeontologist, whose perspective was still not large enough, he researches extra-galactic quasars, luminous objects. The dimensions are beyond human grasp: the human eye can just about see the Andromeda Galaxy, which is 2 ¼ million light years away. The 'Double Quasar', how-ever, is about 10,000 million light years away (pp.77-78, 'Weak Signals'): 'cosmic vicissitudes, cooling expansion; / no need to bugger *each other* up further – / all hands susceptible anyway to the old astral physics.' No other framework would expose the total insignificance of mankind better. Reading:

> The double quasar is the furthest currently detectable object in the universe – if you want to reduce us to as little as you possibly can, then you want the biggest scales available, and mine in *Diplopic* and *C* are rather puny. That initial burst by oxygen-producing algae, manifest in the Bulawayan stromatolites, was all the same an extraordinary event that makes us look rather unremarkable, for all our books and bottles.[5]

Within this antithetical structure, Reading intersperses five purple patches (pp.51, 68-69, 75, 79, 80). In the psychotherapeutic stance, the Reverend Wolly rather unsuccessfully translates the *Lyrical Fragments* and *Lyrica Graeca* (i.e. distichs, Alcmanics and Alcaics after Alcman and Alcaeus).[6] In 1835 he offers the pieces for publi-cation to another Oxford 'Old Boy', the (authentic) editor of *Quarterly Review*, J.G. Lockhart (p.51).

We all grow grey at the temples and
Time's snow creeps down our cheek-bones;
  We should be active while sap
  Courses yet fresh in our joints.

Carpe diem! The classicist Reverend Wolly himself quotes Horace, who also often used Alcaics, to his unsuspecting Sunday congregation (p.68): 'Though we had nothing to do with them, we must / suffer for Sins of our sires' ('Delicta maiorum immeritus lues', *Odes*, III.vi.1). He also refers to Virgil and because of the 'Madness abroad' retreats to his lyrical asylum in 'Claresmould-cum-Cowperly, Snotts.' His home is – like himself – tellingly named; it also houses a 'pale horse' (p.68). The thematic relevance of the Reverend's poetic endeavours is expressed in his second letter to Lockhart, who neither replies, nor ever prints the 'feeble Alcmanics' (p.79) in his magazine (p.68):

> [Far from the clash of arms, having the cure of
> Claresmould-cum-Cowperly, all I can hope is
> these humble fragments translated may lighten
> some reader's heart, as my own is disburthened
> daily engaging in, if futile, harmless
> little unhurtful things...]

In the 19th century, translating classical texts was, according to Reading [LI], 'a nervous tic; everybody was doing that kind of thing then'. He enjoys reading such translations and wrote his own with the help of classicist Mark Pitter. Pitter translated the Fragments of Alcman, which Reading then did into 'bad bits of translationese in the line of a 19th century clergyman' [C]. Reading explained [LI]: 'I got a few very literal and purposefully rather stilted-sounding translations which I then put back into some semblance of Alcaics and Alcmanics. They were purposefully jokey – or meant to be.' The harmlessness of these translations illustrates the book's epigraph, and also links up with the exopoetic function of teaching 'Creative Writing'. As insignificant as versifying may be – at least it does not harm anybody, and it helps the writer.

Like the other stances, these passages also provide Reading with a mask for stilted, archaic and pompous ventriloquism [LI]:

> Classical translation is a genre that I find very useful and very intriguing and very attractive. The idea of any 19th century English cleric having a go at the classics produces a quite amusing result very often. You get endless not very good translations which are hootingly funny by their crassness... On the other hand, I have quite a lot of sympathy with it because in a time when it's very difficult to be grandiloquent and remain serious that's one way of getting over the problem. If ... you're being a 19th century clerical translator, then it's possible to say things in a way which would otherwise be regarded as stilted, even unintentionally humorous... so it's a kind of double-bluff in that way.

The Reverend's mental ease is destroyed when in 1841 the term 'dinosaur' is established and when in 1859 Darwin publishes *On the Origin of Species*, which the pious man can only refer to as 'that book' (p.80). The story of the Creation is tottering, so Wolly (just like his literary creator) has to apply the hexametrical balancing therapy (p.75): 'All I can hope is for solace in these poor impotent strophes.' As if we were reading a 19th-century prelude to *Ukulele Music*, we see times getting worse, the nation in decline, and the Reverend's son killed on 25 October 1854 in the Crimean War ('under Cardigan'). Finally, after over 50 years (1888), the Reverend states towards the end of the century (p.79):

> [Yet I persist in this unhelpful habit,
> sham, atavistic, unwanted, indulgent.
> …
> (… these graspings at dignity through my
> crude adaptation of Alcaeus' metric
> into sad English beyond Elegiac…
> In an old form is there dignity yet there?)…
> …
> I have derived from Alcaeus' metrical
> four-line invention; twisted to travesty,
>   rudely reduced to dactyls, spondees,
>   quantity ousted by Englished stressing.]

Rhapsodistically, some of the translated Fragments go astoundingly well with the events in *Going On*; others remain dark ('simply purposefully badly translated' [LI], as Reading revealed). Some passages can be illuminated: 'Myrsilus' (p.79), whose death is celebrated, is not only a phonological pun, but really was a tyrannical politician, whom Alcman attacked in this Fragment, inventing the image of the sinking Ship of State. Furthermore, the 'Aphrodite' verses (p.74) with their erotic undercurrent may have disorientated the celibate Reverend somewhat – later he mentions in passing 'my loins' fruit'. These puzzling passages are, as Reading explained [LI],

> almost literally rendered from what Fragments remain, which themselves are rather incongruous, and difficult… But it's meant to be completely wackily hopelessly non-translated anyway, and rendering itself comically meaningless, as a lot of these things *are*. This is one of those *raisons d'être* simply because it's quite delightful stuff, to have those weird inversions and so forth. Meant to be funny. Obviously [*laughter*] falls short.

A conspicuously large number of different Fragments are about birds, e.g. about *Accipiter*, possibly to be seen in oppposition to the dove. It becomes evident that the Alcmanic and Alcaic translations of ornithological observations correspond to the function of the nautical weather report of *Ukulele Music*. The signals of the skies announce destruction. Especially significant is the invocation of Jupiter, who outlined the future by means of signs in the sky, bird flight, which was interpreted by augurs. The poet assumes the augur's role (p.74): '*I know the Laws (or the musical modes or / Strains or the customs) of all of the winged tribe.*' The birds flee from the ocean (p.80) as messengers of death, because the final storm from *Ukulele Music* is brewing there (p.80):

> *Jupiter drizzles; out of the Heaven comes*
> *Great storm or tempest; streams of the waters are*
> *Frozen-up. Cast off (strike down) tempest,*
> *Poke the fire, mix the wine, honey'd, don't stint.*

The reaction of retiring to the warm stove is thus condoned by the poet (p.73):

> *Smugly it advocates going on sanely*
> *tendering love at a personal level...*
> [yes, there's a smugness and a paradox to that
> love which discriminates Sweetheart and Swinehound;
> 'Love me, love my madness' – non-acquiescent embracing, it should be.]

The literal proof of 'non-acquiescent embracing' follows in a procedure reminiscent of the 'Poet/Surgeon' as in *5x5x5x5x5*. The book pointedly ends with an explicit image of Christian forgiveness, with the book's first – and now seriously injured – criminal, the Rastafarian, being cradled by the poet's embrace (p.81). While much is made of Reading's indefatigable culling of the 'killing religions', its gentle, fragile counterpoints are usually overlooked. His moral outrage in the other poems is all the more convincing for its mellowing into tolerance and acceptance at the end of the book, and, indeed, in the context of the whole œuvre.

Despite all the doubts uttered in previous books, the poet clearly believes in his art; this is his conclusion, given in the final verse of the volume (p.82): '[Sanity is a feeble weapon / set against lunacy, nobly helpless.]' His 'graspings at dignity' in an 'old form ... beyond Elegiac' result in the introduction and display of an Alcaic stanza (pp.79-80) by means of its prosodic notation. Thus secured, the poet writes the last three poems in the book in this 'fossilised, civilised' form himself (pp.80-82). It is not authentically modelled on Alcaeus' quantitative stanza, which consists of two 11-syllable, one 9-syllable and one 10-syllable Alcaic. It is based on Tennyson's stress adaptation of it, hinted at here in the self-parodying second verse (p.82): [7]

> [Garnering remnants, fossilised, civilised,
> I, mealy-mouthed disruptor of harmonies,
>   strive in an old form (not strong, mayhap),
>   cunningly structural – weakly helpful?]

Reading's approximations of classical quantitative metre in English by simply substituting long/short syllables (pitch, or length) by stressed/unstressed ones (accent) are derived from Cotterill's 1911 translation of Homer's *Odyssey*. As some prescriptive prosodic pundits – Saintsbury, or Standop – would have it, this approximation does not and cannot work in English, which is allegedly iambic/anapaestic by nature.[8] The Elizabethan group 'Areopagus' had attempted writing English quantitative verse. Southey, Coleridge, Longfellow, Tennyson and Swinburne continued the experiment, and Robert Bridges was the last one to try seriously. (Kingsley's and Clough's hexameters are accentual.) Of course, owing to his 'Alexandrinanism' (the resurrection of classical metres and texts), Reading was often asked whether he thought it possible to graft classical metres onto English:

> Well, I think it can be made to work in English. This has been a long-standing debate, especially in the 19th century. It can certainly be made to work in English, or at least an equivalent can be found. Tennyson was able to find equivalents, really (Edgar, p.56).

This same equivalent is also given in Preminger as a basically simple one: 'approximation is rather the substitution of accent for pitch or length'. Matthew Arnold's encouraging suggestions along these lines in *On Translating Homer* also receive refreshing reinforcement from the prosodists Shapiro and Beum:

> It is probably impossible to reproduce in English the quality of quantitative lines...There are, however, a number of sound reasons why an English-speaking poet should study classical prosody and try his hand at imitations: by substituting his native stress for the quantitative principle he may find one or more of the classical forms congenial; and he may be led to pay more attention to the lengths of his syllables, to tempo, and indeed to acoustic quality in general... Such acquaintance was certainly fruitful for Milton and Tennyson; their rich harmonies of vowels are not an especially Anglo-Saxon characteristic... Even when [the quantities do not work out], the verse can be perfectly successful in every respect – rhythm making its ultimate appeal always to the ear rather than to anything else.[9]

Reading (who had not read their book on prosody) confirmed that this was exactly what he was doing as from the mid-1980s [LI]:

> in English, when it's messed about with and you try to use quantity rather than stress... it *can* work and you can find appropriate words, but it tends to become rather flat and is contrary to the whole nature of the language... So it doesn't seem to me to be any worry because you're getting an equivalent and you're... inventing a kind of metre which seems to achieve... magniloquence and...grandeur and out-of-the-ordinary-ness... It doesn't cause me any great soul-searching to think this isn't really authentic classical hexameter or whatever.

Also, one rather ironic argument should be mentioned as to whether stress can replace quantity: it worked once before, when the Latin poets of the 5th century approximated Greek metres by substituting accents – from which the accentual metre of modern languages was developed in the first place.[10] Even Virgil's translations of Homer are read by some as a compromise between quantitative original and Latin stress. These neo-classical metrics and their cadences have a *gravitas* which replaces the light tone of Reading's early works and takes over the function of holding the reader's attention, previously achieved by the virtuosity of forms and artistic manoeuvres. They also came to stay.

Besides Tennyson, Reading names H.B. Cotterill's translation of the *Odyssey* (1911) as the biggest influence on his own 'approximation'. From this he took the caesura after the fourth hexametrical foot, the bucolic diaeresis [C]. It also taught him many other important things:

> Cotterill's approximation to classical metre... [has meant a lot to me]. But what I think of as the important and attractive things about Homer are what Cotterill talks about [in his introduction].[11] ...Cotterill manages to vary the texture between, not exactly the demotic, but between the conversational and the formal, a tension which is not only interesting technically but a constant thing we're dealing with every day. So it's close not only to what poetry does technically but to what a lot of poetry is about: there's a tension between the demotic and formal in speech, as there is between the dignified and the bestial in behaviour (Jenkins, 1985, p.6).

Stet (1986):
Elegiac Celebrations

Sixteen months after *Ukulele Music*, *Stet* was published, a short book of 40 pages, at the same time as *Essential Reading*, a selection from Reading's ten books, edited by Alan Jenkins. *Essential Reading* was well received, and not only by poetry lovers: 'a must for anyone faintly interested in poetry, or not, as the case may be... *Essential Reading* is dark, grotesque, comic – but above all accessible. Buy it, you could get hooked.' And in the *Observer*'s Books of the Year Christmas list, Margaret Drabble named it as one of her three favourites of 1986.[1] *Stet* went on to win the Whitbread Poetry Award, and was shortlisted for Whitbread Book of the Year (won by Kazuo Ishiguro's novel *An Artist of the Floating World*).

When Reading had asked '*but am I Art?*' in *Fiction*, most reviewers failed to meet his challenge, but *Stet* and *Essential Reading* prompted serious engagement with the issues he explored and embodied in his work.[2] 'Well, if Goya and Bosch are art, why not?' wrote Julian Symons. 'Nobody, not Swift, nor Greene, nor Nathanael West has written better about cruelty and vulnerability,' said Jeff Nuttall, while Damian Grant called *Stet* 'a remarkable work, an updated downmarket *Waste Land* which assails us with the sights and sounds of a world gone terribly wrong'.[3]

Stet follows on naturally from *Ukulele Music* and *Going On*. It echoes and develops explicitly from the leitmotif of the monodistich 'post-coronation disintegration' in *Ukulele Music* and joins up with '[Non-acquiescent acknowledgement; present but muted the *OIMOI!*]' of *Going On* ('oimoi' is Greek for 'woe'). ' "What has gone wrong with Britain since the War?" ' asks 'Ex-Soldier, Telford' in a letter to the editor. This disintegration is retraced over the last 33 years, starting in 1952 with the death of George VI and ending in the mid-80s with 'Great Britain's / Satrapess gloatingly self-applauding' (p.96, poem no.37).[4] Reading meets W.H. Auden's request (the detritus has not changed, see poem no.55):

> Get there if you can and see the land you once were proud to own
> Though the roads have almost vanished and the expresses never run:
>
> Smokeless chimneys, damaged bridges, rotting wharves and choked canals,
> Tramlines buckled, smashed trucks lying on their side across the rails...[5]

The most recent past, however, is embedded in the largest possible framework so that nobody fails to see how ultimately insignificant the Now and Here is: Little England is pinpointed within the dimension of a universe in which luminous objects can be detected as far as 10,000 million light years away, and the last 30 years are just as insignificant in a geological perspective when counterpointed by a fossil crinoid 408 million years old (41, p.98):

> Fossil Silurian crinoids infest our cottage's walls of
>   local stone; thin plasterboard separates them from ourselves.

Reading's sardonic injunction 'Muse!, Sing the grotty [scant alternative]' (p.84) sets the tone and is woven through the book as a *ploce* in single monostichs or in the closing verses of other stanzas. Correspondingly, what surrounds it is – for the first time in Reading's œuvre, and later used again for American 'small-town politics' in *Marfan* – a stroboscopic record of the politics of the period: wars and crises (Korea, Suez, the Falklands), armament, the arms industry and English economy, Harriers over Shropshire with nuclear weapons on board, the risk of a collective nuclear suicide, a general election, Royalty, the end of the Cold War, the razing of the rainforests, AIDS, the destruction of a Greenpeace boat by the French Secret Service, as well as the routine atrocities committed every day in England, all presented in drastic directness or hinted at in guarded, lyrical, impressionistic images. This is accompanied by childhood memories and impressions of events in the 1950s, and occasionally refracted by the child's own perspective of those years. Synecdochic moments of happiness – rendered in images of wine, ornithology[6] and the love of the English countryside – often counterpoint the national decline, which is mirrored in the microcosm of Shropshire and works as a metaphor itself. In a secular prayer, the poet wishes for courage and tenacity for his task; emphasised by italics and repeated several times in *Stet* (and in *Going On*), the monodistich sounds like an incantatory mantra (51, p.101):

> [Don't let the Old Ineluctable catch you with you clichés down –
>   *Cope with No Hope without god. / Recognise, not acquiesce.*]

As befits the theme, Reading not only dispenses with poem titles in *Stet*, but, for the first time (in the original edition), also with pagination. However, the compact wholeness thus suggested is a prerequisite for containing the structural fragmentation. Similar to *C*, *Stet* consists of 79 textual units scattered across the pages, creating the structure of a sequence or a collage bordering on a narrative. Both the fragmentation and the superordinate continuity express aspects of the reality which is being examined: a coherent vision holds the fragments together. Reading:

...the actual size of a poetry book is part of a usable medium, and shouldn't be wasted, and I would like to feel that in some way I'm operating as a novelist might...within the framework of a book length... I should hope it's a unified fragmentation, which shouldn't cause too much of a problem to any modernist or after...I think that the fragmentation is... meaningful... because it enables you to bombard the reader with more or less everything that comes along, or everything that's chosen (Bailey, M).

The book's "chronicle" is presented achronologically so that the suspense does not weaken and the outcome remains unpredictable. Furthermore, the reader catches glimpses of connections between units before they are properly recognisable and intelligible, so the incentive to read on is strong. On the first reading, the (antithetical) sources of suspense act indirectly and pre-consciously, thus strengthening one's emotive reaction to the book. At first glance, the antithetical structure of *Stet* is hidden by the strong intermixing of the different elements, while the individual parts and voices are orchestrated with a good sense of dramatic timing and rhythm.

Most of the poems are short, even very short, and most of them could stand on their own. For *Stet*, Reading invented an asynartetic combination of stanzas. The Alcaic stanza introduced in *Going On* (p.80)[7]

[Tum-tee-tee | tum-tum || tum-tee-tee | tum-tee-tee
Tum-tee-tee | tum-tum || tum-tee-tee | tum-tee-tee
Tum-tee-tee | tum-tum || tum-tum || tum-tum
Tum-tee-tee | tum-tee-tee || tum-tum | tum-tum.]

is followed by an elegiac distich (both stanzas consist of dactyls and spondees). These new metra episyntheta – in this combination henceforth called the '*Stet*-stanza' – are introduced in the first poem (1, p.84):

Pyrex, a pie-dish, deep-lined with apple lumps,
deft in the left hand; with the right flopping on
    pall of white-dusted droopy pastry,
        slicing off overlaps, jabbing steam-vents...

'52: Mummy paused, wiped a floured hand and tuned in the wireless –
sad Elgar, crackling, then *death of our King, George the Sixth.*

Reading [LI]:

This unit I was very happy with for a while because it gave me the possibility of doing small things...There was just enough room to handle it, and it was very tightly ordered, but apparently loose, especially to people who didn't really know what was going on...Alcaics are generically similar to the elegiac couplets which follow and make the weighty point about demise, personal and of the body politic (Bailey, M).

A variety of verse forms follows:[8] single Alcaic stanzas (2, p.84); poems consisting of several Alcaic stanzas (26, p.93); doggerel in (catalectic) tetrameters (19, pp.19-20); tetrametric, pentametric, hexametric and Alexandrine monostichs (4, p.84); iambic pentameters (starting to be occasionally loose) (5, p.85); elegiac distichs (12, p.88); single Alcmanic stanzas of varying length (13, p.88); Alcmanic verses in stichich composition, i.e. without the closing hexameter (55, p.103); one halved Alcaic stanza with two hexameters – the first instance of a fragmentation of the two basic stanzas, which Reading will continue forcefully in later books, especially in *Evagatory* (24, p.93); the 'Reading hymn', as explained in *Going On* (the first three distichs of 79, p.116). This list should be sufficient, then, as a response to Whitbread judge Sir Michael Havers' notorious objection to *Stet* that 'it doesn't even scan'.[9] Only the astrophysicist speaks in prose, and descriptions of weapons also seem to have no place in poetry (36, p.96; 38, p.97)

The verse forms are, once again, more varied than they were in *Ukulele Music*, and individual metres are conspicuously reserved for particular voices.[10] How compelling are such assignments? Reading [LI]: 'I seem to remember using different metres for different characters. That seemed to be *a* use of metre and a theatrical, dramatic use to help identify different personae.' The distichs' hexameters, which had repeatedly run over the lines in *Ukulele Music* and had therefore – along with the pentameters – been typographically halved in *Going On*, suddenly almost all fit onto one line again. In view of the various new indentations used in *Stet*, this was to be welcomed.

On the narrative level, *Stet* does without explicit strands of plot. The book is held together by an affinity between individual images and motifs that work together as in a puzzle while the antithetical links between them give them new meaning. Additionally, cohesion is achieved by situational motifs, symbolic objects, and anadiplosis (e.g. 'stet', 'comfy', 'flat oats', 'cleaved crania', 'bivalves', 'Viva', 'Long Life', 'doves'), which recur in many perspectives and situations.

Within this structure, Reading provides a great deal of variety: not only in the different reports, sketches, images and vignettes, but also in the '[supremely orchestrated] change of tone – from numb horror, to farce, to grimmest irony, to lingering pastoral sweetness' (Nuttall) as well as in the diversification of voices, which is at least as elaborate as it was in *Ukulele Music* and *Going On*. The book's autobiographical undertones link up with the present voice of the 40-year-old poet, who muses about the decline of his country since 1952 and, distressed, calls on the printing metaphors for help. At the same time he describes ornithological excursions which he started undertaking with his friend in childhood. This friendship stretches over the same three decades and mirrors almost allegorically the national losses suffered, which, in turn, stand for existential loss – culminating in a violent, shocking, abrupt ending.

This thematic and structural parallel is not executed as well as it could have been, in that it is not made clear enough; possibly this is why it was overlooked.[11] Similarly, the thematic and structural relevance of the very last poem, which is firmly grounded in a typically English setting, has not been recognised; there is an underlying binary principle throughout: *Stet* is half encomium, half elegy on the England of the past.

In another dualistic set-up, the poet has to endure several vicious attacks by the 'anti-poet', his alter ego in square brackets. Operating palinodically, this voice not only reviles 'Poet Pete' because he indulges in personal elegy, but also because he is incapable of ignoring the vile journalistic side of the chronicle – a hopeless inclination which did not lead anywhere in *Ukulele Music* either (5, p.85):

> An acned trio lowers from the front page.
> Cro-Magnon, simian, Neanderthal
> (but the same species as Christ, Einstein, Bach).
>
> [Trite impotent iambic journalese,
> **Reading raps raiders / Poet Pete Protests.**]

The other voices are spared such impertinent disruptions. They include those of two elderly ladies in mourning; a pub philosopher elaborating on politics; other regulars occasionally commenting in Shropshire dialect; the astrophysicist commenting on the universe; and the various citizens who send in platitudinous 'Letters to the Editor' and artless 'Poems of the Week', dripping with bathos. As was pointed out in *C*, not only lethal illnesses are 'impartial': sociopolitical processes concern the whole nation, too, which is why a democratic selection of people's opinions on the subject is presented. 'To recognise isn't to acquiesce', and, as the not wholly literate pub politician puts it: 'All got the diffrent idees like, so we got to accept it.'

These – by now established – "Reading devices" are still forceful and able to carry momentum. Reading's strongly tectonic books, suspended in between lyrical, narrative and dramatic conventions, are very different from other poetry and still too 'exhilaratingly new' (Nuttall). Another reviewer wrote:

> I have no taste for this kind of thing normally, but *Stet* has impressed
> me more than anything else in this review. Its multiple changes of
> tone and speaker are most cleverly handled and its social comment and
> observations are first-rate. It adds up to a strong, memorable whole,
> and against all expectations I ended by applauding it... It deserves a
> wide and generous readership (Lane Fox).

In *Stet* both the lyrical mode and the traditional form of single
poems are re-activated on a broader basis, as though the preliminary
work of questioning and legitimising poetic modes has been con-
cluded and the poet can now wind down a little and write "straight"
poems again. The simplicity is well deserved. Especially as from
Stet many of the poems are constructed in a simple metaphorical
way, sometimes using simple traditional metaphors and deriving
their impulse from an image or implicit simile (10, p.87; 'Harriers'):

> [Bellicose *H. sap.*] Skull-cleaving Harriers,
> distant a field before their ventriloquous
>   stridencies strip dense gold male flowers,
>   hedge-hop me pruning the *Quercus ilex.*
>
> Valorous, some of them, homicides all by grey acquiescence.
> Holm sap is smeared and it smells bitterly on the poised blade.[12]

Complexity then builds up because each book operates (among
other things) as one stately metaphor. Accordingly, the whole œuvre
amounts to a mega-metaphor.

'*Stet*' is a printer's word – from the Latin *stare*, to stand –
meaning 'leave the deleted word to stand as originally set'. It is
used twice (44, p.99; 77, p.115) and explained as 'leave as printed'
or 'let it stand'. Accordingly, in the original edition the title on
the cover was crossed out in red, with the instruction annulled by
dotted underlining. The title is most expressive, as Peter Porter
observes, 'given Peter Reading's intention of reinstating the un-
swervably dreadful into that warp of received beauty known as
poetry'. Of course, the same applies in connection with the use of
language: technical jargon, regional dialects, sociolects, doggerel,
patois and the mock heroic all appear alongside the lyrical and
majestic, or Standard English. The same goes for the material used:
newspaper reports, letters to the editor, snippets of conversation
eavesdropped in pubs, diary entries and pastiche pieces claim their
own space.

Thematically more relevant, though, is how the far-reaching
'stet' metaphor (which links up structurally with the diplopic view
in *Diplopic* and the slashed double-loop in *Going On*) is used to
express the stance of hard-won acceptance. Pathological preaching
in poetry, addressed to autophagous *H. sap.*, is to be deleted, but

is then tolerated after all. The same procedure is applied to the subject under attack (77, p.115; see also 6, p.86):

> brutality ⎱
> Strike out the old obsessive mortality ⎰ ...
> [Physics (unlike text) can't be corrected, though.
>   Let it stand. Ave! Age of Floored Proofs.
>   Stet (no alternative), leave as printed.]

And even this doubles up with another application of the 'stet' directive: the self-confidence which is displayed in the artistic treatment of "reality" is undermined by another "reality".

In the light of this, O'Driscoll's verdict seems a little premature: 'Compared with his other middle and late collections, *Stet* is a book without an agenda, except perhaps to coax a response to his further injunction – "Muse! sing the Grotty [scant alternative]" ' (O'Driscoll, p.217). Of course, the attempt at getting to terms with the status quo is an aim in itself in *Stet*, but it was already the main theme of *Going On* and only touches one side of this book. *Stet* does have an(other) agenda, even if it is only skeletally visible.

The dichotomy of elegy and encomium mentioned above is continued in the subliminal thematisation of courage and fear, and also in the contrast between hard realism and wistful nostalgia. The nostalgic impulse and its relevance in *Stet* may have been overlooked for three reasons.[13] Firstly because the dual structure is not brought out distinctly enough. Secondly because such mellow emotion was not expected of Reading after books like *C* and *Ukulele Music*, the continuity of the works possibly being mistaken for a formula, as if the sensitive voice of *For the Municipality's Elderly* had never existed, and as if poem titles like 'Imperial' had no weight (this was the title given to the opening poem of *Stet* in a magazine publication). Thirdly, and this may be the decisive factor, Reading covers his tracks by artistic transformation of the raw material: 'I may feel nostalgia, as everybody does, about certain things, but I'd hope that my stuff isn't nostalgic' (Jenkins, 1985, p.11). Asked to comment on this point in *Stet*, Reading thoroughly vented his feelings on the matter [LI]:

> Yes, there is a nostalgia. That is the predominant thing. You can't really think of the loss of England without the imperial connotations... Whatever anybody's opinion about the Imperial and the Monarchic is, the end of an era:... any collapse of Empire, as Gibbon has taught us, is *not* a very good thing in many ways because it suggests a collapse of order and of the allegory of good government, or of sound government... You feel that there *are* some things that are a loss. And they stand as a great metaphor, as an Elgarian metaphor... However, you can't consider the nostalgic end of England and things about it which some of us have liked, or would have liked to have been in on, like the topographical

pleasantness of it, without considering all the other things... But I don't think that there's much direct, even implicit, support given, is there, for the *rage* and so forth?

In his essay about pessimism in English literature, Reading expounded the implications and metaphorical background to this national phenomenon in the same straightforward way, the connection to himself implied:

> A poem in Roy Fuller's volume *From the Joke Shop* (1975) contains these lines: 'August itself has undertones of Fall, / Some inexplicable, imperial, / Elgarian sadness.' A feeling of nostalgia and ineffable loss seems to afflict those whose empire has declined or fallen. Even those whom we would not ordinarily expect to profess any kind of imperial sympathy are liable to succumb. [H.G. Wells, for example,] concludes [his novel *Tono-Bungay*] with something very like nostalgic regret for a past era, nation and notion... It is as if Empire (like sanguine youth) stands for all unrealisable potential, all transience, all that is to be irrevocably finished. And each generation senses this anew, identifies the change and decay of the old order as its own special burden of loss (Reading, 'Going').

Reading thus places himself in a long-standing literary tradition. He also described it in an earlier review of Roy Fuller's *Collected Poems*; the qualities he refers to are present in his own books:

> Englishness pervades the 540 pages of this distinguished book. The sort of Englishness I mean is that associated with, say, Elgar – an end-of-an-era profound brooding. The transience of epochs is something of an English preoccupation...The stoical, unhysterical, weighed acknowledgement of self and society is sedulously charted... Reticence, self-deprecation, common sense, comprehensibility, a tendency to conservatism in metre, are English qualities, and the old buffer image... is more accurately the manifestation of the decency, reasonableness, fair play, no-nonsense rationalism for which, historically at least, the nation has been renowned. Not that he is in any way jingoistic, but his regularly espoused values are what were once regarded as national virtues.[14]

This nostalgic sense of loss of 'good English stuff' [C], the underlying mixture of love and grief, is the true theme of this book, is the (hidden) agenda. In one of Reading's later works, *Evagatory* (another lyrical book), it is taken up once more. In this sense Reading should be seen as a specifically *English* writer, as he acknowledges himself, in contrast to more cosmopolitan poets [LI]:

> I *do* think of myself as very English, yes, but I ... have also tried to be as wide-ranging as possible and non-parochial, and I hope and think that I am. And the indication that there's been some support in other countries, well, rather more than in England, tends to support that. There's very definitely an English root to my stuff and my way of writing: there's this overweening sense of a kind of nostalgia as well which I am incurably afflicted with and which I think is quite important, as are the attitudes, irony and humour.

The local and national component is placed in a larger, international, or rather in a metaphorical, existential framework – as it had been before in *For the Municipality's Elderly*, *Ukulele Music*, and *Going On*, and as it later would be in *Perduta Gente*, *Evagatory*, *Last Poems*, *Work in Regress* and *Marfan*. The 'Elgar metaphor' [15] is meant to balance the 'familiar, parochial, local feeling' and 'the wry fondness for it' that Alan Jenkins detects in Reading's works:

> Yes, there's a tension… between 'parochialism', Englishness, if you like, and a desire to be global. I'd like to bridge this but I'm not really able to; unlike James Fenton, say, I haven't globe-trotted. I'm deeply impressed by *Wonder-Book* encounters with distant parts of the world. But this is itself a kind of Englishness, a schoolboy Englishness I was brought up with. I'm English, I like being English, though I'm not very happy about Larkin-like xenophobic Englishness. I'd want to map out a new kind of England, in many ways unpleasant, but with a lot of dotty pleasantnesses about it as well (Jenkins, 1985, p.12).

While horrid events are a fact and regional chauvinism is anathema to Reading, the nostalgic love of England finds reticent expression in lyrical verses, most notably here in a slow gliding-down motion (56, p.104):

> even as that sad realm in the middle was gently expiring
> devenustated but yet, even though feculent, *ours*.

This love also explains the – ultimately – insecure voices in this book, especially that of the poet himself, especially in his reminiscences.

The six-year-old boy, who watches his mother baking, hears the news of the monarch's death on the wireless – followed by sad music from Elgar. Already in this very first poem national events are placed within the domestic framework and charged metaphorically, and the child's perspective continues to colour the daily news throughout – for him an apple-pie and a dead King are equally important. But this is the moment he loses a kind of innocence: a dark, dimly comprehended feeling creeps into his every single experience, a feeling that the adults might possibly not have their world properly under control (39, p.97):

> '56: going home from the Juniors,
> I read the headlines **Suez** and **Crisis Point** –
> crikey! I thought, there must be something
> terribly wrong with the nation's toilets;
>
> soon if the Government didn't act there'd be all kinds of nasties
> gushing up out of the drains, Britain would be [is] engulfed.

Three years earlier, in 1953, little Peter Reading had already been puzzled by the fact that the adults were more interested in the '*Narmistice*' in the Far East – '(I wasn't sure where either of these

things were)' (64, p.110) – than in his seventh birthday, even if
the news of peace made him feel 'comfy inside'. In the same vein,
on one of their excursions to the scrap-yard, Peter and his friend
discover blood-stained blond hair in a car that was involved in an
accident (8, p.86), and then the new monarch, during coronation,
is shockingly observed to twiddle '*its thumbs!*' (11, p.88).

Meanwhile, the teacher of history, '[genuine name, "Miss Clio"
is, by the way]',[16] attempts to instil a peaceful disposition in the
children (31, p.95):

> 'There is no reason, is there, children,
>> why you can't live with other little
>
> children from other countries in happiness?
> You are the ones we are depending on...'
>> We have betrayed her, poor old Dodo –
>>> cleaving of crania, burnt-out Pandas...

However, by encouraging inspired naivety, her endeavours have an
effect. Faced with an underprivileged, criminal family, schoolboy
Peter takes his first steps in responsibility in 'Sociologic' (70, p.112):

> What you should do was share out the money and
> make some new houses so they'd be comfy and
>> teach them to wash to stop their smell and
>>> show them what fun it was, being humans –
>
> once you could teach them to dislike themselves as you did, then clearly
>> things'd be smashing of course – a child of 8 could see *that.*

The moments in which the child's trust is first punctured by
glimpses of worldly understanding are some of the most moving
passages in the book.[17] These moments can also – very occasionally
– provide comforting revelations, as in the far-sighted, lyrical 'secular
ecstasy' of the 12-year-old in 'Luminary', who on a grey winter's
day is summoned for punishment to the headmaster's study, but,
glimpsing a ray of light on the carpet, becomes existentially un-
assailable. The 'oblique shaft, apricot, genial,' falls 'through a grim
dull pane' onto the 'luminous/Axminster' and enchants him, 'ren-
dering misery worldly, nothing' (26, p.93).

Conversely, the poet also discovers an abundance of forebod-
ings in his childhood memories, for example in the charting of
migrations with his friend (7, p.86):

> When (early '60s?) there was an influx of
>> collared doves spreading rapidly through the realm,
>>> monthly we mapped the species' progress
>>>> (hanging for murder was being phased out –
>
> noosed necks diminished/proliferated in inverse ratio),
>> dubbed it the Year of the Noose; unforeseen increase ensued.

Another such example is the Coronation of the 'daft Queen' and
the national success of 'Everest Conquered' in 1953, witnessed by
the infants in a 'gaudily faded Regal'; the double feature on the
flickering screen is a symbol of the beginning of the end (11, p.88).[18]

As for the present, it is laden with doom and decline. The
poet, in an attempt to be stoical, seeks to regard the climatic and
climacteric consequences of the razing of the rain forest as 'merely
cosmic', and equates ethical endeavours with (belated) anxiety
about survival (28, p.94). Prose, however, is all that is warranted
for the laconic description of six gold-plated submachine guns with
gold-plated 9mm bullets costing £9000 each displayed in a walnut
case – made in Essex for Arab Royalty (36, p.96); and it is then
immediately set off by a Thatcher comment on an order for Saudi
fighter planes (*'Marvellous boost to British Economy... / Government
not responsible ... actions of / leaders of other...'* [37, p.96]).

Also, the journalese poems in 'trite iambic pentameters' are just
as drastic and repellent as the ones describing urban violence in
Ukulele Music and *Going On*. They are supplemented by the poet's
experiences of the Shropshire farmers' and workmen's milieu, also
rendered in iambic pentameters, because 'GBH' occurs in rural
circles as well : 'A bloke with whom I once worked at the mill' puts
his wife into hospital ('23 stitches') because of a sandwich she made;
and he is assaulted by her on another occasion: 'Some ententes
rely / much on the reciprocity of malice' (21, p.91). The work
environment itself is also hazardous, '**TRACTOR TYRE BLOW-UP /
KILLS YOUTH**' ('Unveiled', 59, p.107).

The larger symbolic significance is expressed in one image in the
third poem dealing with Reading's work environment (25, p.93):

I had been Crop Inspecting – C2 Pennal
which we'd provisionally bought as seed –
the eleven acres by the railway line,
and in that sheltered corner near the tunnel
someone, quite possibly in love, had been
lying. An Inter-City brayed two notes,
the Buffet car disgorged a Light Ale tin
into the especial, pseudo rural, scene:
holed Nuform, empty Long Life, laid-flat oats.

The discarded beer can from the Inter-City and the punctured
condom from anonymous lovers are everyday symbols of careless
pleasure defiling what has long since become a 'pseudo' form of
nature. The wittily chosen brand names and their accompanying
epithets illustrate the authorial view of modern life, while the
'laid-flat oats' fuse into one image the taking of pleasure and the
crushing of nature.

It is the 'pustular soldiers of the Queen' on that passing Inter-City train who make their voices heard most loudly.[19] With this poem, Reading gives a – as he calls it – 'nod in the direction of' Philip Larkin's 'The Whitsun Weddings' (1958). The genre (it is an 'England-from-a-train' poem) as well as the direct quotes from Larkin's language and imagery (the polluted canals, scrapyards, cooling-towers and patches of green here and there) testify to this intertextuality; 'the last movement of the Movement', as Grant jokes. Reading liked 'The Whitsun Weddings' and 'Aubade'; Larkin's poems are 'characterised by common sense, clarity, demotic jokiness and impatience with airy-fairy aestheticism', he writes in a review of his letters.[20]

'The Whitsun Weddings', among other things, mourns the end of better English times. Thirty years on, Reading's version metamorphoses the newly-wed couples into youths involved in an ugly scene of harassment: a synecdochic example of the brutalisation and shabbiness that have overcome England in the thirty years that *Stet* spans.

The train, now used to evoke associations of a country in decay, moves through a countryside that has deteriorated along with it – something Reading noticed already back in the 1950s when visiting his canal just outside of Liverpool (55, p.103):

> The tramp's scalp's indigo pus-oozing boil;
> sulphur dioxide piss-hued cumulus;
> a mac daubed with puked Chinese take-away –
> drooled noodly detail of a Jackson Pollock;
> furred upside-down tench in a mauve canal...
> I sing the Grotty [no alternative].

Significantly, the tramp is to become the main character in *Perduta Gente*.

It is hardly surprising that the poet begins to notice the first signs of failing health in himself; he makes light of it, putting it down to dyspepsia due to too much drink ('Fit', 14, p.89). Later, with his descriptions of different wines, the poet openly undermines his decision to 'stick to the Perrier more in the future': stet. Two monostichs in French on bitter-tasting wines (17, p.90; 35, p.96) are contrasted with an Alcaic stanza about wine made from delicious sloes that 'sweeten a withering palate, slightly' (49, p.101). Even here the elegiac-encomiastic structure, or agenda, is hinted at. Hymning the sweet fragrance of honeysuckle and hay which mingles with the 'generous finish' of the cru (53) can only – slightly – mitigate the fact that 'Longevity' (14, p.89) is not to be expected – from his body or from the planet – 'Long Lives vibrate, totter towards the edge' (58, p.107). The evidence of general destruction is overwhelming, and we are all to blame: 'Valorous, some of them, homicides all by grey acquiescence' (10, p.87).

Thus the chronicler hastens to give a warning to the young boy about to climb Mount Helicon and drink from the fountain of the Muses. Possibly in a vision, he appears to the boy in the guise of his old, experienced (and coughing) self – or that of the Grim Reaper (69, p.111): '[Prosaically between you and the summit, hacking, appeared a / grizzled agrestic old get, wielding a bloody big scythe.]' The boy understands the premonition: in a paper to his class, the fourteen-year-old forecasts war-like situations in the cities, Wellsian degeneration (73, p.113): 'You could see, in the states and the new slum high-rises, Morlocks / sullenly honing rank fangs; telly-taught, butcherous, brute.' Of course, nobody believes him.

After elegy comes encomium, albeit somewhat brief and qualified – a bittersweet disposition drives the poet on. He is grateful to be here, now, in England (45, p.100). The love of his country expresses itself, for example, in the image of the bedside lamp in his grand-parents' house – on a map of the world, the lampshade testifies to the previous Empire's sphere of power (61, p.108):

Obsolete heirloom, comforting glow of **Generous Empire**
(cruelty and mess, I suppose, may be worse elsewhere than here).

The lyrical, meiotic passages in this poem denoting the 'bleakly rational, bottom-of-the-barrel patriotism' (Imlah), are soon hyper-bolised in the register of uncensored rage. After enumerating distant atrocities, natural catastrophes and madness, Reading aggressively thunders in a preventive-strike stance (75, p.114):

...for some shite god,
possession, border, tenet, goons blast kack
out of each other's chitterlings...I don't care
two fucks for any other pratt. UK's
OK. I'm lucky and I intend to stay so.
What do you want me to do, go batty too?

So far, however, the reader can still "choose" between the different stances and is not influenced in any particular direction. Different personae voice their opinions; after the poet comes whoever is standing next to him in the pub, which happens to be Viv's hus-band. His views on passive politicians' wasting of tax-payers' money were already paraphased by Viv in *Going On*. In this book, he is allowed to speak for himself on two evenings (13, p.88; 54, p.103). His slurred monologue, sounding perfectly conversational in Alcmanic verses, is interrupted – fragmented – several times, and always resumed with a glass of 'Bitter and mild mixed' for which he thanks the publican (nos. 13, 42, 54, 57, 63). At great length, he explains to the 'Mister' (i.e. the silently listening poet, who after the first glass is already addressed as 'mate') how taxes are diverted 'for nucular warflair' (13, p.88) while the money is needed more urgently in the social sector. But then he corrects himself: 'Don't get me wrong now mate', he would not want, of course, that the 'bleeding lunatics step in', like 'them Christian Militias, / them Irish Paisleyists', 'all them old Shreeks with the turban' (63, p.109), 'Ayertolly, / him with the whiskers like' (57, p.105), 'commies [and them other] Dictatorships' – and yet (42, p.99):

> Mind you I don't say I holds with this bleeding
> nucular warflair, don't hold with it me mate.
> Too much of that bleeding lot and an we all be
> dead as a yoyo mate. Bitter and mild please.

The other regulars throw in the occasional colourful comment in Alcaic stanza-scraps (nos. 20, 27, 29, 48): one 'Ex-Army' wants to teach youngsters of today discipline – '*chop their hends orf!*' (27, p.94); another displays his ecological conscience: 'Sensitive things them Topical Rain Forests, / regulates all the world's humility' (48, p.100); as is the well-meaning advice by a farmer to counteract the danger of AIDS with a pint (20, p.91). Finally, the confession of one of the bozo-brothers is very touching indeed (66, p.110; 'Eavesdropped'):

> 'Tell you what, old chap, *strictly* between ourselves,
> I have a *leetle* personal whatsaname –
>   utterly *vital* I drink daily,
>   *huge* amounts, otherwise get so damn sad.'

Sharing the same ground as the pub-goers are the bathetic, amateurishly rhymed, jerkily iambic doggerel verses in the greetings card metre – (catalectic) iambic tetrameters – which are published in *Comfy Home* magazine and supposedly written by 'Contented of Telford, Mrs' and 'McDonald, Mrs (Aberdeen)' – alias 'Miss Prudence' alias 'Uncle Chummy' himself (see *Diplopic*): they are helpless and nationalistic, appalled and apalling. England's reputation is not to be dragged through the mud as long as there are also decent, contented, and pious people about. While hundreds of letters to the editor end up in the bin every day because they have, in a double sense, nothing to say, the published 'poems of the week' – 'Our land is not as bad as all that' (78, p.115) – bravely stand up to the depressing complaints of the *Stet* poet and other muckrakers (see also 40, p.98).

The writer will have nothing to do with unmasked sentimentality or simplified argument himself, but unquestionably they should

have a place in the whole context. One interviewer who also
noticed only the satirical side of the newspaper poems, was told:

> I suppose that they could be thought of as in some ways a bit heartless,
> but they're not intended to be, really. Quite often, the sort of things
> that I'm suggesting is that here are some very worthwhile people, who
> have solutions in a Mrs Gamp sort of way of actually surviving, which
> itself is admirable. And the intention isn't to ridicule them, although
> there is a temptation to do that, of course... and we are, I suppose,
> laughing at such people, at their expense. The overall intention is for
> them to be rather admirable, though there might be other characters
> who appear in the books who are certainly not being dealt with admir-
> ingly...like reps and execs in plastics and packaging [Bailey, M].

Solutions à la Mrs Gamp or Viv are finally offered in *Stet* by
Viv's husband, the pub philosopher, too – albeit after a little detour
(57, p.105):

> All them religerous lot is fernatics.
> Stick all them bleeders together and let em
> blow bloody buggery out of each other –
> Prodestant, Catherlic, Jews Isleramics.[21]
> ...
> All people got their own diffrent religions.
> Obvious, that is like. Obvious, that is.
> No need to kill all them others what aren't yours.
> ...
> All got the diffrent ideas like, so we got to accept it.

His beer is not the only thing that the randomly philosophising
pub bore holds onto during the evening. He hazily remembers a
'quote like so somebody *said* it' about the religious disposition of
mankind and vaguely nourishes hopes for some kind of superior/
superordinate 'Reason' (63, p.109): 'there must be *Something* like, you
know Out There like. / *This* can't be all there is to it like. Course
not.'[22]

The astrophysicist's views are presented as a direct antithesis of
this; on no account does he believe in 'some kind of Reason with
a capital R' (62, p.108). In the interview with him explaining his
work,[23] the first thing to catch one's attention is that it appears to
be presented out of context, is torn into three pieces (nos. 9, 62,
65) and starts and ends in mid-sentence, as if a curtain were lifted
briefly, behind which a lengthy conversation was taking place.
Fundamentally relevant as the knowledge of the physical basis
(and future) of human existence would be for any world view,
most people pay hardly attention to it, considering the matter too
difficult, so one might as well go ahead and talk shop without
considering the layman. But these texts seem to be defined too
exclusively by their antithetical function and, with the exception

of the raw material conveyed, are not very interesting. Also, their length makes them appear a little like padding.

The poet-stance has the last word on world views, like the physicist not accepting the ethical, religious theories of his personae. Life is so simple, isn't it (67, p.111)?

> Simple complexity, dying, euphoria, nastiness, good fun –
> ...
> Ave! no-nonsense astronomers probing Reasonless physics
> [also the modest who just cope with No Hope, without god].

However, the power of this stance is called into question again by three mysterious monostichs (nos. 34, 46, 72): two iambic pentameters, one hypercatalectic, and an alexandrine. According to the poet, these found poems stem from the 'lady's album of 1826' and are 'unexplained':[24] '*All in this place anticipate the Dreadful.*' '*Something ridiculous & sad will happen soon.*' '*This waiting bravely to be badly hurt.*' Towards the end of the book, however, the true explanation of this fake source is revealed (72, p.113):

> [Untrue. *You* scrawl the whining metaphor
> before the scalpel, can't now justify
> expatiation. Call it a day at that.]

Stet: for the vague, theatrical, ominous lament of the poet, who has to mask his fear for the future, for England, for himself and for others so as to be able to bear it. The tenet of 'simple complexity' is only simple as long as disaster does not strike one personally.

And then it strikes. Michael Donahue (Reading's friend since the ornithological childhood days invoked earlier in the book)[25] is killed in a car accident. This is the last piece of evidence and ultimately unmasks the poet: 'tonight, mawkish, I, solo, glut hock' (56, p.104), Reading concedes falteringly in this *apostrophe*; it is Reading's first 'ob.':

> '... terribly sad news... instantly... Motorway...'
> After your mother's letter I turn to a
>   diary, through whose Wetmore Order
>   ornithological recollections
>
> stir, of a friendship early-established and
> special surviving global vicissitudes.
>   Marvellous, those first close-shared eras
>   mist-netting rarities, early migrants.
>
> [Batty/unhealthy – verse at the best of times
> chunters to insubstantial minorities,
>   as for addressing lines to *dead men!*,
>   arrogant therapy/piffle, claptrap.]

East and west coast observatories fêted us
(icterine and melodious warblers,
   thrill of *Phylloscopus bonelli*,
     magnified instants of bright crisp focus)
even as that sad realm in the middle was gently expiring
  devenustated but yet, even though feculent, *ours.*

The friend's unnatural death becomes all the more unbearable as a symbol of the dying process of the whole country. Both the early image of the wrecked small car (8, p.86) and the details of mourning formalities (2, p.84; see also 74, p.114) serve as a foreboding of the violent accident, which is thus embedded in the book as a whole (and even has echoes in *Evagatory*). Reading's two personal elegies to Donahue contain encomiastic verses about birds.

Just as consistently, *Stet* ends with a poem ('Revertal') that begins in the form of the Reading-hymn. '(Inverse of Elegy, this)', the poet discloses in a brief reading instruction. The order of pentameter/ hexameter is reversed exactly in the middle of the poem, thus exemplifying *in nuce* how encomium and elegy on Great Britain are meant to balance each other in this book. (The same may be hinted at in the doves' 'double moaning'.) An elderly lady, evidently Donahue's mother, enters a pastoral, lyrically and lovingly described, and, above all, typically English scene. The warm glowing atmosphere collapses from one moment to the next. As the poet mourns his lost country, she suddenly weeps for her child (79, p.116): '*Oh I miss him so much!*'

Final Demands (1988):
Runes of Transience

Final Demands received a mixed reception.[1] Reading's increasingly elaborate artistic moulds once more provoked almost hostile criticism of his alleged 'game-playing' (Lomas, Forbes, Crawford); by contrast, Margaret Drabble and Carol Ann Duffy pointed to the sincere and sensitive basis of his virtuosity.[2]

In *Final Demands*, Reading developed his style and technique by incorporating new elements, tones, and a musical quality, while also employing devices from previous books. Bernard O'Donoghue was impressed mostly by Reading's 'striking' novelistic technique, combining collage and disparate voices:

> Combined with his metrical compulsiveness, this technique equipped Reading with immense linguistic range, exploited to the full in the expression of his harsh, mordant view of the modern world which refused any consolation or certitude...The most remarkable thing was that, despite the recurrence of the same techniques and themes throughout his highly prolific output, Reading never went over the same ground twice. It would be hard to name another poet whose volumes were as various as *5x5x5x5x5, C, Ukulele Music* and *Stet.*

Final Demands was, as O'Donoghue thought, 'as they say, different again'.[3] O'Driscoll was more reserved this time; he thought *Final Demands* was 'not without impressive writing, especially when Reading is giving personal vulnerabilities their head', but 'For once, though, a Reading volume is less than the sum of its parts' (O'Driscoll, p.216). While both evaluations are apt, the reason given by these two critics for this book's lesser stature (the letters are 'bland' and 'like padding') seems to be peripheral.

The structure of the book – precisely executed subject-matter within a lyrical-metaphorical web – is successful, but the impression of failure can arise because *Final Demands* seems – if seen against the sharp focus of the previous books – directionless, or aimless. This also means that the different lyrical intensity of the poems appears uneven for the first time. While the retreat from "unpoetic" diction is understandable as further artistic development, the less lyrical poems – now lacking a specific function – sit rather loosely with the more lyrical ones. It is perhaps no coincidence that, after finishing *Final Demands*, Reading seems to have endured his first writer's block.

The middle phase, prepared by *Tom o'Bedlam's Beauties*, starting with *Diplopic*, and comprising the impressive *C* and *Ukulele Music* (with *Going On*), culminates in *Stet*. After that achievement, a regenerative break might have been useful, but *Final Demands* appeared 16 months after *Stet*. *Final Demands* is special insofar as it is the (valedictory) link between the middle and later phase, i.e. an important factor for the unification of the whole œuvre. At the same time, this status can also be seen as its weak point, without detracting from the intense and heightened metaphorical and lyrical quality of the book. Neil Roberts makes a strong case for *Final Demands*, which he claims is 'one of Reading's best books'.[4] When asked to comment, Reading only said [LI]: 'I like *Final Demands*, but it seems to have gone down like the proverbial lead zeppelin'.

Reading's 'handwriting' in *Final Demands* is unmistakable. The unpaginated book is a collage of untitled poems and prose, i.e. letters (found material, 'some reworked, some *verbatim*' [C]),[5] and a chapter from a novel (pseudo-found). The collage polyphonically orchestrates the overall subject: 'demise, personal and of the body politic,' as Reading said (Bailey, M). The lyrical intensity of the recurring images was new, as was the fact that the different voices are from several generations going back to the 19th century. Also new is the visual differentiation of the different text genres and voices, which gives the book an unusual layout. Reading had prepared the bromides, and the six typefaces iconically represent and enhance the character of the respective texts. While italics, bold type and square brackets are chosen as usual for the poet's voice, the Romantic 'CHAPTER THE LAST' was printed in a large children's book typeface (in the first edition). The ornate handwriting (English script type) in the letters of a mother around 1860 mirrors the circumlocution in the content; the author's comment '[foxing and the fold of the paper render this paragraph illegible]' (p.140) authenticates it further. Letters by two mothers of 1945 are also presented in two different script types, but – in accordance with their simple language and raw emotions – they are simpler and less artificial. Finally, in the original edition, the letter and military report of Major P. Fashpoint-Shellingem of 1945 were written in a thickly black typewriter print with unappealing layout, producing an ugly, repellent effect (see also the signature, which Reading wrote in bad handwriting).[6]

The eloquent poet-persona is busy with his characteristic 'preoccupation', i.e. the 'on-running meditation on the impotence of his art' (Jenkins), but for the first time this happens indirectly and finds a surprising resolution. Both metrical notations and embittered attacks against sectarian violence, sub-humane 'trogs', 'microcephalic idiots', and 'mad despot captains' are also continued, but these – along with anger-stance and journalese poems – are far less numerous than before. The motif of timor mortis and the lyrical voice connect *Final Demands* with *For the Municipality's Elderly*, and details from *C* and *Stet* here become metaphors for the fragility of human existence: cancer, the AIDS virus, the nuclear accident (predicted in *Ukulele Music*) of 1986 at Chernobyl, and acid rain. As a counterpoint: 'cheerfulness keeps breaking through. We relish Reading's sharp ear for speech varieties, his deft singing of the unsingable: the sounds of flying a kite, of spilling a lorry-load of molasses' (Korn).

But the quiet tones of the previous books are more pervasive here. From *C*, the conciliatory, comforting images are carried over: the cobwebbed bottle of Bual, magical moments of family happiness, and the Laertides vision of a peaceful death. From *Stet*, the pastel painter's sky and the inclination for atheist prayer are continued, as is the use of the *Stet*-stanza; indeed, the lyrical discourse is so unusually prominent that O'Donoghue thought that 'proportionately it is a much more solemn performance', as the relatively many ' "poetly", reflective pieces' prove.

Final Demands stays at a greater distance from the "real world" than was the case before, and its gaze into the heart and mind was prepared for by the lyrical mode in *Stet*. That the pace has become slower and there remains more room for reflection is also evident from the typographical arrangement of the poems. In the first edition, each poem was granted a whole page to itself, which in the case of monostichs, Alcaic or *Stet*-stanzas leaves plenty of open white space.

The verse forms themselves are used much more freely, asynartetically and episynthetically than before, leaving more flexibility for the thoughts and images: an elegiac distich can now turn into a tristich (p.122) or *n*-stich (p.119); an Alcaic stanza within a *Stet*-stanza (p.118) can be lengthened or shortened by including or omitting single Alcaic verses, as the need may arise (p.125), or be turned into a double *Stet*-stanza (p.147). Single pentameters or hemiepes occur (p.131), and the Reading-hymn (p.131) is complemented and followed by an appropriately ambiguous hybrid of elegiac distich/hymn (p.131). Another new invention is a stichic sonnet in Alcaic verses (p.147) – all of these are variations on the dactylic-spondaic basis since *C*, which is further developed in *Perduta Gente* and *Evagatory*. The prosodically empty hemiepes-notation also runs through the book, causing some critics difficulties.[7]

In Duffy's enthusiastic review one formulation stands out: 'Reading's own, uniquely hermetic, verse'. Up to now, Reading's "unpoetic" diction had been lucid and transparent; accessibility (along with the avoidance of 'twee verse') was most important. This begins changing in *Final Demands*. The very first poem employs a new Latinate diction (p.118):

> [Chucked in the Parkray, naff juvenilia…]
> *$P_2 O_5$ drip-fed from a lead pipette*
> *fails to restore dull cotyledons*
> *Liquinured past revivification* [8]

> [Anhydrous *lauriers*. Stubbornly unrevivable old leaves.
> Drying up/not drying out.] — ⌣⌣ | — ⌣⌣ | —

The dried-up laurel seed leaves evoke the yellowing pages of the poems and letters and symbolise the nearing end of creativity (accordingly, these verses are reworked in *Last Poems* [p.118]).[9] The play on words in 'Drying up/not drying out' refers to weakened creative powers through alcohol, and the empty prosodic notation of hemiepes confirm this. Both the book's theme and one of the two main motifs are concentrated in a memorable image: 'instants of tangible loss' (p.139). Personally, nationally, globally – over generations the ghosts of the dead rustle through the book in sepia-brown, dry letters (brown print would have been most suitable for this book), with a metaphorical and natural pendant in the wilted natural leaves – laurel and olive – and in 'Croxley, papyrus and bond' (p.119).[10] With a number of ambiguities, the epigraph already ominously announces:

> [*Clearing the family's papers for next crowd's vacant possession:*
> *brown leaves of letters whose dead still correspond with ourselves.*]

The poet has found a 'long box of letters' (p.150) (the *donnée* of the text, or the pre-text, authentic found material in coffin shape) and tries to decode their sepia utterances. The box also contains an excerpt from the last chapter of a romantic Victorian novel (pp.120-21), written, it is implied, by a young girl called Sophia Mary and found by her sister Emily after her death. She almost burned it, but then followed another impulse and 'committed the dry leaves to the long box' (p.121). A hundred and twenty-five years later, the poet finds them. An episode from the sisters' childhood provides the material for the chapter (originally in big print, p.120):

> Tethered by long ropes to iron pins spiked in the sphagnum, some half-dozen skewbald ponies had been snatching at tufts of the coarse grass sprouting between gorse and ling on the Common where a gaily-painted waggon and grey-green thick canvas beehive-shaped tent betokened the eerie presence of "Mosey" the gipsy and his little tribe…Upon some nearby low gnarled May bushes, richly clotted with their dollops of new curdy blossoms, hung, or rather were pierced by the sharp

thorns, items of bright-hued Romany attire, freshly laundered and arrayed thus to dry, looking like nothing so much as gaudy red, green and blue parakeets perched fluttering.

The flowery beginning is deceptive. The death symbolism, already used in *C*, is gradually interspersed,[11] and different motifs, metaphors, verbal echoes and anadiploses are repeated elsewhere, where later decay is depicted ('Tribe', 'wood-smoke', 'char-crusted', 'forked', 'Woodcock', 'sheets of skin', 'runes', etc.). Gipsy Moses is shown 'tracing the strange symbols with charcoal upon the same sheets of skin or coarse paper'; he had a 'weird manuscript' before him and 'laboriously formed the runes which now, more than ever, reminded Emily of some dimly recollected thing' (p.121). They also remind Emily of the mysterious, illegible 'Roony Stanes', hieroglyphs which have survived over the centuries and been copied from a derelict Priory onto the steps of the Horse Shoe Inn's mounting-block, where the runes urge themselves on anybody who mounts the saddle of the (apocalyptic) horse. (p.121): [12]

> Like those forgotten, or not yet understood, utterances, which one could not help but contemplate as one mounted to the saddle in Bancroft's courtyard, these scripts seemed half to reveal and half conceal some strange sad mystery.
>
> * * * *
>
> Or was this, perhaps, the nature of all things written?

The secret of the runes, hieroglyphs, old papers, and of all literature lies in mankind's attempt to interpret life. This attempt is made via writing, in the hope of being able to understand, to express oneself to future generations, and to leave something permanent behind. Life takes the same course as Sophie's strange story: half understood because it is the same for everybody; half not understood because it is finally incomprehensible. What remains are illegible epitaphs, 'dead leaves': 'we bring our years to an end like a tale that is told' (p.149), as the mother writes on the death of Moses.

As a counterbalance to such gravity, this theme is humorously transposed to the late 1950s: the poet and his school-mates 'strutted the platform *brief candling* it in Thespian piss-take' (p.124). (Childhood reminiscences are rare in Reading's œuvre; they occur almost exclusively in *Stet* and *Final Demands*.) Another reminiscence of this particular stage in a Liverpool park recapitulates this event as 'cockily *Out, outing*' (p.147; see *Macbeth*, V.5.16-22). In another time shift, these children are seen as completely innocent, an incarnation of amusing harmlessness – as opposed to today's graffiti kids, who cannot even spell their 'despair-runes', but know existential fear (p.147).

Building on the metaphorical scope of the novel chapter, it is – after the runs – the *ploce* of the wild fowl caught by the gypsies, the woodcock, which becomes symbolically more intense as it progresses through the book. The brown feathers – 'plumage all straked like dead leaves' (p.121) – provide a mysterious, iconic link between the leaves written on with feathers by the deceased and the dead leaves of autumn (p.139):

> Flushed from meshed rust and ginger dead bracken and
> bramble, a woodcock, russet-barred, uncalling,
>   swishes, explodes up, plumply zigzags.
>   Underfoot: oval of steaming cupped stalks
>
> faintly imprinted in frost-silvered leaf-mould, fecal sac still warm,
>   chestnut-edged buff wisp of down, $\begin{cases} \text{instants of tangible loss} \\ \text{instance} \end{cases}$

The hemiepes follows half way down the page, with a lot of white space to ponder in between, and no full stop for an ending (p.139): 'frail wisps bestraked like dead leaves'. The unusual layout also visualises the sudden departure of the bird: like 'the sparrow brief through the feasting hall' (*Evagatory*).[13] Still, it leaves behind ghostlike traces of warmth: thawed frost where it had sat, a fresh, warm fecal sack – and a feather, 'frail wisps' of itself, another pun which draws together the patterning of the feathers and the lines on the old letters.

A moving parallel image is presented in the three fledgling sparrows which end up in a puddle of spilt molasses at Reading's workplace (p.143):

> Three-fingered Fazzy, hard-case, the Grinderman,
> gathers them gently into his denim bib,
>   nestles them fondly, runs warm water
>   into the millworkers' bog's cracked wash-bowl,
>
> mumblingly croons as he cleanses the sweet down *Frail little poor things*
> [*poor little frail little things, frail little poor little things*].

The inexperienced young birds and the gullible, big-eyed woodcock are 'poor hapless creatures' (p.121), easily destructible – both a painful and unusually tender symbol of vulnerable, fragile, transient human life. The unusual metaphorical arrangement is focussed and founded on the woodcock – natural existence, human communication and artistic transformation are organically merged, interdependent as they are.

At the same time, the narrative interweaves time, place, mysterious allusions and echoes, all underpinned by the book's metaphorical unity. As in a family saga, the plot extends over eight generations of the two familes Bancroft and Hurt. The poet's family is fictitiously presented in the epigraph as descendants of one of these families.

Between January 1857 and July 1862, the versifying, pious mother writes six long-winded letters from Tonge (Leicestershire) to her daughter Emily, who seems to have moved to the 'metropolis' by herself. The letters tell of humdrum domesticity, presents, illnesses and deaths in the neighbourhood, and the mother's anticipation of Emily's visit in May 1857, which however only materialises five years later, by which time the mother is quite ill. Emily by now is the wife of the priest John Shoebridge and a mother of two children and thus busy with the next generation. During's Emily's long absence grave things happen in Tonge. First the grandmother dies, then her own mother closely escapes death from cancer, and in 1859 her 24-year-old sister Sophia Mary dies 'after a very severe conflict with her last enemy Death' (p.145). Emily's mother writes about this almost without punctuation, her clichéd language unable to express how 'distressed' she really is, which means that these domestic catastrophes barely move the reader. For the difficult things in life, biblical stencils are employed: 'Thou great Jehovah, we are weak and frail things but Thou art Mighty' (p.152). Only one genuine (leitmotif) sliver of articulate emotion pierces the encrusted language – 'frail poor little frail beings' (p.145).

In the end, though, the graceful handwriting is undermined by the bombastic Christmas lyrics offered by the venerable Tonge matron and set to 'God Save our Church & State' (p.128):

> Britons once more strike home
> Tell the proud Church of Rome
> That we despise
> All her idolatries
> Masses and Mummeries,
> And pray that she may fall
> Never to rise.

The opportunity is irresistible: cut to the modern variant in Ulster, graffito in 'prettily bright tangerine: MURDER THE FUCKING SHITE POPE'. The other side spray their slogans in 'emerald' on the same 'bleak brick aerosolled dead-end'. And where there are religious fanatics, the 'crazed trog footy fans...baying for mashed flesh and gore' are not far, either (p.129). Here, though, the *Stet*-order is annulled for the first time; these lines about 'microcephalic idiots' have been crossed out by hand, 'as if to say that that which is inadequate as literary discourse still demands to be read' (Sheppard). And in the line 'Three hundred years of intractable nitwits' blather-some humbug', a reference to religious warfare, the 'three hundred' is deleted and replaced by 'four million'. To enable readers unfamiliar with *Stet* to understand the time scale, the reader is then invited to imagine the plaque of history and historiographers, and of this poet in particular, all three likened to 'a failed solicitor' (p.129)

> etched into verdigris *Clio & Co., incorporating*
> *War-Drum & Tub-Thump & Cant'*]
>   kneecapping, spatter and splat }
>   poesy, prattle and prate }

The first letter in the book is written on 9 February 1944 by a descendant of Mr Bancroft, the widowed Mrs A. Bancroft of Breedon-on-the-Hill, a small place near Tonge. Ungrammatical, breathless, and naive, she asks the 'Commanding Officer' to release her son, a Royal Marine Engineer, from the forces, so that he can work on the big estate in Tonge and support her (p.123). A second widowed mother sends an unorthographic begging letter to the same Major ten months later (for which another typeface is used). Mrs J. Hurt, resident of the ominous-sounding 'Ashbourne Park' near Thorpe, would like her son – also of the Marines – back 'on compassionate grounds' (p.136), because she needs him. On the first day of the new year she writes a second, apologetic letter, taking back her request because she fears to have harmed her son's reputation. This mother's two letters are all the more poignant because they are pointless, the reply to Mrs Bancroft by 'Major P. Fashpoint-Shellingem' having already announced in formulaic administrative jargon that the 'higher authority' did not permit such exemption (p.130).[14] T. Bancroft's number indicates that he is in the same regiment as B. Hurt, a painfully appropriate name (see pp.123 and 136).

The Allied Forces invaded Germany in February 1945. Shortly before the end of the war (and the book), a postscript appears: a three-page, single-spaced, '_S_E_C_R_E_T_' report by the Major, dated 5 March 1945, about an 'incident' that happened four days before while the Royal Marines were clearing mines from a road in eastern Holland (pp.154-56). The Major describes the event:

> During the operation some type of Booby Trap was initiated by the right hand clearance party resulting in the death of CH/X104783 Marine T BANCROFT and Po.X. 101922 (T) Mne (L/Cpl) B. HURT … Marine T. BANCROFT was thrown some 30 feet from the site of the explosion into the crater in the middle of the rd; L/Cpl B. HURT was thrown some 60 ft into an orchard adjoining the rd…The bodies …were recovered… and burial effected on the site.

Elsewhere, Reading addresses some readers' uneasy complaint: '["Doesn't he ever write about *happiness?*" – / **Husband & Wife & Daughter – A Pastoral...**]' (p.125). Even if it starts from the death-place of *C* (Callow Valley) with the picnic that had been overshadowed by Charon, it is devised as a genuine answer. In view of the world's status quo, words like 'peaceful' or 'joyful' can only be termed '[mawkish the platitudes]' by this thin-skinned poet, but nevertheless they do apply for a particular '*donnée* of time and *propre* cartography' (p.125):

> Most savoured plump pork pie ever picnicked-on,
> gleaming, the glazed baked crust, like a varnished Strad;
>   relish of Meaux tang, crunch-grained, brittle,
> peppery, fluted columns of celery;
>   hot earthy radishes; crisp frilled lettuce;
> bottles of Bass, beck-cold, effervescent gold,
> yeasty the foam. Plush cushions of whinberry,
> sheep-nibbled, silver-lichened, deep-pillow us...
>
> Paean to celebrate this: [pastoral, cliché, old hat –
> blush at the schmaltzy word] Love [but today it *is*, though, it *is* this].

The pastoral paean – composed of varied Alcaic stanzas and ending with a hymn-stanza (reversed distich), but not addressed to Apollo – follows the 'impotent gratitude' that goes with 'godless well-being', as in an earlier hymn (*Going On*, p.64). The word 'love' in *C* had to travel the maximum distance right the way through a gruelling book; here it is squashed between attack and defence. That is why it has a strong effect, as Potts says:

> When goaded, Reading can produce elegant and beautiful pastoral and elegiac pieces, but he hedges them about with qualification...To an extent, the feeling is expressed all the more powerfully for this reluctance, just as Reading's clinical detachment in many poems makes the atrocities he describes more grotesque (Potts, 1990, p.97).

Of course, the 'sunrise' (p.125) cannot stand unqualified; it has to be followed by a sunset – another '*donnée*' (p.142). Likewise, the 'Thrill of a kite held' in the paean (p.125) finds its negative pole in the imagery of another, rather more dubious 'secular ecstasy Hymn', 'Squalor Magnificat'. As in Hopkins' hymn 'The Windhover', there is a gliding rhythm, supported by the large number of appositions and by the layout; it may not depict a majestic bird, but nevertheless (p.131):

>   ...a *Mirror*'s
> double-page centre-spread, caught in grained wind,
>   lifts on a gritty, urinous-odoured gust,
>   levitates, kite-like, gale-buoyed, higher,
>   rises in slow flaps, graceful, up-spiralling,
>   soars to the 19th storey, with pulchritude
> slaps against, clingingly hugs
>   one of the uppermost panes.

In a second step, this hymn, too, is relativised by its context. The
literal, shocking antithesis to this second paean soon follows (p.132):

> Emerald digits heralding increases
>   glow from the charcoaly VDU screens
>
> nineteen floors up where populous feculence
> blands, with cathartic distance, to picturesque.
>   Suddenly, borne on some freak updraught,
>   double-page-spread of a *Daily Mirror*
>
> (EFFORTS ARE NOW BEING MADE TO ENCASE THE DAMAGED REACTOR)
>   presses against the bright pane,
>   clings, and remains, and remains

'On the same front page: **ARABS IN A-BOMB BID / NHS BOSS
BACKS HIV VIRUS BLITZ**' (p.144) – these now enlarge the narrative
strand. They are three of the four threats which in *Final Demands*
exemplify the precarious stability of human existence on the global
level. While the pub bore annotates the global headlines with pre-
dictable, amusing asides in the Ludlow 'Globe' ('they Middle
Easter lot... once them starts lobbin they fings round mate / no
fuckergonnerav no chance mister', p.144), the poet points to the fact
that these risks are hardly new (p.135): '*Myrsilus dead! Get pissed at
the joyous news!... /... /* Mad despot captains *still* scuttle ships of
state'. For the time being, the only thing for him to do is to counter
the 'Turbulent content' (p.135) with his 'formally elegant' and
'metrically dignified' verses.

'*Ave!,* impartial Viral Democracy' – this had been the sarcastic
aureate exclamation greeting the AIDS virus early on (in an appro-
priately ambiguous stanza form), albeit not as a single new calamity,
but as 'heightening all shared vulnerability' (p.122). The biological
stance is equally distanced: megalomaniacal *H. sap.* cannot stomach
evolutionary competition from another organism (the HIV virus).
Still, the tender voice of the poet also makes itself heard (p.144):
'[Poor kids, twice-vulnerable: some other godly twits' war / your
own too-dangerous love.]' (appropriately with double hemiepes).
The other source of contamination, radioactivity, is mentioned in
the same ironical way (p.131):

> [Grot is a great democrat. *H. sap* consanguined by waste...
> cultural disparates, sub-trog and top prof, Chernobyl/Chelsea
>   – suddenly neighbourly now: mutual Geigered air croaks.]

Finally, acid rain also pelts skulls democratically (p.132): 'acid rain
laced with lethal reactor-leak, / frozen in pills, percusses, fairly /
riddles the brainpans...' [15] Politically, ecologically and medically,
the threats are frontierless and ubiquitous: there is no longer any
escape, anywhere.

The decay of the 'body politic' is accompanied by that of the individual. The exopoetic trigger of this narrative sideline is biographical: in 1986, Reading turned forty. This psychological caesura of incipient middle age stands symbolically for the unavoidable decay on the personal level.[16] In the printer's terminology, the 'proofs' reach Reading's literary persona on his 40th birthday: his photograph on the book's cover is turned into a memorable hyperbolical image, appropriately rendered in elegiac distich (p.122):

> [Punctual, these (with a 40th birthday card) proofs are delivered –
> dust-jacket mug-shot confirms eyebag-puff/jowl-blubber/flab.]

Eerily, the outside world also seems to regard his age as precarious; in accordance with the existentially resignative stance on the global level, however, the invitation for a medical check-up is ignored as being 'Futile pathetic kindly-meant' (p.135), although the warning signs from *Stet* ('tremulous tightness') are now manifest as 'Three-day abdominal pain: dead scared – the liver / the plonk?' (p.137), and although later the relief about the cessation of the pain is after all worth a hymn on the most trifling things. (Only when seen in context, i.e. together, do the stances reveal the emotional complexity behind them; they also signify that it is difficult to find an unambiguous attitude to one's own death, in spite of all brave gestures.)

The poet-persona sees himself as part of a generation continuum binding his family to the dead personae of the letters. For instance, noticing the 'Knobbled amorphous purple grotesqueries' (p.150) of his father during a game of chess refers back to his sensation of 'premature arthritis' in his own hands (p.119); and both Gipsy Moses (p.121) and Mrs Hurt also suffer from this affliction (p.136). Similarly, the poet's death fright also infuses the chess game with his father, who, 'at least for a couple of moves', fights the advancing 'palfrey of pale polished ash' (p.150); (the poem was given the ambiguous title of 'Gambit' in a magazine publication). Thus, the poet's chess game with his daughter seems fraught in retrospect (p.119), and indeed the child's grandfather is not the only one who is close to death: his fingers 'fumblingly clutch at a worn-smooth pawn skull' (p.150) – an image recalling the bald skull of the ten-year-old girl after chemotherapy (which, in turn, links up with the Victorian mother's mastectomy). The runes of mortality are already visible on the child's temples (p.142): '10 years and 3 months old; on the paper white / temple, a turquoise vein like a hieroglyph'.

A sonnet (new: in Alcaic verses) links the "personal" side of decay with the public. The poet with his waxen jowls is not the only one on whom the years show (the dead leaves and transparent skin seem like the first indication of the palimpsests of *Last Poems*). His surroundings are also degenerating, for instance the stage in the park, which once was in the midst of plush rhododendrons. The difference is extolled in symploce (p.124):

> (...Weeds sprouted from the cracked stage.
>
> Weeds overwhelm the wrecked stage...)

Three years later, with another allusion to Macbeth's 'Out, out, brief candle' monologue, the stage is seen as iconically symbolising the short drama of life, and the graffiti are accordingly read as 'despair-runes' (p.147):

> Urinous, burnt-out, relic of civic wealth
> 29 years on: wintery sun projects
> (onto flaked stucco daubed with despair-runes) a
> palimpsest walking shadow. A fingernail
> rot-tests the wreckage, strays to a middle-aged
> wattle of jowl-flab, substance of candle-wax.

The youths are not the only ones guilty of defiling the country. The adults produce 'more ambitious garbage', as Reading wrote in an article (Reading, 'Going', p.33). 'Kwik Save' trolleys (p.124) adorn a public paddle-pool; 'Squashed polystyrene Indian Take-Out trays, / eddying grease-smirched chip-papers, Pepsi cans, / scuttering plastic cups' (p.131) fly and roll unhindered through the streets. Already in *C* garbage was the tangible symptom of the general 'shit' threatening to suffocate the country. The degeneration of mores and the maltreatment of the environment are shocking in themselves, but then they are also presented as a miniature version of the much more dangerous radioactive harakiri. Personally, nationally, globally: again, there is no escape.

So, the 'Final Demands' are formulated – solely on the personal level, because it is the only one where there can reasonably be any hope of fulfilling any wishes. The wish (*'may they not miss me much'*, pp.119, 135) is expressed twice. After this, the other, explicit 'final demands' refer to the practical matters connected with the poet's anticipated death (p.137): '(Access, phone bill, / water rates, overdraft, life insurance)'. On his 40th birthday, he consults his cheque book, because 'the Mrs and kid shan't, at least, be bequeathed debt'. Furthermore, the poet's 'final demands' are perhaps also addressed to the reader's attention, or even empathy. The notion of responsibility – towards oneself, one's family, and other creatures – can also be distilled as another of the 'demands'. Paul Bailey asked the author directly, who explained:

There are quite a lot of final demands; a sort of responsibility pervades the thing a bit concerning family responsibilities, the sort of tension one has between loved ones and one's own well-being; the final demands of the body politic; the final demands of an individual trying to produce another...yet another book, set of verse and what not, and that last one perhaps breaks down (Bailey, M).

In the end, though, the only one genuine 'final demand' is easily overlooked, for all its prominence. The 'last enemy', death, demands of everybody the highest, final price for life.

That the death of the poet is possibly not so far off is indicated in the poem fantasising about suicide (seen already in *C*; see also *Last Poems*). Like a palimpsest, the sepia-coloured leaves show the lines of the dead. The differences between the generations gradually also dissolve, as pain, loss, and grief are constant over the centuries and unchangeable – 'so does he deeply immerse in the fall of past generations, / ...sinks in the lines of the dead' (p.119). Now that he has immersed himself in this double correspondence, the next and last step is traced out (p.153):

> [...when they read this, it may be already done...]
> Low over dim pines, dactylic phrases croak
>   (*Scolopax rusticola* roding),
>   finishing off in a sneeze-like high 'tswick',
>
> [... supine in bracken...] the only other sound is a rattle
>   (barbs in a brown plastic phial): — ⌣⌣|— ⌣⌣|—

The vision: like the woodcock, he hides in the ferns, and like the bird, he will leave 'frail wisps bestraked like dead leaves' (p.139) behind, i.e. the pages of this book. Different from the Christian Victorian ('Oh let us prepare for our last moments', p.146) and in accordance with his pragmatic 'final demands', he hopes for practicality rather than metaphysics – 'pox on all quacks who won't prescribe knock-out drops' (p.157).

The projected end of the poet-persona, of the nation, and of the globe finds its natural equivalent at the end of *Final Demands* in the long prepared death of the word, of poetry, of language. The resounding poems have been accompanied from the very beginning by empty, toneless noises; the rustling, rattling, wheezing, clanging and clattering of omnipresent death is continuously heard throughout the whole book. When he lies down in the leaves ready to die, the poet hears the 'comforting rattle' of the sleeping-tablets; the brutal graffito 'Cadder shag Abo-Gaz, Kiddo de Wanker' (p.124) has a hammering sound; the geiger counter croaks, the dactyls croak, joined by crows (a symbol of impending evil), in the bracken the woodcock rustles, an air-hose hisses, 'pills' of acid rain and radioactive fall-out knock on the skulls, 'Bickering Pepsi tins' clack on the icy canal in the rhythm of an elegiac distich, as in 'Aeolian' (p.124, also 137),

stuttering, blown, tintinnabulant: —— | — ·· | ——
— ·· | — ·· | — || [Bleakly harmonious grot.]

In the end, the final 'rustle of old gratuitous scrivenings' (p.158) comes not only from the found letters, but also from turning the last page of this book; here, what has remained is now crumbling (following the shocking military report). In conclusion, the images and motifs are united: woodcock, mankind, laurier and letter-paper (p.158):

frail wisps of dead bestraked leaves

crackle of anhydrous bay

— · · | — · · | —
Croxley pa pyrus and bond

|| — ·· | — ·· | —

Further down on this last page the second hemiepes appears again as empty prosodic notation, as if it was becoming ever more difficult to find words. Thus, it is unambiguously and resolutely crossed out. The *stet*-order 'let it stand' is annulled in *Final Demands* – a cancellation of the third degree. Some time after the death of the protagonists the written remnants fall to dust, too. Nothing survives – not words, not letters, not poetry books.

At the London launch of *Final Demands*, Reading read extracts from the book, ending his reading by producing a little brown phial from his pocket and shaking the tablets in the rhythm of the hemiepes. The hiatus was there. Reading confirmed this soon after in an interview: 'In fact, I seem to have reached something of an impasse – it's mildly disconcerting' (Bailey, M).

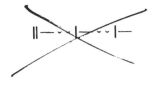

Perduta Gente (1989):
Underworlds

Published in June 1989, *Perduta Gente* was the first of Reading's collections to make an international impact. Not only was it a Poetry Book Society Choice, but it was later combined with *Ukulele Music* in a volume from American Northwestern University Press (1994). More importantly, *Perduta Gente* received added prominence as his most recent collection when Reading won a Lannan Literary Award in 1990. This $35,000 prize is the most prestigious distinction he has received. Launched in 1989, the Lannan programme was established to further 'the careers of emerging and under-recognised artists', 'to foster serious criticism and discussion of contemporary art and literature, and to suggest new, experimental and provocative literature to a wider audience'. The other poets to receive awards that year were Seamus Heaney, Carolyn Forché and Derek Mahon. Reading's was given because he was 'a strikingly original British poet...His writing is forceful and uncompromising, difficult and exhilarating. [His] subjects are topical, daring and often painful' (press release, Lannan Foundation, 11 September 1990 [M]). The Lannan Award also led to reading tours in America (1992, 1994) and a sinecure (Lannan Literary Residency) in Texas in 1998-99 (where he wrote *Marfan*).

The temporary loss of orientation after *Final Demands* had been termed a 'purposeful hiatus' by Reading (Potts, 1990, p.96) – quite rightly, because *Perduta Gente* became the *furioso* beginning of a new creative phase and was in its own right an accomplished work of great authority, attracting much more attention than the previous volume. Reading was invited to read extracts on TV, and was interviewed and reviewed widely as one of the most important poets in Britain; Harold Pinter selected *Perduta Gente* as the best of his three best *Books of the Year*, saying: 'In this brilliant and ferocious poem, Reading looks under the lid at those consigned to the shit-heaps of this country... A *tour de force*'.[1]

Reading had become an inspirational figure for the new generation of socially aware British poets, including *Scratch* editor Mark Robinson, who wrote that *Perduta Gente*

> makes you feel grateful once again that Reading is there making it that little bit more difficult for people to pretend, a little more difficult for

people to write off poetry as a spent force. He is the most important
poet of the eighties, the best chronicler of the breakdown in Britain,
the poet who brings it most alive, who upsets you the most, whilst
leaving you some hope, through his wit and his witness, his gallows
humour, his anger and compassion, his restless need to put the truth
over in a truthful way... The pleasing dissonance that echoes from this
book – pleasing both for its great poetry, and for the simple fact that
someone is saying these things – rings truer than most anything else
you're likely to read this year.

In *Perduta Gente*, socio-political reality is intertwined so closely
with the human condition, and the emotive impact of the book is
so forceful, that readers are *nolens volens* engaged in a dialogue with
the author of this book about matters outside poetry: the state of
our world, *Weltanschauung*, and morals. *Perduta Gente* hits our
sense of accountability hard, and at the same time it is Reading's
most moving book.

Even if he tirelessly repeats that his art cannot effect anything and
in the end is utterly futile, Reading's irrational, manic impulse to keep
writing indicates an unquenchable sense of responsibility that qual-
ifies his sense of hopelessness. Imlah stated that Reading 'emerges
from *Perduta Gente* more certainly one of the very few poets in
England who demand to be read'. Fraser Steel, who had broadcast
poems by Reading on BBC radio, also saw Reading's continual dev-
elopment culminate in the dignified seriousness of *Perduta Gente*:

> *Perduta Gente* is the unmitigated summation of human catastrophe
> Reading has been moving towards. His early work could have been
> taken as the miscellaneous production of a basically comic writer in a
> particularly harsh vein. Through the 80s, single poems have given way
> to composed books which mark out their areas of outrage and pin them
> down for inspection, often with procedures which are ingeniously
> mechanical: [e.g. in *C*], and in the more recent books an array of clas-
> sical metres...is used to manhandle intractable material. It's as if the
> individual lyric, harvested with a sickle, has given way to the heavy
> machinery needed to cut and bail the prairies of enormity which Reading
> faces...The value and importance of Peter Reading's poetry is that he
> gives us the *Inferno* without the *Purgatorio* and *Paradiso*. There is no
> glimpse of redemption... But the ills of humanity, unmitigable though
> inflected by changing times, are Reading's theme, and this time he's
> managed to get most of them in. It will not be popular, and it is not
> tourism.

Douglas Dunn conceded that Reading was the 'harshest observer
in contemporary writing' and his poetry 'bleakly impressive', but
objected that 'his extremism tends to make the real feel like where
minorities live and no one else'.

The "reality" of Reading's poems is often called into question
because he concentrates on what many, perhaps most, people

would want to ignore or resign themselves to. But, of course, to say Reading is distorting or falsifying reality in his work is to miss the point: for one thing, writing is always a form of distortion of reality anyway, a response to the writer's reality rather than a depiction of the reader's. Just as readers leading contented lives cannot deny the existence in reality of what Reading is responding to, his 'lost people' in *Perduta Gente* do not prove the absence of happiness in the "real" world either: both are there. This author feels compelled to respond to aspects of our world rarely faced up to in life or literature, and he does so in very unconventional ways. While this goes some way towards explaining why Reading will never be a bestseller, it also explains the unusually strong impact of his voice, which is 'instantly unforgettable' and unique, as has been noted (Crawford). Reading cannot accept man-made horrors as given and feels a moral duty to look at the so-called 'underside' of the world. Blake Morrison stressed the basic ethical impetus:

> Reading is the Laureate of Grot...; of all the gunge and dreck we prefer to forget... If some readers find his knackered, puke-stained Britain too much to take, he clearly sees no reason to stop describing it until we've done something about cleaning up the mess.

That nature, love, or responsibility are special and part of the overall picture, as some critics object, is stating the obvious. It is something Reading never disputes – quite the contrary: that is what his hymns, pastorals, *For the Municipality's Elderly*, *The Prison Cell & Barrel Mystery*, and *Final Demands* are about, and they contribute as much to the "whole picture" as the contentious *Ukulele Music* and *Perduta Gente*. What he challenges, though, is the notion that insular idylls could be of the slightest relevance for the future of the planet or indeed for those who cannot have peaceful, comfortable lives. In this sense, Reading addresses a reality which is superordinate to any kind of untroubled reality. Reading further challenges the notion that *H. sap*'s sense of responsibility is highly developed enough to secure the survival of the species. In this light, idyllic subject-matter cannot but take second place in Reading's œuvre, with reduced functions.

John Whitworth, who had expressed his admiration for Reading's tough approach six months before, now found himself irritated by *Perduta Gente* and at a loss: 'what does Peter Reading want?'[2] The interviewer Potts handed on this question to Reading:

> Reading shrugs off the question. 'It presupposes that poetry is some sort of tool to engineer something. It can be, but it doesn't need to be as calculating as that. Paintings don't do that; when you look at a Rothko or a Giotto, you're not assailed by the question "What does he want?"

There are certain allegiances, but you don't ask that question... you see the thing, and a kind of vision.' He adds: 'What – to be crassly naive about it – what I want in *Perduta Gente* is an end to the unpleasant circumstances which its heroes and heroines have to put up with' (Potts, 1990, p.95).

In no other book did Reading look as closely at misery as in *Perduta Gente*. In the *Poetry Book Society Bulletin,* Gavin Ewart explained to PBS members why this was so:

> Reading... does for the winos what Kipling did for the private soldier in his *Barrack Room Ballads*. He gives them a presence in literature (and 'don't think it couldn't be you' – a similarity to Kipling's 'single men in barracks most remarkably like you')...There are nasty things here, just as there are nasty things in the war poetry of Owen and Sassoon, and in Chekhov's penal colony. It's better to know, even if Reading perhaps accentuates the negative and eliminates the positive, than not to know. If you know, you can do something about it.

Again, Ewart was addressing the socio-realistic side of the book even if he hastened to add that Reading was not a political writer and offered no solutions. Also, at the Salamanca Festival of Literature in Australia, where Reading was invited in 1989 to read *Perduta Gente* and made a strong impact, discussion concentrated on his social commentary:

> SANDY McCUTCHEON: Everyone has commented on what a stark picture you're painting of Britain, and I wonder what your feelings are about the future of Britain... there's obviously some passion in there for you.
> PETER READING: Yes, it's perhaps a stark picture, but that's because it's unfortunately a stark place at the moment. But I would like to emphasise, really, that in many ways this stands as a metaphor for something much larger than England, which is, after all, only a tiny place. It's to be regarded as a microcosmic suggestion of a more important set of global issues, really.[3]

Reading is here hinting at what is fairly evident from the imagery of the book and its three different thematic strands, starting with the title. Also, it is significant that in this later phase Reading leaves hardly any room for the gallows humour and wit which had so far grounded his works firmly in the visible and audible world and had also provided some counterbalance to the hopelessness. Where there is nothing more to laugh about, the end is in sight. Indeed, soon after finishing *Perduta Gente* Reading sensed a 'Sibelian silence' [C] coming his way. He often mentioned Sibelius in those months. He felt that most of what he had to say had been said.

Perduta Gente initiates Reading's valediction. At the same time, continuity from the previous books is ensured by overlapping subject-matter and technique, while the changes and developments are distinctive and purposeful, with clear aims. It also avoids using strategies that by then might have appeared repetitive and schematic, such as the intrusive square brackets with the author's (self-)critical snarl; the perspective-changing devices used to create distance; the Dickensian exaggeration of characters; and the personae's self-revealing incompetencies and weaknesses. The polyphony and cacophony produced by using different voices and abrupt changes of register and tone recedes into the background. As Morrison says: 'For all its mix of registers, his art aspires to the condition of music, the presiding instrument here the balalaika, plangently wailing its burden of loss.' Single voices are no longer pinned to certain dictions, but given a greater linguistic range; and three different stylistic levels – demotic, neutral, elegiac – are maintained almost throughout, harmonising in a peculiar way. This makes the voices more impressive and convincing, drawing them together more closely so that their impact develops through concordance and superimposition (rather than through contrast and conflict). Thus, the superordinate diction de-individualises the dramatis personae in such a way that even a specialist register like the dosser language can call for some general validity. This, in turn, both mirrors and undermines one of the thematic concerns – that of universal danger.

The lyrical passages in *Perduta Gente* are much more homogeneous than was ever the case in previous books. The element of entertainment and suspense is put aside to make way for a strong unified vision, rendered in 'language as inventive, muscular and startling as anyone's now writing', as Hart says. This vision finds new expression in *Perduta Gente*: despite the highly topical material, it is less immediate than before, despite the intense "pessimism" less extreme, and despite clear warnings less insistent, hence more convincing and more ineluctable than ever before.

Consistent with the rest of the book, the metrics in *Perduta Gente* are unified but loosened up by fragmentation and variation.[4] This adds to the impression of detachment and also slows the pace down. The start of Reading's valediction is marked by a halting, thickening rhythmical heaviness, which peaks in the monosyllabic, monometrical verses of the first and last pages. The metra episyntheta hitherto used are now brought back to the basic form initiated in *C*. Even if it does not often appear intact and is broken up typographically, the elegiac distich is the point of reference of the increasingly independent metres in this volume.[5] Most frequent are stichic hexameters with closing hemiepes or stichic pentameters (at times only appearing as an epyllion). Elegiac distichs are assembled into stanzas, too; and elegiac *n*-stichs, single Adonic-

verses (or, the last two feet of a hexameter), and a hymn stanza
also appear. All pervasive, though, is the weighty single hemiepes: it
is used for emphasis and amplification, and rendered even heavier
by abundant anacrusis and hypercatalexis. When used stichically
(as, for instance, in the last poem), this reciprocus versus can take
on an alarming, authoritative quality in its cumulative repetitiveness
– an adequate, musical cadence for weighty prophecies. However,
what is most important in *Perduta Gente* is the closeness of the
diction to that of the Old Testament prophets, whose verses are
set in markedly short lines, too. The lyrical (rather than narrative)
character of the book and the atmosphere of an 'incontrovertible
end' can also be expressed much better by short lines.

Perduta Gente is a fragmented collage of a fragmented world, a
cubist-like artwork of untitled poems, two prose-strands, and photo-
copied newspaper cuttings and excerpts from authentic secret doc-
uments, which are used like illustrations. O'Driscoll noted how with
this book, 'over which the ghost of Kurt Schwitters hovers, Peter
Reading returns to the realm of visual art' (O'Driscoll, p.218);
Brownjohn describes it as an 'experimental novella... [which] has
been assembled and arranged with the imaginative resource and
technical care of a considerable poet'. At the launch (and at suc-
cessive readings), the newspaper and document pages were shown
as slide projections in between the readings of the prose and poems.
The author's intermittent diary entries in prose (photocopied pages
from a note-pad covered in Reading's handwriting) for a while run
parallel with the extracts from a fictitious biography of Reading
(set in larger print). As in the interview with the astrophysicist in
Stet the prose texts start and end in the middle of a sentence, thus
spilling over into their surroundings, as do the excerpts from the
secret papers, and the poems with no final full stop. The incom-
pleteness of these passages also creates the impression that only a
brief insight is being granted, as if the true dimensions of the dis-
tress cannot be fully depicted or discerned from the comfort of a
desk or armchair.

Like the fragments of letters, the badly cut-and-pasted newspaper
cuttings – depicting top property ads and a militant letter to the
publisher by the notorious 'Ex-Soldier' about 'The Vagrancy Issue'
(all authentic) – all have a clear antithetical function and in this
context take immediate effect. The seven extracts from the secret
document of the 'Energy Authority' are also scattered across the
whole book. The novel-like infiltrative structure not only makes
for diversity, but is thematically relevant. Besides, as Reading said
[LI]: 'As the papers were what was important about the papers I

left them as they were, laid them out on a big table and put them in between the poetry.' These documents are genuine, too, and were indeed unlawfully photocopied, as is said in the book. The real scandal, of course, is that the documents were secret and kept from the public in the first place: they give details about the risks and consequences of radioactive contamination for the employees of a damaged nuclear plant.

Perduta Gente was originally unpaginated for reasons of unification and, as a mosaic, could be read in any order. Read sequentially, it appears more organised than usual, because despite the mixing up of text genres a partial chronology can be made out; also, the narrative plot is relatively clearly defined in this book, backed up by the depiction of similar images and situations from different perspectives, by the two refrains and by the *ploce* repetition of single words.[6]

Tectonically, *Perduta Gente* is Reading's most accomplished book; the novelistic outline, epic scope, lyrical density, and rhapsodic character also help to make it extraordinary. Reading places the book in a great literary tradition, which gives it the portentous, solid foundation needed to help carry the subject-matter. As Virgil's ghost did with Dante 650 years ago, Reading leads the reader through the dark forest of Error and the different circles of Hell. (There is no salvation in Reading's book.) Mostly in italics, the versions (pp.163, 185, 188) of the *Inferno* are a hybrid amalgam of the original and of different translations. Reading admitted that he 'altered, or lifted, phrases' [LI]. The book title is taken from the most prominent passage:

> Per me si va nella città dolente
> Per me si va nel eterno dolore
> Per me si va tra la perduta gente

is the inscription above the Gates of Hell (*Inferno*, Canto III). In Sayers' translation:

> Through me the road to the city of desolation;
> Through me the road to sorrows diuturnal;
> Through me the road among the lost creation.[7]

'Perduta gente' is archaic, polyvalent, resonant, and metrically an Adonius (which goes with elegy). It immediately signifies that not only individual lost people are meant, but the whole species, perhaps even the whole of creation. 'Let us observe and silently pass by' are not original words by Reading, either: they are Virgil's words to Dante every time they have gone through a circle. Reading also uses the Dantesque images of agony – sighing in limbo, crawling and weeping in mud ('slurry'), fire in the sixth circle, 'City of Dis', black wind.[8]

Other literary sources of inspiration not immediately recognisable include the Old Testament apocalyptic prophecies (Lamentations, 1.1ff. and Isaiah, 10.1ff.); these passages are also typographically marked as archaic ('u' instead of 'v', as in Reading's Oxford facsimile King James edition of 1611). Reading was 'haunted by the cadences,' he said; 'there are some extremely resounding bits in it, which seemed appropriate in that context' [LI]. Another translationese passage was taken from a quotation of Aeschylus' *Agamemnon* in *Jude the Obscure*; and a quotation of a novel and two images of radioactive pollution go back to a novel Reading had reviewed, *Grace* (1988) by Maggie Gee.

However, *Perduta Gente* was not triggered by literary sources.

> The first [poems] were a couple of poems about winos, homeless people kipping under the South Bank Festival Hall in London, which is quite a posh concert hall...Just at the back of it there's a kind of rat-run – it's just a dark, uriniferous mess, where a lot of people live. Within the last decade these people have proliferated hugely. What were a few embarrassing individuals have become a huge population, like a little township immediately at the back of the cultural goings-on of London. This has always dismayed me when I've come into contact with these people. I find it very dismaying. The sort of thing one would almost burst into tears about (Edgar, p.57).

While he was pursuing this subject, somebody gave him the secret papers about radiation, and although the link was not clear straight away:

> That was the point at which the two things came together. It seemed to me not to be too far-fetched to suggest that, in the same way that people have a bad deal thrust on them, and they can't do a thing about it, so the bulk of us have a lot of things thrust on us by governments and so on which we can't do anything about. It's just beyond our powers of dealing with in any practical way (Edgar, p.58).

The book opens with the poem 'Last Movement', which is in fact a multiple ending. Along with the "lyrics" depicting stinking wretchedness, the visual imitation of the last five bars of Sibelius' Fifth Symphony (one upbeat is rendered by an extra syllable) and the majestic, expressive pauses in between the six crashing chords exemplify the co-existence of the peak of civilisation and the expendable outcasts. They are in the Festival Hall at the same time, only separated by a few floors. The metres and registers used enhance this point; the concert is described in Reading's hymn stanza, while the synaesthetic 'concert' underneath consists of an elegiac distich followed by a disintegrating distich. The two spheres are also connected by the juxtaposition of Latinate words and slang.

Not much has changed since the North-South divide of the 19th century; at the end of the 1980s, visitors to the Royal Festival Hall could not get to this palace of culture without repeatedly encountering some of the estimated 50,000 homeless people living in the area dubbed 'Cardboard City' or 'Doss City'. (Estimates for the whole of England were six times higher.)[9] Walking past the dark, stinking, cave-like habitations blackened by fires around the Waterloo Station underpasses, it was as if one had entered the Inferno minutes before attending Reading's reading of *Perduta Gente* in the Royal Festival Hall.

This world is portrayed realistically in *Perduta Gente*; the author-persona knows it well. Six handwritten pages from a dosser's diary are given, and the page numbers (101 up to 117) indicate that the diary-writer has been in this position for some time (they are also oblique line references to the first passage paraphrased from Dante). Curiosity about the diarist's identity is satisfied only halfway through the book: the poems warn us that this fate can befall anybody, so it is only logical that the "author" of *Perduta Gente* should become homeless, as cross-references between the fictitious biography and his own accounts verify: nobody 'could have expected that the author himself would have plumbed such depths of filth, depravity and degradation' (p.182). The 'author' thus assumes the role of a persona, and as such is the author of the poems warning us that anybody can become homeless (the same double-twist as in *C*).[10] At the launch, when Reading read the biography passages at speed, it made them appear fleeting, principally irrelevant. At the same time the condensed impact created the opposite effect, i.e. that one could not listen closely enough to be able to understand the true enormity of this man's fate. It became clear in the end that the details did not matter; what did matter was the banal fact that a person became homeless who could not possibly have foreseen or expected it.

The author alternates between a 'Derry' (derelict house) and the crypt of St Botolph, where food and clothing are distributed (p.169): 'It's like a sort of air-raid shelter with us all waiting for something awful to go away, or, worse, to happen' (echoing the ominous monostich in *Stet*). A plot can be traced in outline; the setting is a time which brings warm family festivities to some and icy nights of loneliness to others – between 'Friday 19th, Tues 23rd' (p.172) and 'January, 2 a.m.' (p.178). Some luxuriate inside the Royal Hotel, others sleep on the hotel's kitchen window-ledges, surviving on warmed air from the ventilation (pp.172, 178). The soup kitchens keep them from starving. The 'Poor Sisters of the Mother of God' of St Mungo give out dry bread and soup, enduring severe tests of humility and perseverance (p.175): 'One of the blokes under the fly-over climbed into the van and got his dick out. He's a Brasso addict and was sick all over the chief nun'. Mucky Preece urinates into another nun's face (p.196). These (authentic) incidents [11] ensure that no sentimental notions develop: Reading's dossers really are 'expendables', and their base treatment of the only people who actively help acutely brings home the hopelessness of the situation.

These 'base beasts' (p.175) are the author's company, so he knows their habits. Often he is with an 'old shitty dosser' and his 'missiz' (p.172), who earn their living by 'buskin' in Victoria or Euston underground stations. The three are beyond the dignity of names, but can be identified by their drinks (Strongbow, Carlsberg and Thunderbird). The old man's drunken slurge and begging litany resounds throughout the book – 'gizzera quiddora fiftyfer fuggsay' (p.174)[12] – but the reader's potential sympathy is prohibited by his violent kicking of his 'missiz', 'bellowing "fugg-bag, / fuggbagging fuggbag"' (p.191). Also, the details of the 'missiz' accident on the escalator where she breaks a leg and loses an arm, as well as the details surrounding her death have to be pieced together like a mosaic (pp.165, 174, 191, 197), which heightens the narrative tension.

As with previous books and their specialist areas of focus, *Perduta Gente* acquaints the reader with the lore and lingo of dosserdom: the down-and-outs sleep in the spike (dosshouse) or do a skipper; they are called dipsos (dipsomaniacs) and dispos (dispossessed), winos, alcos, bums, scumbags and tosspots; they drink 'meths', i.e. 'Blue' (causing blindness and death), followed by a 'bottle-bank cocktail' or Brasso, 'Melted-down boot polish, eau de Cologne... surgical spirit, / kerosine, car diesel, derv...' (p.203). Eating a Trebor Mint after Brasso on bread 'takes off the heat and the taste' (p.203). Drugs are mentioned, too; pain-killers are affordable, but one resident of the derry is also into expensive 'H and Coke and D.D.A.s and skin-popping and main-lining' (p.205).

The description of this miserable world is grotesquely counterpointed by the newspaper cuttings of militant letters by the notorious ex-soldier on the 'Vagrancy Issue' (p.166) suggesting a 'Remedy' against parasites and criminals: cut 'DHSS cash' (p.193), also 'chop off [their] arms' (p.166). The cut-out words 'Cut dole' acquire the reverse meaning as 'dole' is later used in the sense of 'doleful', or 'dolent', a neologism. More grotesquely still, the articles that would like to see the dossers dead protect them physically from dying from the cold at night (p.165): layers are placed between clothing, 'night attire proper for doing a skipper in icy December / under the Festival Hall' (p.193). The other part of the newspaper, 'Wound

round a varicose indigo swollen leg' (p.193) in stinking layers of
trousers, advertise '*bijou* / River-View Flatlets'; property pages warm
the homeless sleeping by the river (pp.161, 199): 'London's most
exciting apartments all have river views, £330,000 to £865,000 –
Talk Terms Today or regret it for the rest of your life'. A 'most
startling penthouse £2,500,000' comes complete with kennels and
'maintenance free storage containers' (p.199); in these the author
sleeps.

Squalor is not absent from the countryside, either. 'Derelict barns
in south Shropshire are fetching six figure prices', a newspaper
reports (p.161): these barns have adjacent pig-pens, inhabited by a
descendant of Tucker's from *C*, who also has an authentic [C],
but heavily ironic name: Mucky Preece. (Boris the Swine and the
author sleep in pig-pens, too.) He, too, puts the newspaper to good
use as toilet paper.

These stanzas are further intensified by the literary superimposition
– stanzas from Dante – with which they alternate, leaving no doubt
as to the location of this world (p.163): '*Now we arrive at the front
of the ruin*'[13] is the start of the tour through Hell, where terrible
moans from the futile are heard in the darkness. Here, the ruin is
the derelict barn, which is, of course, (hel)l-shaped. '**Money no
object to buyer of L-shaped picturesque old barn / seeking
the quiet country life**' (p.163). Dante's tour proceeds across the
Acheron to Limbo, the first circle of Hell, where the non-Christians
do not even utter a moan, '*Now we lie sullenly here in the black mire*'
(Canto IV, 13 and 22-42). And so to Mucky Preece's pigsty. The
barn changes hands for £222,000 (p.161), bringing about Mucky
Preece's homelessness (p.180), driving him to London (p.209),
where another interlacing of Dante's and Reading's stanzas describes
the infernal emergency night-shelters, and the damned in the vesti-
bule of the 'tormented Sad'. An imagined Hell is supererogatory,
as we already have one on earth (p.188).[14]

Reading aptly uses the old Testament prophets' voices to con-
front those accountable for these hellish conditions. The first and
last stanza of the core poem of this book (p.185) are adaptations of
the *Lamentations* and the prophecies of Isaiah, with echoes of words
and phrases from Dante.[15] The national glory of Jerusalem – and
London – is over, because God's wrath will send a storm to earth
(Jeremiah, 30.23) to destroy all. The Day of Judgment – 'the day
of the storme' – is imminent: 'Something is in the air' (p.185),
which is not just radiation, just as it was not only apocalyptic in
Ukulele Music ('Something is in the wind: terrible storms', p.45).
Thus, the ambiguous 'dole' is ever-lasting, the 'sorrows diuturnal'

(Canto III, 2). In this poem, the Biblical prophecies provide the frame for Dante's and our own Hell, and the author's prophecy is placed at the centre: that we will not awaken from this nightmare.

'All bad things come in threes', one could say of *Perduta Gente*. Reminiscent of the triad of Inferno-Purgatory-Paradiso or perhaps even the Holy Trinity, the wails and descriptions are phrased mostly in steps of three adjectives or three nouns: 'Bankrupted, batty, bereft' (p.173), '*children and women and men*' (p.188), 'shrieks, lamentations and dole', 'lost livers, roof-trees and hearths' (p.212), etc. The accumulating repetitions convey the impression of irrefutability and resignation, thus underlining the central thought. 'Gagged, disregarded, unsought' refers to both the narrative level and the metaphorical level and accordingly occurs twice in the book. All triads prepare for the end, where people await 'chamber or bunker or vault' and words are reduced to the ultimate incantation 'woe vnto woe vnto woe' (p.213).

The stocktaking also proceeds in threes. Not only in the city and country, but also by the sea there are homeless people. They erect ramshackle shelters in the dunes, which are destroyed by a JCB in yellow-black uniform to ensure the survival of other species ('**Reserve of Endangered / Natural Habitats**', p.167), while a 'regular clank of a bell / tolls from a wreckbuoy, swung by the reflux' (with echoes of John Donne and Eliot's 'The Dry Salvages'). One thing always leads to another; the 'undesirables' are chased away three times in all. Mucky Preece's mother (p.180), 'a lone hag gippo' in a trailer and with a pony, is driven away to London by cruel schoolchildren revived from *Tom o'Bedlam's Beauties* (p.162):

> But when she skedaddled, a stain,
> delineating where she'd been,
> etiolated and crushed,
> blighted that place and remained.

The 'crone scumbag' ends in a cardboard box, herself 'etiolated and crushed' (p.212); and the eviction of homeless families from the squat by bailiffs in yellow hats completes the picture (p.170).

There are also three vignettes documenting comparable misery abroad. For a long time, Reading had not been able to travel abroad for financial reasons, but in the 1980s he was invited to give readings in Sarajevo and Kiel (on the Baltic); images of both cities are used in *Perduta Gente*. The third foreign setting is a birchwood on the southern edge of Moscow.[16] *Perduta Gente* is not merely a socio-political comment on the conditions in England: the problem is international, global.

These realistic images have at the same time an intense metaphorical dimension. The motif of the city as a symbol of Hell is a literary convention that enables Reading to strengthen the existential basis of *Perduta Gente*. For this reason, Sarajevo, Kiel and Moscow are not named, but allegorised as 'the city', specified in 'Through me the way into the doleful city'. Of course, Dante's 'città dolente' in the inscription on the Gates of Hell rhymes with 'perduta gente', drawing the two images even more closely together. Thus, in the Moslem 'Turkish end of the city' smoke from grilled meat fills the air, evoking an image of Hell. Beggars are there too, 'manifest mendicant mountebanks', extorting money from the visitor while 'Muezzins were Tannoying dirgefully' (p.179) – the lamentations are omnipresent. The homeless in Germany raid litter bins, envy the ducks their bread and spend the night under the spans of the university library (p.183). Both these images prepare for the Russian scene, which the word 'tenebrous' connects with the personae under the Festival Hall; there, too, the 'sloshed spirit hissing in ash' links their abysmal lives to the Gates of the *City of Dis* (p.171):

> Often at dusk in the birch woods beyond the
>   gates of the city,
> you see the glimmer of fires of the hapless
>   dispossessed losers.
>
> One of these, russetly lit from beneath by
>   fulminant embers,
>   howls through the tenebrous gloom –
>   something concerning smoked fish,
>   black bread and vodka, I think.
>
> Distant, a plangently-played balalaika ac-
>   companies wailing
>   vocals whose burden is loss –
> Gone are the youthfully beautiful whom I
>   loved in my nonage;
>   strength and vitality, gone;
>   roof-tree and cooking-hearth, gone.

The Dantesque situation merges with previous imagery of impending doom, which was also accompanied by a string instrument (*Ukulele Music*). Additional biblical references – fish, bread, and wine – and the archaic re-creation of Anglo-Saxon imagery and language suffuse this lamentation for a lost and once intact life, making it a memorable song whose refrains charge the book with tension.

Via Boris the Swine the narrative connection with the Chernobyl reactor is introduced: he worked there until the accident, which first featured in *Final Demands* (pp.132, 176): 'remember the headline / **(Efforts are now being made to encase the / damaged reactor)**?' After the dirge about man's existential unshelteredness, the

second balalaika song refers to the irreversible, perpetual threat
presented by man's destruction of the planet; it is amplified through
sombre repetition and the variant 'those having precognition suffer
madness beforehand' (p.212) – no empty prophecy, as the author's
fate will show.

The existential elevation is marked by grave translationese, an
almost verbatim quotation from *Jude the Obscure*, which in turn
quotes the chorus in *Agamemnon*;[17] when, after everything in the
sense of tragedy has happened, only this knowledge remains (p.176):

> Nothing can ever be done;
>   things are intractably thus;
> all know the bite of grief, all will be brought to
>   destiny's issue;
> those who have precognition suffer
>   sorrow beforehand;
> bodies are bankrupt, the main Expedition has
>   left us behind it.

Thus, the Russian *perduta gente* are the tangible link between the
three thematic levels of this volume: being homeless, being exposed
to radioactive contamination, being part of the tragic human con-
dition. The Western version of the Russian balalaika dirge is given
as 'plangent the harp-twang, the *Hwaet!*', italicised to identify it as
an echo across the nations and a lament of the (timeless) reasons
for despair, in Anglo-Saxon alliteration, '*vanished, the vigour I valued; /
roof-tree and cooking-hearth, sacked*' (p.173). The interconnected
three countries and the three levels of calamity carry on from the
'democratic', global threats of previous books, which the homeless
author summarises in a hexametrical epyllion (p.201):

> Wind that disperses the Cloud is a blow for
>   Federalism,
> fairly enfolding Muskovite, minaret,
>   *Einkaufszentrum.*
>
> Scoffing our tea, bread-and-marge and secreted
>   surgical spirit
> here in the crypt of St Botolph's it feels like a
>   fallout-shelter.

Unlike in *Stet* and *Final Demands*, the atomic catastrophe is not
a faceless menace: the 'first two victims' (p.181) are Boris the Swine
and a physicist, who both worked at a nuclear plant. Seven torn
snippets of a secret document from the 'Energy Authority' are
reproduced in a rough, ugly manner, and in impassive scientific
jargon they reveal the consequences of radioactive contamination,
the 'Mortality of employees' (p.177), and the radioactive pollution

of the atmosphere after the 'ernobyl ac' (p.181) and a series of smaller incidents (obviously kept secret). Especially nasty details are pasted upside-down, and the contours of some lines and individual letters are shredded – the content is leaking out. The 'Probable Effects' (p.186) in contaminated employees of power plants (nausea, diarrhoea, vertigo) seem harmlessly 'flu-like and are the same as the (three) symptoms caused by meths and Brasso; the official prognosis is 'erious effects improbable' (with eerie phonolexis). Only at the very end does the word 'cancer' appear (p.211). The technical details mentioned in passing offer information no less nightmarish concerning half-life and transportation (pp.186, 189); and the new detectors (which sound like new metres and accordingly give the author hallucinations) measure employees' contamination, which had not before been registered 'by our older field foot monitors' (p.202). Of course, the authorities are not interested in individuals, but in the 'total stochastic risk' (p.211), but still the last sentence comes as a shock in its absoluteness (p.211): 'and death as early as 2nd week with possible eventual death of 100% of exposed individuals.' The formulaic phrase 'approved by' closes this chapter.

The other texts elucidate narrative connections. A Cockney, unfamiliar with both higher education and homelessness, talks about a young relative who was hired as a physicist at a nuclear plant, but now 'lives in a squit with no rent, / eed had a radio dose' (p.184). The ex-physicist does cocaine and mixes 'bottle-bank cocktail' with the author, who reports in his diary (p.195):

> he used to work at some atomic power station... but he got the sack for telling the newspapers about some radio-active leak, and he'd stolen all these papers – Top-Secret – from the Power Station, and he couldn't get work and then his wife died (cancer) so he came to this.

Again, the link between two motifs is given in one persona. The last piece of the mosaic: the physicist gives the papers to the author, who publishes them in *Perduta Gente*, whereupon he is questioned by the police (p.191). Now that the public knows about its contamination, there are nothing but questions (p.194): 'Why did the PM deny there was any contamination?...Why was the public not told?' But even in this situation the authorities know exactly what (not) to do (p.194): 'These are the questions which residents meant to raise at the Meeting, / had it materialised.' (see also p.41).

In parallel with the secret documents, five excerpts from an academic biography (based on the author's diary, his poems, and a witness account) describe the last months of his life. The use of the literary pretext of Dante's *Inferno* thus receives a macabre justification – the author himself has descended to Hell. The reasons can only

be deduced from the author's warnings and the other fates; a com-
bination of bad luck, despondency and depression suffices, with
alcohol to finish things off. Repeatedly, intently, and angrily (in
the notorious square bracket), the author warns his readers not to
be too complacent, 'Don't think it couldn't be you – / bankrupted,
batty, bereft' (p.14). (Most ironically, in 1992 Reading himself
became 'jobless, bereft of home, skint' within a matter of months.)

The author's preoccupations are forced upon him by evidence
from all and sundry (p.168):

> author's last review which speaks of 'post-Chernobyl reindeer piled in
> a ruck in the tundra ... trains with their burden of sinister finned flasks
> [rumbling] ominously on and on through a benighted city where trash
> amasses, the loonies and dispos [*sic* (presumably dispossessed)] prolifer-
> ate and the resident strumpet of the Globe opines "If you ask me, this
> planet is fucked; not just me, love, the whole planet, fucked".' This,
> scribbled as circumstances permitted, between the derry (derelict house)
> and St Botolph's crypt where the destitute alcos

The 'last review' is Reading's favourable assessment of Maggie
Gee's novel *Grace* (1988), which investigates the transportation of
spent rods through England.[18] Gee's radioactively contaminated
reindeer after the Chernobyl accident and the weekly transportation
of 'ten metric tons of nuclear waste' from Sizewell, Bradwell and
Dungeness 'on their way to reprocessing in Cumbria, where even
more waste will be produced' in steel flasks with leaks discharging
'low-level radiation' through the heart of London by night – this is
all authentic.[19] The trains with their deadly content 'hurtle perpetually
on / through the benighted cities where trash a- / masses' (p.204).
The darkness of the city recalls the Kimmerian city of death in
Ukulele Music, but 'be-nighted' also implies 'being kept in the
dark', insinuated also by 'a city / hugely unconscious' (p.206). The
strumpet's diagnosis is reiterated by the author: 'not just me but
the whole planet, fucked' (p.204).

As a dosser without a future who possesses secret documents
about leaking reactors and knows about radioactive trains leaking
into London back gardens, the author is gradually losing the will
to live, as is evident from his biography. Already sunk deep in the
underworld mire, he is however still writing neutrally descriptive
or gravely lamenting poems. The world under the Festival Hall –
the place where there are no more choices – has steadily grown
into a metaphor for the naked existential conditions of life itself;
the author leaning on Beckett (p.180):

> sometimes it seems like a terrible dream, in
>   which we are crouching
>   gagged, disregarded, unsought

in dosshouses, derries and spikes,
and from which we shall awake,

mostly it seems, though, we won't.

In the long run, this is unbearable. The reader can close the book, but the author is trapped in it and inevitably turns into the ' "morose old hypochondriac", as one reviewer dubbed his literary persona – which projected affectation was to become increasingly the reality' (p.198). He does not despair of his *personal* lot, but of the ways of the world (p.198): 'the burden of his monody, rarely coherent, seems to have been Black Dust, "Pancake" Contamination Meters, Smear Meters, Clean Zones and stochastic risk' – quotations from the secret papers which drive him insane, aptly phrased in poetic terminology ('burden', 'monody'). The metaphoric likeness between homeless dossers, citizens exposed to radioactivity, and all mankind in its existential unshelteredness becomes an irrefutable verity (p.191):

> That he was now physically and financially derelict... seems to have concentrated his notion of the 'slurry-wallowing degraded dispossessed' as a metaphor for all of *H. sapiens* involuntarily subjected to that other 'excreta' and thereby, irrespective of position in society, dispossessed of

In the end, even the very last shelter is taken away from the dispossessed, and from the author; the space is obviously needed for better housing and people. The 'Derry' squat – which so far had been a shelter to the author, the appalling Euston couple and the equally disgusting Mucky Preece, but also to entire families – is broken up at 3 a.m. by police (in yellow-black), bulldozers, and bailiffs (pp.170, 187, 205, 209): 'Sleep-fuddled dissolutes, still dressing cold dis- / consolate bratlings, / struggle with carrier-bags' (p.170). The evening beforehand, the pitiable wretches consume their last supper: a fire is lit from wooden banisters, Mucky Preece cooks 'cat stew' in a bucket, his only possession (p.196), and the author contributes rotten veg from market detritus (p.205). The dead rats of the house are kept in preparation for the bulldozers – 'got ready to chuck them at those bastards' (p.205) – but due to the fire started by the keepers of the law, the evacuation succeeds (p.209). The unconscious 'missiz', dumped with the bins outside the 'Derry' because of her non-stop meths-induced vomiting that robs the others of sleep, is burnt to death (pp.164, 190, 209). Helpless, driven away, burnt: one more allegory on the destiny of mankind on its way to Hell.

The evacuation of people is also presented from the other side's perspective (p.187): 'one nutter stayed'. He – the physicist or the poet – bombards police and bailiff with rats, screaming 'Don't think it couldn't be you.' Then (p.187)

was he came to the window and emptied a briefcase
    full of these *papers,*
  hundreds of fluttering sheets
  caught in the wind off the sea,

shipment of radioactive materials,
    health implications,
  Smear Meter, that sort of stuff
  printed on papers ripped out,

which the wind blows through the 'dead silent Borough' (and *Perduta Gente*).

After so many well-prepared parallels in the narrative, metaphors, and phonolectic cross-referencing throughout the whole book, this (fifth) link merges the different narrative strands in the tidiest possible manner (see also pp.201, 185, 207). The reactor or train accident sends a deadly radioactive cloud through London, which like the papers moves inaudibly through the still night, while above, in the Festival Hall, Sibelius' symphony with its 'incontrovertible end' is played at the same time that the author disperses the secret papers from the fourth floor of the nearby derry. Art and reality become one in the 'five brays of expiry' (p.210):

Wind that disperses the Cloud (a blow for De-
    mocracy) favours
Palace twerp, propertied yuppie and news-wrapped
    dosser with doses
equal in Geiger croaks. Shreds of (marked **Secret**)
    papers are scuttering
  over the wrecked party-lawn's
  panic-vacated marquee
  and under the Festival Hall,
  drift against cheap sleeping-bags,
  cardboard, plonk bottles and stiffs:

               rads,[20]

               stront,

               risk,

               leak,

               contam

It would not be Reading writing this book if the two parallel 'brays of expiry' were left visually unconnected. The book ends with a palimpsest of both (pp.160, 210) printed paradigmatically on top of each other, thus bracketing the whole book: the double concert after Sibelius of similar sounds and similar fates is merged in time, place, and typography (p.214): 'squit / rads, honk / stront, piss / risk, meths / leak, dis tress / con tam'.

The last two poems before this final palimpsest, which anticipates the end of *Last Poems*, synoptically draw the conclusion based on the evidence. As in the Sibelius symphony, for the heightening of coherence and cohesion all previous motifs and some of the triple enumerations in grave hemiepes are concentrated once more in an auto-cento.[21] The author's madness now seems as normal and unavoidable as the madness of the world, which faces the greatest imaginable catastrophe while producing badges saying '**Have a Nice Day**'.

Only the author is no good at escapism, and things are going downhill fast (p.196), 'Week of continuous Blue, / total amnesia'. Physical decline sets in, his symptoms correspond to those of radioactive contamination, and after the destruction of the derry he vegetates in a 'defunct fibreglass storage bunker'. The distance between concert-goer and fatally sick down-and-out, between Festival Hall and Hell is not all that great. The 'madness' suffered from 'precognition' (p.212) hastens the end. The biographer, unmoved as always, notes the last sign of life (p.208):

> how the author was last encountered in the concourse of Euston, pediculous, intoxicated beyond capability, plunging and bucking like a demented warhorse – the side of his head oftentimes cracking against the tiled floor, blood and contusion already in evidence, a (profoundly embarrassed and irritated) companion struggling to hold

His death is of course also implied by the fact that the biographer is in possession of his diary, papers, and poems; and his continued descent into Hell is foreshadowed by the image of the unidentified corpse under the Festival Hall in the very first poem (p.160).

The last poem dissolves the realistic setting; the image of the contaminated earth fades into a metaphysical no-man's-land, a waste land of the homeless and the naked wretches, Dante's Hell and Beckett's earth – the place is emptiness, the time is unendingness, and the voice of the 'crazy invisible exegetist' merges with that of Dante and the prophets – and laments unto eternity (p.213):

> Dusty, crepuscular, vast;
> ranks of unfortunate supines fading
>   into infinity;
>   chamber or bunker or vault
> seemingly lacking extremities; coughing,
>   puking, diarrhoea;
> drone of the crazy exe-
>   getist intoning
>   Woe vnto woe vnto woe
>   vnto woe vnto woe vnto woe

Shitheads (1989):
Translationese Exercises

The day before the publication of *Perduta Gente* Peter Reading
announced that henceforward he did not wish to produce another
'Peter Reading'. He was 'apprehensive of repeating [him]self', so
'for the time being' there would not be a new book. True, three
poems had been commissioned and written, but they were uncon-
nected. But before too long, Reading discovered they had some-
thing in common after all, and at the beginning of November 1989
he announced a

> very short limited edition of about a dozen poems, which... I found
> myself with. They are all slightly separate and they all have titles. I
> wasn't going to expand them into anything larger. But they all, as it
> turned out, go together. They include some translations of short pieces
> by Catullus into the original metres – hendecasyllabics and elegiac dis-
> tich – and some of my own. They're all about unsatisfactory people.
> It's called *Shitheads* (Edgar, p.59).

Shitheads was published six months after *Perduta Gente* and reviewed
in a few big papers.[1] The pamphlet only had 12 unpaginated
pages in the original edition, with nine new poems (or rather eight
poems and one piece of prose) and translations of seven poems by
Catullus. The Bloodaxe edition printed 'Prouerbes xiij. iij.', 'Ye
haue heard this yarn afore' and 'Parallel' in *Evagatory*, where they
had also been reprinted in earlier editions. This chapter discusses
the poems as part of *Shitheads*, where they first appeared.

'It will be a translationese exercise' [C], Reading had announced.
This refers not only to the translations of the Catullus fragments,
but also to his own poems, which contain elements of translation.[2]

Reading had met Michael C. Caine, the publisher of this pamphlet,
at the dinner following the launch of *Perduta Gente*, and a few
months later took up the invitation to submit something to his
small press, because it suited the *intermezzo* character of *Shitheads*.
The translationese exercise became a 'a nice job, fast'. The volume
was supposed to appear before Christmas, 'in a limited posh edition,
hard-bound' [C]. However, publication on 21 December 1989 was
not quite achieved, as Caine wrote in a letter [M]: 'I needn't have
worried as sales went v. well because of the 2 reviews... – but mainly
the *Sunday Times* including a poem with the publisher/author's
address.'

A year after publication all the copies had been sold. Two hundred standard and 40 specials had been planned; the editorial note mentions a 'limited edition of 200 copies', signed by the author. However, only 177 copies came back from the London 'Hand + Eye' printer Phil Abels; according to Caine, '23 copies were lost through his faulty guillotining' [M]. Of the special edition, 31 copies exist.

That Reading's booklet was brought out by a publishing house calling itself 'Squirrelprick Press' is noteworthy because in *Going On* (1985) the first poem contained this satirical reference to the preciousness of some small-press publishing (p.49):

[Squirrelprick Press is producing my
latest, *Blood Drops in Distich*,
    hand-deckled limp-covered rag,
    Special Edition of Ten.]

In retrospect, it can be seen that a publisher of that name was more than welcome both as a joke and for reasons of coherence, and Caine was prepared to take it on for the publication of *Shitheads*.[3] The book's epigraph thus refers back to *Going On*, ironically couching the abrasive title of the present work in the punning terminology of the small press:

[Squirrelprick Press is producing his latest (a light intermezzo),
    Shitheads, a thing of great charm; hand-deckled, Limited, limp.]

Another joke concerned the actually very lavish design of the book, meant to contrast sharply with its subject-matter.[4] *Shitheads* is, as the title makes plain, a satirical invective, though 'less savage than much of Reading's recent work' (Porter). 'Reading's formal skills are well-known – his control of line is extraordinary – but he adds to this the most elegant sense of outrage currently at work' (Duffy). This quality creates a most natural connection with Gaius Valerius Catullus, seven of whose epigrammatical invectives are placed in translationese in the middle of the pamphlet.

Catullus's erotic verses and his stinging attacks on personal enemies, political opponents and Julius Caesar himself, are not normally introduced to young learners of Latin and so are not widely known. Catullus was also the first Roman poet to have consistently adapted Greek metres to Latin (as Reading was doing in his own language), and he is said to have given new impetus to Latin poetry through his adaptation of Alexandrianism, with its special emphasis on form, structure and technique, later taken up by Tibullus, Propertius, Ovid, Horace and Martial. Their poetry aimed to replace stiltedness, long-windedness and the formal style with wit, brevity, informality, but mostly with elegance and erudition. What was also unusual was that poetry seems to have been an integral part of these young poets' lives.[5] Such qualities were highly attractive to Reading, as was Catullus's mastery of light verse and his originality and flair, which Peter Whigham says consists of his ability to combine the old with the new, to transgress genre boundaries, and to do this most idiosyncratically. In *Nothing For Anyone*, Catullus had already been nominated a hero (p.114), though, as Reading has said, theories about Catullus are to be seen approximatively, as 'he was constantly altering what he was doing, like everybody, really' [C].

The acknowledgements mention a 'collusion with M.W.S. Pitter'. Pitter had already helped Reading with translations of Greek poems for *Going On*; they had been literal, purposefully "bad" translations of Alcman and Alcaeus. As in 1985, the classicist Pitter translated the poems as closely as possible,[6] and Reading, who with the help of a dictionary can understand Latin texts [C], this time transposed the raw version into the genuinely poetic medium: 'the Catullus was as serious as we were capable of' [C]. Translating Catullus into 'approximating metre' (which apparently has not often been done) was 'lots of fun' [M]: 'There are many translations of Catullus into English; my own…merely tried to take a few that are not commonly (if at all) translated, and to do them in something like the original metre.' Catullus' short poems nos 33, 40, 43, 79, 89, 93, 103 were thus rendered in the same metres Catullus had used (substituting lengths by stresses): the first three in hendecasyllabic verses ('hendecs'), the others in elegiac distich. Reading wrote [M]: 'The versification is pretty close.'

It is not uninteresting to compare Reading's translations with those of one or two other authors. The recent translation by Jakob Rabinowitz follows the 'spirit and sense of the text' (rather than form or tone), as he writes in his preface.[7] Because Rabinowitz sees Catullus as a kind of anarchic rebel and sexual freebooter, his poems are accordingly slangy and "provocative", while the translation by Whigham of 25 years earlier sounds more serious and steady.[8] Whigham's is more comparable to Reading's version, but both Rabinowitz's and Whigham's renderings lack the metrical fidelity and the forceful tension resulting from the original metres.

Reading described the aim of the translations as follows [C]: 'in *Shitheads* we tried, really, to do something of what we'd thought the Catullus things were like. Fiendishly difficult, I'm told, by Pitter and one or two others, to actually put your finger on: a curiosity of style, of stance, and so forth. And we just tried to do those in the appropriate metres.' Really hearing the three hendecasyllabics in poems 33, 40, and 43, though, is not easy for an unpractised reader. Reading admitted [C], 'yes, they are difficult to hear. But this was partly… because there is this great difficulty of syntax, of tone. The metre itself is a slightly difficult one to attune to anyway, and this seems to be one of the things that makes bits of Catullus very curious to actually catch.' However, with the help of Tennyson's example (quoted below) and a little practice Reading's poems can be read (and spoken) rhythmically and fluently; there is a syncopated drive, an impatient urge forward. In his example, Tennyson not only heeded the approximative distribution of stresses, but also paid attention to the quantity of the syllables: 'All composed in a metre of Catullus's (— — [⏑ — , — ⏑ or ⏑ ⏑] — ⏑ ⏑ — ⏑ — ⏑ — ⏑).

The reference to Catullus is not directly given in *Shitheads*; the acknowledgements just mention two 'Englished versions of Catullus' as having previously appeared in the *TLS*. As before with the Virgil-Dryden-Reading adaptations in *Diplopic*, the seven translations are merely headed 'Englished' and then individually entitled with their numbers (in Roman numerals). In the poems chosen here, foes, rivals, and an array of deplorable individuals come under attack: Vibennius, Ravidus, an alleged beauty, Lesbius, Gellius, Caesar, Silo.[9] Some of the poems go well with some of Reading's own tirades (or rather, vice-versa). For example, echoes of 'Translationese' (p.217) can be heard in no. XL (p.218):

Little Ravidus, what sad brain disturbance
makes you fling yourself into my sharp spiked verse?
What misguidedly-invoked god, raised rashly,
is preparing to rouse a crazy dispute?
Or you'd maybe just like your name made public?
What's the matter, eh? You want fame at all costs?
You shall have it then, since you've shown a fancy
to love *my* love – and you'll pay yearly for it.

In elegant verses, Catullus censures the same kind of defects and evils as Reading does: dishonesty, greed for money, arrogance, degeneracy, autocracy. *Shitheads* can thus be read as an aside to Reading's œuvre.

With the exception of one block of prose (set as a neat 'slab' in the original edition, thus a concrete poem) and the poem in 3-stress metre (p.217), Reading's own poems are written in various antique approximative metres: elegiac distich, an (extended) Alcaic stanza, a *Stet*-stanza with added hemiepes, hexameter and pentameter, a stichic hendecasyllabic stanza, two Alcmanic stanzas and finally numeric-syllabic stanzas of tanka-verse length.

One commissioned poem, the dunciad 'Designatory' (p.216), an extended Alcaic stanza with the typical, distancing adjective-title, became the title poem and provides the imagery for the book. The title page of the original edition featured a woodcut, showing the image in vivid detail:

> Ours is that thriving company noted for
> caps (worn by prankster drolls) on the peaks of which,
>   gleaming, repose the simulacra,
>   sculpted in plastic, of great big dog turds.
> Thus we are designated: **Shitheads**.[10]

The book lampoons a series of 'unsatisfactory people': con-men, job-cutting managers, yuppie computer executives, noisy weekend trippers, and 'Costa del Parvenu' holiday-makers; more familiar Reading targets include the fanatical fundamentalists and Thatcher. Reading's invectives function as a prologue and epilogue to Catullus's poems; they focus on comparable offences and offenders.

Shitheads had started out as three commissioned poems, all included in the book: 'Prouerbes xiij.iij', 'Ye haue heard this yarn afore', and 'Designatory'. 'Prouerbes xiij.iij' (p.235)[11] is a *Stet*-stanza with added hemiepes which matches the batty old Oxford college tradition of Hunting the Mallard with the persecution of writers such as Salman Rushdie, whose *Satanic Verses* (1988) prompted the Ayatollah Khomeini to pronounce the notorious *fatwa* in 1989.[12]

> He that infults Our Mallard muft pay for it;
> hee that reueres falfe pochard and blafphemous
>   wigeon and fmew knows not Y^e True Quack
>   which was reuealed to vs by Our Drake's beak.
>
> Therefore a Iiffy bag plump with correctiue plaftic explosiue
>   plops on ye mat with ye mail, blafts his child's face into pulp.
>
> [Hee who keeps fhtum ftays aliue.]

The phonolectic proximity of 'Mallard' and 'Allah' links religions and silly totemism, while the diction and orthography, like the concluding proverb, link the Old Testament with modern life. As Reading said [LI], 'that particular proverb is really quite an amusing rendering of something that hasn't much changed'.[13]

'Ye haue heard this yarn afore' (p.225) is, as the title indicates, a remake of one of the nautical stories from *Ukulele Music* (p.22), but the title is also an exhortation or admonition, as the urgent problems *have* been described before, to no apparent effect. The difference here is that the killing of the island birds is not caused by hunger, but sadism ('feeking diuerfion'), and Reading anteposes a new stanza (also in the narrative 3-stress metre), which legitimises the new version and, syntactically, follows on directly from the title (set as the first line in the Bloodaxe edition, p.225):

ye haue heard this yarn before
(but I'm minded on it againe
thefe daies of fqualls and rank clouds
and raines as is uitriolic –
pines fhorn ftark as mizzen-mafts
wi neuer a frolicfome fowl –
and ye top-gallant air all rent):

Then the original, only slightly changed poem follows, a reversal of the story of Creation, which with its allusions to the modern context – radioactive clouds, acid rain, defoliated trees, ozone hole – makes the destruction of birds some centuries previously seem relatively harmless.[14]

The other poems are geared more towards Catullus. 'Holidaywise' (p.216), which introduces the 'Costa del Parvenu' holiday-makers complete with cars and cigars, calls termagant spouses 'trulls' in an allusion to Catullus's names for diverse society ladies. The title 'Holidaywise' exposes the linguistic level of this class, alluding to Betjeman's 'Executive', just as the prose text 'Translationese' which follows (p.217) describes the identity-crutches of such an 'Executive', a member of staff in Reading's place of work, the animal feedmill. As in Catullus' poems, authentic names are given, even though the attack is always also meant generically (p.217):

> Junior Executive Computer Manager [sic], it isn't that I am coy about using your real name (Kydd), my dear, damp-eared callow fellow, but that I suspect my readers, ignorant unsophisticates!, of never even having heard of you!... how I admire your *savoir vivre* when you light up another of those slim panatellas; how impressed I am by your shinily-polished slipper-like shoes (tasteful, with their little gold tassels)...Can you imagine that?! No, of course you can't.... [Poor young chap, whom I so much esteem, you have dashed yourself slap-bang into this slab of hard-edged prose.]

Perhaps more damning than the tone of voice is the implication that Kydd would not understand the use of elevated language in the first place. The first 'Managerial' follows from this and it too mentions an authentic name (p.217):

> Smith (a sobriquet much in vogue with con-men)
> and your Board of Directors, bumpkin straw-heads,
> and your quorum of exec greysuit shysters
> [whose sub-literacy ensures my safety],
> you have earned our esteem in these blunt hendecs;
> for your management of us (six years, thank you)
> systematically has reduced our travail
> and secured us a future wholly workless.

Hurford commented: 'Whether this is Britain's future or the poet's remains unclear, but the equivocation boldly implies that they are one and the same. *Shitheads* is a rare, funny and serious book of poetry; furiously self-employed, resisting redundancy.' Reading, however, became redundant very soon after – the second 'Managerial' (p.220) reviles the same 'Exec.' for spending '13 grand' on a company car on the same day he 'saw fit to lay-off three hapless employees: / millworker, driver, a clerk – also-rans not worth three fucks'.

Reading had expressed his dislike of arrogant, poorly educated parvenus many times before. A millworker for many years, he had had ample opportunity to see and experience the condescending demeanour of his supposed superiors. The invectives in *Shitheads* are thus to be seen not only in the context of Reading's œuvre, but also in the context of his private life: 'I am a simple man who gets insulted hugely in the normal course of events' (Jenkins, 1985, p.11). But the denunciations are also aimed at a larger context. Only weeks before his dismissal, BBC interviewer Daisy Goodwin asked him questions about his workplace:

DG: Do you write about this place and working in this place much?
PR: Only in a general metaphorical way. As I mentioned before, the
         whole place, to some degree, stands as some kind of lumpish
         metaphor.
DG: For what?
PR: [*clearing his throat*] Feculence.
DG: I don't know what 'feculence' means.
PR: Shittiness.

The disparaged people in *Shitheads* are also personae embodying the existence of 'feculence' in the world at large, just like the downfall of England in *Stet* and other books generally stands for the end of the world. In this sense, all Reading's books are metaphorical, including *Shitheads*.

In the original edition, *Shitheads* ended with the lampoon 'Parallel' (p.231), half of which consists of macaroni-verses in creative fatras style (termed 'Desperanto' by Maxwell in his review);[15] they are rendered in a syllabic stanza form hitherto unknown,[16] and in the Joycean sense they enhance the meaning given in the other half, an ametrical "translation" of this patois-hotchpotch, which can be understood as a caustic comment on Thatcherite politics:

Ni iscts vots marrypappa	Nor was your spouse
grignaleto, ne.	a pipsqueak – far from it!
Mas vots pollytiq	But your many wise policies
saggio sauvay	were saving your islet,
vots salinsula	your filthy isle, and
insulapetty,	made all equal with nil.
et fair tutts egal mit-nochts.	

This is the first and last time that Reading referred so explicitly to Thatcher in a poem (one other poem in *Stet* refers to Thatcher's arms industry policy). In the preamble to the *Evagatory* reprint of the poem, England was called the 'sad realm farctate with feculence' (p.231).

Blake Morrison had already written in his review of *Perduta Gente*:

> Reading first hit his stride with the collection *Fiction* in 1979, the year Mrs Thatcher came to power, and in a series of almost annual poetic reports he has stalked her like a bad conscience ever since. If what he writes is too learned, ironising and fatalistic to be protest poetry...it's also true that no other poet, except perhaps Tony Harrison, has as sharp an eye for the underside of Eighties Britain.

Reading had dealt with this particular subject-matter in more detail than anybody else, and with *Perduta Gente* had created a conclusive climax. Unsurprisingly perhaps, the 'intermezzo' of *Shitheads* was followed by a long writer's block. After that, Reading resumed his slow farewell, with book titles announcing a drawn-out retreat: *Evagatory, Last Poems, Work in Regress, Ob.*

Evagatory (1992):
Out, out

In February 1992 Chatto published *Evagatory* and *3 in 1* – a reprint of *Diplopic*, *C* and *Ukulele Music* in one volume[1] – a week after Reading's dismissal from the animal feedmill, which had received some coverage in the press.

His writing had not been going well for a while. The day after the launch of *Perduta Gente*, he had said: 'Awful are the times like today when it's over and you have nothing to do. Apart from domestic, moral, and financial worries there is the worry "what do I do next?" ' [C]. The second half of 1989 had been spent with *Shitheads*, but in 1990 Reading was low on energy, resilience, and creativity. He started work on a new book, but progress was slow.

> It started life... as an intention to produce a mixture of a picaresque Odyssey travelogue... I'd been reading *Gil Blas*... and felt that the idea of a picaresque rather appealed to me. Well...I've fallen miserably short of that idea, not least in length, but the idea of wandering and repetitive occurrences of the same voice under different ostensible cir-cumstances I have managed to keep... prevalent (O'Donoghue, M).

Reading's state of mind at that time is recorded in an interview with Robert Potts:

> 'Nothing has meant more to me than writing. Without any satisfaction – indeed, with great dissatisfaction – I feel I'm facing the end...if I can finish this, I've nothing else to say.'... More than once he said that he would most likely fall silent. This has seemed for a long time the logical conclusion of a poetry which constantly suggests its own redundancy... There are various reasons why Reading feels he will 'fall into Sibelian silence', not least the absence of any posterity, any future reader to write for...'I'm writing now for mutated arthropods...Species are always superseded by others, but this is more accelerated than any of us would have thought. It has been precipitated at a vast rate...Two hundred years ago, when we would have been able to exercise some control, something could have been done,' but now the matter is out of our hands. Hence the tendency towards silence. Not only is poetry an irrelevance, it also contributes to that situation by demanding the razing of the rainforest for paper (Potts, 1990, pp.95-97).

This interview was given in August 1990, two months before Reading was uplifted by the Lannan Literary Award, which enabled him to finish *Evagatory*. Like Beckett, who ends his trilogy with 'you must say words, as long as there are any... you must go on, I can't go on, I'll go on', Reading went on. He saw this himself as part of a Beckettesque tension which becomes increasingly difficult to play along with. The logical thing would be to pack up... It's an alarming prospect. I keep hoping I may try something completely different. But of course I don't know what that is (Potts, 1992).

Even after the publication of *Evagatory* Reading still voiced the same doubts – even to the point of audible embarrassment when *Evagatory* and its 'great predecessors' were praised by Bernard O'Donoghue in an illuminating radio interview. The first question had been whether Reading still believed in poetry:

It isn't the word I'd have used, 'belief'...This is a very difficult question to answer because I don't quite know why one persists with this or with any kind of art. I felt this about painting when I was a painter, and if you question the whole idea of the likelihood of any audience, then it's very difficult to vindicate. So I'm not quite sure but it's something which I simply feel I'm – to put it rather pompously – almost an agent for, that it's almost as if it has nothing to do with me (O'Donoghue, M).

Reading was invited by the Lannan Foundation to give a reading of *Evagatory* in Los Angeles in April 1992, which boosted his reputation in America.[2] The book also received high praise from the reviewers, who by now rated Reading as one of the most important poets writing in Britain.[3] 'For some years now Peter Reading has been maintaining a Doomwatch on our perturbed and poisoned planet in a running verse journal' (Porter); '*Evagatory* is not so much an eleventh-hour plea as a thirteenth-hour shrug' (Maxwell); alluding to the 'Prouerbes' poem, Greppin wrote in the *TLS*: 'Peter Reading's poetry is powerful, often moving, and very original. This is Y^e True Quack.'[4]

Reading had been allowed to create the cover for *Evagatory* himself (his collage appears in a black and white version on p.241 of *Collected Poems 2*). In a Schwitters-like *Merz*, significant fragments of quotations and of a one-way train ticket are pasted on top of each other, announcing the author's leave-taking. *Evagatory* is a distancing adjective form stemming from 'evagari' (Latin), meaning rambling, roving. 'Evagation' also denotes (archaically) mental wandering (with the added meaning of 'a diversion, an extravagance', 1649), as well as the act of wandering (away) (1691). The title provides the framework for this book: the author sets off on a final odyssey through the demolished world and in the end retreats into inner immigration, into his mind, wandering away from human life, the world, and the solar system altogether. *Evagatory* is more abstract, lyrical, euphonical, elegiac and reticent than any of his previous books.

Despite its unsurpassable existential pessimism, this book aroused less controversy than its predecessors. In his interview, O'Donoghue mentioned the lyricism of this 'serious, Beckettian sort of book', as in lines such as 'Surely Odysseus roamed these blithe isles, / parsley and iris cushioning meadowlands':

> I'm very pleased that you say that because I feel that, and it was, I suppose, an intentional part of it – 'musical'... I'd have said, in preference to 'lyrical', because there are connotations that 'lyrical' has which I would again wish to avoid... and of course it's held together, lyrically, if you like, by the metrical device of these dispersed Alcaics (O'Donoghue, M).

In another interview, Reading qualified this strongly lyrical, or musical, quality: 'While aspiring to "Tennysonian grandiloquence" in his new work, he is swift to undercut potential pomposity: "It's got to be punctuated with the fact that you know this is a bit barmy, you know it's not on to adopt this voice all the time. The high-serious tic mustn't get too carried away" ' (Potts, 1992).

Reading's use of language had changed. Except for the first volume, individual later poems, and *Final Demands,* he had not used poetic diction much – it would not have been adequate for his subject-matter. In *Going On* there had been lyrical bits (partly in satirical function), and in *Final Demands* the lyrical vein became established. *Evagatory* condensed the language anew (and was also shorter than previous books): Reading's syntax became more asyndetic, more loaded with nouns and qualitative adjectives, his style more symbolical, brachylogical and metaphorical (p.224):

> Pipe Clay Lagoon, wet silver ellipse of sand
> pulsing in lightwaves, pure cerulean dome,
>   indigo-bruised smooth straits of turquoise,
> bloodshot-eyed *Larus novaehollandiae*

The poem titles (in magazine publications) were all adjective derivatives, an abstracting, distancing, depersonalising device. There are few verbs in the simple forms (instead, many participles), few articles, and no more pronouns. 'The book's language is, as one would expect, acute, disturbing, and extremely resourceful; its tetrameters are as sure-footed as they are heavy-hearted; its quality of spatial awareness is of the very highest' (Maxwell).

Reading's intention to avoid producing another 'Reading' was not entirely followed through: this book is another sequence of unpaginated poems, prose, and (this time) drawings, all about his major theme; but Reading still manages to find 'fresh uniquely disturbing ways of saying the few essential things on his mind' (Maxwell).

Evagatory is tectonically even more unified and more musically arranged than previous books. The (mostly) lyrical voice is totally distanced, depersonalised, elliptic, but above all unusually monodic. What is more, the book is carried by a vision more intense than ever before, permeated by the oldest pre-text available in the Anglo-Saxon tradition on this bleak theme, *The Wanderer* and *The Seafarer* (9th century).[5] At the same time, the theme of transience and stoic hopelessness refers back to his own pre-text, his first book of poems, and anticipates [*untitled*] (forthcoming).

The unity of the volume is achieved by means of several factors (unified in themselves) working together: the facets of the theme, the hypertextual links to a literary tradition, the intratextual musical echoes of single verses of the core-poem in other poems, the over-layering of motifs and images, the logical resolution, for which an adequate image is selected, and of course the ongoing metrical variation on the Alcaic stanza and the almost exclusive use of logaoedic (and aeolic) verse (there are also two prose texts and two poems in 3-stress metre). In this book, Reading uses 'dispersed Alcaics', as he calls them; although they do not form full Alcaic stanzas, the three basic Alcaic lines are used in any order and number. As before, these Greater or Lesser Alcaic verses are distinguished by different indentation.

The picaresque frame situation turns the poet into the persona of the wanderer, presenting vignettes of a doomed world. The demoralised poet observes the world like a 'Spectator rather than as one of the species' (*Spectator*, I), taking in the signs of the approaching end, while the local birds' cries of fate are heard from skies of the most beautiful colours and with the enjoyment of del-icious food and wine providing the only *bonvivant* counterbalance: 'Only a troubled idyll now possible' (p.229). The light is going, darkness approaching.

Evagatory is a very "English" book. The basic metaphors – eating, drinking, wandering – are taken from the earliest Anglo-Saxon poems of the heroic tradition. The Germanic banquet in the mead-hall exemplifies the success of a society in a hostile environment, and is socially central;[6] but just as the wine in *Evagatory* is enjoyed under darkened, polluted skies, the banquets in the Anglo-Saxon elegies *The Wanderer* and *The Seafarer* appear only indirectly in *Evagatory* as reminders of earlier, better times. The speakers of these two companion poems are exiled from the *cynn* (tribe, king-dom) that defines their identity, and ponder the transience of life. Whereas Christians derive consolation from their belief in eternity, men in the heroic world had comfort in *lof* – 'fame in one's life-time' (*For the Municipality's Elderly*), but *The Wanderer* also pro-jects a ruined city without 'after-speakers', i.e. the vision of a depopulated earth of the eschaton (last days) – such as Reading describes in *Evagatory* a thousand years later.

Wyrd or *wierd* (fate) destroys all.[7] The prevailing moods of the pre-text, fear and despair, have turned to resignation and deep sadness in *Evagatory*, because the end is already too close. The Christian bracket or *consolatio*, which occurs alongside the 'bleak truth' of the pre-text, is rejected; it plays no part in *Evagatory*. The following description by Bede can be seen as the philosophical and metaphorical seed of *Evagatory*; a council is called on the occasion of King Edwin of Northumbria's conversion in 625:

> And one of the King's chief men presently said: 'Thus seems it to me, thou King, the present life of man on earth against that time which is unknown to us: it is as if thou wert sitting at a feast with thy chief men and thy thanes in the winter-time; the fire burns and the hall is warmed, and outside it rains and snows and storms. Comes a sparrow and swiftly flies through the house; it comes through one door and goes out another. Lo, in the time in which he is within he is not touched by the winter storm, but that time is the flash of an eye and the least of times, and he soon passes from winter to winter again. So is the life of man revealed for a brief space, but what went before and what follows after we know not.'[8]

The 'flight of a sparrow brief through the feasting-hall' is borrowed as one of the refrain *ur*-verses of *Evagatory*, a metaphorical burden both in the literary and literal sense; and the setting for *Evagatory* is provided by the contrast between *cynn* and *wraecca*: the 'fire-lit, gold-adorned, beer-warm hall' on the one hand, and the 'exterior darkness of sea and moor'[9] on the other. In a Germanic tavern, the wanderer recounts in 'a drunk salt's slurred dirge' his 'sea-borne sorrowful history, / winters of toil through tempests, foam frosts' (p.233). Winter, hail, night (the agents of 'wierd') come down polluted in *Evagatory* as 'wind preternatural, pissing acid' / 'vitriolated downpour' and 'pulse of warning light' / 'last light' / 'dark'.

This fate is the same for every *eorl*, as the wanderer muses; the wanderer and seafarer (sometimes in the third person) thus merge into the persona of the *eard-stapa* (wanderer), who for long years sails the earth and in the Anglo–Saxon poems starts his lament with 'Oft must I alone each early morn / bewail my sorrows' (line 8). In *Evagatory*, the 'wandering dosser' who visits different coasts of the earth is an aged *scop* (poet), a 'snow-haired elder', who drunkenly sings his fate and night-thoughts in nostalgic elegies (sometimes in the third person, as the 'quondam Parnassian'): '...dawn of each day I bewail my sorrows, / how I was sundered in youth from homelands' (p.233).[10] Like the wanderer over a thousand years earlier, today's wanderer no longer has an intact *cynn* to return to. However, his *lord* did not simply die – he has led the country (and the world) to ruin.

Reading felt that this literary 'nostalgic tradition' including 'certain English stereotypes' was encompassed by Roy Fuller's phrase 'some inexplicable imperial Elgarian sadness', and he identified with this tradition 'very strongly', too (O'Donoghue, M). However, a strong abstraction from this English line makes itself felt. Even though Reading refers to the increasingly uninhabitable 'island' on which the autophageous 'poor mad islanders' destroy themselves, his 'Albion' is – as in *Stet* – a metaphor for the future of the planet as well as for the unstoppable machinations of the almighty 'wierd', just as the places visited are virtually interchangeable and therefore stand for everywhere: 'Sydney, *The Age* screwed up in a trash-bucket' (p.222) is also 'England, *The Times* screwed up in a trash-bucket' (p.229).

More than any other of Reading's book, *Evagatory* is firmly embedded in the context of the entire œuvre; in an intratextual *tour de force* of amplification, numerous links with almost every previous book are made, so that echoes start accumulating.[11] It also contains four poems from *Shitheads* (slightly adapted), three of which were written before the book was geared towards Catullus ('Ye haue heard this yarn afore', 'Prouerbes xiij.iij', 'Designatory'), plus 'Parallel'. This device of auto-cento and the reiteration of earlier poems is also to be found in *Last Poems* – with these two volumes, Reading is working towards a modernist ending to his œuvre, unifying it by means of a circular, closed structure and by numerous cross-references.

Despite this fastidious intratextuality, *Evagatory* is a decidedly idiosyncratic book and tightly structured within itself; Maxwell wrote that 'its effects augment alarmingly at every reading'. Because the book's structure is so complex, step-by-step delayering is needed to make it more transparent. The wanderer's different stops are usually introduced with a verse about the coastal topography, thus emphasising the close connection with the seafarer; and these two ancient elegies are paralleled by two very personal elegies (for Roy Fuller and Michael Donahue), which, however, are also examples of the *'flight of a sparrow brief through a feasting hall'* (p.227).[12] Many poems and texts appear in units of three; and there are three steps away from England and back again, not so different from the tectonics of a five-act tragedy.

The wanderer first visits three places in Australia and Tasmania.[13] From a bar in Sydney harbour he witnesses a spectacular 'carcinogenic sunrise / (**15% of population…**)' (p.222) and in the beach setting of Pipe Clay Lagoon he describes a 'pastoral picnic under an ozone hole' (p.p224, 229). In 'Antipodean' he overhears the anthro-

pomorphic talk about the 'Convict Ruins' in the Hobart 'Ship
Hotel' bar, and how the cockatoos 'wailing their weird *wee-yu my-la,*
are / really the ghosts of sun-charred hanged cons' (p.222) – two links
which introduce the next poem: a pastiche dramatic monologue in
3-stress metre spoken by 26-year-old bushranger Wil Westwood in
a strong Australian accent and archaic diction. (The setting in time
is 1847).[14] It is his farewell letter to the *'kindley Chaplaing / whot
preechis in Port After: / Sir, I gets hangd this day'* (p.223):

> *Strong ties of erth wil soon*
> *be renched, this burnin fever*
> *of life wil soon be kwenched,*
> *   …from cup*
> *of mizry hav I drank*
> *from 16th yeer…*
> *   … the sweetest drarft*
> *is that as takes away*
> *mizry of livin deth.*
> *   …I now*
> *do bid the world A Due*
> *and all as it contaynes!*

The poems then describe places in the former Yugoslavia.[15] There,
the 'frost-haired elder' is drinking into the night again – 'crno vino, /
visokokvalitetno vino' / 'vinjak' (red wine, high-quality wine, brandy)
– and in 'soft-breathed translationese', Jasmina translates his words
accompanying his lyre, a hymn-like exodos, 'Song's Weight' (p.224):

> This is his song's weight, Time's malice castigates
>   not only me (whose beard grows snow-hued,
>   bones become joint-sore, dulled eyes gum-filled),
>   also fair governments, concepts, zeniths,
>   all which we valued nears expiry.

Before 1989, only lamb was grilled on skewers; now 'kindred are
skewered on sharp-spiked ash-spears' (p.233) is the horrific parallel.
In Trebinje (p.225) a 'nightingale, one hour richly mellifluous / under
this vitriolated downpour', sings ('Dalmacijan'). In the third poem,
Jasmina translates the 'lyrical twang from a grizzled oldie' again
(p.225), who in Café Dalmacija on the Adriatic sings his nostalgic
jeremiad about the equally 'lachrymose' Odysseus (also 'Dalmacijan').
The world depicted here so lyrically has the potential to be very
beautiful indeed.

At the third stop, there are three related poems again, used as
points of reference later. The poet-persona casts anchor near two
islands – in the Indian and Atlantic Ocean – and describes the trapped
and tortured creatures on them: birds perishing from violence (on the
'Mafcarenhas Iflande', p.225) and from civilisation (in north-east

England, p.227); Anglo–Saxons suffering from violence and civilisation, too (p.226).[16] The fate of the degenerating gulls presages what is awaiting another species, *H. sap.*: 'all that remains, their last year's shit's stink' (p.227). The wanderer remains on this particular island for a long time and visits another coast. There, trash and trashy behaviour combine to form a memorably squalid night image without sound (p.236): 'Waded ashore, St Pancras Isle, 2 a.m., / kneedeep in poly burgerboxes, / black plastic bin-bags, spat snot, spilt pils.'[17]

The newspapers ('the sumps of society') present further details about the 'corporate concentrated slurry', '... mayhem and muck of a / clapped-out, subliterate, scrap-stuffed fake state' (p.230):

```
        23.3 million vehicles,
        29.8 million drivers,
 300 000 maimed on their ludicrous
        tarmac p.a., 5000 flenched dead –
             fortunate, then, that it doesn't matter
 (for they are far too philoprogenitive).
```

The prose report about the 'poor mad islanders' (p.229), which at the launch Reading read like radio news briefly switched on and off (and which was marked by big letters in the original edition), seems like a postlude to the global catastrophe brought about by a combination of different destructive acts. Not only are other-believers eliminated (p.235), but killings also occur from mere negligence or, indeed, just for wanton fun (p.232):

```
 East End of London, where the indigenous
         practise a noteworthy brand of homicide –
 fruit and veg hurled from speeding limos. [...]
         Turnip tops septuagenarian shopper,
 Juvenile jogger culled by cabbage.
```

Again, the 'Snow-haired, an elder, dulled eyes gum-filled' remains, who with his 'sweet-toned curious instrument' sings of the demise of the 'sad realm farctate with feculence', 'whose fame was fabled' (p.231). The poet sits in his wicker-chair outside his cottage 'in the last corner receiving sunlight' (p.236) reflecting on his 'sad shire / running to exponential ruin', listing synecdochical examples. 'Albion' is no longer one – Reading uses the poetic name for England here for the first and last time (p.229):

```
 England, The Times screwed up in a trash-bucket,
        gliding astern, the Thames, the old prides,
        end of an era, nation, notion,
            Albion urban, devenustated
        (one of those routine periodic
 faunal extinctions [cf. the Permian]),
 arthropod aberration (posterity).[18]
```

From his estranged home country he travels away again, first to a forest in Sarawak. In Borneo, what remains of the British protectorate is only a weak lamp; real traces of life are left only in the Malayan limestone caves by bats ('faeces of which are sifted by cockroaches'), before darkness takes over: 'one-and-a-half miles into the labyrinth, /... wheeze of a Tilley lamp near expiry. // Guideless, directionless, lightless, silence' (p.232). Consequently, the next vision presents images of sedimentation in matrices (Niagara and Tende, p.237). At the last stop – dark *Ratskeller* of two 'Germanic' cities – the bard intones his doleful dirge once more, again in 'translationese', once as the 'Seafarer' (p.232), once as the 'Wanderer' (p.233). The 'wandering / dosser drones on', drunk and memorable:

> no man grows wise without many winters spent
>   pondering folly of worthless world's-gear,
>
> awful the apprehension of earth-ending,
>   crumbled the mead-hall, no laugh lasting,
>
> where are the heroes, word-hoarders, feasting-feats? –
> gone back to dark as though they had never been,
>
> life is a loan and bank accounts transient,
>   kindred are skewered on sharp-spiked ash-spears,
>
>   all of this world will be Weird-wreaked,
>   emptied...

This Germanic elegy is as depersonalised and abstract as the other is personal and immediate. In the next *Ratskeller* the 'slurred dirge' is heard among a 'babel of strange-tongued wanderers': the bard is not the only lost person. The dirge, though, will not be heard for much longer. 'Reflective' (p.240) draws the bard close to the author (as does the other 'Reflective', p.236):

> Quondam Parnassian, muse prolific,
>   Master of Troubled Idyll, charted
>   province of hyperborean bleakness...
> fell into silence, like great Sibelius
> mute till the end, reflective of soundlessness.

The remaining poems and drawings deal with the last act of the 'evagation', inner emigration. With unusual directness and precise imagery Reading retrospectively sums up his career as a poet. This is the odyssey of his œuvre (p.227):

> Perilous trek, unarmed, unaccompanied:
>   set out from Cranium, through uncharted
>   swamp, to arrive at Lingua Franca,
> thence to this Logaoedic Dependency.

The drawing of a skull's profile which follows (p.241) was on the opposite page in the original edition and looked *out* of the book: the skull is filled with a piece of a map of London. The network of streets not only represents the brain's contortions, but is the empty formula for the people who live there, just as the prosodic notation (of an Alcaic stanza) spilling out from the jaw is the empty formula for the 'Lingua Franca'. Another explanation is given on the next page (p.229):

Cranial voice loquacious/inadequate
    (translationese from life to lingo):

It is implied that just as the song of the wandering poet was translated three times from one language into another (pp.224, 225, 233), and just as Reading transposes the old Saxon pre-texts into the 20th century, the entire work of a poet is one of creating new language, of translating, always approximatively – from cranium into verse, from 'life' into 'lingo'.

Halfway through the book (p.234) the *ur*-poem finally appears ('Cranial').

region of hyperborean bleakness;
cranial voice loquacious/inadequate
    feebly ∫ translating life to language;
          ↳ reducing
I, like my sad realm, farctate with feculence
    (one of those routine periodic
faunal extinctions [Permian, Holocene...],
flight of a sparrow brief through the feasting hall),
    all that remains, their last year's shit's stench;
etiolated eyeless crustacean,
        guideless, directionless, lightless, silent

It runs vertically inside the skull; correspondingly, the jaw emits 'thence to this Logaoedic Dependency' instead of empty metrical signs. The *ur*-poem is in fact an auto-cento, a synopsis organising the book like a musical theme: all eleven verses are quotations from other poems, or they are quoted in other poems, the cross-referencing going back and forth. The *ur*-poem is rendered twice more in variations, forming another trio; and the last variation is printed three times in overlap, visualising as in a palimpsest the echoing, receding voice of the poet: '[thence to this silence, total, Sibelian]' (p. 239).[20]

The skull, too, appears a third time on the opposite page (p.238), this time looking out of the book in the other direction. By now, its contours are shaped by fragments of the *ur*-poem printed across and on top of each other, simultaneously providing a visualisation

of the 'perilous trek' filling the poet's head. One third time the
poet speaks of himself in the third person, a distancing effect that
the wanderer had also used to help gain composure in view of the
impending fate ('Reflective', p.236): 'Shamrustic lair of quondam
Parnassian / (lapsed into silence like great Sibelius, / mute till the
end reflective of wordlessness)'. Finally, he makes one last joke
(the only one in this book), 'only a troubled idyll now possible, /
few of the better years remaining... / '55 Margaux, '61 Léoville'.

In the radio interview with O'Donoghue Reading started by
reading this *ur*-poem; in the background, very bleak music could
be heard (one of Shostakovich's late string quartets, the 15th). In
another interview, Reading revealed:

> The approach I favour is that of late Shostakovich – the late quartets
> of Shostakovich – which is about complete blankness and confrontation.
> The only kind of consolation that's offered here is that sense of shared
> nothing, if you like: that this is the human lot. To listen to those
> quartets – and the late Beethoven quartets, for that matter, do the
> same thing – is to be slightly comforted in knowing that humanity is
> not alone in this, that this is what we have to face, a sort of facing the
> void, which is bleak but I think that there's a sort of heroic approach
> (Edgar, p.56).

Towards the end of the book, dissolution begins in the fifth and
last act of evagation. A second pastiche poem in 3-stress metre
using the nautical diction of the 18th century has strong Old
Testament overtones, which alienating device makes the subject –
the consequences of the Gulf War as an image of the Last Judgement
– all the more apocalyptic, further intensified by the "naive" pre-
sentation and the archaically typeset orthography. The Seafarer has
reached the last coast of his life, on which the avian heralds of fate
are already perishing in 'fome fticky tar'. Eerily, after a collision,
it is not the Seafarer's ship that crumbles, but the rock, like pitch-
black meringue (p.237):

> now preternatural fqualls
> did moderate, and ftrange vapours
> defcend in ferruginous fog,
> an oppreffiue heat, withal;
> then did we verily know
> we had entered vnto Y^e Gulph.[21]

'All that remains, the stench of their excrement.' This tetra-
metrical (Alcaic) monostich, printed in the original edition at the
top of an otherwise empty page (p.240), not only refers to bats
and birds. Isolated like this, its effect was calculatedly shocking.
Maxwell was impressed:

[This] one-line page... looks, like so much of Reading, gratuitously out of context, but in its place near the end of the book, as a forlorn, feeble aftershock, it creates one of the most painful, sizzling silences possible on a page. Reading's intelligence about white space, about linebreak, bold type, italics, and the whole arsenal, succeeds, among other things, in turning the laboratory-tested sedatives of '80s 'L=A=N=G=U=A=G=E poetry' not to mention the spillages of '60s free versedom to a waste of good paper, or to what he memorably terms the modern tabloid: 'corporate concentrated slurry'.

The book's remaining pages laconically note the end of the world and the end of Reading's writing, i.e. the long foretold storm and his evagation (in the three remaining Alcaic verses, thus complementing the monostich): 'sea-level newly pole-augmented, / mutated arthropods, algae, UV, / force 12s dispersing disbound **Collected Works**' (p.240). In the end, the visual level takes over as the linguistic one loses ground. The poet has a one-way train ticket which appears several times in a *Merz* (p.241) (it blots out the quotations of *ur*-poem verse fragments more than on the cover of the original edition). In a last three-step movement, the news of the irrevocable departure of the speaker, poet, wanderer, seafarer, author is announced. A badly cut-out newspaper article with annotations scrawled in Reading's hand (p.242) testifies to the fact that the concern for beauty in form is finished. Instead, factual information is given about a spacecraft steering towards the heliopause, where the gravitational effect of the sun ceases to operate. By the year 2010 or 2020 the spaceship named 'Voyager', like the 'Wanderer' on board, may still have 'almost 10 years of contact with the Earth before they run out of power'. When the plutonium generators are exhausted, the capsule will drift on forever. After 40,000 years, the 'Voyager' will 'meet' the star AC+79 3888 ('at distances of trillions of miles') and, after another 250,000 years, will drift towards Sirius, the brightest star in the universe.[22] A badly reproduced drawing with further hand-written notes and crossings-out of years then graphically depicts the trajectory (p.243).

Finally, on the last page these annotations appear for the third time as a poem (p.244). This is tripartite again, with each part set in diminishing print – the trajectory seen from a quickly increasing distance, 'drifting, 290 000 / years beyond launchpad, in towards Sirius', with no final full stop. It is an impressive metaphor for the irrevocable retreat into the poet's own cranium, into total exile, 'Sibelian silence'.

Evagatory may not be 'incomprehensible' (Reading's disqualifying epithet for bad poetry), but nor does it fulfil what was once his aim: to create 'accessible, readable, entertaining' books (with subtleties for those who can see them or take the trouble to). Reading [LI]: 'Yes... I'm sorry about that, but this is a very common tension – you're labelled elitist. But I don't think that it's possible to do anything sophisticated in art or science unless, ipso facto, it becomes rather complicated in its eloquence.' When another interviewer asked which audience he could reach with this book, Reading replied:

> I suppose that, to a large degree, you could say that most poetry has very, very little audience, and this is one of the points of impotence which one is very conscious of. And I suppose the more sophisticated you get in things like verse forms and structures, the more remote... you become. However, if the thing is to be successful I think that some measure of sophistication is necessary, and it doesn't need, perhaps, to interfere with any 'message' that might be getting across to an audience (Bailey, M).

The increasing metaphorisation and increasing use of rarely used words, often of Latin origin, and the abstraction and high degree of literariness, paired with the absence of reflexive, metatextual elucidation, would make it difficult for an uninitiated, new reader to understand *Evagatory*. Because of its strong unity, Reading's œuvre is indeed best read chronologically. Reading commented [LI]:

> I think you could say that anybody coming to, say, the last three Beethoven string quartets without having heard anything of him would find them very difficult as well... I do regard all these *opera* in many ways as a single thing. And this is one of the reasons I'm a bit dismayed when things go out of print because I think it would be nice to have them all looked at in one context. I agree, really, that *Evagatory* is 'difficult'. Does it disturb me? No, I don't think it does. I think that anybody reasonably sophisticated could follow *Evagatory*, but I know for a fact that one or two people very close to me... have said that... they read *Evagatory* first and were completely taken with it but found it difficult, and then read a couple of other things, read *3 in 1*, came back to *Evagatory* and found it perfectly simple and wondered why they'd had the slightest difficulty. But I suppose there are certain formalities and stiltednesses, or apparent stiltednesses, which are a bit difficult to get on with until you know what the ground rules are.

It therefore meant a lot to Reading when the *Collected Poems* came out in 1995-96; at the same time, when asked whether he was not preaching to the converted, he said [LI]:

> Yes, I think that's a very valid criticism, and I would simply agree with you... I don't really think I'm achieving anything whatsoever.

Nor did he think the low print-runs of the original editions – in total, little more than 17,000 books were printed over 25 years – were the reason for not being widely known up to the publication of the *Collected* [LI]:

Yes, these print runs haven't occurred by accident. They occur because it's an unwanted commodity and I accept that. I suppose, to be really honest, most people who fiddle about with Art, are doing so in a terribly indulgent manner and it's a mixture of therapy and self-indulgence. And I don't think I'm an exception to that. There *are* exceptions, I'm sure, but I don't think I'm one of them. Not quite sure why I *do* it, except that it's the only thing that seems to vindicate, or has seemed to vindicate, my existence in some measure. I don't really in the retrospect think that I have achieved anything as far as reaching an audience goes …What am I saying apart from the fact that things are shitty and that nothing can be done about it? That's a very nihilistic attitude and I'm a nihilist…What can I say beyond that?

There are three answers to that. Firstly, aesthetic pleasure in a well-made artistic artefact is one important function of art. To produce this pleasure in his reader is indeed one of Reading's aims [LI]:

I do feel that in a way, though it's not the sort of thing that I'd be too ready to acknowledge because I don't think many people associate my poetry with beauty in a conventional way. But it has – I think… an aesthetic quality of its own, depending on how you define beauty. This again relates to…cadence and music and the sort of magniloquence that I associate with poetry or the way that I tend, in my own mind, to define it. There's a kind of beauty about that, yes, but I suppose people tend to assume other things about beauty… A daffodil or something. Got nothing against daffodils, either.

Secondly, art can arouse and demonstrate empathy, and thirdly it can provide company. Reading agreed that these were also his objectives in art [LI]:

Yes, I think the fellow feeling and keeping company is the very impor-tant thing. That's what I find important about the Arts and the things that I respond to, painting and music, music perhaps particularly, and occasionally writing… It's like the function that friendship achieves – to feel sympathy with your fellowman is very important. Or perhaps it's the most important thing. So in that respect art can be quite important. I don't know whether mine is, though; my particular art – I don't really think that it achieves anything much.

Reading's œuvre has since reached a wider reading public. The question of how much this new popularity can 'achieve', though, is still difficult to answer. Reading once said: 'I think there's a lot of whistling in the dark. That's one of the subjects I've gone on about' (Edgar, p.56). At least in the dark you hear that other – unforgettable – voice.

Last Poems (1994):
In the Echo Chamber

Last Poems appeared nearly two and a half years after *Evagatory* –
which had also taken Reading a relatively long time to write –
after 24 years of remarkable productivity. The lessening of literary
creativity had been marked out in the books of the middle phase
and become explicit in *Evagatory*. *Last Poems* ties up the *opus*,
simultaneously providing an epilogue and enacting the exit by
iconoclastically purporting to be a posthumous collection prepared
by 'John Bilston' after the poet's suicide.[1]

Reading wrote *Last Poems* at a time of great upheaval in his
private life, which seemed to bolster his decision to stop writing.
In February 1992 he had become unemployed, and in the summer
his first marriage ended, which left him very much like his alter
ego in *Perduta Gente*: 'jobless, bereft of home, skint'. However, he
received a grant from the Authors' Foundation for 'a new project'
[C] in August, and also met Deborah Shuttleworth, whom he later
married; *Last Poems* is dedicated to her. The plan to follow her to
Australia for a while was postponed when Reading broke his leg;
this meant another winter in Little Stretton, working on *Last Poems*.

In January 1993 Reading mentioned a 'forthcoming, pseudo-
posthumous thing' [C], of which 30 pages had been written, and
which was intended to be published in the spring. He announced
that he wanted to 'get back to writing individual poems, one doesn't
want to get stuck with doing the same kind of thing for the rest of
time. People expect books now, and I want to be able to write the
occasional poem again' [C]. In February 1993 he joined Deborah
Shuttleworth in Melbourne, noting that this new life made his prior
urge to write irrelevant [LI]. Still, *Last Poems* was completed by
June 1993.

Therefore, the invitation from the well-known visual artist Peter
Kennard in July 1993 to collaborate on an exhibition about home-
lessness and poverty in Britain came at exactly the right time.
Reading accepted gladly because this was a new artistic alternative
and because 'his stuff seemed to me to be about the complete end
of cultural and social humanity – eroded placards, debris of arte-
facts, faded images of words and people &c.' He started work
straightaway: 'I produced 30xA4 sheets "recycled" (grand euphemism)
from previous stuff of mine, from *Final Demands*, *Perduta Gente*,

Shitheads and *Last Poems*, and these sheets were worked on to make them "visual" (enlarged by photocopier, burnt, otherwise damaged, torn &c.)' [M]. Three-dimensional objects were added, such as a bank cash bag or 'books, metamorphosed' [C].

Reading was hopeful about this step (back) into visual art. 'Erosive' was shown at the South Bank Centre in June 1994; and the Poetry Library then bought *Erosive: Thirty-Seven Texts, Hand-Produced by Peter Reading* (1993/1994), which were dated by hand on his birthday, '27.vii.94'. Reading's strangely attractive exhibition artefacts were a development of the last pages of *Last Poems*, but also quotations from many other of his books (with one or two jokes), physically fortifying the strongly intratextual unity of his œuvre. Reading told an interviewer:

> Peter Kennard is really a more political man than I am…The poems of mine which he saw and found particularly striking included a sequence called *Perduta Gente,* the lost people. It centres on homeless people and is located very much around the South Bank. At the time it was written, the area was thick with cardboard boxes and near comatose people under this centre of sophisticated activity. This is what Peter Kennard homed in on and wanted to convey, although it's been slightly cleaned up now, cosmetically at least…It's not really just poems, but bashed about books that I've made, palimpsests, and bits and pieces. Peter has produced placards which have taken parts of my texts and messed about with them. What we end up with is a set of erosive texts, which are physically dilapidating. The implication is that here is a set of Museum exhibits from some defunct civilisation (Clark).

Relics of a defunct civilisation are also found in *Last Poems*, which is only slightly longer than (the rather short) *Evagatory*. For the first time since *Stet*, a book was paginated again, and for the first time since *Diplopic*, poems' individual titles were retained, this presumably a result of the book ostensibly having been put together by 'John Bilston'. *Last Poems* contains a Preface, 23 poems varying in length from three lines to 10 pages, and three palimpsests at the end (photographed collages or eroded texts). It offers a very heterogeneous fund of translations and adaptations of old poems – Reading's own as well as other poets' – interspersed with only five completely new poems, all in meticulous formal order.[2] Despite the outward presentation of the volume as a collection of individual poems, *Last Poems*, too, is a unified work: as in a modernist collage, fragment after fragment is produced until the book itself becomes fragmented and the pages degenerate into a smudge – an image of the fate of literary works, lives, civilisations.

The poems are highly cryptic, musical, elegant, and metaphorical, with a strong sense of the 'tireful lacuna' about them (lamented by the Curate translator in *Going On,* p.80). Reading now looks to his literary soul-mates, as Robert Lowell did in his *Imitations* (1961), which he called 'a small anthology of European poetry'[3] and in which he covered 2,700 years and five languages (from Homer and Sappho up to Eugenio Montale and Boris Pasternak). Reading, too, spans the arc of literary archaeology as widely as possible to make his central subject heard once more through other authoritative voices. Like Lowell, he begins with the most ancient of extant occident literature, and in huge century-long strides takes us through the same 2,700 years of (partly still mythical) human history: Homer, Euripides, Thucydides, Alcman, Ovid, Anglo-Saxon poetry, the Middle Ages, Defoe – Reading.

The death of the last hero (Beowulf) is the starting-point of the book (p.247), and nothing has changed since then: fraud and disappointment, hunger and misery, havoc and pestilence, murder and slaughter – the apocalypse is on the horizon, accelerated in the 20th century. *H. sap.* has not understood or learnt a thing, and so the *wierd* introduced in *Evagatory* can freely take its course. However, as Reading told an interviewer (and had long before made clear, especially in the palaeontological sections of *C*): 'This is a natural course of events, and in a way it's more or less happened before. It's simply another ending' (Clark).

Conforming with the evagation into the poet's cranium acted out in *Evagatory, Last Poems* is more cerebral than its predecessors and deals with elegiac-philosophical ideas. The already sparse visuality of *Evagatory* is here reduced even further; the book adopts the *crepuscolarismo* tone of *Weltschmerz* and abandons the Apollonian/ Dionysian tension of earlier books. One thing, though, is "positive": the gesture of stoically gazing at *wierd* continues from the heroic tradition as best it can, supported by the magniloquent diction which also derives from this tradition. In dispersed Alcaics, 'Euripidean' (p.249) expresses this core of the book in a detailed, powerful, almost gnomic manner.[4] Also, a new soft tone is audible, addressing the mothers of war-faring, perishing children:

> What we have long foretold will before long be
>   fully accomplished, the theme of dirges.
>
> Low, low it lies, imperial majesty,
> vanished the pomp, the high-vaunted vanities,
>   nothing remains, no name, no issue.
>
> Mothers, expire with grief on beholding your
> progeny thus deformed and your lovely ones
>   now become loathsome, pallid, death-waxed.
>   …

Not to be borne, such weight of anguish.
...

Nor may we now reach forth with our impotent
    hands to forestall our headlong downrush,
    having irrevocably acted.

Some, there are, hold that the ills attending
    mankind exceed his joys; per contra,
others opine that his frail life encompasses
more bliss than woe – for how could he, otherwise,
    bear to endure each grief-racked orbit?

As *Last Poems* almost entirely consists of adaptations of poems already in existence and thus presents itself as one large hypertext of different pre-texts, one implication is that Reading has nothing distinctive to add and has reached the self-fabricated end of his writing career: exit the author. On the purely literary level, this is taken to its logical conclusion: one poem is entitled 'Valedictory', Peter Reading, the author of 16 books, ceases to exist, and *Last Poems* is published posthumously. Asked whether he would be able to resurrect himself after this book, Reading said:

> I don't know... I'm reluctant to simply reiterate too much stuff [from] the past. We'll just have to wait and see... I feel the inclination to write something. I feel this stress when I don't do anything but there's not much I can do about it, unfortunately. If nothing presents itself, that's my loss (Clark).

Still, a sense of appeasement, which seemed to be a literary side effect of the new love, asserts this one consolation, as experienced by Lycabas dying beside his dead lover Athis (p.267): 'even in death there is comfort through sharing, / joined with a loved friend'. That some lives are not only spent painlessly, but happily, is also worth mentioning; 'Fates of Men' (pp.253-54) lists different fates in Anglo-Saxon versification (a rendering of the Anglo-Saxon poem of the same title in the *Exeter Book*): 'Divers are the destinies   dealt out by Fate to us.'

More important still for the question of literary resurrection is the fact that even though Reading's move from intratextuality to intertextuality seems to have been the product of deplenished resources, it brought with it new creative possibilities that were eventually to provide a way out of the spiral down towards self-annihilation that Reading had manoeuvred himself into. Unlike for Sibelius, who stopped composing, there is no final *nulla* for compulsive artists of Reading's stature, as there was none for Beckett. To quote another remarkable literary parallel, Robert Lowell's *Imitations* were also written 'when I was unable to do anything of my own... One wants a whole new deck of cards to play with, or at least new rules for the old ones.'[5] Indeed, Reading was galvanised by this new poetic direction of intertextual engagement. In the following three books, *Eschatological, Work in Regress,* and *Ob.*, utterly nihilistic as they may be, the new forms, styles, dictions, themes, and personae encouraged Reading and eased his way towards a new creative phase.

The 'Foreword' to *Last Poems* is signed by 'John Bilston, Melaleuca, 1994'. Bilston says he found the poems in an envelope with the superscription '*Last Poems*' in Reading's hand. He does not introduce himself, and seems to be the same biographer who already in *Perduta Gente* had access to the poet's manuscripts. 'John Bilston' is, however, just as obviously fictitious as the biographer, a Reading pseudonym, previously used three times for reviews and once for a letter to the *TLS*.[6]

As in Pushkin's *Belkin's Tales* or Nabokov's *Pale Fire*, the functions of the fictitious editor are clear. First, Reading avoids explanatory notes by the author, which he always deemed unprofessional, but can still publish the exopoetic details he wishes to be known. This signposting of the intertextual character of the book (having Bilston identify some pre-texts) is a clear marker: it tells and enables the reader to enter the communicative process to the full. Secondly, the author's implied suicide becomes more plausible through the editing of the manuscript by another person. Thirdly, Bilston apparently is in Melaleuca (the southernmost tip of Australia): and as Reading was last living in Melbourne and had stopped publishing poems (which was known in literary circles), the possible conclusion is that art and life might have started mingling in a sinister way and that Reading had ended his life in Australia (not just metaphorically as in *Evagatory*), and, literally at the end of the world, had left behind an envelope containing his last poems. Finally, the suicide is intratextually consistent, or feasible, because such a locality was suggested in *Evagatory* and such a scene was anticipated in *C*, where Charon finds a notepad with a last sonnet on the author's corpse. All these considerations aside, the eroded texts themselves symbolise the end of literature.

Bilston annotates the poems by giving their literary sources: Homer's *Odyssey*, Ovid's *Metamorphoses*, Anglo-Saxon poems from the *Exeter Book* and *Beowulf*.[7] Reading had discovered antique and Anglo-Saxon poetry as a student and now came back to it with a vengeance. The intertextual engagement with classical heritage is accompanied by an increasing enthusiasm for the 'heroic twang' of epic heroic literature, and so he assimilated both the tone and the diction of the original texts. In the words of Matthew Arnold, the 'Grand Style' is achieved 'when a noble nature, poetically gifted, treats with simplicity or with severity a serious subject' (Preminger). Reading explained this literary lineage [LI]:

> There are certain dictions I'm anxious to resurrect like the 18th century and earlier ones, the... maritime things, and the anonymous 19th century cleric's translationese of the classics, and... the resurrection of these Saxon things in *Last Poems*. I find those things extremely and curiously moving by their directness and just by the kind of genre they are. They're not like anything we have now, and I ... find them, of course, a very useful device for their metaphorical power and their kind of diction. I ... have always have found that kind of diction in poetry a necessity, a complete avoidance of the everyday. Now I've used demotic language an awful lot, but it's taken up into a context which I think is un-ordinary. And these kinds of stances, these kinds of dictions are all different ways of approaching unordinariness. Increasingly I find magniloquence is very important and I like old-fashioned people like Tennyson because of that: here is a grand gesture. And I would dislike intensely somebody like John Ashbery because he lacks any kind of resonance whatsoever, let alone sense.

Bilston also mentions a handwritten note indicating that 'Euripidean' and 'Thucydidean' should be ascribed to an 'anonymous cleric of the nineteenth century', i.e. the versifying Curate of *Going On*. The artistic advantage is evident: Reading can reproduce the heroic diction of the earlier texts without sounding stilted or archaic *himself*. Intertextual 'versions' can take on so many forms and fulfil so many functions – and they are so relevant to postmodernist concepts of "reality" and theories of language (revolving in the extreme around the 'universe of texts' and Derrida's free play of signifiers, the *regressus ad infinitum*) – that Reading's re-writes will no doubt yield very interesting findings for future poststructuralist critics.

What Bilston does not mention in the Foreword is that in *Last Poems* Reading not only presents a hypertext of a few milestones in Western literature, but intratextually self-references his own *opus*. In almost all the poems that lack an antique pre-text, there are allusions, echoes, or quotations from his earlier books – the last (intact) poem, 'August:' (p.277), is almost totally an auto-cento. A significantly large number of poems refer back to the first book, *For the Municipality's Elderly*, or *Water and Waste*, where, a quarter of a century ago, Reading had started with his theme of the transience and brevity of life.

All the other quotations in the book are also from thematically relevant contexts and images. The new poems are thus soaked in a deep pool of associations and history, which substantiates, affirms and secures them, amplifying their impact considerably. Reading had employed this aesthetic (inter- and intratextual) device before, re-using special iconic images and motifs in multiple echoes, but also personae, objects, evocative words or phrases, and all sorts of other narrative, dramatic or lyrical elements. Reading confirmed this [LI]:

> I've consciously tried to recycle some stuff, but there were some things whose imagery I've found quite important or just wanted to reiterate, as well... Some things have just stayed with me and I do tend to repeat just because I want to repeat them. But also there's a conscious desire to... unify the whole *opera*.

The device of reiteration and cross-referencing is, however, held together by Reading's lyrical voice, which spans an unusually wide poetic range and is polyphonically multi-layered, but never leaves its own continuum; no matter which artistic functions determine the form it takes in individual poems, it can always be traced back to the flow of one and the same individual voice – the spellbinding power of poetry as such. This is what makes Reading so distinctive and what unifies his œuvre more than all the textual artistry taken together.

Last Poems begins with '[Untitled]', a new version of the central poem of *Final Demands* (p.118), in which the old scribbled papers of generations dry up like the poet's laurels. It is now presented in square brackets and Alcaic tetrameters as the prologue to the poems of this book and the human fate they describe; the bond is rotting (an allusion to banknote paper and the human community), and a closing comma opens the arena for the failing 'utterance' one "last time" (p.247):

> [...
> crackle of brittle anhydrous laurel leaves,
> sepia-scrivened crumbled eroded leaves,
> parchment eroded round the sad utterance,
> rotted the frail bond, with it the utterance,]

The eroded ancient papyrus texts may be translated anew in Reading's book, but *Last Poems* itself ends in graphic erosion. The process of decaying and forgetting is unstoppable – but the ironic twist is that such hypertexts will guarantee the survival of literature until the end of the reading world.

After this bracketed prelude, the coronach 'Funerary' opens the beginning of the end; it is a concise adaptation of the end of *Beowulf* (*ll.* 3137-82), depicting the hero's funeral. (It, in turn, brings to mind the burning of Achilles and Patroclus in the *Odyssey*, XXIV, 80*ff.*). The brave warrior Beowulf, who like Odysseus in Phaeoecia conquered three monsters, has been ruling over the Geats for 50 years; as an old man, he fights and kills the dragon which has been destroying his people, but as only one of his twelve knights, Wiglaf, helps him, he perishes in the fight. In *Beowulf*, the warriors say he was '*lof-geornost*', addicted to the undying fame of his deeds: this is the driving-force of heroes, and their most important quality is responsibility towards their followers. With Beowulf, the ideals of heroic society are buried: bravery, intelligence, and strength in the face of any danger; therefore the monsters will return as the ineradicable incarnation of evil and death. In the light of this heroic past the unconditional celebration of reality is no longer possible – and this is where Reading's poem sets in, like the pre-text written in Saxon alliterative metre with caesura. The twelve Geat warriors ride round the barrow, lamenting the hero's death; 'Funerary' is a monument to the last true hero of the Western world (p.247):

> And this is fitting: for fair men to value
> with powerful words   their worthy lord
> when his life, as all men's   must, departs him.
> So the men of the Geats,   Great-Hall-dwellers,
> who'd shared the hearth   with the hero, bewailed,
> claiming their king   was the kindest of leaders,
> the mildest of men,   most meriting renown.

The vision of the impending 'terror, killing, captivity, shame' will come true and his people will be eradicated: heroic society is at an end, because the indispensable total solidarity has broken down – which led to Beowulf's death. The heroic circle of journey, welcome, feast, boasting, armament, battle and reward is over. The Geats, now without *lord* – and thus without protection – will be attacked and destroyed by the Swedes and Franks. Everything else develops from there, and so Reading proceeds to recapitulate the bloody history of Western civilisation.

The following four-footed quasi-sonnet 'Regal' (p.248) about the news of the death of '*His Majesty, King George VI*' (and punning on the cinema name 'Regal', common in the 50s) is a re-write of two poems from *Stet* (pp.84, 88), functioning as a contrasting validation of the thesis of decreasing human potential. Today's rulers no longer deserve an epicedium: 'The Regal, I recall, / was gaudy, faded, had seen better days'. Their entourage is also introduced with a simile in 'Bosnian' (p.250, an intratextual re-write of p.224): modern citizens are like lambs led to slaughter, and 'in the fast-darkening air' are just as real as the 'Hooded Crows' on the other side, evoking sinister associations of medieval executioners. With all the dramatis personae present, the carnage can start in the very next poem.

With zestful ferocity, 'Homeric' (pp.250-53) opens a series of

barbaric slaughters. It is a stichic epic narrative, an adaptation of
the postlude to the climactic passage in which, on his return to
Ithaca, Odysseus kills the usurpers of his house and Penelope's
suitors and then orders 12 servant women to clean the bloody mess
up, after which they are summarily hanged (Book XXII, *ll.* 381-477).
As Tim Dooley shrewdly observes: 'The juxtaposition of "cleans-
ing" with scenes of horrific murder has a chilling contemporary
resonance.'

As a schoolboy, Reading had been fascinated by the best-selling
prose translation by E.V. Rieu (1946) of the *Odyssey*. Later, he was
inspired by the metrics and tone of Cotterill's translation of 1911.
He adopted the bucolic diaeresis, followed Cotterill's rules regarding
the accentuating hexameter as well as the 'simplicity... directness,
and... rapidity' of Homer's original and 'a diction natural, but not
undignified', as Cotterill phrased it.[8] To match the Homeric tone of
neutral reportage is obviously not difficult for Reading; his hexa-
metrical version is both highly formal and orderly and very readable
and poignant in its detachment. Reading's stark portrayal of the
butchery also has to be seen in its context as translation. His own
comment shines through the palimpsest by virtue of ellipsis: there
is no talk of the heroic grandeur of the vengeful Odysseus and he
omits the end of Book XXII, in which the women of the house
fall on the hero's neck, thanking him for his killings. Instead, he
closes with a description of Odysseus' men's attack on the traitor
Melanthius, thereby negating, transvaluing or deconstructing the
original (p.253):

> Plying a keen-edged blade, they sawed his
> nose and ears off,
> carved off his genitals, tossed them aside as
> meat for the mongrels.
> Finally, hacking his hands and his feet off, their
> fury was sated.

Critics of Reading's portrayals of violence should ask themselves
whether they would made the same complaint to Homer that in
his depiction of cruelty he was 'too black and over the top' – and
if not, why not.[9]

The same ellipsis applies to the two long poems entitled 'Ovidian'
(pp.254-59, 265-73). Commissioned by Michael Hofmann and James
Lasdun in 1992 for *After Ovid: New Metamorphoses*, the poems
render 'the brawl over Andromeda' [M] in Reading's 'characteristic
quasi-classical hexameters', as Bilston informs the reader. In the
first 'Ovidian' (after IV, 663-803), Perseus defeats Neptune, frees
Andromeda and recounts how he severed the head of the Medusa.

The second part (after V, 1-235) directly continues from there: the agreed wedding turns into a bloodbath because Phineus – Andromeda's uncle, to whom she had been originally promised – dislikes losing her to Perseus. 'Baying for spilt guts, the rest of the rabble took up their weapons' (p.226),[10] and so an enumeration follows of horrendous atrocities, complete with physiological grotesqueries such as heels drumming floors in the throes of death – rendered in the nonchalant Ovidian tone.[11] But again Reading avoids any show of approval of the heroes such as can be found in other translations.

Also fitting with Reading's themes, the hapless poet Lampetides, invited to the wedding to play the zither – a peace symbol – is killed along with everybody else, thus echoing the fate of another useless poet perishing while plucking his lyre in *Ukulele Music*. Accordingly, the subject of the auto-referential poems which follow is also ruin and death. *Last Poems* shows Reading working towards a 'clean desk' [LI], tying up the loose ends. The different metres pass in review, and diverse previous motifs, lines or poems with foreshadowing functions are now called up to unify the œuvre, forming a tightly woven net of cross-references, and closing around what is intended as the final statement.

'Submission' (p.260), in 'dispersed Alcaics', is a sequel to a poem from *Stet* (p.89) and *Final Demands* (p.137), which mentions a slight pain 'left of the sternum', i.e. in the heart, thus making the thought of death tangible, immediate. Just as in *Final Demands* a medical consultation had been dismissed, so here the poet's wish expresses a 'final submission'; and an image of the 'submission' to the ineluctable is also presented: Reading quotes an excerpt from Daniel Defoe's *Journal of the Plague Year* (1722), in which the plague-stricken crawl under the hedges 'and DIE'.

The next poem, 'Pestilential' (p.260), in iambic pentameter (used mostly as a narrative metre by Reading), gives details from Defoe's fictionalised account of the plague year in London of 1665. 'Blind Piper' recalls 'Poor Tom', while the equally mad Solomon Eagle begging for God's mercy in the most frightful manner is known from the first book (*For the Municipality's Elderly*, p.55), both there and here 'denouncing / of Judgement upon the City'.[12] Just as heroes perish in battle, people of the Middle Ages die from epidemics, and modern civilisations from the ecological consequences of their own actions. The monsters of evil remain – only their manifestations change. Reading's choice of the hypertext medium is very appropriate – nothing else could carry off the idea of palimpsest better.[13]

'St Laurence's' (p.262) is the name of the church in Church Stretton, but also refers to St Lawrence's, the church in Ludlow

(*For the Municipality's Elderly,* p.54), named after the same saint. The reference to the bench and the use of iambic pentameter signal the return to the earliest topography. That in some places a mild April sun comes with ultraviolet danger, is one of today's 'pestilences', with the pointed difference that it is utterly self-inflicted.

'Thucydidean' (p.261) is ascribed to the anonymous cleric and, like the other poems with a Greek antecedent, an epic poem written in hexameters. It lists various natural disasters and describes the pestilence as an example of how endangered, frightened people 'turned to lawless dishonour, / heedless of gods and law for they thought themselves already sentenced – / then there was bloody and slaughterous civil mass insurrection'. This is an almost verbatim echo of the civil unrest and dissolution of social stability resulting from the ban on cars prognosticated for England in *Evagatory* (p.229). This time it is the fall of Athens that leads to the downfall of the mighty, democratic Empire, as chronicled by the historian Thucydides (*c*.460 – *c*.400 BC).[14]

The peak of intratextual cross-referencing, however, is 'Reiterative' (pp.263-64), prefaced by a metatextual comment: '[Churned out in '76, / the eroded, faded text...]'. Reading presents a slightly tautened new version of his 1976 poem 'Nothing For Anyone' (*Nothing For Anyone*, pp.127-29), again in 3-stress metre, in which he refers to the foreseeable end of the industrial world ('Population, Energy, Food') as mapped out by Lord Eric Ashby in 1976.[15] The macabre thing about 'Reiterative' is that it reads as if it had not been written 18 years before, but now, at the turn of the century. The fatal dangers delineated have become all too real, but are still not widely perceived as really life-threatening. Furthermore, humankind has not come an inch closer to a real solution, as is evident from the daily news. Reading, after quoting his monitory poem, draws the obvious conclusion and, with the usual self-mockery, snarls like an authoritarian teacher (p.264):

[That was in '76,
the hackneyed text is eroded,
somebody ain't been listening –
you, at the back, sit up
and fuckingwell pay attention.]

To go with 'Reiterative' there is an illustration created by Reading himself as part of the cover picture on the original edition: it shows a fragment of the eroded poem of 1976 ('Nothing For Anyone') and of the bracketed 1994 postscript written in Reading's hand, all on a yellowed background. 'Fucking-well pay attention' is ominously shortened to 'fucking-well pay' and the line 'insurrection c[ivil a]nd bloody' is doubly underlined. The text is cut off by a block of aggressive black and red paint bearing the title of the book, and superimposed over the text is a blue figure painted in broad, crude brush strokes, shown running away with an arrow through its head. The figure resembles daubed graffiti, the body and arms coming close to a swastika, the head reminiscent of an arrow-pierced heart, exactly the kind of stuff those 'at the back' would be drawing on their desks, instead of listening. Finally, there are the initials of the book's imprint 'CP' (Chatto Poetry), telling the reader to compare the cover with the poem.

After delineating extended parallels in human history Reading finishes with his own persona. 'Alcmanic' (p.264), in Alcmanic verses, is a wistful echo of the harsh monostich 'All that remains, the stench of their excrement' (*Evagatory*, p.240):

[That which remains is incongruous; frail bond
palimpsest crumbling, with it the notion;
utterance utterly lost in hiatus;
all that remains is fragmentary:] *ear-ring*

The mysterious pun 'ear-ring' is indeed an extant fragment by Alcman, and Reading, with the use of preliminary square brackets, associates his own bequest of *Last Poems* with this echoing 'utterance utterly lost in hiatus; / all that remains is fragmentary'.[16] In a poem following soon after, the haiku '[Untitled]' (p.275), he provides the context for this fragment, in which it can get lost yet again: 'A silver ear-ring, / lost last night in the hayfield, / lies in flattened grass.' In passing, it also alludes to the (possibly) doomed lovers in the 'flattened oats' of *Stet*.

A new version of the Anglo-Saxon elegy *The Ruin* is also seen in this light, entitled 'Fragmentary' (p.273). Although it echoes the jeremiad of *Perduta Gente* ('Rooftrees are wrecked'), it is close to the original text, but tauter and more cohesive, reducing the original 49 lines by almost half. The original text is itself 'fragmentary' – both sheets were damaged by fire. Here, the illegible parts of the manuscript are rendered in square brackets as 'Hiatus, lacuna...', thus forming the link to the future erosion of Reading's own works. A Saxon (unfamiliar with stone buildings) describes the ruins of a Roman city abandoned 300 years before (probably Aqua Sulis, i.e. Bath), and meditates on the old stones: 'Those men who might have re-made it lay dead. / What was once fought for is wasteland now.'

Another fragment follows. 'Shard' (p.274) evokes a fragment of an Athenian amphora and is Reading's hexametrical counterpiece to Alcman's '*ear-ring*'. The lamenting 'snow-haired elder' from *Evagatory* appears here as the 'antique/lyrist', of whose poetry only this burden is allegedly extant: '*Sweet wine passes between the lips of amative partners…*'. The wistful memory of a love-and-wine-drenched summer has autobiographical roots, as delineated above; after a long winter's wait for the loved one, 'fructose is concentrated', not only in the ice-wine. 'Exilic' (p.275) is the companion poem describing the summer-winter contrast from the woman's perspective. Presented as a version of the Anglo-Saxon poem 'The Wife's Lament', it is a close translation of the original. Unlike the wife unjustly exiled by her husband, this exiled woman yearns for her lover 'in a land inaccessible'. '*Only death should divide us*' is a quotation from the original, but also presented as the author's "fragment" by the use of italics. She fears: 'Alien feelings / that he no longer loves me as formerly / fill me with fear, forlornly I pine here.'

The interpretation of what seems to be an unusually private digression comes in 'Midnight,' (p.275), which in iambic pentameter follows on from the poem in *Evagatory* (p.225) where a nightingale's song provides a 'richly mellifluous' counterpoint to the 'vitriolated downpour' heard at midnight from a Trebinje hotel; at the same time it suggests the literary end (p.275):

Midnight,

       a hotel bedroom, open window,
sibilant tyres on rain-washed asphalt streets
whispering a repetitious *finish, finish.*
You stroke your lover comprehensively,
who purrs contentment, clings to your neck and sobs.
Sibilant tyres on rain-washed asphalt streets
whispering a repetitious *finish, finish.*

Another confirmation of Reading's private motivation to turn his back on writing is given in the monostrophical 'Valedictory' (p.276), which antonomasically announces the end of his career in 3-stress metre: 'This buffer's in full retreat, / had more than enough, wants out'. (Again, an envelope structure is employed to exemplify the circular course of Reading's œuvre.) His early sarcasm and self-deprecation are distinct in this poem, and with these the 'esoteric subculture' mocked in the early books comes alive once more, not having changed to its advantage over the years, just like politics: 'each successive bulletin / is more wacky, sad, obscene'.

The culmination is 'Idyllic' (p.276), the third, hexametrical variation by Reading of the leitmotif Homeric scene of peaceful sleep. The dreamed suicide of *C* by overdosing on sleeping tablets after an excellent bottle of wine, which in *Final Demands* re-surfaced as a comforting vision, is now to be carried out at last. Two significant stanzas are added to the long-standing fantasy, anticipating the

actual circumstances of his death: the late discovery of the well-
hidden corpse and the 'kingfisher-blue pulsating strobe and bray of
the tumbril'. The image of the bodily remains of the poet-persona
is thus the logical conclusion of the book. (As a fortuitous after-
thought, though, the place of his death is 'Melaleuca', named after
the variety of tree from which an omnipotent essential oil is procured
[*Melaleuca alternifolia*] – it seems to have healing power even over
suicide.)

The last poem, 'August' (p.277; commissioned by the *Housman
Society Journal*), substantiates the pseudo-irreversible end:

August:

>   the steady thresh
> of an advancing harvester;
> the dark swift departing;
> ash in Ludlow church,
> HIC IACET A.E.H.;
> last light is pressing the panes;
> les lauriers sont coupés.

A dead poet, another dying in nature,[17] and a distillation of ageing
quotes from earlier works all merge to form a fastidious final image
that is moving and minimalistic. Only the last line is not intratextual:
the use of French at first suggests that Reading – as an ex-writer –
is now in need of translation himself, like the classics he translated.
However, it turns out to be the reversal of a translation of a pre-
text used in another poet's *Last Poems*. A.E. Housman's epigraph,
'We'll to the woods no more, / The laurels all are cut...', was itself
a translation from 'Les Cariatides' by Théodore de Banville: 'Nous
n'irons plus aux bois, les lauriers sont coupés.'[18]

The laurels also bring the book itself to completion by referring
back to the first poem; and the change from the initial 'frail wisps
of laurel leaves' (p.247) to 'lauriers coupés' expresses Reading's
literary fate and life up to this point. The laurels – as the symbol
of the poetic spirit – no longer adorn his brow, just as the laurel
symbol of victory, peace and literary excellence itself has become
obsolete. Indeed, 'Les Lauriers' was introduced in *Tom o'Bedlam's
Beauties* as a nursing home for the mentally deranged.

The end of the author can only be followed by the disintegration
of his texts. The last three pages illustrate the erosive process
befalling two poems, which describe the expected literary and social
process of dissolution. The blurb of the original edition stated:

> Renowned for his innovation with the form and physical surface of
> poetry, Peter Reading opens up new possibilities with *Last Poems*: the
> collection ends mysteriously and movingly with poems which have

crumbled into incoherence, the legacy of a long-vanished poet, but
also a more profound statement about the futility of art.

'Erosive' (p.278) is visual art: it consists of badly typed, cut-up, re-
pasted fragments of the first poem in *Last Poems*, '[Untitled]' (p.247),
itself a rewrite of the central poem of *Final Demands*, which had
portrayed the end of Reading's poetry and of his persona as he
'sinks in the lines of the dead' (p.119). Individual letters already
sink and fade in the title line.

The last two pages (pp.279-80) graphically simulate the process
of erosion up to the point of illegibility. Some letters are thickly
smeared, others have vanished. It is the unheeded warning 'Nothing
For Anyone' from *Nothing For Anyone*, which new readers can also
identify through the new version in this book ('Reiterative'). As in a
palimpsest it barely shines through, evoking the multiply rewritten
pergament papers translated in this book.[19]

Both Reading's early books and the rich tradition of Western
literature gleam through this "last" work, *Last Poems*. This kind
of continuity – new books re-creating old books, revivifying the
forgotten past by means of modern adaptations, generations creating
and superseding one another – offers the ultimate literary consola-
tion, which was anticipated in the human consolation of shared
death (Lycabas and Athis, p.267). One statement about poetry by
T.S. Eliot is enacted and visualised by Reading here: poetry is the
collective memory of humankind. This is literature as stable and
affirmative as it can be.

Eschatological (1996), *Work in Regress* (1997), *Ob.* (1999), *Marfan* (2000): Last Things

To have one's poems published in a *Collected* so early in one's lifetime is highly unusual and a great honour. Reading's *Collected Poems* was published by Bloodaxe in two volumes on his 49th and 50th birthdays (in 1995 and 1996). As Michael Hofmann wrote: 'if anyone deserves the accolade it is Reading: prolific, distinctive and controversial...he has customised the language more radically than any other poet of the moment'.[1]

Another book that alerted readers to Reading's stature was *The New Poetry* (Bloodaxe, 1993), in which he featured as a seminal contributor and key poet. The publishing climate is still turning in his favour: he was published in volume 3 in the second series of *Penguin Modern Poets* (with his own choice of poems), and then given substantial showings in two other important recent anthologies, Sean O'Brien's *The Firebox: Poetry in Britain and Ireland after 1945* (Picador, 1998) and *The Penguin Book of Poetry from Britain and Ireland* (1998), edited by Simon Armitage and Robert Crawford.

Accompanying this widening of his readership, there has been a shift in appreciation; more readers and critics have discovered the gentler and funnier side of Reading and qualified their views, noting also that here was a poet who could hold their attention over 300 pages at a stretch.[2] The previous talk about 'doom and gloom' had among other things come from the simple fact that most readers, not knowing all his books, were unfamiliar with 'the potency and range' (Gidley) of this 'formidable œuvre' (O'Neill), which needs to be read in its entirety, as one huge epic poem.

With a few notable exceptions, reviewers agreed that this *Collected* established the reputation that had been slow to develop, and concluded that Reading had become a major British poet. Simon Armitage introduced him for *Stanza on Stage* at the Birmingham Readers' and Writers' Festival (1996), where he read from his early works:

> Reading's *Collected Poems*...confirmed his reputation as the most innovative, sophisticated, and original poet of the past 30 years. Throughout his writing career, Peter Reading has single-handedly stuck to the task of examining the society we live in through endless consideration of the language it uses and misuses. Some of his work has been described as gruesome, discomforting, and alarming, but there is also a wit and

an exhilaration to the poetry…and a tenderness as well made all the more moving by the subjects that surround it. It is all too easy to talk about the importance of certain poets, but for me Peter Reading forms that vital link between the generation that preceded him, and the one about to follow. And because he is unique, he is also without comparison, and therefore without equal.[3]

The *Collected* included a new collection, *Eschatological* (1996), the first of three books to appear after the pseudo-ultimate *Last Poems* in quick succession: *Eschatological* (1996), *Work in Regress* (Bloodaxe, 1997), and *Ob.* (Bloodaxe, 1999; including *Chinoiserie*, published as a pamphlet by The Bay Press in 1997). The new books generally present 'The Mixture as Before',[4] i.e. the sombre and rhapsodic pondering of 'lives, loves, deaths' in ever shorter, starker poems moving through personal and historical time. As Reading has artistically and threateningly fabricated 'creative extinction [as coterminous] with personal extinction',[5] and as he emphasises his probably premature demise in private conversation too, the wait for another book has taken on an uneasy, uncanny quality over the last few years.

However, even if *Ob.* shows Reading at his most depressive, purporting to prepare his own obituary, that has not prevented him leaving his fabricated death-bed to write a vigorous new collection, *Marfan* (2000), a compelling travelogue exploring the Texan-Mexican border country, incorporating photographs by Jay Shuttleworth, resounding with Reading themes and suffused with mordant humour. And he has just completed a subsequent collection, much of this also drawing on his perceptions of America, to be titled [*untitled*] (due from Bloodaxe in 2001).

Two uncertain yoke-fellows, despair and resilience, have always co-existed in Reading.[6] But his resilience seems stronger again, urging him to write more despite his announcement that he would not write another poem after his 50th birthday [C]. The stance of finishing had been exaggerated, typical of Reading's extreme positions and intense integrity – he has an artist's unconditional mania. His persistence is not 'heroically at odds with his terminal outlook' (Potts), for the simple fact that for Reading life consists of writing. The pull, the passion, the obsession cannot be resisted; he cannot do anything else.[7]

His new, creative exploration of the potential of intertextual writing has interesting historic parallels, fits in fascinatingly with current literary theory, and is at the same time an organic development of a modernist device that Reading had been attracted to very early on. The inheritance from artists such as Jasper Johns

and Rauschenberg manifests itself in his writing as the found poem,
first used in *Nothing For Anyone*, with the new context automatically
providing a change of perspective. The next step was to invent
found poems, such as the poems 'from the Spanish of' in *Fiction*
(p.159), 'from the Russian of' (p.186) or 'after' (p.198) other
fictional "authors" (wines, sherry) in *Tom o'Bedlam's Beauties*.
After the very first conscious intertextual links were made with
Eliot and Larkin in *For the Municipality's Elderly*, single hypertex-
tual 'versions' of earlier pre-texts and genres followed in *Diplopic,
C* and *Stet* (Dryden's translation of Virgil, metrical conventions,
and Larkin's England-from-a-train poem respectively), as well as
an abundance of literary allusions. The subsequent use of more
extensive hypertextual allusions and parallels call up entire literary
traditions, such as the *topos* of Rome burning in *Ukulele Music* (or
the fall of Athens in *Last Poems*), or, indeed, the old intertextual
practice itself, as in the 'bogus translations' of Alcman and Alcaeus
in *Going On*. In *Shitheads* Reading started a straightforward 'trans-
lationese exercise' by enlisting the help of a classicist and then
turning the close translations into poems. With the palimpsests of
Evagatory and *Last Poems* as a visual preparation, Reading goes
one step further in the last four books, coming into "his own"
again and writing remakes of classical authors in a double projec-
tion: he draws on the similarities between them and him in their
historical or personal situations and in their philosophical outlooks,
and he transposes not only their language, but also their epoch,
consciousness and genre.

To investigate in detail both the presence of pre-texts and the
multiple forms, structures and functions of Reading's hypertexts
and their intratextual relatedness within the whole œuvre is a sep-
arate task best performed by a classicist (with, ideally, a knowledge
of Chinese). It is only such a scholar who can with any reliability
ascertain, for instance, to what degree Reading affirms his foils,
negates or modifies them, which stylistic or technical idiosyncrasies
he captures, and to what extent he submerges his foils in his own
voice. The rest of us can still enjoy Reading's poems on the terms
given – but for this a basic familiarity with the concept of inter-
textuality is still helpful.[8]

Intertextual theories and their philosophical implications are
fascinating in themselves, but of little practical value when it
comes to doing substantial work on individual texts that do not
clearly relate to other texts. Therefore, German and American
studies in particular have narrowed intertextuality down to texts
which identifiably interact with one or more other texts. To be more

precise: we call a text intertextual, if, for a successful communica-
tive process, the writer wants the reader to recognise the intertextual
relations, and the reader can rely on intertext signposting, i.e.
markers (open or hidden), from the author to help his under-
standing – as is the case with Reading's books. (Unsurprisingly,
Reading's œuvre is also itself open to intertextual treatment, as the
transposition of his poems into other genres – film, art, music, and
drama – shows.)

This Alexandrian tradition of going back, of translationese stock-
taking, has been current practice for centuries: interestingly, it
occurs mainly in phases of cultural decline and seems a necessary
pre-condition for new creative phases. Through antiquity, the
Middle Ages, the Renaissance up to our own age, it may feature
more or less strongly, and be welcomed, repressed or negated: what
changes are the functions such intertextuality fulfils in the relevant
cases. In English classicism, Dryden and Johnson gave the theor-
etical justification for it and provided examples. As Dryden said of
his 'versions' of Virgil and Juvenal: 'I have endeavoured to make
Virgil speak such English as he would himself have spoken, if he
had been born in England, and in this present age.' [9] (Seen in this
light, Reading's translations of Dryden's translations in *Diplopic* are
funny indeed.)

The most famous examples of intertextual poetry in this century
were by Ezra Pound and Robert Lowell. The controversy about
Lowell's *Imitations* (1961) was preceded by the one about Ezra
Pound's *Homage to Sextus Propertius* (1919). Both were attacked by
classical philologists such as William Gardner Hale for their low
level of creativity and their translation "errors", although long
before this Dryden had influentially distinguished between three
types of translation (Preface to *Ovid's Epistles*, 1680):

> First, that of metaphrase, or turning an author word by word... from
> one language into another...The second way is that of paraphrase, or
> translation with latitude...The third is imitation, where the translator
> (if he has not by now lost that name) assumes the liberty not only to
> vary from the words and sense, but to forsake them both as he sees
> occasion; and taking only some general hints from the original, to run
> division on the ground-work, as he pleases.

Pound consequently pointed out the critics' narrow focus, saying
'there was never any question of translation, let alone literal trans-
lation. My job was to bring a dead man to life... doubling of me
and Propertius, England today, and Rome under Augustus'.[10]

Lowell's *Imitations*, like Eliot's *Waste Land* and Reading's latest
books, are intertexts about isolation, death, moral disintegration,

and fragmentation, and they are about re-writing the history of meaninglessness and futility. They negotiate between the 'vertical' (diachronic) dimension of intertextuality, that is to say the literary heritage or textual genetics, and its 'horizontal' (synchronic) dimension, which is the current poetic discourse or the translator's own poems, thus creating a relationship between the two. This relationship is dramatised by quotation, translation, imitation, adaptation, or allusion. The intertextual dialogue between two writers, cultures, or languages involves demands and concessions, an appropriation of some areas and a secession of others; the borders between the pre-text and hypertext can either be distinct (as in the collage of the *Waste Land*) or blurred (as in the *Imitations*), which directs the dialogic tension either outwards or inwards.

This is the literary background to Reading's own adaptations, which cover the same vast stretches of literary time, conduct the same Bakhtinian inner dialogue and polyphony, and also strive to attain classical status. In this light, all his poems are in a sense one.

Pound thought that whole layers in poetry were untranslatable: of the music (*melopoeia*), imagery (*phanopoeia*) and the connotation and associations of words (*logopoeia*), only imagery could be directly translated (the music only sometimes, but connotations of words never, only in finding equivalents). In his opinion, considerations of heroic style or metre were 'dead technicalities' and secondary.[11] This is where Reading sharply differs: he pits his metrical prowess against free verse. In his "translations", the heroic style and classical cadences and metres are paramount.[12]

Eschatological (1996) as a title is a distillation of the book's agenda: scatology, classicism, and the contemplation of three of the Last Four Things: Death, Judgement, and Hell. (In its first draft, the title was *Scatological,* and it ended with three increasingly burnt manuscripts of the last poem '[Untitled]', which in Anglo-Saxon metre sings the end of the world and eternal torture in Hell [M].)

Eschatological follows naturally from *Last Poems*: on the one hand, it is a partly self-sufficient book and can be synchronically read as the typical Reading sequence with a polyphony of voices, personae, contrasts and parallels. At the same time, this is the horizontal foil for the intertextual dialogue, because its ground-note and unifying theme of preparing for what Hopkins called 'no worst, there is none', together with its leitmotifs and imagery create interaction between the poems, which means that then the vertical, intertextual dimension can add layers of meaning and new functions. The appropriation of a historical pre-text invokes the relevant author's entire aura (see Lucretius); the collation of different poems by an author (see Aeschylus) creates a new text; and multiple intertextuality is achieved when more than one source is targeted at the same time (the classics, the Old Testament, and Anglo-Saxon poetry in the 'Choric' poems). All these procedures help to bridge the gap between the old texts and today's readers. Furthermore, the diachronic reference to genres and literary conventions (antique epic, Anglo-Saxon lament, modernist collage, modernist free translations) fortifies the poems with an ingenious comment on generic links within literary history.

The allusion to the death horror in *C* (p.288) is counterpointed within and by 'Lucretian' (p.287-91), a fascinating, telescoped, very free remake of *De rerum natura* ('On Nature'), a renowned didactic poem in six hexameter books (Reading treats one book per section). Lucretius was the most important advocate of Epicurean philosophy in Rome. While 'passionately convinced that his doctrine was needed to free the Roman mind from superstition and fear of death, Lucretius confined his psychagogic outbursts to clearly discerned "purple patches", letting reason carry the argument through the rest of the poem. The resultant transitions are often jarring...' (Preminger, p.439). Lucretius' poem delineates Epicurean natural philosophy: ideas about the origin of the world, the course of history, and the strictly causal laws of fate, which inflict pain and evil on man indifferently. Coggrave had recommended that Reading read Lucretius [M], who saw nothing terrible in death ('Lucretian', III). Epicurus' voice becomes part of Reading's: 'Epicurus, empiricist hero, / first took a cool look at religion' (I, p.287), which intertextually supports Reading's own derision of 'the unpopularity of common sense. Elementary Darwinism isn't very popular either, in the 20th century, in Britain, or America' (Jenkins, 1985, p.11). At the same time, 'How much idiot evil / gormless theists engender' (I, p.287) is a reference to the Lucretian hexameter '*tantum religio potuit suadere malorum*' from *De Rerum Natura* (I.101) which was first paraphrased in *Stet* and then reiterated in *Work in Regress*, where again Reading's 'heroes', the scientists, are under attack (p.30):

> Islam (that loudmouth jackass the Prince of
>   Wales has advised us)
> offers alternative values to wicked
>   Westernist Science.
> How many times does one have to reiterate
>   worldly Lucretius?:
> *Tantum religio potuit sua-*
>   *dere malorum.*

Religion-induced evil, 'Lucretian' reminds us, is to be witnessed from antiquity (Agamemnon) to the inquisition (Tomás de Torquemada) and the 20th century (Khomeini). Love-induced madness is also given a savaging (IV, p.289-90); but here the absence of common sense is derided in a comical and grossly exaggerated parody of infatuated behaviour. However, when it comes to the frailty of children, the madness is once more chilling, as in 'News' (p.292):

> Nothing, fond parent attempting to shield your
>   child from the onslaughts
> waged by quotidian strife (we observe you
>   on tonight's shitshow
> try, with a frail and futile attempt at
>   resuscitation),
>   can counter the cunts with the creeds,
>   barriers, borders, beliefs.

Eschatological shows Reading casting last glances over his shoulder and erecting a pyre of all the images of "Last Things" he happens to see on earth. Some of these "Last Things" are spotted in mundane existence and presented iconically in a starkly sarcastic tone, such as the detritus of consumerist habits and their 'con-men' equivalents ('Corporate', pp.285-86), or the Nature Reserve in 'Leasts' (p.285), likened to the place where Reading's father was incarcerated in Japan during the Second World War.[13] Pre-empting criticism one more time in 'Epitaphal', he reminds readers that he never invents such things (p.293): 'You thought him cruel? No more than you should think / a Turkey Vulture cruel – vocations differ.'[14]

At the more celestial end of the scale, reverence is the ground-bass, as in the sequel to the description of Beowulf's funeral (p.283) or Reading's homage to his late friend Gavin Ewart (p.284). There are more re-makes of Anglo-Saxon laments and of Chorus passages of the *Oresteian Trilogy* by Aeschylus, himself an intertextual writer (whose work was also translated by Lowell). Reading also comes back to the corpse of the gypsy he once found as a boy near the canal, this time describing it in graphic detail (p.293); and as an epilogue he quotes the slightly adapted haiku epigraph of *Ukulele Music* (p.296, see p.11), thus neatly bracketing *Collected Poems: 2* with a *déjà lu*: '[No fatuity / of which *H. sap* can conceive / remains unfulfilled.]'.

Eschatological presents the assortment of different forms we have come to expect of Reading. The hexameters with bucolic diaeresis are typeset in yet another new way, i.e. in two lines with a break after the fourth foot and less indentation than before (p.282):

> There is no thing in the archive of angry
>   heaven – affliction,
> terror, distress – but unfortunate man must
>   bear the weight of it.

A strangely hybrid form comes into existence in 'Lucretian' (p.287), which presents two verses as one through indentation, each of which contain three stresses (p.287):

> When men were oppressed by the gods,
>   scared shitless by superstition,
> Epicurus, empiricist hero,
>   first took a cool look at religion...

After the accentual approximation of earlier books, Reading here quasi-approximates hexameter by way of stress and emphasises this by indenting the six-stress line exactly like the accentual hexameters in this book (and in *Going On*), while making the proximity to stressed metre clear by dividing the verse after the third foot.

Another unexpected choice was made for 'Choric' (p.294). So used to Reading's consistent metrics, the reader at first hears a wild mix of dactyls, trochees, and iambs, therefore tries to read it as stress-metre – but then stresses vary from two to five. Surprise: 'Choric' is unmetrical, the first free-verse poem in decades and 'a bit of a weirdo' [C], as Reading conceded, adding that in Greek tragedy the choruses also apparently sometimes lapse into unidentifiable metrics.

One elegiac distich is reserved for Reading's laconic threnody for Ewart (p.284; in the next book, there is another one, p.36). It is set in four lines with double indentation, which makes it look like Reading's Alcaic stanza, and underlines the generic relatedness of all these classical metres, also adding an intratextual dimension to the metrical field.[15]

Less complicated and more familiar to English readers, Anglo-Saxon alliterative metre is easily identified by its caesura,[16] just as straight iambic pentameter is easily recognised ('Epitaphal', p.293).[17] Last, but not least, the haiku still is a favoured short form, used here for the postscript (p.296, see also the epigraph in *Ukulele Music*).

The next book, *Work in Regress*, also uses syllabic verses, stress-metre, iambic pentameter and dimeter, elegiac distich, haiku, hexameters, Anglo-Saxon alliterative verse, tankas, and, like *Eschatological*, includes one amorphous poem. As with the metrical ambiguity of some poems in *Eschatological*, poems occasionally seem open to different metrical readings again and spin a few delicate threads between syllabic, classical and stress metres, seemingly touching all at once, as in 'Fireworks' (p.17), or 'Salopian' (p.48). Another inroad into new territory is represented by the three poems 'From the Chinese' (pp.33, 44, 47), which Reading developed in his next sequence, *Chinoiserie*. Here, however, the 'versions' are not yet strictly syllabic, but random, loose, short verses, quasi-syllabics.

Work in Regress (1997) and *Chinoiserie* (1997) were widely reviewed together.[18] The cover of *Work in Regress* shows a steel etching of Reading by Peter Edwards.[19] *Work in Regress* was another Poetry Book Society Choice and one of ten titles shortlisted for the 1997 T.S. Eliot Prize. The title is both descriptive and self-ironic, keeping things on hold while the book testifies to Reading's singular faith in poetry.

In this volume, Reading is still unwaveringly committed to epic grandeur and idiom, revitalising the wisdom of ancient Greek, Latin, Anglo-Saxon and Chinese poets in sinuous, resonant, contemporary 'versions'. (That these are not literal translations is indicated by the distancing '-an' in the poem titles). Mimnermus, Callimachus, Theocritus, Propertius, Catullus, Horace, Theognis, Ovid, Li Po and Langland are also comparable foils that lend more force to Reading's own 'brief catalogue of "lives, loves, deaths", their great remoteness in time underlining the timelessness of the poet's concerns', as Alan Jenkins says in the *PBS Bulletin* in his interview with 'John Bilston':

> But do you share my feeling that in the face of encroaching disorder, the orderliness of Reading's verse makes its own statement; and further, that in a valueless and virtueless present, as here, antiquity itself becomes a virtue? 'Succinct, sir.'... [Talking of the] sparer textures and a sometimes painfully direct expression of personal sadness, anger and despair... Can we find a parallel here with other modern artists – Rothko, Shostakovich, Beckett – who found themselves... moving inexorably towards the point... (presumably) of artistic self-extinction? Or is Reading experiencing an (understandable) depletion of the resources that have sustained him through the writing of roughly one book per year for the last quarter century? 'I don't accept "understandable"; he should work harder.'

Indeed, 'Desperate Circumstances / demand disparate measures' is an allusion to *Hamlet* (IV.3.9) and the epigraph's punning "explanation" of why he still has a new book ready almost every year – he cannot help it, and *his* way of coping happens to be a metrical one.

Work in Regress is only a slim volume, but certainly has no sense of fatigue about it. For instance, 'Fireworks' forms one concentrated haiku with nothing to spare (p.17):

> The shelling is heavy tonight;
> if we survive till tomorrow
> there'll be nettle soup and black bread.

The range of poems is impressive: there are short, strong, tight, stripped-down pieces as well as funny, powerful long ones, and satirical versions alternating with utmost seriousness. Crispness, vibrancy, clarity, and a dark grace take the place of Reading's recent harrowing harshness. Also, the quirky humour and brilliant wit are back, as is his 'mad brio', as Scammell termed it, i.e. his appetite for devastatingly vitriolic maledictions (a genre also savoured by the ancient poets); these qualities were also admired in the *PBS Bulletin*: 'As ever, Reading's scorn for the invincibly ignorant is a righteous hammer blow, but his humour and (dare one say it) enthusiasm do at times bear at any rate a remote resemblance to lightheartedness' (Padel/O'Brien). There is even some straightforward personal feeling to be shared again; Reading's sympathies have always been larger than he has cared to be known, but here they surface in touching haikus, revealing open tenderness all through the book, and all the more poignant for their brevity. '*En Attendant*' (p.40):

> I have been here now
> for long enough to know that
> you will not turn up.

Looking at 'A Shropshire Lad', though, John Kerrigan thought 'the gently rueful subject-matter comes as a bit of a surprise... this muted remake of Housman atmospherics...this tribute to A.E.H.'s lyricism about the lads who lie in Shrewsbury prison'. While Kerrigan's diagnosis of Reading as a reactionary xenophobic moral authoritarian is rather off the mark (he generalises from what are isolated stances), he has a valid criticism with his point that Reading's use of paradoxical extremes 'discourages the poet from addressing the tiresomely complicated sphere of incommensurabilities and compromises in which most human life goes on' (Kerrigan, pp.13, 20).

What interests Reading more are thoughts of regret, sorrow, exile and 'grim demise'. They coexist with both the bruised, startling expression of yearning love and the acceptance of the inevitable. In addition, the focus on ugly details of contemporary urban life (pp.18, 22, 28) is all the more alienating for being placed in the heroic context of ancient texts. However, the point made in reviews and in the interview quoted above – that antiquity is the foil of perfection to contemporary sordidness – does not withstand close scrutiny, because Reading re-writes authors who stand for very different historic and poetic phases within the Greek and Roman traditions. This was the beginning:

> Poetry was uniquely important in ancient Greece, as a means not only of expression, but also of communication, commemoration, and instruction. As early as the 9th century BC, the bard was thought to possess

keener than normal insights into the nature of man and gods; in later centuries, the poet of ability was regarded as the peer of the philosopher and statesman (Preminger, p.326).[35]

The earliest extant Greek poems, Homer's Ionian epics, embody the values of a feudal society and extol the tragic human condition. In the 7th century there followed lyric poetry (choric and monodic), expressing personal feelings of friendship and love (Alcaeus, Sappho). Additionally, elegiac poetry was used for various purposes, not just lament, but the expression of opinions on any kind of subject. After *Last Poems*' 'Homeric' and translations of fragments by Alcaeus in *Going On,* Reading now continues with 'Mimnermian, [Mimnermus (*fl.* 630 BC)]' in elegiac distich (p.20):

When the brief blossom is done, to die is
    better than living
        haplessly plagued by the dread
        of penury, grief and the grave.

Painful longevity, chance death early,
    death of one's children –
        infinite is the ill-luck
        on the Olympian list.

Preminger thinks Mimnermus of Colophon (7th century) was 'perhaps the most skilled of the elegiac poets... He is better known to us, through the extant fragments, as a writer preoccupied with the despair of youth's fading, and the deeper horror of the ugliness of old age and the finality of death' (Preminger, p.328).

At roughly the same time, the Megarian aristocrat Theognis was in the throes of penury. 'Theognian [Theognis (*fl.* 530 BC)]' (p.41), also in elegiac distich, highlights financial worries of the most privative kind that Reading has also shared since being made redundant: 'Penury batters us, even the boldest / into submission' (an echo of the medical 'Submission' in *Last Poems*, p.260).

Preminger goes on to say that with the stabilisation of the Greek world in the sixth and fifth century, personal poetry was 'eclipsed by the rise of the drama', especially the tragedies, as in the three great tragedians of the fifth century, Aeschylus, Sophocles and Euripides. These are of no concern in *Work in Regress*, as there were various re-writes entitled 'Choric' already in *Eschatological.* Now things started changing, though:

Towards the close of the 5th century...with the rise of science and philosophy, the faith of the Greeks in the value of poetry as a vehicle of truth began to decline, a trend underlined a little later by Plato's attacks on the poets as mere technicians who possess no real knowledge (Preminger, p.329).

This new interest in conceptual knowledge engendered historical and philosophical prose, which put poets in a dilemma.

> Consequently, the Hellenistic period is notable for the emergence of poets who emphasised elegance of style and beauty and novelty of technique... No longer did the poet feel that he was the voice of the community... or that he was bound by strict and important moral obligations to his society... [The Alexandrian Callimachus, one of the three major Hellenistic poets besides Apollonius and Theocritus was] a precise formalist who composed in several genres... He is at his best (at least to modern taste) in the epigram. This traditional form, which is based on the elegiac couplet...received a rare polish from the terseness and wit of the Callimachean technique (Preminger, p.329).

Terse and polished, too, Reading's 'Callimachan' (p.37) recalls in only one elegiac distich Philip of Macedon (whom Athens feared), burying his small son. The image of losing a child becomes a leitmotif in this book. This traumatic experience is shared by many other parents in this book (and indeed, as Isabel Allende unsentimentally pointed out to another grieving mother, by the majority of the women who have ever lived – with the negligible exception of a minority of today's privileged modern Western women, living in maximum shelter).

Under the Ptolemaic patronage in the new Egyptian city of Alexandria the museum and library was founded as a nationally sponsored academy, attracting many poets, Callimachus, Apollonius and Theocritus being the most famous. Theocritus is a 'crucial figure in the development of pastoral poetry, for his catalytic skills fused an energetic folk art with the rich inheritance of Greek literature to create bucolic verse which... many feel is unequalled in the ... genre. With these three major writers... of the 3rd century BC, the great age of Greek poetry came to an end' (Preminger, p.330). In 'Theocritan (XXVII)' (pp.52-53), Reading deconstructs his pretext and the genre it stands for by turning it into a pseudo-bawdy pastiche, as Dryden had done before him. The ludicrous effect is achieved by denying the shepherds the contemporary diction employed elsewhere, so that the transposition falls flat, as does the supposedly erotic encounter. Perhaps this is also an intertextual comment on the quality and effect of literal translations.

In another travesty, Reading deflates eroticism by the use of another linguistic register: 'Horatian' (p.27), a haiku free-associating on possible consequences of '*Nunc est bibendum*', rather bluntly, if not clinically, presents a rhyme (cheesy pudendum) that will stick in the mind, like it or not. In formal precision and various metres, Horace (65-8 BC) also treats 'love and wine lightly, life and death deeply, and the Augustan virtues from the approved Stoic point of view' (Preminger, p.440).

The Latin poets get into their stride in *Work in Regress*, too. 'Catullan (CIII)' (p.45) is the second, looser version of the same poem already translated in *Shitheads* (p.219), and the drastic change in register makes this a very different poem, exploiting the freedom any translator has. There are also two poems each 'after' Propertius and Ovid. Reading's two version of Ovid were particularly admired: 'Ovidian' (pp.24-26) is 'the triumph of these classical renderings. Its realisation of Ovid's bleak and frozen exile in Tomis glitters with vivid detail and ice-sharp formal and metrical exactness' (Murray). The impact of Reading's renderings of Ovid is especially effective for both the strength of the original and a particular affinity on Reading's side with the last of the great Roman elegists, allowing him to use "his own voice" at its most powerful. Ovid was banished from Rome for writing too openly and abundantly on amatory themes, and languished (and died) in exile in Tomis on the Black Sea at the mouth of the Danube, where the climate was harsh and the villagers lived in dread of the marauding invaders every winter, recounted by Reading in his sorrowful long poem.[20] The much shorter 'Tristia' (p.51) presents the same facts in a totally different way: chillingly compelling in its bleak despair and masterful style and syntax, it refers to Ovid's last collections, the *Tristia* (Sorrows), in which Ovid returned 'to the elegiac form, protesting or admitting guilt and complaining of his bitter life in his Gothic outpost' (Preminger, p.440).

A bitter life of a different kind is addressed in Reading's Propertian poems. Sextus Propertius is supposed to be the 'most violent and original of Roman poets in his structure, language, and imagery... Though protesting, he was persuaded... away from the intense, introspective poems on his mistress which comprise his earliest collection to..."official" poetry... as a vehicle for retelling incidents from Roman history' (Preminger, p.440). Reading went for the passion: 'Propertian (III.viii)' (p.31) is a splendid rendition of a violent row between lovers, but the connection with the other 'Propertian (IV.vii)' (pp.58-60) retrospectively casts a more complex shadow on the scene. Cynthia has died – but sleep and a 'quiet life' apparently desert the poet again in his grief-stricken state. She appears to him as one of the 'apparitions... / from Elysian regions' (p.60), but reproaches him for sleeping soundly and not even pretending to grieve. Her indictment matches the violent image of her in the other poem, but her perspective is irreconcilable with the poet's, just as the poet's stances in the two poems are irreconcilable with each other, thus testifying to the intensely volatile and complicated nature of this relationship, and implicitly pinpointing the fact that in the realm of human relationships, all one gets are translationese 'versions', and they, too, can only be read against each other like texts, but never gauged against what is dubiously termed "reality".

Texts and lovers endlessly relate to each other until they virtually relinquish their separate status. Similarly, the deceased are like palimpsests to the living. 'For all its variety, *Work in Regress* is an elegiac book, much (and movingly) preoccupied with the death of friends' (Jenkins). The book opens with 'Three' (pp.11-16), an epic obituary list from Reading's lifetime, 1946 up to 1996. There is a funny, slightly mad zest to it, because it mixes grave, humorous and trivial matters indiscriminately (as they would occur in life), and because its literary foil (the lists of brave deeds in old heroic poetry) makes it look utterly inappropriate and comically picaresque. The title 'Three' refers to the genesis of the poem on the one hand (it was commissioned by BBC Radio 3 to celebrate fifty years of existence); it also denotes another set of 'threes': Births, Events, Deaths (compare 'lives, loves, deaths'); it also commemorates three dead friends: George MacBeth, Michael Donahue and Gavin Ewart, all of whom also wrote poems.

Like Radio 3, Reading was 50 in the same year, but there are other links: George MacBeth first invited him to read on the Third Programme in 1970.[21] MacBeth's soothing theory about dead friends being the same as distant ones is now supported by Reading remembering friends in his books, and further corroborated by the Propertian tag '*Sunt aliquid manes, letum non omnia finit*' (Book IV.7; translated as 'Ghosts *do* live; / death doesn't end all'), with which another dead friend, Donahue, once prefaced one of *his* poems, mentioned in 'Easter Letter' (p.47, *CP1*).

As one reviewer phrased it, the Latin tag is repeated like a mantra. It was presented at readings as Reading's taped voice – which was what the BBC produced in the first place, providing a sense of a ghostly experience today. The taped voice of 1997 also makes the point that, like the ghosts of friends, Reading can return to haunt readers,[22] and that his invented death does not end all.

This is a mellow line for Reading to take; faithful remembrance, keeping people and emotions alive, if only in one's memory, and thanking people is a long way off the nihilistic stance. More elegies for the dead follow, or for vanished loved ones, as in the poem addressed to his first wife (p.19), the only poem in free verse. In this light, the old poets do not just 'add ballast to Reading's *miserere*', as Scammell wrote, but keep him company, importantly.

In the poems without any direct historic pre-text, intratextual references abound. '[Untitled]' (p.54), for instance, is the second thanksgiving to his parents (see p.117, *CP1*); the harsh 'Nomenclature' (p.23) has a mellower antecedent in 'Nomenclator' (p.39, *CP1*) and stresses the idea of 'versions' again; [23] the 'Nips' (p.29) sparkle as they do in *Diplopic*, but Aunt Prudence's advice 'Give up the drink' links up explicitly with the burlesque 'Gula' (Latin for 'throat', 'gullet', or 'appetite', pp.34-35), an extract from Langland's *Piers Plowman* in alliterative metre with caesura (commissioned by the South Bank Centre as part of its 1996 Poetry International Festival). After the most outrageous gluttony and attendant consequences, Glutton finally promises 'Abstinence' to 'my auntie... / (though I've loathed the old hag . for as long as I've lived).' In 'Shakespearean' (p.22), a story grafted on a verse from *Julius Caesar* (II.1.14) indirectly amplifies Reading's invectives on his bosses in *Shitheads*. '*Raphus cucullatus*' (p.38) is another variation on the narrative recounting the capturing of birds by sailors (p.22 and p.226, *CP2*); and '[Untitled]' (p.43) is an algamam of several previous poems (especially p.230, *CP2*). Finally, 'Salopian' is a pure auto-cento, collated by re-writes of different parts of the first book, *For the Municipality's Elderly*.

Nicholas Murray wrote:

> The self-satisfied blandness of much in the contemporary poetry scene has led to an exaggerated picture of Reading as 'controversial' and a 'laureate of grot', putting himself somehow beyond the pale of civilised norms by his ruthless exacting of a full look at the worst. In fact, notwithstanding the exhilarating savagery of his satire... there is at the heart of this collection, for all its furniture of bleakness, a profoundly human centre and an exemplary commitment to the art of poetry.

However, after so many forceful poems, Reading still introduces doubt as to his creative powers in 'Seed' (p.21; entitled 'Rosebay' in its first draft):

> Onto the pile of the Axminster fluffs of
>   willowherb settle.
>   Autumn: the wanton swing-doors
>   splay to admit this spent seed.

One recognises in the tone and image a poem from *Final Demands* (p.137) where 'Under a clay weight dumped on the leather-topped / desk in his study, final demands... / flutter in rose-fumed draughts from the garden'. Penury is draining – and his poetic powers are ebbing, too. (The 'spent seed' as an image of diminished creativity originates in Psalm 137: 'By the rivers of Babylon').

Towards the end of the book, in 'Distich' (p.61), Reading takes this up again, suggesting that he is about to 'do it', i.e. to stop writing/ living. Jenkins detects a 'deep and inconsolable sorrow lies behind these lines', but knows better than most: Reading

plays quite knowingly with our alarm at the prospect... At artistic van-
ishing point, all that remains are a (faultless) distich and the poet's
remains...this evinces the ultimate sophistication of a poet at the height
of self-awareness, though (self-confessedly) low in creative powers.[52]

Reading recycles the old stance of fading away, perhaps following
Eliot: 'The progress of an artist is a continual self-sacrifice, a con-
tinual extinction of personality... the more perfect the artist, the
more completely separate in him will be the man who suffers and
the mind which creates; the more perfectly will the mind digest
and transmute the passions which are its material.'

First published in a limited edition in 1997, *Chinoiserie* forms the
middle section of *Ob.* The first "Chinese" poems had appeared in
Work in Regress ('From the Chinese', pp.33, 44, 47). Reading had
announced the book as a 'new private thing'; the cover says the
poems are 'transcriptions from Li Po', which means that they are
bogus versions, something also hinted at by the playful title. They
were inspired by Li Po in so far as they are Reading's response to
Waley's (and others') translations of Chinese poetry, not the origi-
nals. Quite a few poems can actually be traced back to Li Po, but
most are Reading's own, made foreign. They are intensely lyrical,
imagistic, hedonistic, personal, and peculiarly transparent poems in
the elegiac mode about drinking wine and watching life and love go by,
and preceded by an epigraph celebrating '(*Deborah: ten   thousand
sighs; / ten thousand nights'   golden wine!*)'. Poem 41 (*Ob.*, p.45):

> Singing girls,   their faces rouged,
> drunk, turn to   the setting sun.

For Reading, this Chinese form was advantageously aloof enough
to enable him to do something new: 'it is difficult to say anything in
such a short space...but it enables one to do a different aspect of
oneself' (C). Poem 46 (p.47):

> Green spring, but I   grow white-haired
> on this bank of   the Yangtze.
>
> My shadow here,   thoughts elsewhere,
> my poor garden   choked with weeds.
>
> What to do so   late in life
> but sing my songs   and forget?

Reading carries on his own metamorphosis in fresh surroundings,
as can be seen from the poems which have quite obviously moved
a long way from the original source, most notably in the ambigu-
ous poem saying 'Though you   married me / any   sot would
do'; or in this sarcastic piece (poem 37, p.44):

How gaunt   you've become!
Are you   suffering?

Is it   Terminal
Acute   Poetry?

Li Po lived in the 8th century during the T'ang Dynasty and wrote spiritual and narrative poetry. 'Li Po's ideal was the kind of blithe, unobligating companionship he enjoyed with the moon and other objects of nature, as contrasted to entangling and emotion-filled human ties – hence his unconventional call for a "friendship without feeling".' [24]

Before his time, the Chinese had written symmetrical syllabic poetry with a pause dividing each line in the middle. Li Po and his two contemporaries Wang Wei and Tu Fu used an asymmetrical measure, writing lines of 2:3 and 3:4 monosyllabic words (instead of 2:2, 3:3, or 4:4), in the so-called Shih form:[25] its dirge was 'drown away the woes of ten thousand generations', which is a leitmotif in *Chinoiserie* ('ten thousand' cups, nights, and sighs). In turn, Reading sometimes reverses Li Po's syllabics for variation, introducing the 4:3 stanza, and weaving in detached images of his own experience of troublesome night thoughts and drowned sorrows, looking at both the general and his own drinking condition, bracing himself against 'extirpation' with the consolations of 'verse, viticulture, love', '("in order of merit", he remarks sardonically)'.[26] *Chinoiserie* thus has poems syllabically divided into 2:3, 3:4, or 4:3, mostly in stanzas of two to four unrhymed couplets (reminiscent of the clerihew), but also in monostichs, tristichs, or quatrains. Poem 24 (p.39) stands out metrically and typographically because it is set like a pyramid in steps of 3-5-7-9 syllables, almost in the middle of the 49-poem sequence. The most notable deviation from the original source is the absence of rhyme. Chinese poetry, of course, does rhyme; in fact it would be hard put *not* to rhyme, since most syllables end on a vowel.

Reading uses Li Po's lyricism and imagery as an imaginary pre-text, but also as a mask, or a stance, to give a voice to his rather more quiet and tenderly wistful side, which could hitherto only occasionally be heard behind the clanging noises of the more important Big Issues. For Reading, Li Po's landscapes and the rich symbolic associations of images of birds or trees would ring a familiar note on the one hand, and point him towards a new, rather more mythical angle on the timelessness of his old woes on the other.

Reading had first come across Arthur Waley (1889-1966) and his renderings of Chinese poetry when he was 16 and reading widely. Waley himself had read classical Japanese and Chinese poetry while working as a librarian's assistant, and later he became the well-known translator of Oriental texts with more than 20 volumes to his credit, receiving the Queen's Medal for Poetry in 1953. While Reading's adaptations are all in strict syllabic metre, the literal translations by Waley are lines with 5 stresses and a number of unaccentuated syllables in between. Waley remarks in a Preface: 'Out of the Chinese five-word line I developed between 1916 and 1923 a metre, based on what Gerard Manley Hopkins called "sprung rhythm," which I believe to be just as much an English metre as blank verse. The Chinese seven-word line is much more difficult to handle and I have not attempted any long poems in this metre.' (Waley's 'sprung rhythm' was invented seven years before Hopkins was published.) Two translations of Li Po by Waley:

'In the Mountains on a Summer Day'

Gently I stir a white feather fan,
With open shirt sitting in a green wood.
I take off my cap and hang it on a jutting stone;
A wind from the pine-tree trickles on my bare head.

'Self-Abandonment'

I sat drinking and did not notice the dusk,
Till falling petals filled the folds of my dress.
Drunken I rose and walked to the moonlit stream;
The birds were gone, and men also few.[27]

In the same Preface he admits to having been dissatisfied with the results of his many attempts to translate 'other great T'ang and Sung poets... [namely] Li Po, Tu Fu and Su Shih'. It would need a Sinologist to assess Waley's Sprung Rhythm translations and Reading's syllabic adaptations of these *as* adaptations; generally, the poems will have to be regarded "independently", as was done before with Pound's and Lowell's adaptations.

The fact that Chinese poetry appeals to people who normally do not usually read poetry would also suit Reading. Waley explains that 'it mainly deals with the concrete and particular, with things one can touch and see – a beautiful tree or a lovely person'.[28] Another Orientalist, Burton Watson, gives more details about T'ang Poetry which make it appear very modern indeed: it is marked by 'remarkable accessibility', 'directness, moderation, and great visual clarity', avoiding rhetoric, fancy, myth, and ego-abstractions, and instead depicting occasional, 'strikingly realistic and personal' experiences at the T'ang Dynasty court (often involving the palace women), employing language that is 'conventionalised, self-effacing, and low-keyed'.

This would also suit Reading at this stage: after the heightened linguistic register of his books since *Evagatory*, Reading's poems are stripped down again to simplicity in style and diction. Most important, though, and congenial to Reading's own stance, is the Chinese poet portraying himself as a person full of 'melancholy or apprehension'. The typical T'ang poem is a 'poem of grief', reiterating, as Reading has done, 'look what happens to man', and ending on an anti-climactic note. Pondering particulars of mankind, nature, and eternal nature, however, counterbalances the pain and frustration and achieves a 'tone of transcendence'.[29] Judging from these descriptions, Reading's versions are very true "translations" indeed.

Reading also uses this foil in his "own" (as opposed to "translated") poems in *Ob.* (1999), where it takes the form of epiphaneous encounters with birds – an astoundingly mellow turn. These are among the longest of the 27 new poems which frame the Li Po versions.

While Reading's predominant concern – 'That last   journeying / in pain   and in fear.' ('Ob.', p.61) – is as prominent in this book as it was in *C*, it still has to make room for the poetic transformation of new experiences. *Ob.* is dedicated to William Johnston, a member of the Lannan Foundation who had invited Reading for readings in the US, and in 1997 and 1998, took him bird-watching in the Gulf of Mexico, Canada and the mountains of Arizona. This is where the last great Apache-chief Geronimo went into hiding: spectacular mountains had formed in different formations after a gigantic earthquake, and there Reading saw species of birds and migrations on a scale he had not witnessed before. It was evident he had not experienced anything as exciting since going birding with his friend Michael Donahue, and many marvellous poems and an extraordinary prose passage ('Veracruz', p.27) were written in celebration of these up-lifting moments, 'this generous transience' and 'joyful time'.

However, echoing a hexameter from *Perduta Gente* (p.206), the epigraph '(*Those having precognition suffer / terror beforehand*)', sets the depressing ground-note for this book. A large number of poems hypnotically circle around ageing and imminent death in a variety of tones, supplemented by pseudo–death-bed recollections 'under the oxygen tent', and the paraphernalia attendant on the poet-persona's death and funeral.[30]

The first poem, 'Meanings' (p.11) introduces uses of the abbreviation *Ob.* (obsolete, obscene, obolus; obiter dicta, 'said in passing') while tiptoeing around the implied reference to 'obiit' (he died).

The vision of suicide by an overdose of sleeping-pills ('Found', a found iambic pentameter from a medicine pack) is followed by the vision of his friends gathering after his funeral, presented in '?' in the form of an Anglo-Saxon Riddle used before in connection with madness (*Tom o'Bedlam's Beauties*):

> Soon and silently,   in a dark suit...
> Men at the mead-bench,   meditate, name him.

As this is presented as a *fait accompli*, the other poems can only intensify the terror: sombre birthday thoughts ('51st', p.16), miserable sleeplessness and dark night-thoughts,[31] horrific nightmares ('Everglades', p.50), melancholy remembrance of 'joyful time' turning sour ('Medieval', p.57). The severe depression peaks in the long poem 'Coplas de Pie Quebrado' ['Stanzas with a Broken Foot'] (pp.13-15),[32] a variant of *Sweeney Agonistes*' 'Birth, Copulation, Death', where Reading adopts such a relentlessly morose and embittered stance ('the journey is full of shit'), further intensified by the insistent Mimnermian refusal to accept old age with a little grace, that one expects the ambulance's blue tumbril on the very next page. The parallel 'Axiomatic' (p.58), a collection of Readingish epigrams about old age presented with a touch of self-deprecation, redresses the balance a little. However, despair is piled on so thickly, and the previous existential and intertextual dimensions are so much reduced, that this strand of the book approaches a state of nightmarish, thanaphobic paranoia.

It is probably due to this overall, introspective drift, started in *Chinoiserie*, that Reading includes some very nakedly personal lines in *Ob.*, something so sedulously avoided before.[33] Both the sniping at fatuous ignoramuses and the explicit sexual memories are calculatedly startling in their bluntness;[34] through this one-dimensional authenticity – the stripping of all stances – readers witness the simple fact that, after having addressed a number of dead friends in recent poems (done self-disparagingly in earlier years), Reading now takes the next step and starts talking freely to people he knows, or knew.

Some will cringe at the experience: Reading did work as Visiting Tutor (Writers' Fellowship) at the University of East Anglia from January to June 1997. Looking at students' poems in workshops ('Workshop', p.18) is at best a double-edged experience for this writer, as the ambiguous line 'keep up the good work' demonstrates – the line had been used before in *Diplopic* where a decrepit journalist condescendingly manages the kiddies' column (p.212). In contrast with the Sunderland academics whom Reading befriended in 1981-83 (see *Diplopic*, *5x5x5x5x5*, and *C*), his new colleagues fare rather badly, making the poet-persona look smug also ('In the SCR', p.19):

> The puerile academic quips,
> the smugly learnèd repartee
> withstanding little scrutiny.

Equally unrestrained, the relentless maledictions on students ('Catullan', p.20), poetry lovers ('At the Reading', p.19), Tony Blair ('Shropshire Lads' [p.25], a re-write of *Work in Regress*, p.46), and commercialism ('[Untitled] In this Stygian city...', p.28) alternate with candid declarations of loving remembrance ('Recollection', 'Mnemonic' [p.23], 'Copla de Pie Quebrado' [p.49], or respectful elegy ('[Untitled] A reach of Severn' [p.26]), about an unknown Shrewsbury Lieutenant and with allusions to Reading's late poet-friends). As regards relationships, not much seems worth mentioning in between.

Other poems reap the benefits of the richly stratified ground Reading has previously prepared for himself. The repulsive, murderous dramatic monologue of an old South American fascist ('Coplas de Pie Quebrado', p.56) is reminiscent of the General's apologia in *Going On* (p.59); 'Melancholic' (p.54) is another successful re-write, touchingly rendering extracts from Robert Burton's *The Anatomy of Melancholy* (with clear auto-textual references); 'Flyer' (p.18), ridiculing another poet, could be read as an attack on Ted Hughes (see the title 'Frog's Breath'), whose anthropomorphic poems Reading detests; [35] and 'Little Ones (I.M., *G.E.*)', another poem remembering Gavin Ewart and using one of his titles, presents Ewart-like 'flyweight poems', complete with rude pentameters and bawdy innuendo. [36]

Metrically, these poems are varied, using the favoured forms of the last few books: hexameters, iambic pentameters, 'stress quasi-hexameter', or 6-stress metre, stress metre, haiku and tankas, a quatrain in dactylic tetrameter, syllabic metre, elegiac distich, Anglo-Saxon verse, and the syllabic Li Po metre.

The last poems successively become shorter: the final death struggle, then the chilling monostich, Reading's epitaph. 'Stone' (p.62): 'Where *gravitas* nor levity can stir him.' [37] The cover of *Ob.* shows a photograph of Peter Edwards' plastercast of Reading's head, an imitation death-mask with attendant classical connotations of the famous dead. [38]

Despite all this drumming and flailing of arms, as if Reading were awaiting execution, the core remains firm: a singular commitment to and belief in the art of poetry. For this reason, one poem title in particular stands out: 'The New Book': 'Small and dangerous / like a *sgian dubh*.' [39]

That New Book became *Marfan*, written during a sinecure sponsored by the Lannan Foundation. Reading spent a year in the USA, writing a 'straightforward topographical travelogue' [C] about Marfa, the small Texan town where he lived.

> *The bails are scattered, the last man run out.*
>
> *Wisden* recalls the English ignominy...
> A solitary, voluntary exile
> respires hot, fan-rotated desert air
> in a southwestern public library.

Marfan was published by Bloodaxe in 2000 with photographs by Jay Shuttleworth and with Reading's own collages. In the book-length sequence, Reading immerses himself deeply – *not* in the lines of the dead, but in a completely new element. He investigates, researches, observes, and describes rather harshly, but also humorously, the history, geology, topography, folklore, politics, religion, superstitions, art, commerce, and contemporary life and strife of the American-Mexican Rio Grande border in Presidio County:

> US 90 East, Marfa to Alpine:
> you drive through the volcano of Paisano –
> just breccia 35 million years old,
> caldera, and pale rhyolite, and you.

Mystery stories about *ignis fatuus*, poignant personal tales about the Great Depression (appropriately rendered in the Southern drawl), reports from the *Big Bend Sentinel* about borderline enforcement and local VIPs, the voice of a deranged, stuttering man professing to receive signals from the CIA about the White House, and echoes from *Perduta Gente*, all rendered in very loose iambic pentameter, alternate with poignant visual artwork and vignettes of highways, prisons, cemeteries. The issues of injustice and poverty loom large, but the humour is definitely back:

> When this gets published I shall have to be
> beyond the City Limit on a Greyhound.

While in Marfa, Reading also produced three new pamphlets, which are to be included in [*untitled*] (forthcoming from Bloodaxe): *Apophthegmatic* (The Bay Press, 1999), *Repetitious* (Laertides Press, USA, 1999), and the pamphlet *Copla a Pie Quebrado*, (produced in 1999). *Apophthegmatic* (unpaginated; edition of 150) means 'like pithy sayings'; it is inspired by syllabic Chinese poetry and uses natural images to ponder the brevity of life and the poet's anticipated death (the subject matter of *Ob.*, too), incorparating eroding replicas of some of the poems, which read (and look) like epitaphs: '*Hic Jacet:/ Who Blindness/ & Senility/ Exhausted*'. It consists mainly of haiku, tankas, and fragments of those, but also improvises on Chinese metrics by presenting poems of two or three lines written in invented syllabic patterns (e.g. 2,4,2 or 3,6,3).

> Bittern stiff in reeds,
> for ninety minutes we watch -
> in that time just three
> cautious slow-motion high-steps,
> three dagger stabs, three tadpoles.

The notable metrical exception is a self-deprecating aside in two hemiepes: 'Badass and not nice to know – / you have got used to the role'. Images of birds, 'the old reaper', 'Mortimer Forest' and other quotations (mainly from *For the Municipality's Elderly*) cross-reference Reading's œuvre once more.

Repetitious (unpaginated; edition of 250), written in straight iambic pentameter, can be seen as a six-page, intratextual summary of Reading's œuvre full of allusions to and repetitions of lines from *For the Municipality's Elderly*, *C*, *Ukulele Music*, *Evagatory*. In a nutshell:

> A snow-haired elder strung his instrument,
> the burthen of his song: malicious Fate
> fucks up the aspirations of Mankind.

At the same time, Reading chose the name 'Laertides Press' for this publication (the publisher was Cleveland University Press), which points to the other rhapsodic strand in this pamphlet: all poems intertextually link up with the Odyssey. Thus, *Repetitious* is also a new example of "diplopic" writing by Reading. It ends with a memorable, near-rhymed re-write of Reading's poems that describe the Homeric idyll of finding unending sleep under an 'olive and oleaster grafted flush' – a symbol of peace.

The pamphlet *Copla a Pie Quebrado* was given to the Lannan Foundation, whose Art Department produced it in an edition of 250 in 1999. It is a paradoxically attractive four-page pamphlet in gatefold format combining eight striking colour photographs of a dilapidated, depopulated Marfa with poems written in a new kind of dactylic/spondaic stanza (three trimeter lines plus closing hemiepes), Reading's adaptation of an old, Spanish stanza:

> *Copla a Pie Quebrado,*
> metric, the final foot broken –
> fitting for History fractured
> in an aridified dump.

On returning to England, Reading completed his new book, to be titled [*untitled*] – which will not contain the new Marfan photographs – and then received a two-year Continuation Grant from the Lannan Foundation in January 2000. Recently, he has produced another artwork, *Six Poems* (in an edition of 5, signed and numbered): each poem is handwritten on an A3-size page and combined with two photoprints of graffiti taken with a disposable camera; each page is in a portfolio. The texts are closely related to the photoprints and are also partly recyclings from [*untitled*], which is about the transience of texts. The sixth page accordingly has no words or photoprints on it, just a circular blank which can be seen as nought, a typical Reading gesture towards the futility of his art. One of the five copies was given to Patrick Lannan, one was sent to Patrick Taylor of Dublin's Taylor Galleries, and two will be sent to a book dealer in London. The fifth one was sent to the Arts Council's Poetry Library, and Reading remarked about this latest piece on transience [C]: 'I'd like one reposited in the Archives there.'

As this guided tour through Reading's literary territory makes clear, he is one of today's most dedicated, gifted, inventive and obsessive poets. In a long-sustained development, he has pushed back poetic boundaries – linguistic, thematic, metrical, structural – by transgressing current demarcations of genre and taste, experimenting with countless tones, dictions, perspectives, poetic styles and an impressive range of historic pre-texts, relentlessly questioning established values (not least the value of poetry) and focusing uncompromisingly on contemporary and global issues of great significance. Added to this, there is his existential, epic reach, and his persistence in a bleakly humane vision while confronting the void. All this has had an impact that impels readers to either fall for or recoil from his work. But regardless of whether or not he suits readers' literary tastes and regardless of opinions about the functions of art, his intensely passionate œuvre is a powerful, unique, at times cathartically traumatic reading experience. In its expression of part of our consciousness of our age, and in its bravura, idiosyncrasy and originality, it is an outstanding contribution to the most important and moving poetry of the late 20th century.

GLOSSARY

These definitions are drawn from sources including Preminger's *Princeton Encyclopedia of Poetry and Poetics* (used by Peter Reading), which is also one of the main sources behind Robert G. Shubinski's Internet glossary at http://shoga.wwa.com/~rgs/glossary.html

abstract poem: poem made of sound-patterns, or using non-referential sound patterns.

accentual metre: verse based on the number of accented syllables only (not on the total number of syllables).

acrostic: usually a poem in which the first letters of each line or stanza form a new word when read downward; there are many variations: medial letters may be used (mesostich) or final letters (telestich).

Adonic, Adoneus: verse consisting of a dactyl followed by a spondee or trochee (like the last two feet of a dactylic hexameter).

aeolic verse (after the Greek dialect of Alcaeus and Sappho): set of metres combining dactyls and trochees.

akyrological (*Gr.* 'non-literal speech', *impropria dictio*): poetic expression by way of imagery and topoi.

Alcaic strophe (after Alcaeus, 7th-6th century BC): 4-line stanza of the aeolic type; lines 1 and 2 ('Greater Alcaic') contain 11 syllables, line 3 contains 9 syllables, and line 4 ('Lesser Alcaic') 10 syllables. Reading follows Tennyson's example, *see* p.158 & note 7 (p.289) to *Going On* chapter.

Alcmanic strophe (after Alcman, 7th century BC): stanza consisting of catalectic dactylic tetrameters and ending with a dactylic hexameter (*see* p.144).

allitero-assonances: both the opening consonant and the following vowel are repeated in other stressed syllables.

alliteration: the repetition of initial sounds (usually consonants) in two or more words of a line, producing a noticeable sound effect.

alloeostropha: stanzas of irregular length (opposite of strophic stanzas).

alpha-omega metaphor (*Gr.* 'A-Z'): metaphor covering opposite extremes (e.g. heat/cold, beginning/end).

Amoebean verse (*Gr.* 'responsive verses'): verses spoken alternately by two speakers.

anacoluthon (*Gr.* 'wanting sequence'): change of syntax within a sentence that leaves the beginning uncompleted.

anacreontea (after Anacreon, 6th century BC): light lyrical poems on wine, love and song.

anacrusis (*Gr.* 'the striking up of a tune'): one or more unaccentuated syllables at the beginning of a line, not part of the metrical pattern.

anadiplosis (*or* **epanadiplosis**; *Gr.* 'doubling'): repetition of a prominent (usually final) word of a colon, clause, line, or stanza at the beginning of the next for emphasis.

anapaest (*Gr.* 'beaten back'): a metrical foot of two unstressed (or short) syllables followed by a stressed (or long) one.

anaphora (*or* **epanaphora**; *Gr.* 'carrying up or back'): repetition of same word(s) at the beginning of successive phrases.

anaptyxis: inclusion of an extra vowel (to gain another syllable).

annominatio (*paronomasia*): change of a word to obtain additional meaning(s), as in a pun.

antanaclasis (*traductio*): the witty repetition of a word in different connotations, or a pun on homonyms.

antistrophe (*Gr.* 'counterturning'): repetition of words in reversed order.

antonomasia (*Gr.* 'naming instead'): the substitution of a proper name by an epithet or appellative, or the use of a proper name for a class or type.

aposiopesis (*Gr.* 'becoming silent'): an abrupt halt midway in a sentence, which does not get finished (*see* **anacoluthon**).

apostrophe (*Gr.* 'to turn away'): addressing a dead /absent person /object/ abstraction as if it were alive/present.

asynartete (*Gr.* 'disconnected'): a classical verse composed of independent cola.

asyndeton (*Gr.* 'unconnected'): omission of conjunctions.

aubade (*Prov.* 'alba', *Germ.* 'Tagelied'): a dawn song, often expressing the regret of lovers at parting.

auto–cento (*Gr.* 'self' and 'patchwork'): composition of passages selected from one's own work.

autophageous (*Gr.* 'devour oneself'): self-destructive.

autotelic (*Gr.* 'self' and 'end'): having an end-purpose in itself.

barbaristic (*Gr.* 'using foreign words'): faulty use of language, solecisms.

brachylogical: short, concise, saying much in few words.

bucolic diaeresis: diaeresis after the fourth-foot dactyl in a hexameter.

burden: central topic, often repeated in a refrain.

cacomorphous (*Gr.* 'bad, harsh', 'shape'): discordantly arranged ('cacophony', discordant sound).

caesura: in classical metrics, a word end within a foot (*see* **diaeresis**); in modern prosody, a rhythmic break or pause within the poetic line, dictated by semantics or natural speech patterns, not metrics, and used for investing strict metres with the movement of informal speech.

catachresis (*Gr.* 'misuse'): misapplication of a word, especially in a mixed metaphor.

catalectic (truncated): omission of the last (generally unstressed) syllable(s) in a line (*see* **hypercatalectic**).

choree (*Gr.* 'pertaining to dance'): *see* **trochee**.

choreophrasis (*Gr.* 'dance', 'saying'): phrases repeated as if in a dance, going in circles, *see* p.96.

choriamb: *Gr.* 'consisting of a choree and and iamb'.

colon (*Gr.* 'limb', *pl.* **cola**): a single sequence or distinct clause, may be composed of a number of feet or metra.

concrete poetry: forms of verse in which the visual aspect (shape) plays an essential part (*see* **kalligram**).

consonance: repetition of the final consonant sound of a stressed syllable.

copla de (à) pie quebrado (*Sp.* 'stanza with a broken foot'): any variation of the *copla de arte menor* (octosyllabic verse) in which one or more lines have been reduced to half-length and/or half-lines have been added (originally with ABcABcDEfDEf rhyme scheme). See pp.262 & 265.

coronach: funeral lament or dirge.

crepuscolarismo: melancholy, tired-of-life manner of speaking.

dactyl (*Gr.* 'finger'): metrical foot of three syllables, the first of which is stressed (or long) and the other two unstressed (or short).

deca (-syllabic, -strophical): *Gr.* 'ten' (syllables, lines).

deixis, deictic (*Gr.* 'refer'): words which particularise either themselves (i.e. names) or associated general nouns (i.e. demonstrative pronouns).

désinvolture: stylistic casualness, frankness, straightforwardness.

diaeresis: in classical prosody, the coincidence of a word-ending with the ending of a metrical foot.

diaphora (*Gr.* 'difference'): in rhetoric, explaining the difference between two things.

dimeter (*Gr.* 'of two measures'): line consisting of two measures.

dipody (*Gr.* 'two feet'): in classical verse, a combination of two metrical feet constituting a single measure.

dit(ty), lai: short, simple song.

dramolett: short drama.

drôlerie: amusing, odd sketch.

elegiac distich: *see* pp.131-32 and note 8 (p.287) to *Ukulele Music* chapter.

ensalada (*Sp.* 'salad', hotpotch, medley, mishmash, can also mean colourful): poem consisting of lines and stanzas of varying length and rhyme schemes.

envelope: poetic device in which a phrase or image or poetic technique is repeated so as to enclose other material.

epanaphora: *see* **anaphora**.

ephemiride: chronological notes on daily events.

epicedium (*Gr.* 'funeral song'): song of mourning in praise of the dead, sung in the presence of the corpse, as distinguished from *threnody*, a dirge not limited in time or space .

epiphora (*or* **epistrophe**): the ending of a series of phrases with the same word(s).

episyntheton (*Gr.* 'compound'): metre composed of cola of different kinds.

fatras: irrational or obscure piece of verse, full of fun, word-play and nonsense.

Fescennine verse (*origin Latin*: either derived from *fascinum*, a phallic emblem worn as a charm, or from the town of Fescennium): crude, ribald or abusive song or invective verse.

foot: a measurable unit of poetic rhythm, in which *arsis* (*Gr.* 'lifting up') and *thesis* (*Gr.* 'setting down'), or their modern counterparts rise/stress and fall/ no stress alternate in a specific pattern; the feet used in English are the **anapaest** (˘ ˘ −), **dactyl** (− ˘ ˘), **iamb** (˘ −), **spondee** (− −) and **trochee** (− ˘).

Georgics (*L.* 'agriculture', from *Gr.* 'earth' and 'work'): didactic poem, usually for instruction in (agricultural, rural) skills, art or science.

haiku: Japanese lyric form, usually of 17 syllables in 3 lines of 5-7-5 syllables.

hemiepes (*Gr.* 'half-hexameter'): dactylic trimeter catalectic ending in a long syllable (− ˘ ˘ | − ˘ ˘ | −).

hemistich (*Gr.* 'half-line'): half line of verse divided at the caesura, usually forming an independent colon.

hendecasyllabic (*Gr.* '11-syllable'): line of 11 syllables of a certain metrical scheme (*see* pp.208-09), also called Phalaecean (after Phalaikos, 4th century BC).

heterocosm: *Gr.* 'other universe'.

hexameter (*Gr.* '6-measure'): classical 6-foot catalectic dactylic line; Reading mainly uses |− ˘ ˘ |− ˘ ˘ |− ˘ ˘ |− − |− ˘ ˘ | − − | (spondee replaces dactyl in fourth and sixth foot, but can occur in others), *see* pp.131-32 and note 8 (p.287) to *Ukulele Music* chapter.

homoeomeral (*Gr.* 'having like parts'): parts which are metrically the same, or repetition of same stanza form.

hypercatalexis: additional syllable(s) after the final complete foot in a line .
hypertrophied, -trophic (*Gr.* 'over, beyond', 'nourishment'): abnormally enlarged by overnourishment.
hypertext: *see* p.245*ff.*
hypomnemna (*Gr.* 'over', 'memory'): eye-witness report, remembrance.
inter-, intratextuality: *see* p.245*ff.*
iamb: metrical foot of a unstressed (or short) syllable followed by an stressed (or long) one.
ithyphallic (*Gr.* 'erect phallus'; 'ode and dance performed at Dionysus festival'): short verse with the appearance of three trochees.
lampoon (probably *Fr.* 'lampons', 'let us drink'): an abusive satire attacking an individual, motivated by malice, and intended to distress.
litotes (*Gr.* 'plainness, simplicity'): figure, related to meiosis, employing understatement for the purpose of intensification, or affirmation by the negative of the contrary (e.g. 'Few atrocities... remain unfulfilled', epigraph to *Ukulele Music*).
logaoedic verse (*Gr.* 'prose-poetic'): mixed dactylic and trochaic cola (or mixed anapaestic and iambic).
macaroni-verse (prob. indicates crude mixture – like that of flour, cheese and butter in macaroni – and its burlesque appeal): mingles two or more languages together for comic effect, or incorporates native words into another language.
malapropism (*Fr. 'mal à propos'*, 'inappropriate'): misapplication of words, from Mrs Malaprop in Sheridan's play *The Rivals.*
measure: a metrical group or period, may consist of the dipody as in classical verse or of the foot as in English verse.
meiosis (*Gr.* 'lessening'): underemphasis for greater effect, considered more generic in application than litotes; also ironic understatement.
Melpomene: the Muse of Tragedy.
Meredithian sonnet (from George Meredith's *Modern Love*): 16-line sonnet-variant rhyming abba cddc effe ghhg.
metalepsis (*Gr.* 'exchange, confusion'): positing the cause of something as the effect (kind of metonymy).
meta-poem (*Gr.* 'beyond, after, along with'): poem commenting on (or exposing the artificiality of) poetry, the writing process, or any level of language; self-reflexivity; communication on communication.
metonymy (*Gr.* 'change of name'; *L. 'denominatio'*, 'misnomer'): a figure, closely related to, but more general than, *synedoche* (a part of something stands for the whole, or the whole stands for a part), in which one word is substituted for another which it is closely associated with.
metra episyntheta (*Gr.* 'compound metre'): metre composed of cola of different kinds, e.g. elegiac distich.
mid(dle)-rhyme (internal): rhyme occurring within the same line.
mise-en-abîme (*Fr.* 'thrust into the abyss'): textual structures which mirror themselves, e.g. stories within stories doubling the narrator's narrative; in deconstruction theory: a way of illustrating the endless play and instability of signification and indeterminacy.
monometer (*Gr.* 'one measure'): line consisting of single metrical foot or dipody.
monostrophical (*Gr.* 'one stanza'): poem consisting of one stanza or of stanzas of the same form.
mosaic rhyme: rhyme in which two or more words produce a multiple rhyme.
numeric metre: metre invented by Reading which is based on a numeric principle (e.g. 10x10x10, or 5^5).

onomatopoeia (*Gr.* 'word-making'): the formation of a word in imitation of the sound of the thing denoted, such as 'sizzle', but generally any word whose sound is suggestive of meaning.

paean (*Gr.* 'healer', i.e. Apollo): choral songs in honour of somebody (originally of Apollo or his sister Artemis).

palinode, palinodic: poem of retraction; strophe and antistrophe, or other patterns that retract something said before .

parabasis (*Gr.* 'coming forward'): during an intermission in classical Greek drama, the chorus, alone and out of character, came forward unmasked to deliver to the audience views which the author felt strongly about.

pattern poem, *or* **kalligram** (*Gr.* 'beautiful', 'writing'): poem set in a visual shape so as to represent a physical object or to suggest motion, place, or feeling in accord with the idea expressed in the words.

pentameter (*Gr.* 'of 5 measures or feet'): classical pentameter (not to be confused with regular English pentameter) should mean a line of 5 measures, but in antiquity was applied to a dactylo-spondaic line consisting of two equal parts (2.5 + 2.5 feet = in fact 2 hemiepes, so strictly speaking a catalectic hexameter), *see* pp.131-32 and note 8 (p.287) to *Ukulele Music* chapter.

persona (*L.* 'mask'; dramatic character following the masking conventions of classical Greek drama): role constructed by narrator or implied author of a text.

perspectivation (point of view, focalisation): controlling information according to whether or not it is viewed through the consciousness of the narrator(s) or character(s).

Phalaecean: *see* **hendecasyllabic**.

pleonasm (tautology): redundancy, the use of more words than necessary.

ploce: the weaving of several repetitions of one or more words through a passage of some length.

poésie engagée (*Gr.* 'to make', Fr. 'engaged'): poetry written in the cause of something (e.g. socio-political ideas).

poète maudit (*Fr.* 'poet', 'bad-mouthed'): poet who is hated, envied, or feared for his gifts and/or uncompromising search for truth.

poeta doctus (*L.* 'learned poet'): a poet who displays knowledge of literature, writing, and many other fields of interest.

pre-text: *see* p.245*ff*.

quartet (*It.* '4'): first two 4-line stanzas of the Italian sonnet (the other two are *tercets*).

quatrain (*Fr.* '4'): 4-line stanza, usually rhymed.

quatorzain (*Fr.* '14'): stanza or poem of 14 lines, e.g. a sonnet.

quodlibet (*L.* 'what you please'): humorous medley of tunes, poetic potpourri.

reciprocus versus (*L.* 'reciprocal verse'): a verse which is in the same metre when the order of the words is reversed, e.g. a hemiepes $|-\smile\smile|-\smile\smile|-|$.

reverdie (*Fr.* 'back', 'green'): dance poem celebrating the coming of spring.

rhapsodist (*Gr.* 'stitcher'): poet who mixes his own work with the recitation of others, or who abridges his own poetry; in ancient Greece, a wandering minstrel or court poet who recited (extracts of) epic poetry, or his own poems, interpolated with others'.

rhopalical (*Gr.* 'club-like', 'thicker toward the end'): wedge verse in which each word is one syllable longer than the previous word; Reading applies this principle to lines.

Sapphic stanza: an aeolic verse form named after the Greek poet Sappho (7th-6th century BC), defined in note 14 (p.284) to *Diplopic* chapter.

septenary (*L.* 'of 7'), *or* **heptameter**: metrical line of 7 measures, usually trochees.

silloi, sillographical (*Gr.* 'squint-eyed, malicious'): satiricial poems or lampoons directed against doctrines or schools.

Spenserian stanza (as in *The Faerie Queene*): composed of 9 iambic lines, the first 8 being pentameter and the last hexameter (alexandrine, a line of 12 syllables), rhyming ababbcbcc.

spondee (*Gr.* 'used at libation'): metrical foot of two stressed (or long) syllables.

spoonerism (after Rev. W.A. Spooner [1844-1930]): a transposition of initial sounds so as to form some ludicrous combination (e.g. Spooner: 'half-warmed fish' instead of 'half-formed wish'); or the "accidental" transposition of whole words, *see* **malapropism**.

stance: *see* p.145.

Stet-stanza: *see* p.158.

stichic (*Gr.* 'row, line'): a stich is a line of verse (derivations: hemistich, monostich, distich, tristich, etc.); stichic verse is composed in recurrent and homogeneous lines (as opposed to stanzaic verse of varying length and movement).

syllabic metre: verse based on syllable count (the number of syllables in each line), not stress.

syllepsis (*Gr.* 'a taking together'): grammatical kind of ellipsis, in which one word is used to refer to two or more words, only one of which it agrees with grammatically; one part of speech related to two others in different ways, to witty effect; originally, a predicate which is true only of one of the two subjects it is connected with.

symploce (or *complexio*): the combining of anaphora and epiphora.

synaesthesia (*Gr.* 'together', 'to feel or perceive'): (description of) a perception of one sense modality in terms of another; metaphor of the senses.

tanka: Japanese lyric form of 31 syllables in five lines of 5-7-5-7-7 syllables.

tetrameter (*Gr.* 'of four measures'): line of four measures; the English tetrameter is a line of four feet.

tétramètre (*Fr.*): 12-syllable classical alexandrine, which has 4 divisions to the line and a caesural pause after the sixth syllable.

Thalia: the Muse of Comedy.

topos (*Gr.* 'place', *pl.* **topoi**): commonplace; fixed or formulaic expressions, phrases, quotations, images, emblems, motives, literary techniques or concepts.

trimeter (*Gr.* 'three measures'): line consisting of three measures, or feet (English trimeter).

triple metre: any poetic measure consisting of three units, such as syllables or feet or measures.

tristich: *see* **stichic**.

trochee (*Gr.* 'running'), *or* **choree**: metrical unit in quantitative verse of a long syllable followed by a short; used for rapid movement.

Ubi sunt (*L.* 'where are...?'): motif of great vogue in medieval Latin and Old English poetry emphasising the transience of life or fragility of beauty; a poem listing at great length the names of those dead or gone, often noble heroes or beautiful women.

vers de société (*Fr.*): poem written in an urbane, animated manner, often ironic light verse about contemporaneous subjects.

volta (*It.* 'turn'): the place at which a distinct turn of thought occurs (e.g. the transition point in a sonnet).

NOTES

Peter Reading *(pp.9-19)*

1. Robert Potts, 'An Interview with Peter Reading', *Oxford Poetry*, 5/3 (December 1990), p.96. Henceforward: (Potts, 1990).

2. Page 289: 'that first fright of Death – lost in thick fog/ and with the tide coming in rapidly/ over the mud-flats in the river-mouth...'

3. Alan Jenkins interview, 'Making Nothing Matter', *Poetry Review*, 75/1 (April 1985), p.5. Henceforward: (Jenkins, 1985).

4. Stephen Edgar interview, 'Whistling in the Dark', *Island*, 43/44 (Winter 1990), p.59. Henceforward: (Edgar).

5. Interview with Ian Hamilton on *Bookmark*, BBC2 TV (1 November 1986) [M]. Henceforward: (Hamilton, M).

6. Interview with Paul Bailey on *Third Ear*, BBC Radio 3 (1 March 1988) [M]. Henceforward: (Bailey, M).

7. 'A Symposium: Forms and Influences', *TLS*, 27 April 1984, p.463.

8. Lannan Reading Series [Video], 'Lannan Foundation presents Peter Reading', 21 April 1992 [M]. Henceforward: (Lannan Video, M).

9. Peter Reading, 'Muse at the feed mill', *Observer* (11 June 1989), p.42, henceforward: (Observer, 'Muse').

10. Interview in: Ysenda Maxtone Graham, 'Poets Cornered', *Sunday Telegraph* (3 March 1991), p.1. Henceforward: (Y. Graham).

11. Susan Press, 'Poet ploughs lone furrow', *Liverpool Daily Post* (3 March 1991). Henceforward: (Susan Press). And Edgar, p.56.

12. Peter Reading, 'Going, Going: A View from Contemporary England', *Island*, 42 (Autumn 1990), pp.33-34. Reading gave this paper at the 1989 Salamanca Writers Festival in Hobart. The title is taken from Larkin's poem about ecological destruction, and 'expresses an extreme change of attitude (increasingly common of late among his countrymen blundering in post-war grot), from the cautiously confident to the confidently hopeless, from shoulder-shrugging complacency..., through dawning awareness...to a vision of Albion urban, devenustated, fallen: "I just think it will happen, soon"' (p.35). Henceforward: (Reading, 'Going').

13. Reading, 'Going', pp.33, 36, 37 (the familiar phrases are from *Evagatory*, written at the same time).

14. Robert Potts, 'Poet Pete ponders his last protest', *Guardian*, 6 February 1992, henceforward: (Potts, 1992), p.30. And Peter Reading, 'Freelance', *TLS* 7 February 1992, p.12. Henceforward: (Reading, 'Freelance').

15. Daisy Goodwin, *Bookmark*, 'Day Jobs', BBC2 TV (22 January 1992) [M]. Henceforward: (Goodwin, M).

16. Quotations from Joanna Coles, 'Poet's overall objection goes against the corporate grain', *Guardian* (21 January 1992), p.20; 'Corn Law', *Daily Telegraph* (21 January 1992); 'Poet sees no rhyme or reason in uniform', *Evening Standard* (24 January 1992), p.18; Potts, 1990; Reading, 'Freelance'; see also local press reports in the *Shropshire Star*: '"Fancy dress" row may cost job' (24 January 1992) and 'Poet facing sack in row over overalls' (29 January 1992).

17. A few weeks after his dismissal Reading told this 'very silly and mildly amusing matter' deadpan to the audience after the reading in Los Angeles; there was a lot of laughter. Asked, 'and this makes the literary news in London?', Reading replied, 'oh well, it's a very small country' (Lannan Video, M).

For the Municipality's Elderly *(pp.20-39)*

1. The Solomon Eagle episode in 'Easter Letter' (p.55), for instance, is taken from an authentic source (Daniel Defoe's fictional *Journal of the Plague Year* of 1722); it was rewritten again in *Last Poems*.

2. Auden borrowed part of Sophocles' pithy saying for the death refrain of his 'IV' (September 1936), *The English Auden: Poems, Essays and Dramatic Writings, 1927-1937*, ed. Edward Mendelson (London, 1977), pp.205-06.

3. Two poems were not printed in any book: these were 'Modest Appraisal' (*Ambit*, 42 [1970], p.50), a sonnet and dunciad on Adrian Henri; and the mock-reverdie 'Sumer is icumen in' (*Ambit*, 45 [1970], p.37).

4. Gavin Ewart, 'Reading Peter Reading', *PBS Bulletin*, 141 (Summer 1989), p.1.

5. Dannie Abse, 'Travellings of the soul', *TLS*, 28 February 1975, p.214; Martin Dodsworth, 'Eastern windows only', *Guardian*, 28 November 1974; Henry Graham, 'Elderly White Earth', *Ambit*, 61 (1975), p.54; Alasdair Maclean, 'Matters of concern', *TLS*, 23 May 1975, p.552; Peter Porter, 'Authentic voices', *Observer*, 19 January 1975; Terence de Vere White, *Irish Times* (details unknown).

6. This was the first poem in *Water and Waste* (p.42); Reading "explains" the parallel: 'being has changed from the bore/ of perpetually thwarted joie de vivre/ to a sense of inert indifference'. Exactly in the middle of the poem (verse 15), the word 'love' functions as the inconspicuous hinge between the two opposing halves, just as the speaker is looking at two views of the same river from a bridge.

7. Reading never allows poetic licence to replace the findings of the natural sciences as the basis for his observations of the factual world. Accordingly, scientific terms are strewn in now and again (see also the chapter about *Diplopic*): 'asphyxiate' (p.29), 'stroboscopically' (p.38), 'naphthalene' (p.52). The references to Darwin, Archimedes and Mount Wilson, where in 1920 the discovery was made that the universe is expanding, serve the same purpose.

8. In *The Less Deceived* (London, 1955), p.26; and reprinted the following year in Conquest's *New Lines*. Larkin's adaptation of the epic Spenserian stanza (seven stanzas with nine iambic pentameters each, without end-Alexandrine, and with its own ababcadca-rhyme scheme) dissolved the tradition metrically, too. Reading echoes Larkin in places; the speaker of the poem is also modelled on Larkin's, 'something of an old buffer' [LI]. Larkin himself also did not want to be mistaken for the persona of the speaker, as he made clear in an interview (*London Magazine*, vol. 4 [November 1964], p.74). In *Stet*, Reading wrote another reply to another famous Larkin poem, 'The Whitsun Weddings'.

9. 'Faithful and simpleton are singing/hope for the dead', while 'Eli, Eli, lama sabachthani?', the agonised cry for help from Jesus, gets 'stuck' as an isolated, unanswered monostich in anachronistic Hebrew between a hearse and faded bones; and the 20th century chocolate egg is long covered in dust.

10. 'Lapse' functions twice as part of an envelope: with respect to the extremes of death by heat or cold and to the seasons. 'Genesis', the beginning of human history, in this volume is the last thing to be mentioned. The reversal of important doctrines is underlined by the allusion to Michelangelo's 'Creation': the Big finger here produces 'decay'.

11. Note especially 'Juncture' (pp.59-60), a surprising sideline and an answer to Frost's 'The Road Not Taken' – here 'a parsleyed cul-de-sac/narrow gauge alternative': 'Spring has returned to me; you can't'. Asked about this, Reading

said [LI], ' "The Road Not Taken" is one poem that I was very familiar with and liked very much... yes, that was very likely twiddling around somewhere in the back of my mind'. Time appears circular all of a sudden, 'now your unexplained appearance/.../leaves behind a trail of sleepers/drawn out from infinity' (the 'sleepers' re-occur in several books).

12. Alan Jenkins, 'Peter Reading', in *Dictionary of Literary Biography*, ed. Vincent B. Sherry (Detroit/Michigan, 1985), 469-75, p.470. Henceforward: (Jenkins, *DLB*).

13. In the four sentences (four stanzas, 5-4-5-4 verses, i.e. two falls) a dactylic-spondaic falling rhythm can be heard, which is appropriately uplifted anapaestically-iambically by the final safety of 'though it did, the sluice', which furthermore receives fortification by the end rhyme and metre of the last verse.

14. Michael Alexander, 'Poetry and place', *Literature matters*, 13 (May 1993), pp.4-5.

15. Definition by Dr Johnson of 1799 quoted in *The Princeton Encyclopedia of Poetry and Poetics*, ed. Alex Preminger, enlarged edition (Princeton, 1974). Henceforward referred to as 'Preminger'. (*The New Princeton Encylopedia* was published in 1993.)

16. T.S. Eliot, The Family Reunion (II,1): 'There is nothing at all to be done about it,/There is nothing to do about anything,/And now it is nearly time for the news.' This became an incantatory *ploce* in *Perduta Gente*, which goes back to the Chorus in Aeschylus' *Agamemnon*. See also Auden/Isherwood's *The Ascent of F6* (1936): 'No, nothing that matters will ever happen;/Nothing you'd ever want to put in a book', which Reading quoted in 'Going', p.34.

17. 'Provided', 'I suppose' (pp.29, 30, 34), 'if', 'likely', 'almost', 'perhaps', etc. Reading, while cataloguing art-slides ('Primavera', p.41), is not absolutely sure yet: 'Nothing of me is likely to remain/among these records of two thousand years'/obsolete art, reduced, collecting dust.'

18. Dennis O'Driscoll, ' "No-God and Species Decline Stuff": The Poetry of Peter Reading', in *Contiguous Traditions in Post-War British and Irish Poetry*, ed. Cedric C. Barfoot (Amsterdam, 1994), 199-218, p.203. Henceforward: (O'Driscoll).

19. These specialist references also have occasional thematic functions in that some of the artists quoted also dealt with the question of death.

20. Martin Booth, *British Poetry 1964-1984: Driving through the Barricades* (London, 1985), 158-60, p.158. Henceforward: (Booth).

21. Tom Paulin, *Minotaur* (London, 1992), 285-94, p.288. Henceforward: (Paulin).

22. 'I didn't know death had undone so many' and 'sighs are exhaled' are echoes of Eliot and verses from the *Inferno* (Canto III), as is the inscription on the Gates of Hell. In *For the Municipality's Elderly*, Reading alludes directly to this myth (see also 'Deepwood Lane', p.56, re. Dante's Canto I), which is followed up in *C* (Charon) and in *Perduta Gente*. The Waste Land death's 'knock upon the door' is echoed by the publican: 'HURRY UP PLEASE IT'S TIME' (and see p.62). See also p.33, 41, 45. The verses 'When the world ends' and 'last light is pressing the panes' are verbatim quotations from *The Waste Land* and *Prufrock* ('fog is pressing the panes'), repeated in the last poem of *Last Poems*.

23. For example, 'New Year Letter' (p.47) takes its title and philosophical train of thought from an epistolary poem by Auden of 1940 (W.H. Auden,

Collected Poems, ed. Edward Mendelson (London, 1976), Part V: 'New Year Letter', pp.159-93); see also the Auden refrain in 'Dead Horse'.

24. Six out of 35 titles are foreign-sounding. See also the epitaph 'Qui caecus et senectute confectus' ('who was exhausted by blindness and senility'). 'Sunt aliquid manes letum non omnia finit' is a quotation from Sextus Propertius, translated and extended in 'Three' (*Work in Regress*). 'BY.ADAM.IN.TE. DVST.ILYE.' (continuing: 'in Christ I have the victory'). 'Nomenclator' quotes Renaldo d'Aquino: 'donna mia ch'io non perisca' ('may I not perish'). Dante's inscription on the Gates of Hell is quoted shortly afterwards (Canto III: 'per me si va nella città dolente', 'through me the way into the doleful city').

The Prison Cell & Barrel Mystery *(pp.40-54)*

1. Colin Falck, 'New Poetry', *The New Review*, 3/26 (May 1976), p.59.

2. See 'Kwickie Service' (p.74), 'Us in The Ship' (p.74), 'Trio' (p.77).

3. 'Peter Reading writes...', *PBS Bulletin*, 88 (Spring 1976), p.2.

4. Peter Porter, 'A whiff of sulphur', *Observer* (11 April 1976), p.32.

5. Martin Bax, 'The Prison Cell & Barrel Mystery. Peter Reading', *Ambit*, 67 (1976), p.67; Martin Dodsworth, 'Genial strength', *Guardian* (20 May 1976), p.14; Colin Falck, 'New Poetry', *The New Review*, 3/26 (May 1976), p.59; Desmond Graham, 'Neatness and Truth: Recent Poetry', *Stand*, 18/2 (1977), pp.729; Peter Porter, 'A whiff of sulphur', *Observer*, 11 April 1976, p.32; D.M. Thomas, 'The Adamic silence', *TLS*, 23 July 1976, p.910; 'Peter Reading: The Prison Cell & Barrel Mystery', *British Book News* (May 1976), p.380.

6. See for instance the chapter about lyrical fictionalisations in Neil Corcoran's study *English Poetry Since 1940* (Harlow, 1993), pp.244-60.

7. 'Early Stuff', 'Mem-sahib', 'Correspondence', 'Luncheon', 'Ballad', 'Duologues', 'Soirée' and 'Ménage à Trois'.

8. Meiosis is used here to mean enlarged litotes (see Glossary), not ironic understatement, as some dictionaries define it.

9. 'The Post House' is a popular pub in the centre of Liverpool, which Reading frequented in his student days and later visited occasionally. 'The old spectacular' refers to the old shows of the Music Halls.

10. The first line of the next stanza is indented and thus completes the five-stress line. Uncertain readers can count the stresses in retrospect and thence are aware of the principle which is promptly corroborated in the next poem, this time with three stresses. (Emphatic italics also help identify stresses.)

11. The title poem sequence uses different numbers of stresses, but significantly introduces a third stress when 'The cold' reminds the unfaithful husband of his wife, completing the trio. 'Widow' has three stresses for the three perspectives involved, and the same is true of the three syllables for each of the three personae in the syllabic 'Trio'. Two stresses for double meaning in the ithyphallic 'Mycologia', for the two personae in 'Us in The Ship' (tending towards the choriamb used before), which number is doubled for the same personae in 'Kwickie Service'. Logically, four stresses also for the first two dialogues in 'Duologues', as well as for the four lovers' interchangeable quartet 'Correspondence' (six stanzas, eight lines each) and for the four personae in 'Ménage à Trois' (the stress number is doubled as the protagonists' stress escalates while there is no more room left for unstressed syllables). 'Prolonged Look' mirrors the decreasing appeal of the lover in decreasing numbers of stresses.

12. Syllabic metre is typical of Romance languages, Polish, Japanese, and Chinese, but was also used in England after the Restoration until *c.*1740. Since then, it has been revived only occasionally, e.g. by Robert Bridges, Dylan Thomas, W.H. Auden and Marianne Moore, and more recently by Thom Gunn and George MacBeth. While its advantages for English remained un-identified, its difficulties are agreed upon: the reader has to pause artificially after every line so as to notice its rhythm. In 'Trio', Reading avoids the problem by having the colon end with the end of the line as often as possible so that the pause no longer seems unnatural.

13. The enumeration of the house numbers '61/ 63/ 65/ next one's hers/ 69' (p.78), for example, not only heightens suspense, but also avoids a four-syllable word. On p.80 anaptyxis in a song is marked by an accent ('fixèd star'), thus drawing attention to the syllabic principle.

14. The husband has selected 12 daffodils and 12 irises for his bouquet. The wife's sentence, however, only lets the daffodils "through" to his old flame: yellow symbolises jealousy and infidelity, daffodils are "fallen" flowers (originally lilies) and grow on the banks of the Acheron – the dead take plea-sure in them. The blocked-off iris, on the other hand, is the messenger of the Gods and Goddess of the rainbow, the bridge between Heaven and Earth. The colour violet stands for true and faithful love. Even if Reading did not consult *Brewer's* treasure chest, as he said [C], critics will take pleasure in doing so: Ivor H. Evans (ed.), *Brewer's Dictionary of Phrase and Fable* (London, 1870, 15th, revised ed. 1995).

15. The condescending, undignified vocabulary used by the wife to describe the ex-lover's situation ('got him', 'drunk', 'flat', 'hooked') is counterpointed by the ex-lover's gentle words, all circling around one word, 'love' – however, they are not printed on the same level, but mostly somewhat lower down, indicating an inferior position.

16. His evening call comes too late to have any impact or effect a change: 10 o'clock (not 9).

17. Matching the double meaning of the fungi the verses have two stresses each. The first two stanzas give the expressive Latin names *Mutinus caninus* and *Phallus impudicus* (belonging to the 'Phallaceae' family: *Dog Stinkhorn* and *Common Stinkhorn*). The closing *Destroying Angel* is the popular translation of *Amanita virosa*, a highly poisonous common toadstool, which can kill, but whose white flesh in turn is destroyed "sexually" by the phalli-fungi.

18. The title poem – a kind of aubade – condenses in lyrical imagery the seven basic situations of the unfortunate love, which are elaborated in other poems: the chance meeting (2), the rekindled love (3), the resuming of the past (4), the sobering (5), the approaching end (6), the last meeting (7), the melancholy gloom (1).

19. Porter. In their recent articles (see Bibliography), O'Brien and Kerrigan assume that the poem exhibits 'xenophobia' – as if Reading had never parodied British accents, or never written his harsh anti-xenophobic poems: the foreign accent is not what the poem is about, but it fulfils two opposing functions: to create both an anecdotal atmosphere and a touch of authenticity.

20. See the related poem in *Nothing For Anyone*, p.110.

21. Many famous lovers are invoked for this mundane story: 'Euridice and Orpheus', 'Leda and the Swan', 'Hero and Leander'; similarly incongruous is the list of innovative painters with the telling names (Les Fauves, Les Nabis, Intimisme); ironic, too, 'Cybernetics' (there can be no case of control here).

Also, a list of painters of the late 19th and 20th centuries is appended and jargon and specialist terms are strewn in to evoke the Liverpool Art College atmosphere ('Dip AD' was the 'Diploma in Art and Design', and 'ATD' the 'Art Teacher's Diploma').

Nothing For Anyone *(pp.55-71)*

1. Martin Bax, 'Nothing For Anyone. Peter Reading', *Ambit*, 73 (1978), p.89; George Mackay Brown, 'The dark wood', *Scotsman*, 24 (September 1977), p.3; Gavin Ewart, 'Accepting the inevitable', *TLS*, 25 November 1977, p.1381; Joan Forman, 'Presenting the female Muse', *Eastern Daily Press*, 11 November 1977, p.26; Shirley Toulson, 'Peter Reading: *Nothing For Anyone*', *British Book News* (January 1978), p.60; Robert Welch, 'Interminably, he flutes', *Yorkshire Post*, 17 November 1977, p.8.

2. Ewart. This review among others was quoted from in the poem 'Opinions of the Press' (*Fiction*).

3. The quotation is from Ovid's *The Art of Love* (I.633), and also quoted in *Romeo and Juliet* (II.2.92): 'At lovers' perjuries, / They say, Jove laughs'.

4. Brownjohn was the editor of the fifth 'Poems for Shakespeare' anthology for the World Centre for Shakespeare Studies. For a detailed analysis of this poem, see Isabel Martin, 'Postmodernising Shakespeare: A Palimpsest Poem', pp.185-99, in *Historicizing/Contemporizing Shakespeare*, ed. C. Bode & W. Klooss (Trier: WVT, 2000).

5. In his own hundred or so reviews Reading showed little patience with so-called 'dark' poetry which refuses to offer any decoding clues, thus seemingly satisfied with its own company and not too interested in sharing experiences with readers. 'Difficult' poetry is something else; here Reading sometimes bluntly confessed in his reviews: 'I don't understand this' [M].

6. Sir Harold Hartley was the first to publicise the alarming prognoses about the future of human society (especially Western industrial nations) in 1954, in the first Fawley Foundation Lecture at Southampton University (*Science & Society: the Pattern of the Future*). Since then, the core problems of 'Population, Energy, Food' have become more urgent far faster than predicted by Hartley. These three words are quoted by the leading biologist, environment expert and educator Lord Eric Ashby, F.R.S., in his 21st Fawley Foundation Lecture (1976), which updates Hartley's prognoses and also refers to the Club of Rome report *The Limits to Growth*. Reading refers to this source, which was printed in *Encounter* ('A Second Look at Doom', 46/3 [March 1976], pp.16-24), in a note to the poem. In another note he refers to the 1974 book by the brothers Cecile de Witt and Bryce de Witt about the Black Holes in the universe. With 'CIPEC, OPEC', Reading refers to the first copper crisis (1973) and the first oil crisis (1973).

7. Reading paraphrases Lord Ashby here (Ashby, pp.17-18, 22-23), who adjusts the perspectives in explaining the natural decline and fall of *every* culture and ultimately of every species. (He also recommends Edward Gibbon, *History of the Decline and Fall of the Roman Empire* [1776-1788], which Reading duly read and referred to later in *Evagatory*.) Henceforward, Reading makes this his own yardstick, as is evident in the following books (especially *Diplopic, 5x5x5x5*, and *C*).

8. Now Reading has moved towards Paulin's territory. Paulin writes: 'Soccer violence is now a permanent feature of British culture, and British football

fans are feared and hated throughout Europe (at the time of writing [1988] twenty-nine supporters of Liverpool's football team are awaiting trial in Brussels for causing many deaths and injuries in a riot there two years back)...The British abroad are notoriously unpopular, and British visitors to Europe now find themselves strangers in a continent where they used to win battles with clothyard arrows and other weapons. No one living in Britain now can fail to observe the jeering brutalism and demoralized separatism with which large sections of the island's white population confront the various ethnic minority groups within the country' (Paulin, p.288).

9. The words 'apes' gore' are echoed in *Going On* (p.77) and in 'Ovidian' (*Last Poems*).

Fiction *(pp.72-80)*

1. Alan Brownjohn, 'Cosmic, Comic, Casual, Careful', *Encounter*, 53/5 (November 1979), pp.70-77; Neil Curry, '*Fiction*. Peter Reading', *Ambit*, 80 (1979), p.81; Robert Greacen, 'Peter Reading: *Fiction*', *British Book News* (November 1979), p.954; Edna Longley, 'Catching up – Poetry: 1: The British', *TLS*, 18 January 1980, pp.64-65. Curry, Brownjohn and Longley were annoyed: 'the jokes [are] so obvious that they become too tedious to bother with'; 'hardly more than a small batch of sardonic jokes and wheezes'; 'Reading's definite mordancy limits him to the lucidly entertaining verse which has almost talked him out of poetry'.

2. 'Fiction' is also discussed by Peter Hühn, who maintains that its complexity matches that of postmodern American novels by Barth, Pynchon, and Vonnegut, while the poem parodies such literature (and itself) at the same time (Peter Hühn, 'Postmoderne Tendenzen in der britischen Gegenwartslyrik: Formen, Funktionen, Kontexte', *Literatur in Wissenschaft und Unterricht*, 28/4 [1995], 295-331, pp.312-13).

3. Robert Crawford is a notable example: his angle cuts him off from those features which would put the reflexivity into proper perspective, e.g. hermeneutics, morality, or irony. The flatness of his approach leads to literal readings, as with 'Opinions of the Press' ('His work is obsessively self-reflexive – "*but am I Art?*" is its central question', Robert Crawford, 'Cut-Ups', *London Review of Books*, 2/23 [7 December 1989], p.26). Neil Corcoran's reading is a much more valuable contribution (*English Poetry Since 1940* [Harlow, 1993], 'Hiding in Fictions: Some New Narrative Poems', 244-257, pp.245, 247), but Dennis O'Driscoll deals with this aspect of Reading's work best (O'Driscoll, p.200).

4. Jenkins, DLB, p.472. 'Norna of (the) Fitful-head' is Ulla Troil's nickname (Walter Scott, *The Pirate*), a semi-deranged woman supposed to have supernatural powers, especially over the winds, or, as the disrespectful allusion would have it, over Ted Hughes. 'Dis' is Latin for Hades, and 'Garden City' stands for a devilish non-city. 'Pun & Ink' is fictitious.

5. This concrete poem visualises what the title promises, with attention quickly decreasing, barely registering the calamities: 'Do' and his bloody accident still provide more *frisson* than general annihilation ('early retire', an echo of the newspaper headlines in 'Nothing For Anyone', p.128).

6. O'Driscoll describes the opposition as 'colloquial colour and newspaper black-and-white' (O'Driscoll, p.201); it is a register-collision that Reading uses for its linguistic richness and perspectivising potential, and forms the structural basis of *Diplopic*.

7. 'Clues' operates like a condensed crime story. It provides clues both for the strange happenings surrounding this Adlestrop-like stopping of a train and for the whole book, forcing the reader to participate. Reading had originally created 'Clues' as one of the drawings for the book (all rejected by Secker). The answers: 'Shortened grape of Jerez': P.X(iménez) (see 'In State'); 'Stationary, but not at a station': emergency stop, during which this crossword is being tackled; 'Cows on the railway line, Stokesay Castle' (near Ludlow, see 'Parallel Texts'); '*Un pom led me* to writer's disguise': anagram of Nom de Plume; 'Toll or fee split softly to hoax': d-u-e plus 'softly' (p=pianissimo); 'Iberian prof ': 'Don'. In this context, see also 'Parallel Texts' and 'Notes': the 'Notes' verify the answers with the reference to '2nd Class Singles', i.e. the train journey, and with 'Don, Nomdeplume, Dupe'.

8. See the initiation poem 'Early Morning Call' (p.138); the 'Proposed Increases' for tombstome prices (p. 140); 'An Everyday Story of Countryfolk' (p.147); 'You Can't Be Too Careful' (p.150), a satirical found poem (from a brochure of the 'Animal Health Department', for customers of the feed mill, Reading's place of work [C]); 'Madamooselle – A Conversation' (p.151), as witnessed by Reading: 'It was an absolutely verbatim rendering of an over-heard conversation in a Shropshire pub' [C]).

9. See the satires about provincial art in 'Festival' (p.145) and 'Interview' (p.160). 'It's a Small World' (p.139) is a persiflage in triplets of the jargon and affected demeanour of 70s alternative politicising (compare 'Address Protector', p.122). 'Mystery Story' (pp.162-64) originated in a practical joke, which saw Reading invited to a dubious poetry reading to Huddersfield. Reading [LI]: 'That's completely true. It's just very slightly altered. And it turned out that the perpetrator of this practical joke was a friend of mine who's now dead – Michael Donahue [whose name might have prompted 'Don'] – and A.E. Hound is (which is what he first signed himself as) an anagram of Donahue, so I should have got this. But I was thrown, really, by the connotations of A.E. Housman and so on (I lived in Ludlow at the time) [Housman is buried there]. But the Baudelaire and so on is correct. My response as Donaldson is slightly grander than I managed to muster at the time, but this is what it turned out to be.'

10. 'Mens Talents in Difcours Shadowed out by Muficall Inftruments' (pp.156-58), a 'more or less' found prose-poem from an authentic 1713 source [LI], is enriched by the fictitious author 'D. Donaldfonne His Booke Anno Dom 1713 in the author's poffeffion'. Here, Reading substitutes the old swash 's' with the typographically similar 'f' for the first time, the alienating effect of which highlights the old age of the text, as do syntax and orthography. (In *Perduta Gente*, the substitutions of 'u/v' and 'i/j' are added.)

11. Steven Weinberg, *The First Three Minutes. A Modern View of the Origin of the Universe* (London, 1977), p.150*ff*: 'Whichever cosmological model proves correct, there is not much of comfort in any of this. It is almost irresistible for humans to believe that we have some special relation to the universe, that human life is not just a more-or-less farcical outcome of a chain of accidents reaching back to the first three minutes, but that we are somehow built in from the beginning... It is very hard to realise that [our world] is just a tiny part of an overwhelmingly hostile universe. It is even harder to realise that this present universe has evolved from an unspeakably unfamiliar early con-dition, and faces a future extinction of endless cold or intolerable heat. The more the universe seems comprehensible, the more it also seems pointless. – But if there is no solace in the fruits of our research, there is at least some

consolation in the research itself. Men and women are not content to comfort themselves with tales of gods and giants, or to confine their thoughts to the daily affairs of life; they also build telescopes and satellites and accelerators, and sit at their desks for endless hours working out the meaning of the data they gather. The effort to understand the universe is one of the very few things that lifts human life a little above the level of farce, and gives it some of the grace of tragedy.'

12. Knowledge of Slavonic languages helps (Niznegorsky means 'being on the lower side of the mountain') as well as the recollection that Reading started quoting wine names in *The Prison Cell & Barrel Mystery*. The 'Notes' provide a clue: 'Kokur Niznegorsky – One of the more agreeable White Russians', and 'See Johnson, ISBN 0 85533 002 3 (1971)' refers to Hugh Johnson's *World Atlas of Wine* with the wine's "production number" and the vintage.

13. It is the name of the main grape used with Pallamino for Jerez ('Sherry'). Even without this knowledge, the doubtful identity of the General laid out in 'In State' (p.159) – 'Sobre la muerte del generalísimo el excelentísimo Sr. Conde de Torregamberro' – is ample warning: his name, translated, means 'Bullshit' (and 'conde' could be heard as 'cunt').

14. 'Peter Reading writes...', *PBS Bulletin*, 111 (Christmas 1981), pp.2-3.

15. The reviewers quoted are Gavin Ewart (review of *NA*), George Mackay Brown (*NA*), Robert Welch (*NA*), Shirley Toulson (*NA*), Peter Porter (*ME* and *PC*), (n.n.) (*PC*); D.M. Thomas (*PC*), Martin Bax (*PC, NA*), Desmond Graham (*PC*).

Tom o'Bedlam's Beauties *(pp.81-91)*

1. A.A. Cleary, '"Tom o'Bedlam's Beauties"', *Thames Poetry*, 2/12 (March 1983), p.32; Neil Curry, 'Tom o'Bedlam's Beauties. Peter Reading', *Ambit*, 89 (1982), p.73; Martin Dodsworth, 'Shivery looks', *Guardian*, 11 March 1982, p.11; Gavin Ewart, 'Poetry in Britain 1978-81', *British Book News*, 2 (June 1982), p.336; Alan Jenkins, 'A Barbarous Eloquence', *Encounter*, 59/2 (August 1982), pp.55-61; Grevel Lindop, 'Madness stroke sanity', *TLS*, 18 June 1982, p.662.

2. Quoted by John Whitworth, 'The Poetasters' Tabloid Tease', *Poetry Review*, 80/1 (Spring 1990), p.79.

3. 'Peter Reading writes...', *PBS Bulletin*, 111 (Christmas 1981), pp.2-3.

4. *The Letters of William and Dorothy Wordsworth: The Early Years 1787-1805*, ed. Ernest De Selincourt (Oxford, 1967), p.354.

5. Jenkins traces a more recent genealogy for the book (*DLB*, p.473): 'Reading clearly owes something to Ewart's example, behind him stands Auden again, and behind him one of Auden's masters, Skelton. So Reading can align himself with a strong team of social commentators and satirists.'

6. See Wordsworth, p.358.

7. *New Oxford Book of English Verse*, ed. Helen Gardner (London, 1972), pp.369-371.

8. This is Reading's version of *Riddle 35* ('Mec se wæta wong') of the *Exeter Book*, trs. Michael Alexander (*Old English Literature*, ed. Michael Alexander [London, 1983], p.82). St Aldhelm had adapted the riddle from the Latin original *De Lorica* (mailshirt); the Anglo-Saxon solution is 'coat of arms'. Reading first uses this Anglo-Saxon form in 'Remaindered', which is the poem before '?' (p.168) and the last poem in *Fiction*.

9. And more splits: on the first page, the quote 'wyrda cræftum' from *Riddle 35* alludes to this source, identified in the last note; however, the note misleadingly refers to the last poem, which has nothing to do with the source.

10. The 'Notes' lead to some of the cross-references: 'W.P.C. Elliott, Cheltenham Chronicle, 17.12.1973' is fictitious and could be an invention by the Brigadier ('Colonel Fashpoint Shellingem/ (retired) of Cheltenham Spa', p.202); 'His 'n Hers Boutique, Paisley dressing-gown' (see p.188); 'Charles Farrar Browne, 1834, Maine, New England': authentic, see 'Artemus Wardrobe'; 'Telegraph, 27.4.1979': fictitious; 'Johnny Weissmuller, 75-year-old ex-champ': see 'Some of Their Efforts', 'chimp'; 'terminal sonnet "Extruding absent-mindedly remorse"', see 'Alma Mater' with its explicit invitation to look for connections; 'G. Ewart, "Two Nonsense Limericks"', and 'Sonnet found in a Deserted Madhouse, Anon.' are authentic, but do not bear directly on this book; 'Riddle 35, The Exeter Book' (see the first, not the last '?'). Sylleptic wordgames often are double-edged, like 'Dispatch Clerk', 'Greenback', 'Capability Brown', 'Doctor Snyde', or titles like 'Concord', 'Between the Lines', 'Wandering', 'Artemus' Wardrobe', 'Song of the Bed-Sit Girl' or 'Commitment'.

11. 'Concord Dry Cleaners, Welshpool' is authentic, inviting an ironic title. The poem's background was also authentic [LI], a 'little prank I got up to at work while I was fighting the old ennuie'.

12. See 'Between the Lines', 'Tom o'Bedlam's Beauties', 'Wandering', 'Commitment', 'Notes'. As 'Visit' (p.189) appears in the first half of the book, the grave described might be Tom's, with heightened deceit in the epitaph. The Shakespeare sonnet 'Commitment' (p.206) is soaked in punning black humour: 'About the time of my *affaire* with Gerry, / Tom went right off the rails'.

13. 'Peruvian Jungle by Kayak' and the other titles are plainly fictitious, but, as Reading explained [LI], 'they are the sort of things that you may have seen in the kind of wonderbooks for boys which were produced until comparatively recently, designed to fire us with enthusiasm for exploring and to find out things of Empire. And they were written by these sort of people and they had these sort of titles.'

14. See 'Alma Mater' (the teachers were from Reading's old Alsop Grammar School), 'Some of Their Efforts', and the 'Notes'. His death is implied by the allusion to Dylan Thomas's villanelle 'Do Not Go Gentle...' and the phrase 'terminal sonnet'. The sonnet was [LI] 'the most sort of lunatic thing I could think of then off the top of my head, on the spur of the moment, as "in Japan they eat fish raw". This is as mad as I could get it.'

15. Unlike Jesus in the allegory of Christophorus ('with hitched-up skirt'), she drowns in the Styx without victory because no one seems to owe her anything.

16. 'Phrenfy' (pp.194-95), the narrative of the writer's housekeeper, Mrs Ridgeway, does not mention his name. The 'Master' is Jonathan Swift, who saved a third of his income to finance the 'St Patrick Hospital for Imbeciles' (opened 1757). The account is based on Samuel Johnson's *Lives of the English Poets* (1779-81), and Swift's 'All folly' comes from Johnson, too.

17. The anacreontic 'Four Poems' (pp.186-87) are presented as translations from Kokur Niznegorsky (the White Russian wine of *Fiction*). The poems are declarations of love to wine and love-making. The motto is taken from Crabbe's *The Parish Register* (1807). Silvaner Feodosiisky is also a wine.

18. 'Koshu' is the name of a grape and 'Sanraku Ocean' a Japanese wine firm.

19. *Shipwrecks and Disasters at Sea; Narratives of the Most Remarkable Wrecks, Conflagrations, Mutinies & c.* (London, 1856). The cannibalistic episode chosen here, with the same title, gives authentic details, 'just rendered into my verse' [LI]. The collection also contains the narrative about Alexander Selkirk or Selcraig (1676-1721), whose fate inspired *Robinson Crusoe*.

20. This seems to be a gift: before the launch of *Perduta Gente* in 1989 I asked whether he was not going to rehearse the poems written in a tongue-twisting drunken slur. He grinned: 'You mean I should get us another beer?'

21. Reading, *PBS Bulletin*, p.3.

Diplopic *(pp.92-107)*

1. Press release by the organising Poetry Society.

2. A.A. Cleary, '"Diplopic" by Peter Reading', *Thames Poetry*, 2/13 (October 1983), p.51; Gavin Ewart, 'Confronting the bogeymen', *TLS*, 30 September 1983, p.1061; Gavin Ewart, 'Peter Reading: Diplopic', *British Book News* (November 1983), p.706; D.J. Enright, 'Books of the Year', *Observer*, December 1983; John Mole, 'Expanding Elements', *Encounter*, 61/4 (December 1983), p.60; Michael O'Neill, 'Colliding Styles', *Poetry Review*, 73/3 (September 1983), pp.72-73; Peter Porter, 'A bumper book of horrors', *Observer*, 3 July 1983, p.29; [RP], 'Poems to shock', *Coventry Evening Telegraph*, 19 August 1983, p.20; 'Top honours for Little Stretton poet', *Shropshire Star*, 27 October 1983; George Szirtes, 'Comedy of Terrors', *Literary Review & Quarto*, 66 (December 1983), pp.53-54.

3. 'Peter Reading writes...'. *PBS Bulletin*, 117 (Summer 1983), p.3.

4. 'From a Journal (*c.*1917, in the author's possession)' is fictitious [C]. At the Plymouth meeting of the 'British Association for the Advancement of Science' in 1841 Owen coined the term 'Dinosaur'. 'He' is Carew (see p.244).

5. Reading had been to a Kennington (1888-1960) exhibition in London and elaborated his annotations on the sketch of a dead German (p.219).

6. 'The Terrestrial Globe' and 'The Big Cats' show jealousy as the reason for the homicide, which is ambiguously mixed up with a little death and corroborated by the pun 'rec.' (wreck) and the three meanings of 'slough' (a muddy hole, degeneracy, dead skin).

7. Reading was reading Waugh at the time [LI]: 'Well, that was really a *Black Mischief* job... I may have hyperbolised slightly about the going back to the jungle...this irate mother got on the phone and spoke to somebody or other [at the Poly], giving a bollocking: "What have you done? I gave her to you in good faith!" That's quite gen!'. 'Chalky' (Sunderland lecturer Bert Nutter) was Reading's source of African anecdotes (see 'chicken buggery', and *C*, Unit 7).

8. 'A fictionalised true story. That is to say, the girl was deaf rather than blind' [LI].

9. 'Editorial', 'At Home', 'Ex Lab', 'Between the Headlines'. The column 'Uncle Chummy's Letter Box, Kiddies' Column' is taken up in later books. 'Adam (9)' was the son of Reading's new friend, John Coggrave; he wrote to *The Sunderland Echo* about his pet rabbit, because children received 50p for three published letters. During one of the lunches in *The Vaults*, Coggrave imagined 'Uncle Chummy' as a hung-over failed hack, 'crapulous' in his morning state, groaning with dismay at the influx of juvenile correspondence. As 'Miss Prudence', he fakes readers' poems to earn £5 prizes in *Stet*.

10. 'I cringe at the vast majority of "nature" poems because they, for the most part, tend not to do their subject-matter justice. I mean almost anybody who handles nature, Anne Stevenson, for example, and I'd include Ted Hughes in that. They run the risk of sounding terribly mawkish by things like anthropomorphism and just general misinformed attitudes to various fauna and flora. I would sooner read a biologist on the subject' [LI]. The followers of 'that haiku frog' (p.230; *Ob.*, p.18) incensed him (the reference is to the frequently translated poem about a frog jumping into a pool, ascribed to Matsuo Basho [1664-94]).

11. 'War Artistes' and 'Mnemonics'. 'Englished' (pp.236, 237). 'Rhypheans' is intertextual, directly taken from Dryden's *Georgics* translation ('Such are the cold Rhipæan race').

12. In 'Englished (iii. 349-83)', Reading takes up Virgil's amused dismay about the way in which the Northerners treat wine, 'cleaving the frozen Lafite' (in Dryden: 'With axes first they cleave the wine; and thence,/ By weight, the solid portions they dispense'; *The Works of John Dryden*, vol. XIV, edited by Walter Scott (London, 1808).

13. The cross-references are to pp.218, 220-22, 224, 242-44, 214, 228-30; the 'discreetly labelled building' refers back to *Tom o'Bedlam's Beauties*.

14. It consists of three hendecasyllabic Lesser Sapphic verses ($-\smile---\smile\smile--$) and one Adonic ($-\smile\smile--$) and was also used by Alcaeus and Catullus, two of Reading's later models.

15. The 5-7-5-7-7 tanka syllables are made the numerical principle of a sequence of five parts containing exactly those numbers of tankas, thus becoming the 'Super-Tanka', as Reading points out.

16. 'Found' is exaggerated from a true event: Reading discovered a dazed, bruised girl lying in her blood one night near his house in Sunderland [C].

17. 'Martin Amis interviewed by Christopher Bigsby', in *New Writing*, ed. Malcolm Bradbury & Judy Cooke (London, 1992), p.177. This interview is remarkable to read for the similarity between the two writers.

18. Robert Crawford, 'Cut-Ups', *London Review of Books*, 2/23 (7 December 1989), p.26. The second epithet is by John Mole (review of *Ukulele Music*, see there), the third by Michael O'Neill, who described *Diplopic* as 'a well-told sick joke'.

19. Quoted in *Modernism: 1890-1930*, ed. Malcolm Bradbury & James McFarlane (Harmondsworth, 1976), p.327. Unfortunately, the source they quote is not the right one.

20. Graham Greene's autobiography, *A Sort of Life* (Harmondsworth, 1971), p.134.

21. Vincent B. Sherry, 'Poetry in England, 1945-1990', in *Columbia History of English Poetry*, ed. Carl Wordring (Columbia, 1993).

22. Sir Stephen Spender, 'Foreword', *Forward Book of Poetry* (London, 1993), p.7.

5x5x5x5x5 *(pp.108-11)*

1. The booklet was not reviewed on its own, but was included in: Mick Imlah, 'Thanatoptic designs', *TLS*, 4 January 1985, p.10; David Hart, 'Reading between the lines', *Arts Report* (West Midlands Arts), April 1985. See O'Driscoll, pp.199-218, and Jenkins, *DLB*, pp.473-74.

2. Reading has often been asked in interviews about his habit of listening in on conversations: 'Sort of eavesdropping on buses and pubs and generally

where I go is quite interesting' (Hamilton, M). As Reading never got a driving licence, he spends a lot of time on public transport.

3. Reading [LI]: 'Archie Andrews was first in line for the *ABC of Non-Entities*. He was a ventriloquist's dummy, operated by a man called Peter Brough, who was an Australian. During the 50s he was at his zenith. And, incongruously enough, for a ventriloquist and his ventriloquist's doll, they used to have a radio programme, which was very popular, I think...'

C (pp.112-27)

1. 'Shocking but True: Peter Reading writes...', *PBS Bulletin*, 123 (Christmas 1981), pp.2-3. Reading refers to James Thomson's atheistic agony in *The City of Dreadful Night* (1874), and to De La Rochefoucauld's maxim 'Neither the sun nor death can be looked at with a steady eye', which is also the epigraph to psychiatrist John Hinton's book *Dying* (Harmondsworth, 1967), which Reading used.

2. Alan Bold, 'Stricken by the big C', *Scotsman* (8 December 1984), p.5; Robert Greacen, 'Peter Reading: C', *British Book News* (March 1985), p.181; Mick Imlah, 'Thanatoptic designs', *TLS*, 4 January 1985, p.10; Alan Jenkins, 'Noises of apocalypse', *Observer*, 23 December 1984, p.29; Dennis O'Driscoll, 'Beyond a Joke', *Poetry Review*, 75/1 (April 1985), pp.15-16; Carol Rumens, 'Antiseptic Whiff of Destiny', *Literary Review*, 83 (May 1985), p.52; Jaci Stephen, 'Ways of dying', *Times Educational Supplement*, 10 May 1985, p.26; Julian Symons, 'Lines from the sick room', *Sunday Times*, 13 January 1985, p.45; George Szirtes, 'Recent poetry', *Critical Quarterly*, 27/2 (Summer 1985), pp.51-55; 'Verse to make you sick?', *Liverpool Daily Post* (no details).

3. Reading was charged with 'pathological obsession' (Bold), 'morbidity' (Imlah), 'voyeuristic relish' (Paulin), even 'relish in vomit and pus' (*Liverpool Daily Post*). Greacen found *C* 'distasteful' and too negative.

4. All references in this chapter are to the 100 'units', which will have to be numbered by the reader. Page references are added where necessary.

5. Note the slang connotations of 'to tuck someone up' and 'to tucker someone out'; 'Char' is also a post-WWII expression for 'vagrant'. 'Tucker' was also the authentic name of a homeless man in Sunderland whom Reading knew [C].

6. Reading's Charon's literary ancestors are in Virgil (*Aeneid* Book VI), Dante (*The Inferno*) and MacNeice ('Charon').

7. His daughter writes a clairvoyant poem about it: 'we saw a pale grey poniy / Daddy fel asleep by the streem' (32). Later, in hospital, Charon carries the 'Master' over to his last destination, the operation room (66). After the operation the same 'Romany' is present again with his 'mysterious poles' (70); he carries away the corpses (93).

8. Reading said the data in *C* was checked [LI]: 'A lot of those statements come from statements which doctors have made [in Hinton's book, for example].'

9. Elisabeth Kübler-Ross is a doctor, psychiatrist and internationally renowned thanatologist.

10. Unit 5 is autobiographical [C]: 'When I was a boy and read that section of Book V where shipwrecked Laertides crawls under two close-growing olives ...exhausted and finds shelter, I was deeply and permanently influenced.' (The 'metamorphosed' cushion alludes to the Latin pendant, Ovid's *Metamorphoses*). The spiritual comfort of this obsessive poetic memory is reiterated in *Final Demands* and *Last Poems* ('Idyllic').

11. Reading said he did not know Roger McGough's 13-line sonnets (*Unlucky for Some*, 1981, and *Waving at Trains*, 1982). The jokey allusion is to 'On First Looking Into Chapman's "Homer"'.

12. 'Oh weep for Adonais he is dead' (Shelley on Keats, *Adonais,* 1821), in Spenserian stanzas; and 'Sleep after toil, port after stormy seas, Ease after war, death after life, doth greatly please', the closing Alexandrine of the Spenserian stanza invented for *The Faerie Queene* (1.9.40).

13. Compare this technique with postmodern devices like *sous rature* ('two or more... mutually-exclusive states of affairs are projected by the same text'), *forking paths* or *metalepsis* ('the violation of narrative levels'), Brian McHale, *Postmodernist Fiction* (London, 1987), p.101, p.120. Rumens enumerates other intersections with (post)modern techniques: 'shifts of narrative focus, flashbacks, interior monologue, quoted excerpts, even an alternative dénouement'.

14. The authors quoted are the editors of the *Field Guide to the Birds of Britain and Europe*; the 'noble buzzard' is Anne Stevenson's. The 'Plashy Fen School' is taken from Waugh's novel *Scoop* (London, 1938), p.30.

Ukulele Music *(pp.128-43)*

1. Charles Boyle, 'Not Cricket', *London Magazine,* 25/8 (November 1985), pp.79-83; A.A. Cleary, 'Reviews of New Poetry', *Thames Poetry,* 2/16 (March 1985), p.41; P.J. Kavanagh, 'Christmas Books I. Books of the Year', *Spectator* (30 November 1985), p.29; John Kerrigan, 'Bouquets of barbed wire', *Sunday Times,* 8 September 1985, p.45; John Lucas, 'Gruesomely Gooey', *New Statesman,* (20 September 1985), pp.29-30; C.B. McCully, 'Voices Off', *PN Review,* 51 (1985), pp.73-76; John Mole, 'Conceit and Concern: Recent Poetry Reviewed', *Encounter,* 66/1 (January 1986), pp.55-62; Blake Morrison, 'Dialect does it', *London Review of Books,* 7/21 (5 December 1985), pp.14-15; Peter Porter, 'Cassettes of atrocity', *Observer,* 1 September 1985, p.19; Simon Rae, 'Black and over the top', *TLS,* 10 January 1986, p.34; S.J. Wiseman, 'Peter Reading: *Ukulele Music*', *British Book News* (September 1985), p.559; David Wright, 'Poetry's public voice', *Sunday Telegraph,* 15 December 1985, p.12.

2. Neil Corcoran, 'Junk Britain: Peter Reading's *Ukulele Music*', in *English Poetry Since 1940* (Harlow, 1993), pp. 254-57. Paulin, p.291. Kavanagh. Potts, 1992, p.30.

3. Fraser Steel, 'Travelling the Word', *Encounter,* 74/1 (January-February 1990), p.47.

4. Edgar, pp.56-57. The entry 'Politics and poetry' in Preminger's *Princeton Encyclopedia of Poetics* illuminates this connection: 'Poetry deals with man's whole sentient being, with his ideas and with his response to what is happening in the world around him, and it is not surprising that for centuries poets have attempted to shape into art their understanding of political ideas or to render permanent their perception of the political process... Political poetry is poetry that deals with public themes or public figures, with events that extend beyond the concerns of the individual self.' Reading could be termed a political poet only in this sense, just like Homer, Aeschylus, Dante, Shakespeare, or the Romantics.

5. Reading had dedicated *Ukulele Music* to John Christopher, a colleague at Sunderland, who had given him his charlady's note [LI] 'about the budgie, it was more or less verbatim. I only got that small one and did the rest from then on.' Viv was first mentioned in 'Eavesdropped' (*Nothing For Anyone*).

6. See Michael Ball, Fred Gray, Linda McDowell, *The Transformation of Britain. Contemporary and Economic Change* (London, 1989), or Alan Sinfield, Literature, Politics and Culture in Postwar Britain (London, 1989), especially regarding the 50% rise in criminality (p.380) and the general threat of poverty 'for large numbers of ordinary people' (p.417).

7. See Karl Shapiro & Robert Beum, *A Prosody Handbook* (New York, 1965), Chapter 8, 'The Uses of Metre', pp. 66-85: expression of feeling, formalism, engaging interest, sensuous vividness, unity and variation, variation for emphasis, securing attention, heuristic function, order, mnemonic value.

8. In the elegiac distich, the dactylic hexameter is followed by a dactylic pentameter: $-\,\smile\,\smile\mid-\,\smile\,\smile\mid-\,\smile\,\smile\mid--\mid-\,\smile\,\smile\mid--\mid\mid-\,\smile\,\smile\mid-\,\smile\,\smile\mid-\mid-\,\smile\,\smile\mid$ $-\,\smile\,\smile\mid-$. The hexameter usually has five dactyls and one spondee, while any dactyl but the fifth can be substituted by a spondee, too. For a retarding effect, the fourth and sixth dactyls are often substituted by spondees, as shown in the notation above. The pentameter consists of two hemiepes divided by a caesura, i.e. twice two-and-a-half feet (strictly speaking a catalectic hexameter).

9. Substituting stress for length, Reading strictly follows the form of the distich in this book; in later works, it is used more freely, becoming fragmented in the end. The first stress is unnatural in English, necessitating inversion, which heightens the grave effect and does not permit redundancies. The hemiepes also 'carries weight and emphasises things' [LI], because the falling cadence is also a reciprocus versus, which works best with monosyllabic words and masculine endings. Occasionally, when the syntax runs counter to the hemiepes to avoid monotony, the effect can be intense or ironic (see the 5th and 8th distich, p.11, or 'this Great Country', p.15).

10. This authentic episode, in which an elderly lady was injured, occurred in Liverpool, where Reading was waiting at a bus-stop: 'But none of us *did* anything, for this sort of occurrence is no longer unusual.' The episode of the spitting boys in a shopping area in London SW11 was also witnessed by Reading. 'Again, nobody *did* anything' (Reading, 'Going', p.33).

11. The faceless lion is of course a symbol of Great Britain; in front of it, Arabs queue peacefully alongside Jews, while 'tabloids blown underfoot headline a couple of global débâcles'. The idiom inside this image – to place oneself in the lion's mouth – describes the human species' conduct. This episode may have been inspired by a passage in Leonard Woolf's autobiography about his visits to zoos in foreign countries. In *Stet* (p.93) Reading used Woolf's words about the Jerusalem zoo almost verbatim.

12. Interview with David Hart, 'Reading between the lines', *Arts Report* (West Midlands Arts), April 1985, quotation from unpublished manuscript [M]. Reading could not be broadcast on BBC for this reason.

13. For the precise figures, see Alan Sinfield, *Literature, Politics and Culture in Postwar Britain* (Oxford, 1989), pp.368, 367.

14. O'Driscoll, p.207. See also Potts, 1990, p.95. The poem refers to Auden: '"No summer sun will ever/ dismantle the global gloom/ cast by the Daily Papers, / vomiting in slip-shod prose/ the facts of filth and violence/ that we're too dumb to prevent"' (quoted in Reading, 'Going', p.37).

15. In *Perduta Gente*, this echo of Virgil's words to Dante (*Inferno*) is quoted directly: 'all we can do is observe and silently pass by.' (The parabase 'D'ye see' is always employed when the Captain has something of particular importance to communicate to the reader.)

16. MacNeice in 'Bagpipe Music' (1937): 'The glass is falling hour by hour,

the glass will fall for ever,/ But if you break the bloody glass you won't hold up the weather.' He refers to Auden's poem of 1936 (which had also been the pre-text for Reading's 'Dead Horse'): '...dance while you can. / Dance, dance, for the figure is easy / The tune is catching and will not stop / Dance till the stars come down with the rafters / Dance, dance, dance till you drop' (*The English Auden. Poems, Essay and Dramatic Writings, 1927-1937*, ed. Edward Mendelson [London, 1977], pp.205-06).

17. This poem was entitled 'Background music' in a magazine publication. It also has an affinity with Reading's last painting, which shows two performing musicians in a chequered cell-like room.

18. Jenkins, 1985, p.12. These are based on the same accounts of *Shipwrecks and Disasters at Sea*, which figure in *Tom o'Bedlam's Beauties*, where the Captain is also an inmate: 'it actually went back to some 17th century events...It was a book which I had had for a long time, picked up from a second-hand shop when I was an art student and had always just thoroughly enjoyed reading' [LI].

19. See one of the verbal echoes binding this strand to Viv's (p. 20: '*my Tom plays the bones to tunes of George Formby*'). 'Xysterical' is a neologism created from 'hysterical', 'xylophone' and 'xyster' (instrument for scraping bones).

20. The Japanese name of the mate on the 'Lucky Dragon' who notices the catastrophe points to the Japanese stanza form. Between 1946 and 1958 (or 1962) the USA carried out 23 atom tests in the West Pacific.

21. The ukulele handbook explains (p.44): 'the beginner may find his fingers just a little bit stiff and clumsy but this disappears quickly after a little practice!' Reading [LI]: 'That's the case with any metre, I think, that you learn to live with it and can handle it after a while without thinking too terribly...' After a while, Viv has had enough of this '*Allergic Dis Talk*', '*I'm going back to me prowse*' (p.43), but in her very next communication she falls back into elegiac distich without even noticing it (p.45) – that is how 'nat'ral' it can be.

22. The biblical source of the storm is Jeremiah (30.23); see also the Jeremiade in *Perduta Gente* (p.185, 207) and Isaiah's words (10.1-4).

23. The Cimmerians, nomads from South Russia, in the 8th century raided Assyria and Asia Minor, where they destroyed everything. According to Homer (Odyssey, XI.14) they lived in a land beyond the ocean where the sun never shone. Reading's neologism 'unvisible' hints at that.

24. In 'Canto I', Pound writes an 'Anglo-Saxon' paraphrase of Andreas Divus' Latin paraphrase (16th century) of Homer's *Odyssey* (which makes Reading fourth in line). Reading [LI]: 'it's fair to say that it was in mind, though, because it is something that I [read] – and it is one of the more lucid bits of [Pound] that you can actually understand.'

25. Although no text has been translated more often into English than the *Odyssey*, O'Brien calls this passage an 'Ovidian moment'; *The Deregulated Muse* (Newcastle upon Tyne, 1998), p.127.

Going On (pp.144-55)

1. For references to reviews of *Going On*, see the reviews of *Ukulele Music* (the books were reviewed as one).

2. What Reading thinks is 'top-secret' ([LI], 'I'm extremely sentimental and sensitive, but one doesn't want everybody to know that'), can be gathered from every book he has ever written. Cleary also thought this in her review.

Reading [LI]: 'I want to be able to be that without being bad literature', as he does, for instance, in the lyrical pieces about birds, wine, and picnics.

3. Of all the critical assessments of Reading that fail to see the functions of certain artistic devices and ignore the difference between what happens in "art" and in "life", the two most misconceived contributions are by Hugh Buckingham in the (American-edited) 5th edition of *Contemporary Poets* (ed. Tracy Chevalier (Chicago/London, 1991), and by Sean O'Brien ('The Poet as Thatcherite' in *The Deregulated Moose* [Newcastle upon Tyne, 1998]).

4. 'True Duck' is taken up in a poem in *Shitheads* written apropos Salman Rushdie's death sentence (set to music by Jeremy Drake). *Australopithecus* lived 1.5 to 5 million years ago and is as related to apes as to humans.

5. Jenkins, 1985, p.11. Coggrave always told Reading that he was subject to 'galactic intimidation' [M].

6. The original fragments used for *Going On* are in: Denys Lionel Page, *Lyrica Graeca Selecta* (Oxford, 1968): Alcman pp.1-28 (Fragments 1-47), Alcaeus pp.55-96 (Fragments 107-190). (Translation: *The Greek Lyrics. The Lyrical Fragments* also contains Fragments by Alcman). The monodic lyricist Alcaeus was the most famous of the Aeolian poets; very little Aeolian verse survives. Alcman was Spartan (also 7th century BC).

7. Tennyson's 'metrical gymnastics', as Reading put it [LI], included this Alcaic poem about Milton: 'O mighty-mouth'd inventor of harmonies / o skilled to sing of time or eternity / God-gifted organ, voice of England / Milton, a name to resound for ages.' (Tennyson/Swinburne, *Attempts at Classic Metres in Quantity*, 1863). (The misprint 'weekly' in the *Collected* should read 'weakly'.)

8. George Saintsbury, *A History of Prosody from the 12h Century to the Present Day* (New York, 1961). Ewald Standop, *Abriß der englischen Metrik* (Munich, 1989).

9. Karl Shapiro, Robert Beum, *A Prosody Handbook* (New York, 1965), pp.156-157, p.158.

10. Further evidence: whether the Saturnian, one of the earliest Latin metres, 'was quantitative or accentual remains an unresolved problem' (Preminger, p.740).

11. See Cotterill's translation in: Walter Leaf (ed.), *Homer's Odyssey* (London, 1924). In his illuminative introduction, Cotterill explains how exactly to catch the effect of Homer's hexameters, and he also says (p.9): 'what I longed to do was to reproduce the original... in its simplicity, its directness, and its rapidity – characteristics that...were scarcely discernible in the metrical versions that I had seen.'

Stet *(pp.156-72)*

1. 'The man whose pen even insults himself', *Evening Gazette*, 16 December 1986; Margaret Drabble, 'Book of the year', *Observer*, 30 November 1986, p.21.

2. Robin Lane Fox, 'Poetry enjoys a new upswing', *Financial Times*, 7 February 1987, p.12; Mick Imlah, 'Hard and hope-free', *TLS*, 8 May 1987, p.487; Peter Porter, 'English, their English', *Observer*, 9 November 1986, p.28.

3. Julian Symons, 'The brass tacks approach', *Sunday Times*, 9 November 1986, p.55. Jeff Nuttall, 'Poetry', *Time Out* (26 November 1986). Damian Grant, 'An Englishman, an Irishman and a Scotsman', *London Review of Books*, 9/9 (7 May 1987), pp.22-23.

4. As *Stet* usually has several untitled short poems on one page, I have

numbered them consecutively for identification: starting recto ('Pyrex, a pie-dish...') with no.1 and ending verso on p.116 with no.79.

5. From W.H. Auden, *Poems* (1930), his first book.

6. As Grant says, 'Orwell maintained that fishing was the opposite of war; Peter Reading seems to offer bird-watching as the antithesis to atrocity.'

7. The increasing indentation visualises the falling cadence. Simultaneously, Reading's system of different indentations helps a reader with an untrained or unreliable 'musical ear' to identify certain metres or stanza forms.

8. The following numbers refer to the poems where these verse forms are *first* used; there are, of course, other poems with these verse forms.

9. Quoted from the judges' TV discussion about the Whitbread Award in John Gaskell, 'Brewer's book', *Sunday Telegraph* (18 January 1986).

10. The Alcmanic stanza introduced in *Going On* suits the pub bore very well as the length can vary and go on a bit; doggerel-platitudes are best served by the greetings card metre. The *Stet*-stanza is compactly welded to contain imagery and reflection about the particular theme in a very concentrated form. The single short Alcaic stanza (also from *Going On*) takes over the function of previous tankas and haiku, i.e. delivers epigrammatic observations, little vignettes and short glimpses. Finally, the iambic pentameter is kept neutral and thus carries a matter-of-fact presentation of facts, which is only occasionally enriched by auctorial comments.

11. Grant is the only one to recognise the binary structure, but only discusses it with respect to style and narrative. In his review only the 'outer plot' is scrutinised.

12. One example of many elaborate metaphors may suffice: here it is the Holm Oak (symbol of Great Britain's power) which is trimmed by the man with the axe and loses its sap from below and which loses its power of regeneration from above by the male blossoms getting stripped. In this poem various allusions, links to other poems, puns and metaphors are concentrated, e.g. in 'skull-cleaving', 'Harriers', '*Quercus ilex*', 'sap' und 'poised blade'. The explicit parallel in no.42 is almost superfluous, even if the unity of the book is thus emphasised. See other parallels, as in no.59, in which the sound waves 'judder a fossil bivalve free' from their 400 million-years-old rock matrix, which, in turn, falls onto the wrecked 'Viva' car (8), or the sonic wave parallelling the apprentice's violent death: both the entire nation and the individual are victimised.

13. Paulin, who came to see Reading as a radical, is the only critic to identify this nostalgia, or rather, one facet of it: 'Reading's hatred of technology and commercial jargon points to a nostalgia for an "organic" culture buried under acres of light industry on the fringes of Britain's towns and cities' (Paulin, 1992, p.290).

14. See Peter Reading's review of Roy Fuller, *New and Collected Poems 1934-84* (Secker), 'The English Decline', *Poetry Review*, 75/3 (September 1985), pp.64-65.

15. Elgar, too, offers both elegy and encomium (in *nobilmente* movements and 'Land of Hope and Glory'). Possibly this is one of the reasons for Elgar's appearance in poem no.33 as one of the national heroes, alongside Shaftesbury, Dickens, Florence Nightingale and Faraday.

16. Clio is the muse of history, who invented heroic and historical poetry.

17. Generally, the unveiled personal element in this book seems to affect the reader rather strongly, perhaps because it is usually masked.

18. Ironically dubbed the 'last real British achievement', the expedition was only *led* by Colonel John Hunt. The fact that the first men on the summit were not British (Sherpa Tenzing Norguay was Nepalese and Sir Edmund Hillary from New Zealand) adds even more poignancy to the image of faded British imperialist glamour. In 1993, this poem was turned into a new version (like no.1) and given a punning title ('Double Bill'). In *Last Poems*, it was reworked again and entitled 'Regal'.

19. Some reviewers regard this poem as the centrepiece of the book (which would mean ignoring the 'secret agenda'). O'Driscoll, p.217. In a magazine publication it was entitled 'Traveller's Fare' (cf. Charon's toll for the under-world).

20. Peter Reading, review of Larkin's *Letters* (ed. Anthony Thwaite), 'Hapless old fart', *Island*, 55 (25 June 1993), p.53.

21. Reading, with his sillographical gift, can never resist attacking religious fanatics. First he takes up the zoo-metaphor of *Ukulele Music*: the hexametrical Lucretian line *'tantum religio potuit suadere malorum'* is (hexametrically) rendered as 'Heights of pernicious stupidity grow from molehills of nonsense' (24). This is a quotation from Leonard Woolf, *Downhill all the Way: An Autobiography of the Years 1919-1939* (London, 1967), p.43, where he observes that zoos are mirrors of the respective countries, as in this case in Jerusalem (1957): 'The architecture of the zoo seemed a ramshackle replica of the surrounding streets, and long-haired monkeys gazed at one, it seemed to me, with the self-satisfaction of all the orthodox who have learned eternal truth from the primeval monkey, all the scribes and pharisees who spend all their lives making mountains of pernicious stupidity out of molehills of nonsense.' Lucretius is again invoked in no.67 (*De Rerum Natura*, I, 101: such are the heights of wickedness to which men are driven by religion).

22. Edmund Burke (1729-97), 'Man is by his constitution a religious animal' (*Reflections on the Revolutions in France*).

23. Like the palaeontologist before, the astrophysicist has 'no interest whatsoever in our local system, in isolation' (9) and also calls religion 'mumbo-jumbo'. He is 'Quite happy to accept Reasonless causal physics' (62). With his radiotelescope, he records radiating hydrogen atoms while they are moving through the universe at high velocity in interstellar clouds of gas. The search is for the great explosions of the quasars, the most remote luminary sources currently known, 10,000 million light years away.

24. The 'Lady's Album of 1826' had indeed been the (authentic) source of the reticent lines in '"Iuppiter ex alto..."' (*Nothing For Anyone*).

25. Michael Donahue died in 1985, the year before the publication of *Stet*.

Final Demands (*pp.173-86*)

1. Jonathan Barker, 'Poetry '88', *British Book News* (November 1988), p.820; Martin Booth, 'Transcending the pain', *Tribune* (22 April 1988), p.8; Margaret Drabble, 'Antique and contemporary savagery', *Sunday Times*, 6 March 1988, p.5; Carol Ann Duffy, 'Stain upon the silence', *Guardian*, 11 March 1988, p.23; Peter Forbes, 'Operating systems go', *Independent*, 7 July 1988, p.15; Alan Jenkins, 'Bar-room philosopher', *Observer*, 20 March 1988, p.43; Eric Korn, 'Singing the unsingable', *TLS*, 15 April 1988, p.419; Herbert Lomas, 'The Poetic Enterprise', *London Magazine* (July 1988), pp.92-96; Bernard O'Donoghue, 'Letters from Tonge', *Poetry Review*, 78/2 (Summer 1988), pp.62-63; Robert

Sheppard, 'Time's the whole sequence', *New Statesman*, 116/2981 (13 May 1988), p.31.

2. Lomas; Robert Crawford, 'Cut-Ups', *London Review of Books*, 2/23 (7 December 1989), p.26. Drabble: 'arid exercises do not enrage and disturb as Reading enrages and disturbs. His vision of life is profoundly compassionate ...This is not cleverness. It is poetry.' Duffy: 'a sense of compassion (where one perhaps expected anger) is what one receives most strongly on reading *Final Demands*; the cleverness, the assured deployment of poetics, are secondary here, which is as it should be. The poetry is in the pity.'

3. O'Donoghue. In an interview with Reading, O'Donoghue was told later: 'I haven't really aspired to be a novelist, and I don't think I've got the skill to be a novelist, frankly... all I've tried to do is make it possible to do some novelistic jobs within the framework of what I can get away with, if you like, on somebody's poetry list, and I've got away with murder in the past (interview on *Spectrum*, 'Bernard O'Donoghue and Peter Reading', BBC Radio Oxford, 12 April 1992 [M]). Henceforward: (O'Donoghue, M).

4. Neil Roberts, 'Poetic Subjects: Tony Harrison and Peter Reading', in *British Poetry from the 1950s to the 1990s: Politics and Art*, ed. Gary Day & Brian Docherty (London, 1997), 48-62, p.59.

5. Eric Korn: 'I have a godfather's... tenderness for Peter Reading's *Final Demands*. A year ago I was rooting through bookshop detritus when I found a sheaf of Victorian family letters, fumblingly speaking of distresses, hinting at passions. They were not commercial: but it seemed to me they might set Reading ruminating. I scattered them in his direction; now I feel like Johnny Appleseed. The old cores I threw have produced orchards.' The names in these letters are authentic [C], so the mention of 'Mr Bulstrode and Mrs Cross' is a nice coincidence, evoking rich associations of provincial town life in the 19th century.

6. The 'Major's' letters are from Diana Reading's father's estate and were probably written by him; the mothers' letters had been addressed to him. 'They're slightly fictionalised by me and accentuated, but they're founded in truth, as is the final report' [LI].

7. Herbert Lomas seemed not to recognise Reading's hexameters and pentameters. Korn's examples in his eulogy were also dubious. This was pointed out in a letter to the editor ('"Final Demands"', *TLS*, no.4440 [6 May 1988], p.503), signed 'E.W. Gray', giving Reading's parents' address (Gray is his father's first name). The letter was written by Reading, who wanted to avoid the embarrassment of correcting a reviewer he valued [C]. Korn's reply was published in the *TLS*, 20-26 May 1988, p.555.

8. The juvenilia is 'Horticulture', a poem from *Water and Waste*. It showed the old 'A. Barns., B.A.' killing his flowers with 'Liquinure', and here the image, worthy of preservation, is reworked – before the Parkray is lit with it.

9. The laurier as the plant of Apollo symbolises 'the spirit of prophecy and poetry, hence the custom of crowning the Pythoness... and poets, and of putting laurel leaves under one's pillow to acquire inspiration...The laurel in modern times is a symbol of victory and peace, and of excellence in literature and the arts' (*Brewer's Dictionary of Phrase & Fable*). Soon after, Apollo's violin appears as the polished old fiddle of Gypsy Moses (p.121).

10. Even the smallest details have thematic connotations. Croxley Heritage is 100 percent recycling paper of the highest quality – a worthy carrier of the 'recycled' texts (and generations) of the volume. Papyrus creates a natural

link with the process of writing, just as the 'bond' paper indicates 'final demands' of a financial nature.

11. Compare the death symbolism of the 'pale horse', the 'Romany', the colour green (see the chapter on *C*) and then the symbolism of the leitmotif words 'ash', 'char' and 'dead leaves'. The horse of the Apocalypse also appears in the poet's game of chess with his father (p.150): '(tongue-lolling, wild-eyed) the crazed palfrey of pale polished ash' (punning on 'ash', too). (The colourful gypsy clothes already had death connotations in the suicide scene in *Tom o'Bedlam's Beauties* [p.199]).

12. Coggrave, an expert on Joyce, wrote that 'Reading is a reader of *Finnegans Wake*' and quoted from p.18 [M]: 'This ourth of ours is not save brickdust and being humus the same roturns. He who runes may rede it on all fours'. Apparently, Reading once quoted the first 20 pages of the *Wake* to Coggrave verbatim [C]. The phrase 'half to reveal and half conceal' is also a reference to Tennyson's Introduction to 'In Memoriam'.

13. Reading explained the background [LI]: 'I just felt obliged to record this experience. I flushed one up; all that was left behind, down in this warm place that it had sat in in the frost, was a breast-feather and a little fecal sac that it had dropped as it took off. They take off very abruptly and zigzag through the trees. Very exciting and primitive little birds'. The poem was entitled 'S. rusticola' [Scolopax] in a magazine publication.

14. The old military man with the homonymically brutal name was already introduced as 'Peregrine Fashpoint-Shellingem' and inmate of an asylum in *Tom o'Bedlam's Beauties*.

15. 'riddles the brainpans of vassals/viscounts' echoes '?' (*Tom o Bedlam's Beauties*), the riddle about another 'democratic' (mental) illness.

16. By Reading's 12th book, some critics still ignored all stances and narrative levels, e.g. Forbes: 'But mostly it is the morose old hypochondriac Reading taking a dim and distant view of things.'

Perduta Gente *(pp.187-205)*

1. Anna Adams, '*Perduta Gente*. Peter Reading', *The Green Book*, 3/3 (Autumn 1989), pp.88-89; Alan Brownjohn, 'Memoranda from Cardboard City', *Sunday Times*, 9 July 1989, p.14; Robert Crawford, 'Cut-Ups', *London Review of Books*, 2/23 (7 December 1989), p.26; Douglas Dunn, 'Last lines of defence', *Evening Standard*, 3 August 1989, p.34; Gavin Ewart, 'Reading Peter Reading', *Poetry Book Society Bulletin*, 141 (Summer 1989), pp.1-2; David Hart, 'Brief Reviews', *People to People*, 9 (Autumn 1989), p.22; Mick Imlah, 'Doses of radiation', *TLS*, 25 August 1989, p.916; John Lucas, 'Hallo to the art of poetry', *New Statesman* (1 September 1989), p.34; Blake Morrison, 'South Bank shower', *Observer*, 18 June 1989, p.44; Jeff Nuttall, 'On Recent Verse', *Time Out* (23 August 1989), p.46; Harold Pinter, ('A special eight-page supplement recommends the best buys for giving and reading this Christmas)', *Observer*, 3 December 1989, p.65; David Profumo, 'Heart's rag-and-bone-shop', *Sunday Telegraph*, 20 August 1989, p.38; Mark Robinson, 'Reviews', *Scratch*, 1 (November 1989), p.37; Fraser Steel, 'Travelling the Word', *Encounter*, 74/1 (January-February 1990), pp.47-51; John Whitworth, 'But What Does He Want?', *Poetry Review*, 79/3 (Autumn 1989), pp.40-41.

2. Whitworth. Before: 'John Whitworth interviewed by John Whitworth, 'Judicious Prodding by Whitworth', *Poetry Review*, 79/1 (Spring 1989), pp.6-7.

See also Whitworth in *Poetry Review*, 77/1 (April 1987), p.41, p.52.

3. Interview on *In Tempo*, 'Peter Reading interviewed by Sandy McCutcheon', ABC Radio, Hobart, 9 December 1989 [M].

4. For the first time, anacrusis and hypercatalexis (a large number of them, too) are tolerated in the tidy 'antique' metres. 'It was getting a bit looser' [LI], Reading confirmed. This was the first step towards the dispersed Alcaic verses in *Evagatory*.

5. This is now the fourth variant: after distichs on one line (*Ukulele Music*), the typographical trithemimeres-break (*Going On*), and then the whole verse lines again (*Stet, Final Demands*), the hexameter in *Perduta Gente* is given with bucolic diaeresis as in Cotterill (see the chapter on *Going On*). This means three indentations in each distich (and its variants), the last being reserved for splicing the pentameter; it makes them easier to read, just as the metre facilitates the pronunciation and stress of the many Latinate words (e.g. 'etiolated'). Reading's argument was that [LI] 'in an English printed book of normal octavo size it's very difficult to get complete hexameters in'; he also considered the division after the fourth foot as 'logical'.

6. Verbal echoes like 'skedaddle/skedaddler, yellow and black, tenebrous, squatting, city, rats' create parallels between the different episodes, and the repetition of words such as 'expiry, foetid, tenebrous, tumbril, exhaling, etiolated, crushed, blighted' strengthen text cohesion phonologically.

7. Dorothy L. Sayers (trs.), *The Divine Comedy* (Harmondsworth, 1949 [1984]).

8. 'The sullen [men] sighing' is Reading's introduction to the vestibule; 'Dis' (Hell) itself has 9 more circles. See *A Dictionary of Biblical Tradition in English Literature*, ed. David Lyle Jeffrey (Michigan, 1992), pp. 341-43, about the literary treatment of the topography of Hell.

9. Alan Sinfield, *Literature, Politics and Culture in Postwar Britain* (Oxford, 1989), has the details of homelessness in Britain (pp.409-12, 448). See also Andrew O'Hagan, 'Walk on by: Andrew O'Hagan goes begging', *London Review of Books*, 15/22 (18 November 1993), pp.9-14.

10. The biography quotes from diary pages, and some quotes recur in poems; these were therefore written by the homeless author (pp.182, 191).

11. Reading commented [LI]: 'That actual account comes from some sociological account of such dossers that I picked up... So that's pretty literal... somewhere along the great shelves of... public libraries,... there were some tape-recorded interviews with one or two bozos, and so there were some first-hand accounts... about how to survive... And the assault on [the nuns] was from the account from one of the practitioners of meths anyway if I remember rightly.'

12. Begging at that time was prohibited by penalty of £50 or three days' incarceration. Most beggars never had more than £10, so the penalty could only be paid by more begging. In 'Operation Taurus' in 1991 several hundred beggars were arrested; most were aged 17 to 29, and more were under 16 than over 60 (O'Hagan, *LRB*). Note also the present Labour Party's 'zero tolerance' approach.

13. After a hendecasyllabic verse from the *Inferno* (Canto III, 16). The remaining stanza refers to Canto III, 22-23.

14. *Inferno*, Canto III, 47-48, 64, 37, 22, 26, 23, 131-32, 28, 56, and especially verse 51, the last sentence, 'let us not speak of these; but look, and pass'.

15. See God's warning to Jeremiah (30.12-30.16), who in turn warns Jerusalem in the Lamentations (1.1-1.2): 'How doth the city sit solitary, that was full of people!', etc. For the last two stanzas, see Isaiah (10.1-10.4): 'Woe unto them that decree unrighteous decrees, and that write grievousness which they have prescribed; To turn aside the needy from judgment, and to take away the right from the poor of my people, that widows may be their prey, and that they may rob the fatherless! And what will ye do in the day of visitation, and in the desolation which shall come from far? to whom will ye flee for help? and where will ye leave your glory? Without me they shall bow down under the prisoners, and they shall fall under the slain...' (King James Bible).

'Woe' is used in Dante's Canto III, 84; 'Let us descend' comes from Canto IV, 13 and V, 1; 'al doloroso ospizio' is the place of pain.

16. The story of a lonely walk through the Moscow woods at dusk and the discovery of men at campfires drinking vodka and eating smoked fish was mine. Reading was working on another book then (January 1988), but still asked for the 'copyright' [C].

17. Thomas Hardy, *Jude the Obscure* [1896] (Harmondsworth, 1982), p.413. *The Agamemnon of Aeschylus,* trs. Louis MacNeice (London, 1936), p.15: 'Things are what they are, will finish / In the manner fated and neither / Fire beneath nor oil above can soothe / The stubborn anger of the unburnt offering. / As for us, bodies are bankrupt, / The expedition left us behind / And we wait'.

18. Peter Reading, 'Compulsively moribund', *TLS*, 30 September 1988, p.1068.

19. See the 'Acknowledgments' in *Grace* and the journalist's research (*Grace,* pp.2-3, 13, 29).

20. 'Rads' is the unit for absorbed radioactivity. On the opposite page the Energy Authority informs us that 450 rads suffice to kill 50% of contaminated individuals.

21. It reiterates verses from pp.160, 163, 171, 173, 207, 162, 170.

Shitheads *(pp.206-13)*

1. Carol Ann Duffy, 'Bright trickles', *Guardian,* 12 July 1990, p.22; Chris Hurford, 'Resisting redundancy', *TLS,* 21 December 1990, p.1383; Peter Porter, 'Muses on an expedition', *Observer,* 20 May 1990, p.59.

2. 'Prouerbes xiij.iij' (p.235) is an adaptation of the Biblical Proverb; 'Holidaywise' (p.216) recreates fashionable parlance; and 'Translationese' (p.217) translates poetry into prose and draws a parallel with a poem by Catullus. 'Ye haue heard this yarn afore' (p.225) is an adaptation of an earlier poem by Reading; the two poems entitled 'Managerial' are translations of one another (pp.217, 220); 'Vagrants' mentions the difficult Birmingham accent (p.220); and 'Parallel' (p.231) gives a translation of itself.

3. Caine kept renaming his publishing house anyway, because he could not settle on one name (previous names included Scargill Press, Krassivy and Livres d'Enfer).

4. Caine [M]: 'The book was done very classically... to heighten the irony between the classical design & the seemingly obscene words.'

5. For a good introduction to Catullus' life and work, see Peter Whigham, *The Poems of Catullus: A Bilingual Edition* (Berkeley, repr. 1983; Harmondsworth, 1966). It is interesting to note that the poetic qualities he praises in his introduction are similar to Reading's.

6. Reading and Pitter used the (monolingual) edition of Michael Austin (ed.), *Catullus (Gaius V)* (Oxford 1958 [1991]), which was part of the Clarendon

Press series Scriptorum classicorum Bibliotheca Oxoniensis, in which the Alcman fragments had been published, too. Reading adopted Austin's numbering of the poems in *Shitheads*.

7. Jacob Rabinowitz, *Gaius Valerius Catullus's Complete Poetic Works* (Dallas/ Texas, 1991).

8. Compare Reading's version of poem XCIII (p.219): 'I'm not over-sedulous, Caesar, in trying to win your approval, / nor do I seek to enquire if you're a white man or black' with Rabinowitz' version (in his order, no.103): 'CAESAR? Caesar who?' Whigham's version lies in between the two: 'Utter indifference to your welfare, Caesar, / is matched only by ignorance of who you are.'

9. Ravidus was one of Clodia's ('Lesbia') other lovers, as was 'Lesbius', her criminal brother. Gellius, who here is also accused of incest, was L. Gellius Poplicola, presumably also a rival for 'Lesbia's' favours and later (36 BC) consul. Caesar is the emperor himself, whom Catullus attacks in some poems for his alleged pederasty and patronage of Mamurra.

10. A friend of Caine's, Colin Kennedy, had modelled the woodcut after a photograph taken by Edward Martin in 1987 on Blackpool promenade; it showed a stall full of baseball caps, some with a plastic turd on the peak and the word 'Shithead' on the crown – they were sold to and worn by holidaymakers.

11. Jeremy Drake (genuine name), a Paris-based composer, set this poem to music in 1990.

12. Reading's personal opinion of Rushdie's apology at the time was uncompromisingly hard, thinking it 'rather wimpish that he tried to renege what he'd said' [C]. Rushdie had obviously written a good book ... and what was after all the reason for writing if not '100 percent commitment' [C].

13. 'He that keepeth his mouth keepeth his life: but he that openeth wide his lips shall have destruction' (Proverbs 13.3).

14. Simon Rae had asked for a poem for his anthology *The Orange Dove of Fiji* (London, 1989; the title referring to a threatened bird species), and Reading gave him this, which he had already written. The anthology was reviewed in the *TLS* among other places: Simon Carnell, 'The saving image', *TLS*, 15-21 December 1989, p.1392. Another "green" anthology, in which Reading features prominently, is by Norbert H. Platz, Birgit Fiddelke, Anne Unfried (eds.), *Sustaining the Earth: An Anthology of Green Poems in English* (Kiel, 1998).

15. In these Eurospeak macaroni-verses one can identify Yiddish, French, English, Spanish, Italian, German, and baby language.

16. The 7-5-5-5-5-5-7 syllables make seven lines per stanza, of which five always contain five syllables. This is obviously derived from the tanka (5-7-5-7-7), which Reading had often used before.

Evagatory (pp.214-27)

1. Three years before, at the 'Poetry World Festival' in Toronto, Chatto's then poetry editor (Andrew Motion) had suggested Reading change to Chatto; by that time, Reading's dissatisfaction with Secker's poor marketing and PR work had come to outweigh his hitherto strong 'feelings of loyalty' [C].

2. The reading of *Evagatory* and parts of *Diplopic* was video-taped for the (continuing) Lannan Literary Series [M]. Reading used slides and an audio-

tape for a representation of the skull and of the last pages. The three voices (Reading's, Jenkins' and Imlah's, then Chatto's poetry editor) speak the same text over each other, or alternate rapidly, and the sound eventually becomes more muffled and distant. At the end, Reading throws the book away and abruptly leaves the stage.

3. Peter Forbes, 'Poetry for the '90s', *British Book News* (October 1992), p.671; John A.C. Greppin, 'Yᵉ True Quack', *TLS*, 21 February 1992, p.21; David Hart, 'Brief Reviews', *People to People*, 16 (March 1992), p.20; Hugo Giles, 'Reading, writing and epic wanderings', *The Mercury*, 17 October 1992; Hermione Lee, 'Poor mad islanders', *Independent on Sunday*, 16 February 1992, p.30; Glyn Maxwell, 'Desperanto', *Poetry Review*, 82/2 (Summer 1992), pp. 53-54; Sean O'Brien, 'Farctate with feculence', *Sunday Times*, 22 March 1992, p.10; Peter Porter, 'Doing what comes naturally', *Sunday Telegraph*, 23 February 1992, p.12; Eileen Shaw, '3 in 1. Peter Reading', *Northern Star*, 17-19 March 1992; Greg Williams, 'Pages reek of burning anger', *Eltham Times*, 13 February 1992; Greg Williams, 'Ivor focuses on the golden age of cameras', *Bexleyhead & Welling Times,* 27 February 1992; 'A Guide to Summer Reading: ...our selection of 40 leading titles... from this year', *Independent on Sunday*, 19 July 1992, p.33; Keith Brace, 'A nation on the right lines', *Weekend Birmingham Post* (no details).

4. Porter; Maxwell; Greppin. One Ronald Walker wrote a disgusted letter about Greppin and Reading (24 February 1992, M), asking for Reading to be informed of his criticism, who duly used it for 'To the Editor', printed exclusively in the *Independent on Sunday* (5 July 1992), p.7: 'The Editor, the Times Lit Supp, Dear Sir, / I feel compelled to say that your reviewer / disgusts me by his praise of one P Reading. / I have to wonder whether yr reviewer / can recognise a poem when he sees one! / He quotes the words 'All that remains, the stench/ of excrement' and calls it a 'one-line poem'. / Is this obtuseness or some obscure joke? /... / ...It's time / someone protested at this sunken level / of taste and judgement in the 'literature' / you are purveying. I remain yrs truly, / 'Offended Sensibility', Evesham.'

5. The original elegies are in the *Exeter Book*: W.S. Mackie (ed.), *The Exeter Book*, Part I and II (1934).

6. Michael Alexander, *The Earliest English Poems* (Harmondsworth, 1966 [repr. 1975]), p.63. Alexander's explanations are important in so far as Reading's knowledge of Old English poetry came primarily from his book [C]; it is the source of Anglo-Saxon concepts and quotations in *Evagatory.*

7. Alexander, Preface: '*wierd*: this all-important word is related to *weorthan*, to be, become or happen. It means "what is, what happens, the way that things happen. Fate, personal destiny, death".' Reading uses the Shakespearean spelling 'weird' (see the 'weird/wierd sisters' in *Macbeth*).

8. *Historia Ecclesiastica Gentis Anglorum by Beda Venerabilis* (*c.* 672-735), translated by Alexander, p.64.

9. Alexander, p.64.

10. There are further echoes in *Evagatory* of *The Wanderer* and *The Seafarer*, e.g. the *Word-Hoard* in the *Ubi sunt* poem in *Evagatory*, taken from the *Wanderer* ('Where is gone the horse? where is gone the hero? where is gone the giver of treasure?', line 92), or the anticipation of the cuckoo signalling spring on land, or the fear of unavoidable fate.

11. The nostalgic line started in *Stet* with Elgar, which gives the poem for Roy Fuller ('Elgarian sadness') its rightful place here. The significance of the

nautical weather report from *Ukulele Music* is carried over, as are the signs of fate in the skies of *Going On*, which give the *vates* poet his augural role. The 'wandering dosser' motif was used in *Perduta Gente*, and the 'carcinogenic sunrise' alludes to *C*; and a brutal episode from *Ukulele Music* is incorporated, complete with the quotation 'inferior / beings infest and despoil earth' (p.233). There are allusions to the ecological collapse of *Nothing For Anyone*, to the car accident of *Stet*, and verbal echoes of *Tom o'Bedlam's Beauties, For the Municipality's Elderly,* and *Diplopic.*

12. 'Provincial' (p.234) shows Reading's 'grief gush[ing] raw again' at the death of his best friend; the link is to p.230. '*I.M.* R.F.' (p.227) is a pure cento, quoting from Fuller's *Home and Dry* and *Available for Dreams,* and referring to Edward Gibbon, *The History of the Decline and Fall of the Roman Empire* (1776).

13. In November 1989 Reading had given readings in Sidney, Hobart and Melbourne.

14. The deportation of convicts to New South Wales lasted from 1788 until 1840, and to Tasmania until 1853. Westwood's story is authentic (see Hobart Museum), but Reading said [LI], 'the letter is mine. The facts are correct, and he wrote to a chaplain saying some of those things.'

15. Reading was invited to the Sarajevo Poetry Festival in May 1987.

16. With the opening line 'Came to an island farctate with feculence' (p.226), 'Behavioural' echoes 'Designatory' (*Shitheads*) and Pound's *Cantos*; it also recycles motifs and episodes from *Stet, Final Demands* and *Ukulele Music.*

17. The title 'Provincial' was also given to the third poem on p.227, the second on p.232, and the one on p.234; it amplifies the synecdochical function of the individual places and is derived from the 'Province of hyperborean bleakness' (p.234), the cranium and existential waste land which featured in the first 'Provincial'.

18. The poem is a follow-up to the end of H.G. Wells' 1909 novel *Tono-Bungay* (London, 1961), p.413: 'Light after light goes down. England and the Kingdom, Britain and the Empire, the old prides and the old devotions, glide abeam, astern, sink down upon the horizon, pass – pass. The river passes – London passes – England passes...'

19. All of Reading's metra episyntheta and their variations follow from it. The 'dispersed Alcaics' now used in *Evagatory* are the adequate metre for 'dispersing disbound **Collected Works**' (p.240). Neatly enacting his own end, Reading announces the *Collected Poems* (itself a gesture of finality), only to envisage them blown asunder by the 'gathering maelstrom'.

20. '[thence to this silence,]' was the title of an installation by Reading of six poems from *Evagatory*. It was shown in the Stedelijk Museum (Amsterdam) to celebrate its centenary (15 September – 29 October 1995). Reading opened the exhibition with a reading on 16 September, and the museum issued a pamphlet containing those poems.

21. The details are modelled on Richard Jefferies, *After London* (Oxford, 1980 [1885]), pp.200-01: strong wind, a cliff, great heat, strange sun, black sand, buttersoft rock, the 'gulph'. The 'Gulph' denotes the Dantesque Gulf (*The Inferno,* Canto XI, line 68), 'Nether Hell', as well as the whirling storm engulfing everything.

22. Sirius is also called 'the Dog Star' – it is interesting, though somewhat bathetic in context, to note that the poet could be seen as going to the dogs at a time of year when public poetry readings were celebrated in ancient Rome: Sirius ascends in late summer.

Last Poems *(pp.228-42)*

1. The book impressed reviewers: Alan Brownjohn, 'Variety acts', *Sunday Times,* 25 September 1994, p.11; David Clark, 'Essential Reading' (with interview), *What's On,* 22 June 1994, p.27; Tim Dooley, 'Homeric horrors', *TLS,* 8 July 1994; Dennis O'Driscoll, 'Verse Wallah Toys with Premature End', *Poetry Review,* 84/4 (Winter 1994/95), pp.21-22; Anthony Thwaite, 'A life's work in a single volume', *Sunday Telegraph,* 21 August 1994.

2. The five new poems are 'Alcmanic', 'Shard', 'Midnight', '[Untitled]' and 'Valedictory'.

3. Lowell, quoted in the 'Introduction' by Manfred Pfister, 'Imitation und Intertextualität bei Robert Lowell', p.317, in *Intertextualität: Formen, Funktionen, anglistische Fallstudien,* ed. Ulrich Broich & Manfred Pfister (Tübingen, 1985).

4. 'Euripidean' is an adaptation of different Chorus passages from different tragedies by Euripides (480-406 BC), the youngest and most "modern" of the Attic tragedists.

5. Quoted by Pfister, p.332.

6. Bilston's reviews: 'Straying acetically', *TLS,* 15 January 1988, p.69; 'Frets and Fevers', *TLS,* 5 January 1990, p.18; 'Chronicles of Albion', *TLS,* 8 May 1992, p.20. Reading had come across the name in an address on the day he was looking for a pseudonym [C]. The letter to the editor was written to the *TLS,* correcting the mistake about wine in Greppin's review of *Evagatory.*

7. Reading's diction, allitero-assonances and consonances are no less resonant than Michael Alexander's translations, see *Beowulf* (Harmondsworth, 1973), pp.150-51, and *The Earliest English Poems* (Harmondsworth, 1966), 'The Ruin', pp.30-31, 'The Wife's Complaint [Lament]', pp.81-82; see also W.S. Mackie (ed.), *The Exeter Book* (1934), Part II ('The Fates of Men', p.26).

8. H.B. Cotterill, *Introduction to Homer's Odyssey,* ed. Walter Leaf (London, 1924) [1911], p.9. See also the chapter on *Going On,* pp.154-55.

9. In a similar discussion of violence and art, Tony Harrison listed 'Homer, Aeschylus, Sophocles, Euripides, etc, author of Job, the various epics, the Tains, the Beowulfs, Dante, Shakespeare, Blake. When is violence "violence" and when is it great poetry?' (quoted in: Egbert Faas, *Ted Hughes: The Unaccommodated Universe* [Santa Barbara, 1980], p.198).

10. This echoes 'baying for mashed flesh and gore' (*Final Demands,* p.129), referring to the 'footy fans' who first appeared on 'terraces / dripping with apes' blood' in *Nothing For Anyone* (p.128), which links the 'heroes' to the hooligans – both prototypes of *homo barbarus,* as are the congressional Republicans in *Marfan* 'baying / for bigger fences, more technology, / more agents and the US military / to stem the tide' on the Mexican 'frontier'.

11. Reading commented [LI]: 'I don't think Ovid's stance on battle is heroic in the way that Homer's would be. It's really rather flippant and aloof and a bit of a curious attitude, and I hope not to be a million miles away from that. I *think* I'm right in feeling that there's a curious, almost Olympian detachment and ... manipulative flippancy about it all.'

12. Daniel Defoe, *A Journal of the Plague Year* [1722] (Oxford, 1990), p.103: 'I suppose the world has heard of the famous *Solomon Eagle* an Enthusiast: He tho' not infected at all, but in his Head, went about denouncing of Judgment upon the City in a frightful manner; sometimes quite naked, and with a pan of burning Charcoal on his Head...; and with his Hands lifted up, repeated that Part of the *Liturgy* of the Church continually; *Spare us good Lord, spare thy People whom thou hast redeemed with thy most precious Blood'* (see also p.21 and p.241).

13. Almost as remarkable is the shortcut that "political" (unaesthetic) readings of Reading take in this context, diagnosing "the author" as a reactionary because one of his stances is the Gibbonian apothegm 'All that is human must retrograde'. One might as well quote from 'Sociological' (*Stet*, p.112) – 'What you should do was share out the money and / make some new houses so they'd be comfy...' – and deride Reading for his utopian socialism.

14. Athenian Thucydides wrote of the long war between Athens and Sparta (431-404 BC), translated in 1881 by Jowett. Reading adapted the passage in which Thucydides describes the great plague in Athens during the second year of the war (Book II).

15. Eric Ashby, 'A Second Look at Doom', *Encounter*, 46/3 (March 1976), pp.16-24, which develops Hartley's prognoses and the Club of Rome report *The Limits to Growth*. See also the chapter on *Nothing For Anyone*.

16. See the details on Alcman in the chapter on *Going On*, and *Lyrica Graeca Selecta*, ed. Denys Lionel Page (Oxford, 1968), and the translation *The Greek Lyrics; The Lyrical Fragments*.

17. See Reading's first book; the first syntagma is taken almost verbatim from 'Combine', as are the images of death as an approaching combine (Reaper) and migrating birds, and the reference to Housman's ashes (p.48).

18. The line is better known in France in its adapted form as a schoolgirls' *ritornello* sung and performed in a dance. – Housman had another title which in this intertextual mirror cabinet points back to Reading: 'A Shropshire Lad'. And *Last Poems* was also a posthumous collection by Roy Fuller, quoted in 'Regal'.

19. Gérard Genette first used this image of the 'palimpsestes' to express the endless intertextual relations in the echo chamber of the modern world. Gérard Genette, *Palimpsestes: La littérature au second degré* (Paris, 1982).

Eschatological, Work in Regress, Ob., Marfan *(pp.243-66)*

1. Michael Hofmann, 'Try some tetrameter', *Times*, 8 September 1996.

2. Reviews of Vol. I: John Banville, '*Collected Poems*, by Peter Reading', *Irish Times*, 12 September 1995; Simon Carnell, 'Reading matters', Yorkshire Post, 19 October 1995, p.11; Giles Coren, 'The poet who hates writing poetry', *Times*, 27 July 1995; John Freeman, 'Peter Reading – Collected Poems 1', *Tears in the Fence*, 17 (Spring 1996), pp.72-74; Lachlan Mackinnon, 'A Swift for soiled England', *Independent*, 12 August 1995; John Matthias, 'Bloodaxe Books, Part III: Some Loose Ends and Maybe a Major Poet', *ACM* (USA), 31 (Spring 1996), 197-211, pp.197-204; Sean O'Brien, 'Emerging from the Shadows', *Sunday Times* (no details); Robert Potts, 'Peter Reading', *PBS Bulletin*, 165 (Summer 1995), p.6; Robert Potts, 'England's unofficial laureate', *Guardian*, 11 August 1995, p.5, and *Guardian Weekly*, 27 August 1995; *Publishers Weekly*, unsigned notice, 3 June 1996; Malcolm Rutherford, 'My book of the year', *Financial Times*, 2 December 1995; Ian Sansom, 'Scared Scratchings', *TLS*, 13 October 1995, p.28.

Reviews of Vol. II: Alan Brownjohn, 'Virtuoso who sings the Grotty', *Sunday Times*, 15 December 1996; Matthew Gidley, 'Collected Poems 2: Poems 1985-1996 by Peter Reading', *Raw Edge*, 3 (Autumn/Winter 1996-1997); Michael Hofmann, 'Try some tetrameter', *Times*, 8 September 1996; Michael O'Neill, 'Bricolage and Outrage', *London Magazine*, December/January 1997; Charlie Orr, 'Collected Poems 2', *Understanding*, 7 (1997/8), pp.192-93; David

Wheatley, 'The Kakistocrat', *Poetry Review*, 88/2 (Summer 1998), pp.64-65.

Reviews of both Vols. I and II: John Kerrigan, 'Reading's *Collected Poems*', *Thumbscrew*, 9 (Winter 1997/98), pp.13-24; Anthony Thwaite, 'The verse virtuosi', *Sunday Telegraph*, 26 January 1997. All quotations from reviews in this chapter are from these publications.

3. *Stanza on Stage* at the Birmingham Writers' and Readers' Festival; transmitted on BBC Radio 4, with an introduction by Simon Armitage [M].

4. This is the title of a late book by Maugham and also a quotation from a review of one of Maugham's books.

5. Alan Jenkins, 'Nowhere to go but Elysium', *PBS Bulletin*, 174 (Autumn 1997), p.6.

6. Recent newspaper reports have tended to exaggerate both the levels of his drinking and the depths of his bouts of depression (see Robert Potts, 'Through a glass darkly', *Guardian*, 9 September 1997, p.9, and Hugo Williams, 'Freelance', *TLS*, 24 October 1997).

7. See Giles Coren, 'The poet who hates writing poetry', *Times*, 27 July 1995; Coren does not extract much sincerity out of Reading, except this: 'I would be happy enough living in a barrel, if the climate were a bit better. The most important thing is poetry, more than love, life, all those things. Since school-days, art has been what it's all about, the only thing that makes me feel fulfilled.'

8. As I am no classicist, I shall confine this chapter to the identification of sources, the illumination of the backgrounds, and the study of the structure and intertextuality of Reading's three latest books.

9. Quoted by Manfred Pfister in Ulrich Broich & Manfred Pfister (Hg.), *Intertextualität: Formen, Funktionen, anglistische Fallstudien* (Tübingen, 1985), p.325.

10. Quoted by Pfister, pp.322-23.

11. Quoted by Pfister, p.324, who also quotes Lowell accusing 'strict met-rical translators' of being 'taxidermists, not poets'.

12. When I list metres without comment about their function and impact, then I have already discussed them in previous chapters; but identification can still be helpful to the non-expert. This aside, ascriptions of general "meanings" to metres should be reticent because such assessments are often subjective.

13. Reading turned 'Leasts' into a 'poem and artwork' in an edition of 20.

14. The first draft had 'alligators', but 'vulture' was preferred for its intra-textual reference to the epigraph of *Diplopic*.

15. This is in fact the fifth version of elegiac distich, after different pre-sentations in *Ukulele Music*, *Going On*, *Stet*, *Final Demands*, and *Perduta Gente*. Metra episyntheta are selected for 'Choric' (p.284: two elegiac distichs and one hexameter) and 'News' (p.292: three hexameters and one pentameter).

16. 'From *Beowulf*', p.283; 'Exilic', p.285; '[Untitled]', p.293; '[Untitled]', p.295.

17. However, this metre can also appear rather loose and suddenly, strangely, start oscillating on the border with dactylic tetrameters, as in the very first line of 'Corporate' ('In polystyrene, snug sarcophagi', p.285).

18. Helen Dunmore, 'Let's hear it for forks and shoes', *Observer*, 21 December 1997; Cliff Forshaw, 'Mystics at Breakfast', *Envoi*, 119 (February 1998), pp.160-62; Michael Glover, 'Latin tags, Levi threads', *Independent*, 11 November 1997; Alan Jenkins, 'Nowhere to go but Elysium', *PBS Bulletin*, 174 (Autumn 1997), pp.6-7; Herbert Lomas, '*Work in Regress* by Peter Reading', *Ambit*, 153 (1998), pp.74-75; Roddy Lumsden, 'Reading – Kuppner', *Blade*

(Winter 1997), pp.24–25; 'Chinoiserie by Peter Reading', *Raw Edge*, 5 (Autumn/ Winter 1997), p.27; Nicholas Murray, 'Propertius in Salop', *TLS*, 9 January 1998, p.22; Sean O'Brien, 'On the outside looking in', *Sunday Times*, 23 November 1997, p.12; Ruth Padel/Sean O'Brien, 'Peter Reading, *Work in Regress*', *PBS Bulletin*, 174 (Autumn 1997), p.4; Robert Potts, 'Through a glass darkly', *Guardian*, 9 September 1997, p.9; William Scammell, 'A green and putrid land', *Independent on Sunday*, 2 November 1997; David Wheatley, 'The Kakistocrat', *Poetry Review*, 88/2 (Summer 1998), pp.64–65; Howard Wright, 'Old English', *Brangle*, 3 (1999), pp.15-18. More than one reviewer said that Reading should do the whole of Ovid or Homer.

19. It was produced in 1997 in an edition of 50, is 14x11 inches, bears the holograph of a haiku underneath and is signed by Reading (cost in 1997: £150).

20. 'Wine freezes hard' (stanza 7, p.24) re-writes Reading's 'Englished' in *Diplopic*, a re-write of Dryden's re-write of Virgil's account of the barbaric northeners.

21. The first poem quoted (p.12) is a condensed version of 'Chez Vous' (p.35) from Reading's first book (see also p.86), and the last poem mentioned in 'Three' was read on 'Poetry Now' and is from *Ukulele Music* (p.29).

22. Reading was broadcast as the first of 'five of the finest poets writing in English today', as the announcer said; the five poems are all 'new work, 20 minutes long, with the poet heavily involved in the production process and using, as well as their own words and voices, archive material, location recordings, music, and "found sound"' [M]. The only typographical device in *Work in Regress* equals the fading sound of the Propertian refrain '*Sunt aliquid manes*' (p.16) recorded on tape (also played at readings).

23. *A Second Chance* is a quote from the pre-text; *Pence on the Tongue* is a Reading leitmotif (Charon's Toll); *Grim Charonis* must be the female equivalent to Charon; civic bronze (money) leads to *Persephone*, Greek goddess and queen of the infernal regions.

24. Burton Watson, in his Introduction to *The Jade Mountain*, in *The Chinese Translations*, ed. James Kraft, comprising *The Jade Mountain*, p.24. See also Wong Man, *Poems from China* (Hong Kong/London, 1950), p.25: 'LIPAI (LIPO) – 701-762, known as the fairy poet. He was much favoured at court in the luxurious days of Yang Kuei-Fei, who hated him. He could boast that the Emperor once mixed food for him. Knowing his counsels would not be accepted, he left and spent a carefree life. He is said to have been drowned in trying to catch the moon in the river.'

25. Watson, p. 107 *ff.*

26. Robert Potts, 'Through a glass darkly', p.9.

27. Arthur Waley, *Chinese Poems* (selected from *170 Chinese Poems, More Translations from the Chinese, The Temple, The Book of Songs*), London: Allen & Unwin, 1946, Introduction, and pp.116-17.

28. Arthur Waley, *One Hundred and Seventy Chinese Poems* [1969] (London, Cape, 1918/1962), p.7.

29. Burton Watson, 'Introduction to The Jade Mountain', in *The Chinese Translations*, edited by James Kraft, pp.20-22.

30. Some reviewers wanted to put Reading into the *poète maudit* corner, but there were others who found more subtle answers to the new questions: Alan Brownjohn, 'Boys will be boys', *Sunday Times*, 16 January 2000, books section, p.42; Alan Dent, 'Review: *Ob.* by Peter Reading', *The Penniless Press* (September 1999); Matthew Gidley, 'Reviews: Peter Reading *Ob.*', *Raw Edge*,

9 (Winter 1999), p.25; David Kennedy, 'And, Finally...', *Stand*, new series, 1/4 (December 1999), pp.94-97; Robert Potts, 'Poetry: *Ob.* by Peter Reading', *Guardian*, 14 August 1999; Anthony Thwaite, 'Skills with sadness', *TLS*, 12 November 1999; David Wheatley, 'How To Die', *Contemporary Poetry Review* (www.cprw.com), 2000.

31. 'Nocturne' (p.29) and 'Nocturne' (p.51). With reduced point size with each successive line, the verbal echoes of the first 'Night-Piece' (p.62, *CP1*) diminish (and Bach's '*volles werk*' is now 'Shostakovich's 5th's' dread of Stalin).

32. Reading was reading a Penguin book of Spanish verse at the time, where he discovered the *copla de pie quebrado* (stanza with a broken foot), which was developed during the 14th and 15th centuries.

33. 22 years before, apropos *The Prison Cell & Barrel Mystery*, Reading had quoted Auden's cautionary words to writers about autobiography.

34. The ex-lover featured prominently in *The Prison Cell & Barrel Mystery*.

35. 'Hawk Roosting' was the poem Reading chose as his most hated poem at the 'Heroes and Villains session' of the 1997 King's Lynn Poetry Festival (Hugo Williams, 'Freelance', *TLS*, 24 October 1997).

36. Underneath the rude surface, another intertextual joke lurks in the travesty of Milton's verse 'They also serve who only stand and wait' ('On His Blindness'). By altering only two letters ('wank'), Reading reproduces the old threat that masturbation causes blindness.

37. Here, Reading follows Swift, who had also composed his own epitaph: 'ubi saeva indignatio ulterius cor lacerare nequit' (where fierce indignation can no longer tear his heart).

38. For the cover of *Reading Peter Reading*, Edwards reproduced it in sand, with suitable erosive, palaeontological connotations.

39. '*Sgian dubh*' is Scottish Gaelic and means 'black knife', a small dagger carried in the sock by the Highlanders.

SELECTED BIBLIOGRAPHY

A comprehensive bibliography of all primary and secondary material relating to Peter Reading up to 1994 was published in my doctoral dissertation *Das Werk Peter Readings (1970-1994): Interpretation und Dokumentation* (Heidelberg: Universitätsverlag Carl Winter, 1996), pp.630-83. An updated, full scholarly bibliography of Reading will be made available from Bloodaxe. The following is a selective listing only, but all publications by Reading are included in the first section:

Poetry Volumes and Pamphlets:

Water and Waste (Outposts Publications, 1970)
For the Municipality's Elderly (Secker & Warburg, 1974), INCLUDING MOST OF *Water and Waste*
The Prison Cell & Barrel Mystery (Secker & Warburg, 1976)
Nothing For Anyone (Secker & Warburg, 1977)
Fiction (Secker & Warburg, 1979)
Tom o'Bedlam's Beauties (Secker & Warburg, 1981)
Diplopic (Secker & Warburg, 1983)
5x5x5x5x5, with David Butler (Ceolfrith Press, 1983)
C (Secker & Warburg, 1984)
Ukulele Music WITH *Going On* (Secker & Warburg, 1985)
Essential Reading, ed. Alan Jenkins (Secker & Warburg, 1986)
Stet (Secker & Warburg, 1986)
Final Demands (Secker & Warburg, 1988)
Perduta Gente (Secker & Warburg, 1989)
Shitheads (Squirrelprick Press, 1989)
3 in 1 (Chatto & Windus, 1992), REPRINTING *Diplopic, C* AND *Ukulele Music.*
Evagatory (Chatto & Windus, 1992), INCLUDING SOME POEMS FROM *Shitheads*
Ukulele Music WITH *Perduta Gente* (Northwestern University Press, USA, 1994)
Last Poems (Chatto & Windus, 1994)
Collected Poems 1: Poems 1970-1984 (Bloodaxe Books, 1995)
Collected Poems 2: Poems 1985-1996 (Bloodaxe Books, 1996), INCLUDING *Eschatological* (1996)
Work in Regress (Bloodaxe Books, 1997)
Chinoiserie (The Bay Press, 1997)
Ob. (Bloodaxe Books, 1999), INCLUDING *Chinoiserie*
Apophthegmatic (The Bay Press, 1999)
Repetitious (Laertides Press, USA, 1999)
Copla a Pie Quebrado (Lannan Foundation, USA, 1999)
Marfan (Bloodaxe Books, 2000)
[untitled] (Bloodaxe Books, due 2001), INCLUDING *Apophthegmatic, Repetitious* AND *Copla a Pie Quebrado*

Another, unpublished book exists only in one copy, with 'marbled boards, half-quarter highlights, mock-splendour' [C]: *Rana* was written in 1966 and re-worked with illustrations and illuminations in 1992. It is ostensibly a children's story about a frog ('rana' is Latin for 'frog') who jumped out of the world. It was acquired by the Lannan Foundation in 1992.

Recent Artwork and Exhibitions:

Erosive: Thirty-Seven Texts, Hand-Produced by Peter Reading (1993/1994), a box full of visual-textual art, which was bought by the Poetry Library, London. *Erosive* was also an exhibition in association with Peter Kennard (London, 2-31 July 1994).

Leasts (1994; edition of 20), poster of poem and artwork.

[*thence to this silence,*] (1995), pamphlet produced by the Stedelijk Museum, Amsterdam. [*thence to this silence,*] was also an installation of six poems from *Evagatory* designed by Karel Martens and Roger Willems for the museum's 100th anniversary (15 September – 29 October 1995).

Six Poems (2000, in an edition of 5), six A3-pages of handwritten poem and photographs.

Recordings:

The Lannan Foundation presents Peter Reading (1992; videotape and pamphlet), literary series *Readings and Conversations*. Reading reads parts of *Diplopic* and *Evagatory* in its entirety and is interviewed by Christopher Hitchens and Michael Silverblatt.

The Poetry Quartets: 3 (The British Council/Bloodaxe Books, 1998), half-hour reading by Reading on double-cassette shared with James Fenton, Tony Harrison and Ken Smith.

Selected Interviews:

(The unpublished six-hour interview with Peter Reading conducted by me [4-6 June 1993] was taped and transcribed; parts of it are incorporated in this study as [LI].)

Alan Jenkins, 'Making Nothing Matter', *Poetry Review*, 75/1 (April 1985), pp.5-15.

David Hart, 'Reading between the lines', *Arts Report*, West Midlands Arts (April 1985).

Ian Hamilton interviews Peter Reading, *Bookmark*: Peter Reading / Pat Barker / Kazuo Ishiguro, 13 (no. 1/ LMA N 199 B), BBC 2 TV, 1 November 1986.

Paul Bailey interviews Peter Reading, *Third Ear*, BBC Radio 3, 1 March 1988, 7 p.m.

Sandy McCutcheon interviews Peter Reading, *In Tempo*, Australian Broadcasting Corporation Radio, 9 December 1989, 10 a.m.

Stephen Edgar, 'Whistling in the Dark', *Island* (Australia), 43/44 (Winter 1990), pp.54-59.

Robert Potts, 'An Interview with Peter Reading', *Oxford Poetry*, 5/3 (December 1990), pp.94-98.

Ysenda Maxtone Graham, 'Poets Cornered', *Sunday Telegraph Review*, 3 March 1991, pp.1-2.

Daisy Goodwin interviews Peter Reading, *Bookmark*, 'Day Jobs', BBC 2, 22 January 1992, 8.10p.m.

Susan Press, 'Poet ploughs lone furrow', *Liverpool Daily Post*, 22 February 1992.

Bernard O'Donoghue interviews Peter Reading, *Spectrum*, no. 47, BBC Radio Oxford, 12 April 1992, 2 p.m.

Christopher Hitchens and Michael Silverblatt interview Peter Reading, Lannan Foundation Reading Series on videotape, 21 April 1992.

Peter Porter interviews Peter Reading, *Kaleidoscope*, BBC Radio 4 (precise
    date unknown, *c*. June 1994).
David Clark, 'Essential Reading', *What's On*, 22 June 1994, p.27.
Giles Coren, 'The Poet who hates writing poetry', *The Times*, 27 July 1995.
Robert Potts, 'Through a glass darkly', *The Guardian*, 9 September 1997, p.9.
Alan Jenkins, 'Nowhere to go but Elysium' (interview with 'John Bilston'),
    PBS Bulletin, 174 (Autumn 1997), pp.6-7.

Selected Articles:

'Peter Reading writes...' (about *The Prison Cell & Barrel Mystery*), *Poetry
    Book Society Bulletin*, 88 (Spring 1976), p.2.
'Peter Reading writes...' (about *Tom o'Bedlam's Beauties*), *Poetry Book Society
    Bulletin*, 111 (Christmas 1981), pp.2-3.
'Peter Reading writes...' (about *Diplopic*), *Poetry Book Society Bulletin*, 117
    (Summer 1983), p.3.
'Forms and Influences: Peter Reading', *TLS*, 27 April 1984, p.463.
'Peter Reading writes: Shocking but True' (about *C*), *Poetry Book Society
    Bulletin*, 123 (Winter 1984), pp.2-3.
'Gavin Ewart', in *Dictionary of Literary Biography: Poets of Great Britain and
    Ireland Since 1960*, vol. 40, part 1: A-L, ed. Vincent B. Sherry (Detroit/
    Michigan: DLB, 1985), pp.110-16.
'Muse at the feed mill' ('Poet Peter Reading begins an occasional series about
    writers with unusual livelihoods'), *Observer*, 11 June 1989, p.42.
'Going, Going: A View from Contemporary England', *Island* (Australia), 42
    (Autumn 1990), pp.33-37. A taping of the article read out by Reading was
    made in Hobart/Tasmania (2 December 1989).
'Freelance', *TLS*, 7 February 1992, p.12.
(Untitled, unpublished), Report about his Lannan Foundation Poetry Fellow-
    ship of 1990 (April 1992 [M]).
'Nature Notes': 13 articles in *The Oldie* (1992-93).

Selected Critical Articles on Peter Reading:

Contemporary Literary Criticism, vol. 47, ed. Daniel G. Marowski & Roger
    Matuz (Detroit/Michigan: Gale Research Company, 1988), pp.349-55.
Neil Corcoran, *English Poetry Since 1940*, 'Hiding in Fictions: Some New
    Narrative Poems' (Harlow: Longman, 1993), pp.244-57.
Francesco Dragosei, *Contemporary British Poetry: Patterns from the 1950s to
    the Present Day*, 'The Age of Anxiety: Peter Reading' (Milan: Principato,
    1989), pp.104-15.
Alan Jenkins, 'Peter Reading', in *Dictionary of Literary Biography: Poets of
    Great Britain and Ireland Since 1960*, vol. 40, part 2: M-Z, ed. Vincent B.
    Sherry (Detroit/Michigan: DLB, 1985), pp.468-75.
David Kennedy, *New Relations: The Refashioning of British Poetry 1980-94*,
    'Elegies for the Living: The Poetry of Peter Reading' (Bridgend: Seren,
    1996), pp.120-52.
Isabel Martin, Introduction to Peter Reading's *Collected Poems*, in *Collected
    Poems 1: Poems 1970-1984* (Newcastle upon Tyne: Bloodaxe Books, 1995),
    pp.13-24.
Isabel Martin, 'Postmodernising Shakespeare: A Palimpsest Poem', in *Historic-
    izing/Contemporizing Shakespeare*, ed. Christoph Bode & Wolfgang Klooss
    (Trier: Wissenschaftlicher Verlag Trier, 2000), pp.185-99.

Isabel Martin, 'The Rich Repertoire of Metrics in Contemporary British Poetry: Peter Reading', in *Meter, Rhythm, and Performance* (series: 'Linguistik International'), ed. Christoph Küper (Frankfurt: Peter Lang Verlag, due 2000).

Sean O'Brien, 'The Poet as Thatcherite?', first in *The Devil* (Summer 1996), pp.109-18; reprinted in *The Deregulated Muse* (Newcastle upon Tyne: Bloodaxe Books, 1998), pp.123-31.

Dennis O'Driscoll, ' "No-God and Species Decline Stuff ": The Poetry of Peter Reading', in *In Black and Gold: Contiguous Traditions in Post-War British and Irish Poetry*, ed. Cedric C. Barfoot (Amsterdam/Atlanta: Radopi, 1994), pp.199-218.

Tom Paulin, 'Peter Reading', *Grand Street*, 7/4 (Summer 1988), pp.202-11. Reprinted as 'Junk Britain: Peter Reading' in Paulin, *Minotaur* (London: Faber, 1992), pp.285-94 (with revisions to last paragraph).

Neil Roberts, 'Poetic Subjects: Tony Harrison and Peter Reading', in *British Poetry from the 1950s to the 1990s: Politics and Art*, ed. Gary Day & Brian Docherty (Basingstoke/London: Macmillan, New York: St Martin's Press, 1997), pp.48-62. The extended article is republished in Roberts, *Narrative and Voice in Postwar Poetry*, 'Heteroglossia in Peter Reading' (Harlow: Longman, 1999), pp.167-83.

Selected Reviews of Peter Reading:

(More complete listings of book reviews are to be found in Notes to the respective chapters.)

Alan Bold, 'Stricken by the big C', *The Scotsman*, 8 December 1984, p.5.

A.A. Cleary, '"Tom o'Bedlam's Beauties"', *Thames Poetry*, 2/12 (March 1983), pp.32-33.

Tim Dooley, 'Homeric horrors', *TLS*, 8 July 1994.

Margaret Drabble, 'Antique and contemporary savagery', *Sunday Times*, 6 March 1988.

Carol Ann Duffy, 'Stain upon the silence', *Guardian*, 11 March 1988, p.23.

Gavin Ewart, 'Accepting the inevitable', *TLS*, 25 November 1977, p.1381.

Gavin Ewart, 'Confronting the bogeymen', *TLS*, 30 September 1983, p.1061.

Gavin Ewart, 'Reading Peter Reading', *Poetry Book Society Bulletin*, 141 (Summer 1989), pp.1-2.

Damian Grant, 'An Englishman, an Irishman and a Scotsman', *London Review of Books*, 9/9 (7 May 1987), p.23.

John A.C. Greppin, 'Y^e True Quack', *TLS*, 21 February 1992, p.21.

Eric Korn, 'Singing the unsingable', *TLS*, 15 April 1988, p.419.

Grevel Lindop, 'Madness stroke sanity', *TLS*, 18 June 1982, p.662.

Mick Imlah, 'Thanatoptic designs', *TLS*, 4 January 1985, p.10.

Mick Imlah, 'Hard and hope-free', *TLS*, 8 May 1987, p.487.

Mick Imlah, 'Doses of radiation', *TLS*, 25 August 1989, p.916.

Alan Jenkins, 'A Barbarous Eloquence', *Encounter*, 59/2 (August 1982), p.60.

Alan Jenkins, 'Noises of apocalypse', *Observer*, 23 December 1984, p.29.

Alan Jenkins, 'Bar-room philosopher', *Observer*, 20 March 1988, p.43.

David Kennedy, 'And, Finally...', *Stand*, new series, 1/4 (December 1999), pp.94-97.

Hermione Lee, 'Poor mad islanders', *Independent on Sunday*, 16 February 1992, p.30.

John Matthias, 'Bloodaxe Books, Part III: Some Loose Ends and Maybe a Major Poet', *ACM* (USA), 31 (Spring 1996), pp.197-211.

Glyn Maxwell, 'Desperanto', *Poetry Review*, 82/2 (Summer 1992), pp.53-54.

Blake Morrison, 'South Bank shower', *Observer*, 18 June 1989, p.44.

Nicholas Murray, 'Propertius in Salop', *TLS* (9 January 1998), p.22.

Bernard O'Donoghue, 'Letters from Tonge', *Poetry Review*, 78/2 (Summer 1988), pp.62-63.

Dennis O'Driscoll, 'Verse Wallah Toys with Premature End', *Poetry Review*, 84/4 (Winter 1994/95), pp.21-22.

Dennis O'Driscoll, 'Beyond a Joke', *Poetry Review*, 75/1 (April 1985), pp.15-16.

Peter Porter, 'Cassettes of atrocity', *Observer*, 1 September 1985, p.19.

Robert Potts, 'Poet Pete ponders his last protest', *Guardian*, 6 February 1992, p.30.

Robert Potts, 'England's unofficial laureate', *Guardian*, 11 August 1995, p.5, and *Guardian Weekly*, 27 August 1995.

Robert Potts, 'Peter Reading', *PBS Bulletin*, 165 (Summer 1995), p.6.

Simon Rae, 'Black and over the top', *TLS*, 10 January 1986, p.34.

Carol Rumens, 'Antiseptic Whiff of Destiny', *Literary Review*, 83 (May 1985), pp.52-54.

Fraser Steel, 'Travelling the Word', *Encounter*, 74/1 (January-February 1990), pp.47-51.

George Szirtes, 'Comedy of Terrors', *Literary Review & Quarto*, 66 (December 1983) pp.53-54.

Anthony Thwaite, 'Skills with sadness', *TLS*, 12 November 1999.

David Wheatley, 'The Kakistocrat', *Poetry Review*, 88/2 (Summer 1998), pp. 64-65.

John Whitworth, 'But What Does He Want?' *Poetry Review*, 79/3 (Autumn 1989), pp.40-41.

Selected Shorter Reviews:

Charles Boyle, 'Not Cricket', *London Magazine*, 25/8 (November 1985), pp.79-80.

Joseph Bristow, 'Peter Reading: *Essential Reading, Stet*', *British Book News* (March 1987), p.151.

George Mackay Brown, 'The dark wood', *Scotsman*, 24 September 1977, p.3.

Alan Brownjohn, 'Virtuoso who sings the Grotty', *Sunday Times*, 15 December 1996.

Alan Brownjohn, 'British Poets: The Younger Generation', *Literature Alive*, 3/1 (June 1989), 1-24, pp.19-20.

Alan Brownjohn, 'Memoranda from Cardboard City', *Sunday Times*, 9 July 1989.

Duncan Bush, 'Peter Reading', *Poetry Wales*, 32/4 (April 1997), pp.64-66.

A.A. Cleary, 'Reviews of New Poetry', *Thames Poetry*, 2/16 (March 1985), p.41.

Colin Falck, 'New Poetry', *New Review*, 3/26 (May 1976), p.59.

Cliff Forshaw, 'Mystics at Breakfast', *Envoi*, 119 (February 1998), pp.160-62.

Robin Lane Fox, 'Poetry enjoys a new upswing', *Financial Times*, 7 February 1987, p.12.

Henry Graham, 'Elderly White Earth', *Ambit*, 61 (1975), p.54.

Michael Hofmann, 'Try some tetrameter', *The Times*, 8 September 1996.

Chris Hurford, 'Resisting redundancy', *TLS*, 21 December 1990, p.1383.

John Kerrigan, 'Bouquets of barbed wire', *Sunday Times*, 8 September 1985, p.45.

Roddy Lumsden, 'Reading – Kuppner', *Blade* (Winter 1997), pp.24-25.

Lachlan Mackinnon, 'A Swift for soiled England', *Independent*, 12 August 1995.

John Mole, 'Expanding Elements', *Encounter*, 61/4 (December 1983), p.66.

Jeff Nuttall, 'Poetry', *Time Out*, 26 November 1986.

Charlie Orr, 'Collected Poems 2', *Understanding*, 7 (1997/8), pp.192-93.

Harold Pinter, 'A special light-page supplement recommends the best buys for giving and reading this Christmas', *Observer*, 3 December 1989, p.65.

Peter Porter, 'A bumper book of horrors', *Observer*, 3 July 1983, p.29.

David Profumo, 'Heart's rag-and-bone-shop', *Sunday Telegraph*, 20 August 1989, p.38.

Mark Robinson, 'Reviews', *Scratch*, 1 (November 1989), p.37.

Ian Sansom, 'Scared Scratchings', *TLS*, 13 October 1995, p.28.

William Scammell, 'A green and putrid land', *Independent on Sunday*, 2 November 1997.

Jaci Stephen, 'Ways of dying', *TES*, 10 May 1985, p.26.

Julian Symons, 'Lines from the sick room', *Sunday Times*, 13 January 1985, p.45.

Julian Symons, 'The brass tacks approach', *Sunday Times*, 9 November 1986, p.55.

INDEX

312   INDEX

Bunting, Basil, 22
Burke, Edmund, 291*n*
Burton, Robert, 263
Butler, David, 108
Byron, George Gordon, Lord, 69

C, 9, 12, 22, 24, 83, 90, 92, 94,
97, 108, 111, *112-27*, 128-29, 131,
136, 150, 157, 160, 162, 173-75,
177, 180-81, 184-85, 188, 191,
195, 197, 214, 230, 232, 245, 248,
261, 263, 265, 278*n*, 293*n*, 298*n*
Caesar, Julius, 62, 209
Cain, 133
Caine, Michael C., 206-07,
295-96*n*
Callimachus, 251, 254
Captain, The, 129, 130, 135,
138-39, 141-42, 288*n*
Caradoc, 29
Caesar, Julius, 62, 207, 209
Carew, John, 93, 95
Carroll [Charles Dodgson], Lewis,
72
Cassius [Gaius Cassius Longinus],
62
Catullus, Gaius Valerius, 69,
207-11, 219, 251, 284*n*, 295-96*n*
Cervantes, Miguel de, 12
Chalky, 283*n*
Char [*see* Tucker], 114-15, 285*n*
Charon, 114, 119, 125, 126, 181,
232, (261), 285*n*, 291*n*, 302*n*
Chaucer, Geoffrey, 12
Chekhov, Anton, 190
Chinoiserie, 244, 251, *258-61*, 262
Christopher, John, 286*n*
Chummy, Uncle, 169, 283*n*
Clark, David, 229-31
Cleary, A.A., 81, 91-92, 128
Clio, Miss, 165
Clough, Arthur Hugh, 154

Coggrave, John, 15-16, 99, 144,
248, 283*n*, 289*n*, 293*n*
Coleridge, Samuel Taylor, 154
Collected Poems, 9, 19, 20, 215,
(225), 243, 244, 249, 298*n*, 303*n*
Contented of Telford, Mrs, 169
Cooper, Dr, 63-64
Copernicus, Nicolas, 43, 73
Copla a Pie Quebrado, (262, 263),
264-65
Corcoran, Neil, 128, 279*n*, 286*n*
Coren, Giles, 301*n*
Cotterill, H.B., 13, 154-55, 236,
289*n*, 294*n*, 299*n*
Crabbe, George, 82, 282*n*
Crass [*see* Glibber], 87
Crawford, Robert, 173, 189, 243,
279*n*, 284*n*
Crystal, 94, 95, 96
Curry, Neil, 81, 83, 90, 279*n*
Cynthia, 255

Dante, 34-35, 47, 188, 192-93,
195, 197-99, 201, 205, 275-76*n*,
285*n*, 287*n*, 294*n*, 295*n*, 298*n*
Darwin, Charles, 152, 248
Defoe, Daniel, 230, 237, 299*n*
Derrida, Jacques, 233
de Banville, Théodore, 241
de Kooning, Willem, 14
de Torquemada, Tomás, 249
de Torregamberro, General Señor
Conde, 77, 291*n*
de Witt, Cecile and Bryce, 278*n*
Diana, 51, 292*n*
Dickens, Charles, 12-13, 16, 87,
93, 130, 191
Dine, Jim, 12
Dionysus, 270
Diplopic, 9, 11, 24, 28, 67, 77, 82,
92-107, 108, 110, 111, 112, 116,
120, 124, 126, 134, 150, 161, 169,